The Primitivist Missiology of Anthony Norris Groves:

a radical influence on nineteenth-century Protestant mission.

Robert Bernard Dann

Dr. Robert B Dann received his BA and PhD degrees
from the University of Liverpool.
He has thirty years' experience of primitivist church initiatives
in Britain and overseas.

© Copyright 2007 Robert Bernard Dann

Produced and distributed for:
Tamarisk Books,
6 New Farm Court
Great Barrow, Chester CH3 7LS,
England.
Email: tamariskbooks@yahoo.co.uk

All rights reserved. No part of this publication may be reproduced, stored in a retrieval system, or transmitted, in any form or by any means, electronic, mechanical, photocopying, recording, or otherwise, without the written prior permission of the author.

Note for Librarians: A cataloguing record for this book is available from Library and Archives Canada at www.collectionscanada.ca/amicus/index-e.html
ISBN 1-4251-1001-0

Printed in Victoria, BC, Canada. Printed on paper with minimum 30% recycled fibre. Trafford's print shop runs on "green energy" from solar, wind and other environmentally-friendly power sources.

Offices in Canada, USA, Ireland and UK

Book sales for North America and international:
Trafford Publishing, 6E–2333 Government St.,
Victoria, BC V8T 4P4 CANADA
phone 250 383 6864 (toll-free 1 888 232 4444)
fax 250 383 6804; email to orders@trafford.com

Book sales in Europe:
Trafford Publishing (UK) Limited, 9 Park End Street, 2nd Floor
Oxford, UK OX1 1HH UNITED KINGDOM
phone +44 (0)1865 722 113 (local rate 0845 230 9601)
facsimile +44 (0)1865 722 868; info.uk@trafford.com

Order online at:
trafford.com/06-2760

10 9 8 7 6 5 4 3 2

Table of Contents

Preface	7
Acknowledgments	8
Abbreviations	8
Introduction	9
A Primitivist Ecclesiologist	11
The Development of Groves's Ecclesiological Thought	11
The Ecclesiology of A N Groves	12
The Ecclesiological Influence of A N Groves	13
A Primitivist Missiologist	15
Introduction: a Missionary Missiologist	15
Part 1. The Development of Groves's Missiological Thought (1825-1840)	19
1. Early Missionary Influences	19
John Owen (1766-1822) and the British and Foreign Bible Society	20
Edward Bickersteth (1786-1850) and the Church Missionary Society	20
Pietists and Moravians	21
Edward Irving (1792-1834)	23
Joseph Wolff (1795-1862)	31
William Jowett (1787-1855)	31
Karl Gottlieb Pfander (1803-65) and the Basel Mission	32
Joshua Marshman (1768-1837) of Serampore	34
2. Contemporary Intellectual Currents	39
Missionary Motivations	39
The Romantic Movement	42
Evangelical Primitivism	44
3. Groves's Missionary Experiences	47
Groves's Experience in Eastern Europe and Baghdad (1829-33; aged 34-38)	47
Groves's Experience in India (1833-52; aged 38-57)	48
Initial Impressions	48
Indian Roman Catholicism	50
Earliest Protestant Missions	51
Karl Gottlieb Ewald Rhenius (1790-1838)	52
The Rhenius Affair	57
Groves and Rhenius	62
Groves's Later Missionary Career	65
Conclusion: The Development of Groves's Missiological Thought	73
Part 2. The Missiology of A N Groves	75
Introduction: An Ecclesiologist Overseas	75
1. Missions and Churches	77
Missionary Societies	77
Rivalry and Comity	81
Church Organisation	87
Henry Venn (1796-1873): An Introduction	87
Rufus Anderson (1796-1880): An Introduction	91
The Three-Self Principle	94
The "Native Pastorate"	95
Missionary Appointment	102

Spiritual Leadership	106
Indigenous Initiatives	110
Conclusion: Missions and Churches	113
2. Civilisation and Education	**115**
Cultural Identification	115
Commerce, Civilisation and Christianity	117
Groves's early experience of schools	120
Alexander Duff (1806-78) and English Language Schools	122
Educational Mission	124
Vernacular Schools	126
Social and Medical Mission	128
Conclusion: Civilisation and Education	129
3. Finance and Providence	**131**
Missionary Support	131
Groves's Life of Faith	133
Living by Faith: Groves's Principles	139
Living by Faith: A Critique	143
Living by Faith: Some Early Applications	149
Accountability	154
Tent-Making	162
The Rest of Faith	169
Conclusion: Finance and Providence	170
Conclusion: The Missiology of A N Groves	**171**
Part 3. The Missiological Influence of A N Groves	**173**
1. Groves's Missiology Applied	**173**
Brethren Missions	173
The Scriptural Knowledge Institution	173
The Missionary Magazines	177
Early Initiatives	177
Later Ambiguities	181
Dan Crawford (1870-1926)	183
Jim Elliot	186
Zambian Assemblies	187
Mysore Assemblies	188
Conclusion: Brethren Missions	191
Faith Missions	192
Groves as a Model for "Faith Missions"	193
Groves and Hudson Taylor	193
Co-operation with All Denominations	194
Living by Faith	196
Recruitment of Unordained and Uneducated Men	197
Recruitment of Single Women	199
Internationalisation	200
Premillennialist Stimulus	201
Indigenous Evangelists	202
Conclusion: Groves as a Model for "Faith Missions"	202
Groves in Contrast to "Faith Missions"	202
Pioneering Unevangelised Fields	203
Systematising Financial Support	204

Self-support	206
Establishing Authority Structures	206
Respecting Denominational Traditions	208
Evading Ecclesiological Issues	208
Perpetuating the Church / Mission Organisational Dichotomy	211
Other Influences on "Faith Missions"	212
Conclusion: Groves in Contrast to "Faith Missions"	212
Conclusion: Faith Missions	213
Indigenous Missions	213
John Arulappan (1810-67)	214
Watchman Nee (1903-1972)	215
Bakht Singh (1903-2000)	218
Conclusion: Indigenous Missions	220
Conclusion: Groves's Missiology Applied	220
2. Mission Thinkers, Grovesian and Other	**223**
Primitivism	223
Institutionalism	229
Culturalism	233
Church Growth	236
Primitivism Revisited	244
Indigenous Primitivism	247
Support and Dependence	252
Conclusion: Mission Thinkers, Grovesian and Other	258
3. Groves's Primitivist Missiology: a Hermeneutical Critique	**261**
4. Groves's Primitivist Missiology: a Historical Critique	**269**
Conclusion: The Missiological Influence of A N Groves	**275**
Conclusion	**279**
The Primitivist Missiology of Anthony Norris Groves:	*279*
Bibliography	**283**
Index	**307**

Preface

The period in which, as a young man, Groves developed distinctive views concerning church and mission embraced the years 1825 to 1835. As it happens, this was a highly significant moment in the religious history of the British Isles. Indeed, David Bebbington identifies, in these second and third decades of the nineteenth century, a particular crisis in the evolving religious history of Britain:

> It was a clash between those who inherited the eighteenth-century beliefs in order, design and gradualness and those who, in the iconoclastic spirit of the nineteenth century, wished to substitute the free, the dynamic and the cataclysmic… From as early as the 1820s a new force was in the field.[1]

It is the contention of this book, and of its companion volume, that Anthony Norris Groves was a significant participant in the rise and spread of this "new force", both within the United Kingdom and overseas.

---

[1] Bebbington, *Evangelicalism*, 92

Acknowledgments

I would like to thank Christopher Partridge, Timothy Stunt, Tim Grass, Stephen Chilcraft, Alan Millard, David J Clark, David F Wright, and Janet Dann for their valued help, criticism and inspiration. This book is based on a thesis accepted by the University of Liverpool for the degree of Doctor in Philosophy in May 2006.

Abbreviations

The following abbreviations are used for particular missionary agencies:
- ABCFM American Board of Commissioners for Foreign Missions
- BFBS British and Foreign Bible Society
- BMS Baptist Missionary Society
- CIM China Inland Mission
- CMS Church Missionary Society
- LMS London Missionary Society
- LSPCJ London Society for Promoting Christianity amongst the Jews
- SPCK Society for Promoting Christian Knowledge
- SPG Society for the Propagation of the Gospel

English translations of the Bible are identified as follows:
- AV Authorised Version (King James Version)
- GNB Good News Bible
- NIV New International Version
- NRSV New Revised Standard Version
- RSV Revised Standard Version

Primary sources are indicated in footnotes using the following abbreviations accompanied by the appropriate page number(s):
- D Christian Devotedness (2nd edn., Raven, Belfast)
- J Journal of a Journey to Baghdad
- M Memoir of Anthony Norris Groves (3rd edn.)
- R Journal of a Residence at Baghdad

Secondary Sources are:
- BDEB Lewis, Donald M (ed.), *The Blackwell Dictionary of Evangelical Biography* (1995)
- DNB Lee, Sydney (ed.), *Dictionary of National Biography* (1893)
- FOFM Dann, Robert Bernard, *Father of Faith Missions*
- PMANG Dann, Robert Bernard, *The Primitivist Missiology of Anthony Norris Groves*

Introduction

The subtitle of this book suggests that Anthony Norris Groves exercised a radical influence on nineteenth-century Protestant mission. To justify this, we must firstly ascertain whether he was a "radical", that is, an innovator and a challenger to the status-quo (as distinct from a man representing trends and factions already established in his generation), and then to determine the extent of his influence.

Born in southern England at Newton Valence, Hampshire, in 1795, Groves completed his secondary education in Fulham, near London. After training as a dentist, he set up practice in Plymouth and later in Exeter. It was in 1816, at the age of twenty-one, that he first professed himself "a disciple of Christ", a typical middle-class convert to evangelical high church Anglicanism. Eight years later, his contact with Anglicans and Nonconformists of a more Calvinistic persuasion had led him to a fuller assurance of his personal salvation.

Having married his cousin Mary Bethia Thompson in 1816, he found his increasing desire to serve overseas with the Church Missionary Society thwarted by his wife's determined resistance, until in 1824 she too responded to Calvinistic influences and began to support not only his philanthropic activities but also his missionary interests.

Whilst engaged in dental practice, Anthony Norris Groves became convinced, from his reading of the New Testament, that Jesus intended his disciples, in every age, to take literally the instructions given in the Sermon on the Mount. The result was a small booklet published in 1825 with the title *Christian Devotedness*, in which he encouraged his fellow-believers to give away everything surplus to immediate requirements and engage in proclaiming the gospel throughout the world. It typified Groves's lifelong desire "to read the word of God with a single view to know his will,"[1] and to follow, in the most literal fashion, the teaching and the example of Jesus and the apostles as recorded in the New Testament.

Embarking on a course of theological study in 1826, with a view to ordination in the Church of England and service with the CMS in the Middle East, Groves travelled every three months to Ireland in order to sit his examinations at Trinity College, Dublin. In the course of these visits, he was invited to drawing room meetings for prayer and Bible study attended by Christians of both Establishment and Dissent. He was impressed by his first experience of Christian fellowship transcending denominational barriers, and in the spring of 1827 suggested going one step further. Denying the necessity for an ordained minister to administer the sacraments, he observed "that it appeared to him from Scripture, that believers, meeting together as disciples of Christ, were free to break bread together as their Lord had admonished them; and that, in as far as the practice of the apostles could be a guide, every Lord's Day should be set apart for thus remembering the Lord's death, and obeying His parting command."[2] A small circle of friends began to meet regularly for this purpose.

A few months later, finding on pacifist grounds that he could no longer accept the Thirty-Nine Articles of the Church of England and Ireland, Groves withdrew

---

[1] M11
[2] M39

from Trinity College and abandoned his plans for ordination. In the spring of the following year (1828), he severed his connection with the CMS, and shortly afterwards requested adult baptism.

Unconnected with any church denomination or missionary society, Norris and Mary Groves, with their sons Henry and Frank, set off for the Middle East in June 1829 via St Petersburg. Arriving in Baghdad six months later, they launched what must be considered the first Protestant mission to Muslims in the Arab world. They were assisted for a year by Karl Gottlieb Pfander of the Basel Mission, whose book *Mizan al-Haqq* (The Balance of Truth) would become a classic in the field of Christian / Muslim apologetics. Also with them, acting as tutor to the boys, was John Kitto, who later wrote a series of scholarly works elucidating aspects of Eastern culture for English readers of the Bible.

A year after their arrival in Baghdad, civil war broke out and the city entered upon two years of devastation through siege, famine, warfare, floods, cholera, plague and typhoid, during which two-thirds of its inhabitants were swept away by disease and two-thirds of its houses by floods. After many delays and anxieties, Groves, having lost his wife to the plague, was eventually joined by a small party from Dublin including John Vesey Parnell, Edward Cronin and Francis W Newman (younger brother of the cardinal John Henry). The team established a small medical clinic in Baghdad to supplement the elementary schools in which the idea of vernacular literacy had been introduced using colloquial Bible translations as reading texts for both boys and girls.

In 1833 Groves left to investigate the possibilities for ministry in India, and the following year the Baghdad venture was abandoned.

In India Groves's intention was to visit missions associated with a wide range of Protestant agencies and denominations throughout the sub-continent. Travelling in short stages from Bombay via Ceylon to Calcutta, he generally met with a warm welcome and found opportunities to share his distinctive ecclesiological and eschatological (premillennialist) ideas with missionaries and other expatriates. In the far south, at Tinnevelly, he attempted to intervene in a dispute between the Church Missionary Society and some of its own German agents, led by the Lutheran K T Rhenius, who protested at the curtailing of their right to ordain Indian catechists in deference to the Anglican bishop in Calcutta.

After a brief recruiting campaign in Britain and Switzerland, Groves returned to Madras with a fresh team of missionaries in 1835. Somewhat to his surprise, he found a hardening of opposition to his unconventional views and to his support of Rhenius against the CMS, and his opportunities for pastoral ministry and Bible teaching in English became severely reduced. A Christian farm settlement which he then established at Chittoor suffered serious financial reverses, which largely clouded his later years. In 1853 he died at the age of fifty-eight in the home of his brother-in-law George Müller in Bristol, England.

A Primitivist Ecclesiologist

When he first went overseas in 1829, at the age of thirty-four, Groves was a mature man with well-developed ecclesiological ideas. These have been discussed in my companion study *The Primitivist Ecclesiology of Anthony Norris Groves (1795-1853): a radical influence on the nineteenth-century Protestant church in Britain.*

The Development of Groves's Ecclesiological Thought

The decade from 1825 to 1835 in which, as a young man, Anthony Norris Groves developed distinctive views concerning church and mission was one that marked a turning point in the religious history of the British Isles. It witnessed a popular transition from the eighteenth-century love of rational order to the nineteenth-century demand for the romantic, the dynamic and the ideal. In the vanguard of a new generation of radical Protestants were Groves's contemporaries Edward Irving, Henry Drummond and Joseph Wolff. Although he cannot be considered an intimate acquaintance of these men, there is evidence of some personal contact with them, and he resembles them in many respects. Groves's premillennialist views were probably acquired through his early contact with evangelical Anglicans such as Edward Bickersteth. His primitivist convictions may owe something to his early contact with Jewish converts to Christianity and evangelicals possessing a particular interest in the Jews.[1]

The nature of Groves's subsequent spirituality suggests that Quaker influence in his early years made a lasting impression upon him. A strong emphasis on spiritual unity and co-operation, first awakened by his experience of the "Irish Reformation" in the 1820s, also remained with him throughout his life. His pietistic tendencies might suggest some early contact with Continental Pietists and Moravian missionaries, although clear evidence for such contact is so far lacking.

In tracing Groves's ecclesiastical progression from nominal Anglicanism, through High Church and then Calvinistic Evangelicalism, to secession from the Church of England, we see him following a path taken by others of his generation. Indeed it is likely that the influence of, and precedent set by, contemporaries in Ireland, in the west of England and perhaps also on the Continent, played some part in his personal shift of perspective and loyalty.

Despite this, there are differences between the secession of Groves and that of most of his contemporaries. Particularly striking is the fact that in cutting his Anglican roots he neither sought to join another church denomination nor to initiate a denomination of his own. He adopted and maintained a deliberately non-denominational stance, constrained by a desire to follow "primitive" and "apostolic" practice.

---

[1] See PEANG, 48f, 63ff. In the theology of Judaism, principles are thought to have been revealed through events. A defining experience is given by God on a single occasion, so that all generations may learn from it and act in the light of it. In short, the event sets the precedent and the precedent establishes the principle. For this reason, "Loyalty to the norms and thoughts conveyed in the event is as essential as the reality of the event" (Heschel, 217). A Christian with this Jewish heritage will be likely to consider events recorded in the New Testament as precedents establishing principles. This was the position held by Groves throughout his mature years.

The Ecclesiology of A N Groves

In some respects, Anthony Norris Groves might be considered a typical nineteenth-century Nonconformist in so far as his ecclesiology is concerned. In particular, one would note his rejection of the concept of a national church establishment, a view shared by Nonconformists in general, along with his denial of apostolic succession. But in other respects he differed substantially from the typical Nonconformity of his day. His denunciation of clericism, ordination and sacraments carried him beyond the limits of the Reformed tradition into Quaker territory. His dispensationalism and denial of the Mosaic Law set him sharply at odds with the Puritan heritage of British Nonconformity, and his premillennialism conflicted with its postmillennialist consensus. The disposition of some Nonconformists to engage in denominational and political agitation was, moreover, considerably alien to his own view of spiritual unity and the church's role in the world.

Groves's ecclesiology was built upon the simple idea of the individual Christian learning to follow Christ and encouraging other individuals to do the same. He saw the local congregation as a means to this end, not an end in itself. He had little interest in the things that were traditionally considered essential to "church" – meetings, buildings, finances, organisation, training, ceremony. He offered a fresh and distinctive perception of what the collectivity of Christian believers was, is, and should be, and his ideas fall naturally into three categories: Christian unity, ministry, and influence.

1. *Christian Unity.* Groves believed the true unity of Christians to be spiritual rather than organisational. In his view, the body of Christ in the whole world, as in any particular part of it, should be considered a "mystical body" comprising all genuine believers, whether attached to one of the many diverse church denominations or to none. He refused to identify himself with any denomination or society, believing that to do so would require submission to a "system" restricting his freedom to act according to his own conscience and leading of the Holy Spirit. He nevertheless believed it possible and desirable for a Christian to co-operate with others in any spiritual activity that did not require the individual to act in a manner he or she believed contrary to the will of God. One of his stated aims in India was thus "to become united more truly in heart with all the missionary band there, and show that notwithstanding all differences we are one in Christ, sympathising in their sorrows and rejoicing in their prosperity."[1]

2. *Christian Ministry.* Groves urged the liberty and authority of any Christian man to minister (and especially to teach from the Bible), wherever and whenever he might personally feel led to do so, with the approval of those to whom he ministers. He emphasized the importance of all members of the spiritual body engaging in some form of ministry, according to the spiritual gifts granted to them by God, and he encouraged Christians to offer financial support to men whose ministry they particularly appreciated in order that these might devote more of their time to spiritual rather than secular work. He proposed a simple form of dispensationalism (identifying four dispensations) which would liberate mankind from the necessity to observe the Moral Law of the Old Testament whilst requiring the individual Christian to obey all the instructions of Christ. He particularly

---

[1] M226; see PEANG, 98f.

disliked what he termed "that awful distinction between clergy and laity," "that yoke of mere human ordination, the necessity of a title from man to preach and administer, as it is called, the sacraments, of which not so much as a hint is contained in the New Testament."[1] He proposed an alternative: "For all the varied circumstances that can arise in an increasing empire like this of ours in India, every body of believers, however small, will then feel their full liberty, authority and power, notwithstanding any secular pursuit, to take the office of bishop in the church of God: and every one of the church, however humble his gift, will feel free to minister, as of the ability which God giveth."[2]

3. *Christian Influence.* Groves taught that a Christian will be influential in so far as he or she resembles Christ and holds to the teachings of Christ. A disciple of Jesus will not seek to become influential by advancing himself to positions of power and prominence, but will draw others to follow his example through the evident blessing of God upon his life of simple faith and obedience. The Church, comprising Christians of this type, will be a gathered community of the faithful rather than a state-sponsored establishment. Groves emphasised the Christian's need for personal holiness and the importance of an immediate individual response to progressively increasing "light". Throughout his mature years Groves continued to hold to his earliest convictions regarding Christian devotedness, believing that a Christian should literally forsake all, devoting either himself to the missionary cause or his income to the support of missionaries. He counselled, "While one has that ministration of the Spirit which leads him to go and preach the gospel in person, another shows that he is guided by the same Spirit in carefully supplying the wants of him who thus goes… from the abundance yielded by devoted diligence in his honest vocation, and by rigid habits of self-denial."[3]

The Ecclesiological Influence of A N Groves

We might well feel justified in considering Groves a radical ecclesiologist, whilst admitting greater difficulty in ascertaining the extent of his influence in the United Kingdom, at least in his own lifetime. Some might wish it had been substantially greater. Indeed, if Groves rather than John Nelson Darby had been the pre-eminent voice among the Brethren of the 1830s and 40s, the movement might have followed a rather different course, becoming not merely an additional Nonconformist denomination, but rather an alliance of Evangelicals embracing individuals from every denomination and from none. If this was Groves's original intention, and we have some reason to suppose it was, then we might think his influence in his own generation somewhat slight.

Nevertheless, there were aspects of his primitivist ecclesiology, mediated especially through his brother-in-law George Müller, that found a significant place in the Brethren movement. In addition, his ideas concerning liberty of ministry, active participation in the body, plural unpaid leadership, spiritual unity and co-operation, and his concepts of sacrificial stewardship, holiness, "light", faith and

---

[1] R261
[2] *Liberty*, 74; see PEANG,115ff.
[3] D11; see PEANG, 169ff.

obedience eventually found their way, through Brethren influence, into far wider evangelical circles.[1]

There is no doubt, however, that Groves's personal significance to most of his own generation in the United Kingdom stemmed less from his ecclesiological writings, published after leaving Britain, than from his "romantic" example before doing so. His own secession from the Establishment, his self-sacrificing Christian devotedness, his plans for a mission to Baghdad: these all fell into a brief period of less than five years, between the spring of 1825 and the summer of 1829, and they made more direct impression in his homeland than all his subsequent pages of closely argued prose. Groves was indeed a radical ecclesiologist, and his ideas were not lost on his own circle of personal friends, but, as we shall see, his primitivist influence was considerably greater overseas than in the British Isles.

---

[1] See PEANG, 195ff.

A Primitivist Missiologist

Introduction: a Missionary Missiologist

Among formal academic disciplines, missiology is a relative newcomer. It has nevertheless awakened widespread interest, as Jonathan Bonk observes:

> Anthropologists, sociologists, development economists, communications experts, theologians, journalists, management specialists, computer programmers, educators, historians and even marketing consultants – each confident that his or her particular insight provides an indispensable key to more effective strategies – engage in what has come to be known as *missiology*. The myriad books, journals, articles, symposiums, consultations, conferences, seminars, seminary and college curriculums – all devoted to the development, the delineation and the implementation of mission strategies to reach this or that hidden or neglected or inadequately evangelised or developed people – reflect the earnest and lively interest of Western Christians in the subject.[1]

Many current writers on missiological themes will admit to very limited experience of Christian mission in foreign cultures. Andrew Walls suggests that "A new generation of mission scholars is arising with all the necessary skills and equipment but without the opportunity for overseas service."[2] One might think a lack of missionary experience a serious handicap to a student of mission. In point of fact, "opportunity for overseas service" was a benefit heartily enjoyed by Anthony Norris Groves. Labouring as an active missionary for twenty-three years in the Middle East and India, he learned much from his experience as he applied his ecclesiological ideas to the foreign cultures in which he lived.

The nineteenth-century is often said to have produced three great mission thinkers: the British Anglican Henry Venn, the American Congregationalist Rufus Anderson and the American Presbyterian John Nevius. Of the three, only Nevius was a career missionary, and his experience was limited to China. Although Venn and Anderson corresponded with many missionaries, their administrative work was conducted from the comfort of a city office, and this inevitably lays them open to the charge of being "armchair missiologists", men indeed "without the opportunity for overseas service".[3] Anderson undertook four brief trips: to Malta and Greece (1828), to Turkey, Syria and Palestine (1843), to India (1854) and to Hawaii (1863). But Venn never visited any CMS mission overseas.

Despite this, the historian of the Church Missionary Society, Eugene Stock, describes Venn as the first person ever to propose a strategy for "the development of native churches". Indeed, Stock asserts, "Before he gave his mind to the subject no one had done so. It was an untrodden field. We may search the missionary papers during the first half of the nineteenth century, and search in vain, for any signs that the matter was even thought of."[4] If the historian had read more widely outside the archives of the CMS, he would have known that Zinzendorf, Carey, Gützlaff, Rhenius, and Groves, among others, had given careful thought to

---

[1] Bonk, *Missions and Money*, 70
[2] Walls, *Missionary Movement*, 156
[3] Shenk, *Venn*, 59
[4] Stock, *Hist CMS*, II, 83

missionary methods and "native churches" many years before Venn put pen to paper on the subject.

In fact, Groves possessed a far wider personal knowledge of missionary problems and opportunities than either Venn, Anderson or Nevius. He was concerned with the same issues that they raised, and his conclusions, scattered throughout his journals and letters, are as clear and as coherent as anything they offered to their generation or ours. The fact that his thoughts are presented in letters and journals is typical of Groves himself. Although he was by nature an idealist, accused at times of being far *too* idealistic, his missiology was intensely practical. It grew out of personal experience and was tested in real situations. Though not by training or by inclination an academician, he was a sensitive and perceptive man, and he had qualities that ideally equipped him to evaluate missionary strategy.

To start with, he spent many hours in personal study of the scriptures, prayerfully waiting on God for fresh light on matters of difficulty. This indeed was his daily habit, and with his mind full of what Christ and the apostles had said and done, the life of the early church was fully as real to him in imagination as that of the congregations in which he ministered. As an active missionary, he had acquired the ability to speak colloquial Arabic with fluency. He had discussed the gospel with innumerable individuals from Muslim, Jewish, Catholic, Orthodox, Nestorian, Mar Thomist, Zoroastrian, and Hindu backgrounds. He had personal knowledge of Christian schools, villages and industries in many different places. He had debated missionary methods with scores of workers in western and eastern Europe, Russia, the Caucasus, Mesopotamia and most parts of India. For a period of fifteen years he had watched the growth of indigenous Indian churches under the leadership of John Arulappan. But in addition to all this, there was one quality that made Groves almost unique in his generation. It was his habit of seeking fellowship with Christians from backgrounds quite different to his own. His ecumenical spirit, and his freedom from obligation to any particular missionary agency or denomination, meant that he was open to influences from every direction, without being required to toe any party line, or feign a diplomatic neutrality on any issue, or patch up systems inherited from others.

Twenty years ago Anthony Norris Groves was described as "a neglected missiologist".[1] Since then a succession of missiological works have continued to ignore him. The most recent, designed as "a standard textbook for introductory seminary and graduate-level courses in missiology", claims that its "chapters cover the gamut of missions from theology to history to application."[2] No reference to Groves can be found in any of its 750 pages. There is also no mention of Bakht Singh or Watchman Nee, or any treatment of indigenous missionary movements.

In the case of Groves, there are reasons for the neglect. Among them we might recognise the fact that he was a great individualist (never the leader of an organisation wishing to perpetuate his memory), that his ideas lie scattered throughout his journals and letters (never collected into a systematically reasoned monograph), that the Brethren with whom he has been identified always regarded the New Testament itself as their manual of missionary methods (never feeling the need to supplement it with another), and, finally, that his own missionary efforts

---

[1] Newton, *Groves*
[2] Terry, Smith & Anderson, 1998, ix

ended with some embarrassment. Seen in this light, the neglect was almost inevitable, and yet many ideas attributed to later writers find their first expression in the letters and journals of Anthony Norris Groves. And unlike some more recent missiologists, he actually learned a foreign language, spent most of his adult life in an alien culture, recruited missionaries, established them in pioneer situations and personally led people from other races to faith and to maturity in Christ.

Like most active missionaries, Groves lived in circumstances that hindered the communication of his theological views to a wider public. The longer he remained at a distance from urban civilisation, the fewer would be those who had ever heard of him or of his opinions. He did not, like Venn and Anderson, have an organisational status that guaranteed respect for his ideas. He did not have the leisure, like some other writers, to expound in a persuasive and scholarly fashion the finer points of his theories. And the more he adopted the mindset of an Arab or an Indian, the harder he would find it to reason and to communicate like an Englishman or American. As Kenneth Cracknell observes,

> Missionaries, by definition, were not creatures of libraries. None had shelves full of reference books or access to all the recent publications in the field. Very few missionaries were in a position to pen letters to the editors of theological journals... To reach an accurate assessment of their theological struggle requires patient attention to their diaries and journals, their speeches..., their correspondence..., and when they are available, their published works.[1]

Our efforts must now be directed to assessing this form of "theological struggle" in the experience of Anthony Norris Groves, as we evaluate his missiological writings in the context of his age and in comparison with the views and assumptions of his contemporaries.

---

[1] Cracknell, 1-2

Part 1. The Development of Groves's Missiological Thought (1825-1840)

The developed views of any original thinker will owe something to his personal motivations, to the influence of other people, and to the unfolding experiences of his life. We must trace the impact of these various factors in the case of Anthony Norris Groves during his formative years in Britain (1816-29) and in the course of his subsequent missionary career.

1. Early Missionary Influences

Cracknell identifies "five streams of missionary thought" which converged to mould the generation of missionaries to which Groves belongs.[1] In his case, one of these was undoubtedly influential; one was possibly of some indirect significance; three hardly applicable to him at all.

The first of Cracknell's "streams", the Great Awakening in North America (associated especially with Jonathan Edwards), was so far removed from Groves's early experiences as a High Church Anglican in southern England that we can suppose, in the absence of contrary evidence, that it made no significant impression on him. Secondly and similarly, we find in his surviving writings no echo of the missionary theology of the Puritans (Sibbes, Baxter and Mather). Thirdly, though he later on one occasion referred to John Wesley as "that good man",[2] he seems to have had no personal contact with Wesleyan meetings or missionaries before leaving Britain in 1829. Fourthly, although we might suppose him to have a certain affinity with the German Pietists and the Moravians, and though he knew of such men training with the CMS in London during the 1820s, there is no trace of direct Pietist or Moravian influence in his early writings. Whilst his missiological thought may owe something to his experience of Pietists and Moravians after leaving Britain, it is highly unlikely that his initial missionary interest was derived from them.

This leaves us with the fifth of Cracknell's "streams", for there is no doubt that Groves's earliest missionary interest was awakened by the Anglican missionary societies, and in particular the CMS, along with the interdenominational British and Foreign Bible Society. We shall see that both these agencies were active in the Anglican churches of his youth and early adulthood. The young Groves was therefore a missionary recruit from the same stable as Henry Martyn, and would hope like him to fulfil the postmillennialist vision of the great Charles Simeon for the conversion of the nations and the establishment of the kingdom of God throughout a world progressively civilised and Christianised.[3]

With this general context in mind, we can now trace in Groves's own writings the personal influence of a number of his contemporaries in his early desire to serve as a missionary and on his developing ideas about the nature of missionary service.

---

[1] Cracknell, 3
[2] Groves, *Remarks*, 38
[3] Groves knew neither Simeon nor Martyn personally, although he had read Martyn's biography prior to leaving Britain in 1829 (see PEANG, 42ff).

John Owen (1766-1822) and the British and Foreign Bible Society

In 1804 Owen became a founder member and secretary of the BFBS, a post which he occupied for many years. Groves later recalled,

> When I was between thirteen and fourteen, I used to attend Fulham Church with the school to which I was sent, and all I recollect of my general religious state then was, that it was a common practice with us, to take the smaller novels, such as Fielding's and Smollett's, *within* our prayer-books, to read at church; and yet it was during this state of open rebellion against God, and while walking in open defiance of His holy will, that the first permanent impression was made on my mind relative to missions. It was after a sermon preached by John Owen. I recollect the thought arising in my dark soul, "surely it would be a worthy object to die for, to go to India, to win but one idolater from hopeless death to life and peace." Little did I then think that I was ten times worse than he, as great a sinner and with none of his excuses. The impression soon wore away, yet I never was free from recurring convictions.[1]

Some years later he remarked, "When I was a schoolboy, attending Mr Owen's preaching at Fulham, *India* (I know not how or why) occupied my wishes, for I knew not Christ."[2]

It is to Owen, therefore, that we should attribute Groves's earliest interest in overseas mission, some years before his evangelical conversion. There is no evidence of a particular personal friendship between Owen and Groves in later years, although Groves frequently ordered literature from Owen's successors with the BFBS and sent them news of his activities.[3]

Edward Bickersteth (1786-1850) and the Church Missionary Society

Between 1824 and 1830, Bickersteth served as secretary of the CMS. From as early as 1815, he had been instrumental in arranging for clergy with missionary sympathies to visit churches in many parts of England in order to report on the work of the Society, to raise funds, and, if possible, to obtain recruits.[4]

It was probably through the visits of such CMS representatives to the churches of Plymouth and Exeter that Groves remained aware of the needs and opportunities for work in the East, and especially in India. The fact that the CMS struggled against many obstacles, including the refusal of many clergy to receive their representatives, may have been, to a man of Groves's temperament, one of its attractions.[5] In 1814 Groves enquired with the CMS about overseas service and was encouraged to prepare himself for such work.[6] His marriage later that year frustrated these plans, when he found his wife Mary strongly resistant to them.[7]

---

[1] M23

[2] M242. This John Owen should not be confused with the celebrated seventeenth-century Puritan of the same name.

[3] The BFBS archive contains seven letters from Groves to the BFBS between the years 1829 and 1833 (see bibliography).

[4] Hylson-Smith 213-4

[5] For a number of years no bishop would give his official support to the Society, and few clerical recruits could be found in England (Stock, *Hist CMS*, I, 90). A strong supporter of the CMS and BFBS was Thomas Hitchins, a local clergyman influential in Groves's early spiritual development (see PEANG, 26).

[6] M26

[7] M27

A missionary visitor of particular interest to Groves was Bishop Philander Chase (1775-1852), an American, born in New Hampshire. Currently engaged in a pioneering work on the American frontier, he came to Exeter in 1824, and noting Groves's interest, asked him to consider taking his family to join this work in Ohio. Four months passed before Mary Groves would consent to the idea, but their eventual letter of enquiry brought no response from Chase. Mary then agreed they should apply unconditionally to the CMS for service anywhere.[1]

Shortly afterwards, in July 1825, Edward Bickersteth came from London to visit them. Few educated Englishmen had shown willingness for overseas service with the CMS, and Groves, now with the benefit of his wife's support, seemed to the London committee a man of considerable potential. The committee proposed locating the couple in the Mediterranean area, based initially in Malta where a team was already writing and printing tracts for widespread distribution.[2] Groves was advised to prepare for ordination, whilst continuing his dental practice, by enrolling as a part-time external student at Trinity College, Dublin.

In March 1827 a further letter arrived from the CMS, asking them to reconsider their intended location and launch a pioneer work in the Middle East, based initially in some suitable city in what is now Iraq or Iran. The request came in response to a visit from a Jewish evangelist, Joseph Wolff, who had just returned from extensive travels in the region and spoke of a vast area, stretching through Turkey, Syria and Persia, where Christian scriptures might be received and read with interest.[3] It was thus through his candidacy with the CMS that Groves's attention was directed to the region in which he would, two years later, commence his missionary career.

Pietists and Moravians

Zinzendorf's *Periodical Accounts* of the Moravian missions were read by William Carey before his departure for India,[4] and it is possible that they were also known to Groves, although no documented evidence of this survives.[5] Whilst Groves had little or no personal contact with Moravians or other continental Pietists in his formative years, his ecclesiology developed along very similar lines, notably in his concept of spiritual unity transcending denominational considerations. Zinzendorf himself was a significant innovator in the field of missiology, and one with whom Groves might be thought to have definite affinities.

Zinzendorf repudiated civilisation as a motive for mission.[6] His Moravian settlements were designed to be spiritual colonies rather than European colonies, and he declared, "You must take care that the heathen does not make any

---

[1] M32
[2] CMS Minutes, 9th Aug. 1825; Groves to Bickersteth, 15th Sep. 1825
[3] CMS Minutes, 20th Feb. 1827; M19; see below, 31.
[4] Lewis A J, 94. For an assessment of Moravian influence on Carey's methodology, see Oussoren, 219-269. Walls notes that Carey was aware of earlier missionary initiatives from the continent of Europe and hardly considered his own venture a novelty (Walls, "Eighteenth-Century", 32-3). Smith catalogues some of these European "Protestant forerunners" (Smith, Ibid, 479-80).
[5] See PEANG, 81ff.
[6] Cracknell, 28

connection with the Europeans and their way of living."[1] He urged an attitude of humility towards indigenous people: "You must never try to lord it over the heathen, but rather humble yourself among them and earn their esteem through the power of the Spirit."[2] He expected his missionaries to support themselves through manual labour, even working their passage on board ship to their appointed destination.[3]

Moravian missions ignored the Protestant tradition of an autonomous "national church" in each country, established and protected by the legitimate ruler, for this scheme would logically require the conquest of a nation before a church could exist. They were willing to create an *ecclesiola* in any location, even before there existed an *ecclesia*.[4] What is more, Zinzendorf positively discouraged the creation of a Moravian denomination overseas, instructing his missionaries, "You must not enrol your converts as members of the Moravian Church... you must be content to enrol them as Christians."[5] Many such converts, in fact, joined other denominations.[6] David Bosch describes his practice:

> He was not interested in the formation of "churches" on the mission fields; to him, "church" by definition meant formality, lifelessness, lack of commitment... Mission was, for him, not an activity of the church, but of Christ himself, through the Spirit. In this, however, Christ made use of people of extraordinary faith and courage, of daring energy and persistent endurance. Pietism thus introduced the principle of "voluntarism" in mission. It was not the church (*ecclesia*) that was the bearer of mission, but the small, revived community inside the church, the *ecclesiola in ecclesia*.[7]

Zinzendorf did not regard mission as a specialised activity to be undertaken by voluntary societies but rather as a natural part of church life: "The Moravian Church has always been a mission Church and not just the foster-mother of missionary societies."[8] Indeed, as Moravian colonies were launched overseas, strong links of fellowship and prayer were maintained with the entire company of those who remained behind. As Bosch observes,

> Pietism had an abiding significance for the development of the Protestant missionary idea. First, mission could no longer simply be regarded as the duty of colonial governments. In addition, it was transformed from being a concern of rulers and church hierarchies to being an enterprise with which ordinary Christians could not only identify but in which they could actively participate. Third, Pietism ushered in the age of ecumenism in mission in that it aimed at a Christian fellowship that transcended the boundaries of nations and confessions... Fourth, for one entire century, the eighteenth, Pietism caused Germany to be Protestantism's leading missionary country. This was due in no small part to the leadership provided by people like Francke and Zinzendorf. Last, Pietism demonstrated in a remarkable way what total dedication meant... Ordinary men

---

[1] The quotation is from Zinzendorf (Cracknell, 28, citing references in Hoekendijk J C, *Kerk en Volk in de Duitse Zendingswetanschap*, 1962, 43ff.).
[2] Lewis A J, 92
[3] Ibid. On Moravian principles of missionary self-support, see Oussoren, 237-9.
[4] Spangenberg, 277; see also Bosch, 254.
[5] Lewis A J, 95
[6] Ibid.
[7] Bosch, 253
[8] Lewis A J, 97

and women, most of them simple artisans, went literally to the ends of the earth, devoted themselves for life to people often living in the most degraded circumstances, identified with them, and lived the gospel in their midst.[1]

There is much in this statement that will find an echo in the missiology of Groves. If he had been a reader of German (which he was not), or if English translations of pietist writings had been circulating among his circle during the years 1814-29, we might infer some direct Pietist input to his thinking. Evidence for this is so far lacking, and it seems that Pietism reached Groves by more indirect routes.

Edward Irving (1792-1834)

Groves may or may not have been aware of the fact that in 1818-19, at the age of twenty-six or twenty-seven, Irving had himself seriously considered going to "Persia". This was the exact location where, ten years later, Groves would fulfil Irving's vision for "the apostolic messenger, undaunted and solitary, bearing from place to place the gospel for which he would be content to die."[2] The coincidence, if it be such, is a striking one.

Although there is no evidence of direct contact between Groves and Irving, we may assume that Irving's views were familiar to Groves through his interest in the radical ideas emanating from Albury and his contact with mutual acquaintances such as Henry Drummond and Alexander J Scott.[3]

Irving's missionary interest led him in 1825 to visit some pietist recruits from Würtemburg then training in London, and he knew of two others in St Petersburg. Hearing of a pietist team newly established in Karass "on the confines of Persia", Irving remarked that they "soon found out the unproductiveness of Scottish prudence when applied to propagate the Gospel and are fast reverting to the primitive method."[4] By 1829 Groves, too, was aware of these pietist missionaries and, at least initially, shared Irving's admiration for their "primitive method".[5]

Despite the furore aroused by his advocacy of Christ's own missionary methods, Irving has not generally been considered a missiologist of any great significance. Having delivered his so-called Missionary Oration to the assembled friends and supporters of the London Missionary Society in 1824, he said little more on the subject. Once his discourse had been published the following year under the title *For Missionaries after the apostolical school, a series of orations*, he did not pursue his original intention to issue further volumes on the same topic.

It is worthy of note that five years prior to Irving's "Oration", Henry Drummond had founded his Continental Society (1819) for the support of itinerant evangelists in Europe. Drummond's evangelists have been described as "exemplars of the new style of missionary envisaged by Irving in his LMS sermon – men relying on providence for their support, spreading gospel light in a dark land".[6] But

---

[1] Bosch, 255
[2] Oliphant, I, 88
[3] On Groves's contact with this circle and the possible influence of Irving's primitivism on the development of Groves's ecclesiology, see PEANG, 58ff, 65ff.
[4] Oliphant, I, 309-10
[5] For Groves's mixed feelings about the Karass mission, see *Journal of Journey*, 58ff. For further comment on the work in Karass, see Richter, 98, and Bawden, 23-5.
[6] Bebbington, *Evangelicalism*, 77. On Drummond and the Continental Society, see PEANG, 65ff.

as Drummond's "apostolical" mission predated Irving's address, the latter could be considered not so much a visionary dream as an *apologia* for initiatives already well under way.

Despite his expressed desire to speak and write much more about overseas mission, the fact is that Irving barely progressed beyond the exposition of a single passage, Matthew 10:5-42, in a single sermon. The negative response he received presumably dissuaded him from saying more. From the historian's point of view this is regrettable, for it leaves us largely in the dark with regard to the additional ideas he may have shared privately with friends such as Drummond and Scott, and which were thus, we might suppose, communicated indirectly to Groves. And yet the Oration itself, in both spoken and printed form, was a phenomenon of importance and worthy of analysis, especially in view of the fact that the views it presents so closely resemble those expressed by Groves in the years immediately following its publication.

Describing his romantic ideal of the Christian missionary, Irving commenced with a critique of what he called "the principle of expediency, and… the rules of prudence" which, he claimed, characterised the Protestant agencies currently involved in overseas mission.[1] He was careful to express his sense of brotherhood with "the members and managers of Missionary Societies", considering himself "a true friend to the work in which they are engaged", but he warned of his serious reservations about their methods: "That I consider their plans imperfect and immature is, I trust, no more than they do themselves. That I search the Scriptures for light is, I trust, no more than they do themselves."[2]

There was more to come, and not surprisingly it caused great offence, especially when the LMS committee heard his opinion of their recruiting methods: "Instead of going about to seek men who were advanced in faith to the height of the undertaking, they have gone about to reduce the undertaking to the measure of an ordinary faith, and have attracted to the service many who were hardly fit for a pastoral care in the Church at home, much less for laying the foundation of Christian empire abroad."[3]

Irving then ruthlessly caricatured such missionary societies. Their approach was, "We must accommodate ourselves to the absence of these supernatural means, and go about the work in a reasonable, prudent way, if we would succeed in it; calculate it as the merchant does an adventure; set it forth as the statesman doth a colony; raise the ways and means within the year and expend them within the year; and so go on as long as we can get our accounts to balance."[4]

Stephen Chilcraft sums up Irving's Oration as a challenge to the Society "to cease operating as a business, relying on money, worldly expedience and prudence, and to rely on God alone."[5] Irving himself identified "the leading idea of his discourse" as its intention "to bring back the Missionary to the Apostolical office, to restore the Gospel-Messenger to his dignity of place, to give him back his

---

[1] Irving, *For Missionaries*, xiv. References in Roman numerals are from Irving's preface to the published work, and formed no part of his original discourse. The published preface appears more overtly critical of traditional missions than was his oral address to the LMS.
[2] Irving, Ibid, xxv-xxiv
[3] Ibid, 72
[4] Ibid, xix
[5] Chilcraft, Ch.1

charter and prerogative, to deliver him into the liberty of his office out of the hands of whomsoever would enthral it, to make him the servant of our common Lord, the dependent of our common Father, the mouth and voice of our common Spirit."[1]

Irving went on to offer some positive recommendations. In order to discover how Christian mission should be undertaken, he proposed learning from the apostles: "They had no wages; they depended upon no remittances; they lived all along and altogether upon the Brethren."[2] They were "destitute of all visible sustenance, and of all human support."[3] They lived, in short, "by faith".[4] Irving then explained how the practice of living "by faith" is the direct opposite of living by "prudence" or "expediency":

> This is the age of expediency, both in the Church and out of the Church; and all institutions are modelled upon the principles of expediency, and carried into effect by the rules of prudence. I remember, in this metropolis, to have heard it uttered with great applause in a public meeting, where the heads and leaders of the religious world were present, "If I were asked what was the first qualification for a Missionary, I would say prudence; and what the second? Prudence; and what the third? still I would answer Prudence." I trembled while I heard, not with indignation but with horror and apprehension, what the end would be of a spirit which I have since found to be the presiding genius of our activity, the ruler of the ascendant. Now, if I read the eleventh chapter of St Paul's Epistle to the Hebrews, I find that from the time of Abel to the time of Christ, it was *by faith* that the cloud of witnesses witnessed their good confession and so mightily prevailed; which faith is there defined the substance of things hoped for, the evidence of things not seen; whereas *prudence* or *expediency* is the substance of things present, the evidence of things seen. So that faith and prudence are opposite poles in the soul, the one attracting to it all things spiritual and divine, the other all things sensual and earthy.[5]

In Irving's view, mission should be driven by the Spirit of God rather than by the management of finance: "Money, money, money, is the universal cry. Mammon hath gotten the victory, and may say triumphantly (nay, he may keep silence and the servants of Christ will say it for him), 'Without me ye can do nothing.'"[6] How indeed will the "heathen" regard missionaries who are "hired, paid, accommodated and befriended and in all outward things better conditioned than themselves"? Will there not be a murmuring, "They speak to us of faith, let them show their own. They speak to us of the providence of God, but they ventured not hither without every security"?[7]

The need was for a fundamental change of heart in "those who have built up a system of administration on which they have set their heart to call it perfect". And the result would be "much greater simplicity and larger success".[8] Indeed, Irving feared that, without such change, human management was likely to stifle all that is noble, vigorous and heroic in the missionary cause, "to become the death of all

---

[1] Irving, Ibid, xxiv
[2] Ibid, 59
[3] Ibid, 18
[4] On the concept of "living by faith" see below, 131ff and 192ff.
[5] Ibid, xiv-xv
[6] Ibid, xvi
[7] Ibid, 105-6
[8] Ibid, 129

ideal and invisible things, whether poetry, sentiment, heroism, disinterestedness or faith." Mission must be conducted by faith, he insisted, "But *faith* is born to brave contempt, to defy power, to bear persecution and endure the loss of all things. And in doing so, faith will overthrow the idol of expediency and recover those heavenly and angelic forms of the natural man – poetry, sentiment, honour, patriotism and virtue – which the worshippers of the idol have offered at the idol's shrine."[1]

Here, then, is a Romantic ideal to be embraced by both missionary and supporters, an ideal of faith in God's word and in God's people: "Beholdest thou not that the deficiency of earthly means is balanced by the sufficiency of unearthly promises? and that though there be no purse wherewithal to purchase the means of life, there is an admonition from Heaven to all men to take the unprovided Missionary to their home and give him bread and water?"[2] Irving's vision thus balances the ideal of the missionary's faith against the obligation of every Christian (or perhaps of every man or woman) to provide for him. The fact that the missionary has no purse for money or bag for possessions will show how free he is from acquisitive intention: there is nothing about him to arouse hatred or jealousy. They do not have "fixed and stated salaries, like any other craftsmen, which is the sure and certain way to make themselves not only be reputed but justly regarded as hireling craftsmen."[3] Instead, they will simply enjoy the spontaneous hospitality of those to whom they minister.

Above all, Irving praises "the nobleness of the Missionary character, its independence of all natural means, and indifference to all human patronage, its carelessness of all earthly rewards, and contempt of the arithmetic of visible and temporal things". Such missionaries will "live in simplicity and cleave to no sect or party of men, and know no country… and their tidings are all from heaven."[4]

Such a form of missionary support has the advantage of discouraging worldly men, who have sometimes sought to advance themselves through clerical appointments overseas. Indeed,

> Christ wished none but spiritual men to take this office upon themselves; and of the spiritual men in the church, he wished those who were strongest in faith, and those alone, to venture forth. Therefore, he set the mark to the most unearthly standard and appointed that there should be no purse, that is no pecuniary emolument; no scrip, that is no possessions; no change of raiment, that is no pleasures or accommodations of the body; no staff, that is no ease or pleasure of travel; no salutations by the way, that is no ends of natural or social affection.[5]

A missionary of the apostolical school will enjoy complete freedom. He will "have his refuge and dependence upon the Spirit of God for sustenance, for patronage, for reward and for a rule of procedure."[6] He can follow wherever his Lord may lead: "Inward assurances of God's direction will become so strong, the monitions of his Spirit so audible, the commands of Christ to go forth unto all nations so imprinted in fire upon his heart, and invocations from the perishing souls of the Heathen will

---

[1] Ibid, xvi-xvii (brackets added)
[2] Ibid, 81
[3] Ibid, 64, also 37
[4] Ibid, 42
[5] Ibid, 93
[6] Ibid, 119

wax so loud and frequent in his ear, and his whole inward man become so restless and aroused, that he will have no peace till he arise and go forth."[1]

What then is the role of the missionary society? "Whether... [the missionary's] office shall descend to him of God, or descend to him of men; and whether those that guide the work shall consider themselves as infallible to give law to the Missionary... these are questions vitally concerning both the glory of God and the well-being of man."[2] They were, indeed, highly controversial issues, and worthy of more attention than Irving, on this occasion, felt able to give them.

He raised, instead, the question of miracles, and asks in particular, whether the evangelistic success of the apostles might be attributed to the signs and wonders they performed. He preferred to think it due to "the character of the doctrine and the character of the preachers of the doctrine".[3] And though Irving considered the apostolic miracles to be "like fruits before the harvest", and therefore unseasonable in a world not yet perfected, he allowed the thought that if missionaries of apostolic character were sent out, they might once more see the success on the mission field that was seen in apostolic times.[4]

Mission conducted on these lines would have a further advantage. It would be a force for Christian unity when evangelists spent their energies in preaching Christ to the "heathen" rather than promoting sects and societies among the converted: "The missionaries, from whatever sect proceeding, would tend to unity of spirit and recognise each other as brethren, and bring back with them the happy oblivion of those uncharitable divisions which are fatal to the communion of the body of Christ and destructive to its vigorous exertions and great success at home."[5] Churches, he thought, should be planted, not with "the character of *the order* [i.e. the sect or society] that planteth them", but with "the character of the primitive churches, which were of one heart and mind because the Apostles were obedient to the instructions of one common Lord."[6]

Then if denominationalism has no place in the true Church, neither does patriotism. In Irving's mind, the Christian missionary represents the kingdom of God, not the empire of Britain or the culture of any nation: "He will learn to be of no country, that he may remove political hindrances out of the way."[7] Rather than seeing commerce, education or colonial control as a means of preparing the ground for the Gospel, Irving believed the priority was the Gospel itself: "I admire the steadiness with which the spiritual people of this day have stood out against the ignorant clamour that the heathen must be civilized before they can be Christianised."[8]

Civilization, he thought, may be an actual hindrance to the Gospel, especially when the missionary is supplied by his Society with a weight of costly accoutrements and luxuries:

---

[1] Ibid, 121
[2] Ibid, 83
[3] Ibid, xx
[4] Ibid, xxii-xxiii. Groves, in his *Christian Devotedness*, anticipated the same question and offered the same reply.
[5] Ibid, 127-8
[6] Ibid, 131
[7] Ibid, 96. This was an ideal shared by Groves, at least in theory. He wished to consider himself "a citizen of the world, as far as national attachment goes" (J16; see below, 115ff).
[8] Ibid, 106

> Though a Missionary in the first instance should go forth stocked like a trader, fitted out like a discoverer, accredited like a royal envoy, and three times armed with prudence like a hostile spy, when he cometh into close communication with the Spirit of God and the spirit of the people, in order to be the mediator between these natural enemies, he will, if his mind be open to light, be taught... the utter uselessness of all these useful things to that work in which he has embarked.[1]

Indeed,

> This well-furnished missionary... will by degrees divest himself of all those things which withdraw the people from the word of his mouth or hinder them from apprehending the simplicity and sincerity of his spiritual purpose. He will adopt their dresses, follow their manner of life, eat with them and drink with them, and seek access to them at all their unguarded moments, that he may be always at hand to drop his words seasonably into their ear, and manifest constantly before their eye the influence of his faith over all the conditions of man, instead of merely addressing them now and then with set speeches and abstract discourses... And he will not scruple to take favours at their hand, if that will bring him into closer confidence of their souls, which it doth far more frequently than otherwise; and if not he will work to them for his meat, teach them the arts of his country, do any thing that may bring him and keep him in close and frequent contact with their personal affections.[2]

Comparing the preparation offered to missionary recruits in modern times with the way Christ prepared his apostles for their task, Irving declared,

> It was a spiritual work they had to do, therefore he... spiritualised the men who were to do it. It was Faith they had to plant, therefore he made his missionaries men of Faith, that they might plant Faith and Faith alone; they had to deliver the nations from the idolatry of the Gold and the Silver, therefore he took care his messengers should have none; they had to deliver them from the idolatry of Wisdom, therefore he took care they should be Foolish; they had to deliver the world from the idolatry of Power and Might, therefore he took care they should be Weak; they had to deliver the world from the idolatry of Fame and Reputation, therefore he took care they should be Despised; they had to deliver the world from the idolatry of the Things that are, therefore he took care they should be as Things that are not: making them in all respects Types and Representatives of the Ritual they were to establish, models of the Doctrine which they went forth to teach.[3]

In summary, we see Irving advocating a deliberate return to the missionary methods of Christ's earliest apostles, requiring a simple and frugal missionary lifestyle, a rejection of denominational interests, a freedom from worldly business methods, an emphasis on evangelising rather than civilising, and a dependence on God alone for provision and guidance. The similarities between Irving's views and those of Groves will become evident in our discussion of Groves's missiology.

The possibility that Groves's concept of "living by faith" was derived from Irving is strengthened by the immediate rapport established between Groves's

---

[1] Ibid, 94-6
[2] Ibid, 94-6
[3] Ibid, 28

colleagues in Baghdad and a man sent out to join them in 1833.[1] Erasmus Scott Calman had not previously known Groves, but he had known A J (Sandy) Scott, Irving's former assistant and more recently the editor of Groves's journals.[2] Calman had arrived in England as a refugee from the oppression of Jews in Russia. Here he had met Scott and been baptised as a Christian in January 1831. Ten months later he moved to Woolwich, near London, where he became a personal student of Scott, living with his family and attending his church. Calman, as a missionary, chose to live "by faith", without salary or mission connection. Groves's colleague John Parnell tells us that when Calman subsequently left Baghdad, "he went to Jerusalem, refusing to take any money with him beyond what was necessary for the journey, saying that when he arrived at Jerusalem the Lord would provide."[3] Calman was a man very much to the liking of Groves. Although their paths never actually crossed, Groves heard of his efforts in Baghdad: "Dear Calman is most humble; willing to do and be anything: yea I do praise God from the ground of my heart, as I ought"[4]

There were nevertheless some significant differences in the perspectives of Irving and Groves, and we might credit the latter with being, in general, the more careful scholar of the two. They agree in seeing the salaried missionary (wealthy, comfortable and secure beyond the wildest dreams of those who hear him preach) as a poor substitute for the missionaries of New Testament times. But they differ with regard to the means whereby the missionary will obtain his basic necessities. Irving's emphasis was on the missionary taking nothing with him, trusting that his needs would be met by the hospitality of strangers. Groves, in contrast, would accept nothing of the "heathen". He expected, if inadequately supplied by gifts from Christian friends, to work with his own hands and earn his own living.

Irving stated his belief that the instructions in Matthew 10 are of permanent validity, and the abrogation of Luke 22:36 temporary. Groves, in contrast, seems to have regarded both the original instructions and the abrogation as temporary, and followed instead the example of the apostles as narrated in the book of Acts. This is interesting in the light of his wish to take other instructions of Christ literally (as, for example, to the Rich Young Ruler). If Groves was initially encouraged by Irving's willingness to adopt Christ's own missionary principles, he was prepared to look further than Irving into the wider corpus of New Testament scripture and address more complex issues arising from the extension of Christian mission to a cross-cultural rather than a purely Jewish context. With reference to Matthew 10, Irving asserted, "These instructions are of continual obligation, present the everlasting type of the missionary character, and are not by any human authority to be altered or abridged."[5] Irving proposed that if, as is commonly maintained, Matthew 10:16 and 19 are valid in the present time, then so must be verses 9 and 10 of the same chapter. But he seems to have overlooked verses 5 and 6, which would indicate that the passage in question depicts "a temporary measure during his [i.e. Christ's] earthly ministry".[6] In assessing the validity of Irving's view, we

---

[1] Groves himself, at this point, had just left for India.
[2] On Scott, see PEANG, 67f.
[3] M531-2; Newell, *Scott*, 179-80
[4] *Memoir* 1st edn., 163; cf. M238
[5] Irving, Ibid, 46
[6] Keener, 316

should also recognise a significant difference between an itinerant Jewish rabbi speaking of a Jewish prophet in a Jewish home, and an itinerant Jewish evangelist introducing a Jewish messiah to a Gentile city. The first might well expect to enjoy traditional hospitality among his own people; the second could have no such expectation amidst foreigners likely to view him with scorn and suspicion. Irving's application of mono-cultural mission principles to a multi-cultural situation is highly questionable, and one that Groves, significantly, did not follow.

In addition to this, Irving appears far more dualistic than Groves in separating the spiritual from the material. Whilst condemning the notion of a salaried missionary, Irving retained the idea of a Christian minister – a servant of the Gospel devoted to the work of God and free from worldly concerns. He advised, "From the nature of the Gospel itself, he who propagates the Gospel must be separate from worldly interests, and stand aloof from worldly occupations."[1] Groves, in contrast, was quite willing to earn his own living through secular labour. For Groves, "tent-making" was a normal and desirable part of missionary life; for Irving it was a regrettable concession to particular circumstances on the part of missionaries who would naturally prefer to be "wholly careless of the present world, wholly disengaged from its concerns, that they might be wholly occupied with the things of the world to come."[2]

In conclusion, and in spite of these differences, we might draw Groves and Irving together in what would seem a remarkable fulfilment, by the one, of the vision of the other. Indeed, Irving could be thought decidedly prescient in anticipating the dire consequences that would follow the rejection of truly "apostolical" missionaries:

> I cannot and do not doubt that when they put a city to the ban of God's tribunal, there came upon it, if it repented not, judgments of a signal kind… and I believe in my heart that even to this day, were messengers to go forth into all cities arrayed after the fashion of these instructions, they would act like the test of heaven amongst them, and according to their welcome or their rejection, it would be seen that blessings of peace and prosperity, or commotions, revolutions, sieges, wars and discords would befal [*sic*] those places; not indeed miraculously but in the natural course of things, yet not the less at the command and by the will of God.[3]

Was this not a scenario fulfilled to the letter in the devastation of Baghdad six years later? Yet Groves himself saw the woes of Baghdad as preparatory to acceptance of the Gospel rather than as punishment for rejecting it. He declared, "My heart does not despair for the work of the Lord, for no ordinary judgments seem necessary to break the pride and hatred of this most proud and contemptuous people."[4] He looked for a response, and as his work developed he had no thought of shaking the dust from his feet and leaving Baghdad's wretched inhabitants to their fate.

---

[1] Irving, Ibid, 83
[2] Ibid, 60-1; also 62-9
[3] Ibid, 36-7
[4] R236, 127

Joseph Wolff (1795-1862)

Wolff's personal experience of itinerant evangelism in the Middle East, from 1821 onwards, opened up for both the CMS and for Groves the possibility of commencing a permanent work there.[1] The editor of Wolff's journals from this period noted that "He has given a full insight into the state of Muhammadanism as far as the utmost boundaries of Turkey, Persia and even to Chinese Tartary. Wolff was the first to give an insight also into the state of the Christian churches from Alexandria to Anatolia, Armenia and Persia."[2] It was in immediate response to this information that the CMS enquired of Groves whether he would be willing to undertake the task suggested by the Jewish evangelist.

Though not focusing his efforts particularly on Jews as Wolff did, Groves might thus be seen as a willing recruit to his cause. Indeed, it is likely that Wolff's travels, and the opportunities he had found for widespread distribution of scriptures in many languages, encouraged Groves with the thought that missionary work among Muslims was possible, and indeed highly desirable, in the current social and political climate. Wolff's editor adds weight to this supposition, asserting, "Wolff solved the problem whether it is possible for a missionary to preach the gospel in barbarian Muhammadan countries."[3]

Wolff's subsequent disillusionment with the organisational structures and financial policies of missionary societies is of particular interest to us, for it coincides with similar developments in Groves's thought. Typically, we will find Groves expressing it more graciously, and with a greater concern to give honour where honour is due, but the fact is that Groves had gently severed his connection with the CMS (in 1828) four years before the belligerent Wolff, after long periods of tension, severed his with the LSPCJ. In a public letter Wolff condemned his former friends: "Your disregard for the oracles of those men who spoke as they were moved by the Holy Ghost, and your anxiety to accommodate your preaching according to the feeling of your numerous subscribers has rendered you sinners against the Holy Ghost; and you have called down by your conduct in unison with the Church Missionary Society and also the Bible Society, the curse and wrath of the crucified Saviour."[4] As a parting shot he declared that "the accursed system of expediency... has rendered you sycophants of noble lords." Chilcraft comments, "These stinging criticisms of the religious societies mark an important development in the history of missions... Irving and Wolff highlighted important shortcomings of the societies." And then, "Groves provided a positive alternative that was to pave the way for others to follow."[5]

William Jowett (1787-1855)

Jowett was the first Anglican clergyman to volunteer for overseas service with the CMS (in 1813).[6] He undertook careful research concerning the diverse religions and cultures of the Middle East, and in 1825 Groves read his *Christian Researches* with considerable interest and attention. At the time Groves was

---

[1] See PEANG, 63ff.
[2] Wolff, II, 252-3
[3] Wolff, II, 253
[4] *The Morning Watch*, v (1832), 233-4, quoted by Stunt, *Awakening*, 98
[5] Chilcraft, Ch.1
[6] DNB

anticipating joining Jowett in Malta, and a few months later he would arrange for his young protégé John Kitto to assist there in the work of the printshop.[1] In 1830 he again consulted the surveys of both Wolff and Jowett:

> I have just read through a second time Mr Wolff's journal[2] and Mr Jowett's second volume,[3] and I confess that if my little experience entitles me to give my opinion, I think Mr Jowett's judgement much the soundest as to the nature of the operations to be carried on in these countries; that the missionary corps should be as unencumbered as possible, and ready to remove at a moment's notice. I mean those engaged in the simple evangelist's office, disconnected from all secular callings; but should there be a band of enlightened saints, willing to take the handicraft departments of life as their means of support, and unobserved access to the people, they might remain and carry on their work when other and more ostensible teachers were obliged to fly. And this is doubtless the way the primitive churches were nourished when their professed teachers fled.[4]

Wolff had proposed the establishment of Christian colleges, and Groves saw two problems with this. Firstly he feared that such colleges "would lead much more to the diffusion of universal scepticism than the eternal excellency of the truth of God." And secondly, the expense would be enormous: "The liberality of the Christian public is not up to such undertakings."[5] Paradoxically, it was the "unencumbered" Wolff, rather than Jowett with his printshop responsibilities, whose energies were directed to itinerant evangelism. In fact both Wolff's example and Jowett's judgment confirmed Groves in his initial thinking that the missionary's task must be evangelising rather than civilising.

Nevertheless, Groves subsequently expressed great appreciation for the disciplined labours of Jowett and his colleagues:

> We also greatly want Arabic schoolbooks; but these we shall hope to get from Malta, through the labours of Mr. Jowett. We cannot be sufficiently thankful for having these precursors in labour, who have provided to our hands materials that would have cost much labour and time to obtain; I now begin to appreciate the labours of these dear servants of the Lord, who are silently spending their strength for the use of others.[6]

Karl Gottlieb Pfander (1803-65) and the Basel Mission

Born in Würtemburg in southern Germany in 1803, Pfander was eight years younger than Groves. The son of a village baker, his background lay in the Pietist wing of the Lutheran state church. At the age of sixteen he had already decided to be a missionary and in due course was accepted at the newly established Basel

---

[1] Groves to Bickersteth, 15th Sep. 1825. Kitto worked with Jowett in Malta from June 1827 to January 1829.
[2] This probably refers to *Missionary Journal and Memoir of J W, written by himself, revised and edited by J Bayford* (London, J Duncan, 1824). From this date onwards, Wolff's journals were frequently updated and reissued.
[3] This would be Jowett's *Christian Researches in Syria and the Holy Land*. Groves had already read Jowett's volume on the Mediterranean (Groves to Bickersteth, 14th March 1826).
[4] R188
[5] R189
[6] J134; M87. A little later Groves quoted and commented on Jowett's views concerning clergy and laity (R191).

Mission Institute in Switzerland. His studies here included the Arabic language and the Qur'an, and following his appointment to Shushi in the Caucasian mountains he quickly learned Armenian, Persian and the Tartar dialect of Turkish.

In September 1829 when Groves arrived in Shushi on his way to Baghdad, he found Pfander and his Pietist colleagues men after his own heart. He later wrote, "I never shall forget the dear brethren at Shoushee: their simplicity edified me and their devotion stimulated me."[1] Groves responded with enthusiasm when Pfander offered to help him launch his mission in Baghdad.

Pfander was a strong character and a skilled communicator with considerably more missionary experience than Groves. During the year they spent together in Baghdad, we can discern his influence especially in their joint decision to open an elementary school. This had not been Groves's original intention. Indeed, in 1829 on his way through eastern Europe, he had declared, "Education is one thing, which may or may not be a blessing; the knowledge of God's word is another. To forward the one, separated from the other, I would not put forth my little finger; to the latter, all my strength."[2] Pfander's previous experience of schools in which children were taught to read the scriptures in their own dialect, and his confidence that such could be established in Baghdad, persuaded Groves to accept the idea. It was confirmed in his mind by his realisation that direct evangelistic preaching was not a feasible option for him, in a place prone to turbulent religious passions, with his very limited knowledge of the language: "On consultation, both my dearest Mary, myself, and Mr Pfander thought that the Lord's children and saints must take the work the Lord gives, particularly as there appeared no immediate prospect of other work."[3] The purpose of the school was, of course, to help children, parents and teachers read the Bible.

In addition to this, Pfander's skill in personal evangelism and his boldness in distributing literature was a great encouragement to Groves. A year later he declared, "I cannot sufficiently thank God for sending my dear brother Pfander with me, for had it not been for him, I could not have attempted anything; so that all that has now been done must rather be considered his than mine."[4]

Pfander's influence in Baghdad may also be discerned in Groves's determination to learn the spoken dialect of Arabic rather than a more literary form of language, and also perhaps, in the respect he quickly showed for the cultural sensibilities of the people around him. He remarked, "The time spent in the learning of a language among a people, every thought and purpose and habit of whose lives are diverse from your own, has this advantage, that you become in some measure acquainted with their peculiarities before you are in a situation to offend against them."[5] Realising, for example, that it would displease the Muslims of Baghdad for Christians to occupy an upper room, the family left it unused.[6] Few Englishmen of his generation would be so sensitive. Bradley suggests that the typically condescending attitude of the British Empire toward indigenous peoples "contrasted sharply with the more cynical, and more respectful view of the African

---

[1] Groves to Blumhardt, Calcutta, 22nd June 1834. For more on the Shushi mission and Pfander, see FOFM 115-7.
[2] J44-5; M59
[3] R169
[4] R2; M85
[5] R69; M110
[6] M80

and Asiatic races taken by other European countries."[1] The German's habit of debating on terms of equality with people of other races will have not have been lost on Groves.

Pfander and his Pietist colleagues in Shushi no doubt reinforced Groves's impression that the Basel Mission was an institution worthy of respect. Four years later (1834) he was corresponding with its director and hoping to visit its headquarters: "I learn from Mr. Blumhardt's letters, there are many dear German missionaries waiting to come out, willing to do the humblest work with their hands. I purpose to go to Basle and Elbersfeldt, to see these men. I should like to send one or two pious mechanics to Bagdad: They might get more access to the people than we could."[2] The following year, returning to Britain in search of missionary recruits, he made this Swiss excursion a priority.

Despite this, the sensitive individualistic Groves stood temperamentally at some distance from the Germanic disciplines of Basel. The Mission exerted rigid control over its seminarians, and expected well-regulated obedience to its committee and its director. One outside observer, William Jowett, expressed great concern to the CMS regarding the habit of "mutual watching and reproof" inculcated in trainees at the Basel Mission seminary, which he saw to be a cause of quarrels and lingering hostilities between them once they had arrived on the field.[3]

. We should hesitate, then, to suggest significant influence from the Basel society in Groves's missiological development, bearing in mind also that the Lutheran and Reformed ecclesiology of the Pietists differed significantly from that of Groves. Pfander's influence on Groves was more personal than missiological.

Joshua Marshman (1768-1837) of Serampore

When William Carey took ship for India in 1793, few of his contemporaries would have regarded this as an event of historic significance. At the time, the "consecrated cobbler" was more generally mocked or ignored. On his first visit to the subcontinent, Groves travelled far in order to visit the Serampore trio, which is proof of his high regard for Carey and his colleagues, a regard tinged nevertheless with an element of caution. In anticipation he confessed, "I shall be very thankful to get my prejudices against this station removed. May the Lord prepare my heart not to expect too much from man, but to be very thankful for all that I see is according to His will."[4] On arrival at Serampore in April 1834, he was not disappointed:

> I have just seen poor old Dr. Carey, who is sinking into the grave, after more than forty years' service, leaving the world as poor, as to temporal things, as when he entered it. He leaves his widow and children without a shilling, to the loving care of their brethren. May the Lord give them grace to administer support to them, with such love, that it may be like a balm from the Lord's hands, making the broken heart to rejoice. Never, I think, were men more overwhelmingly belied than these: Not, perhaps, that they have done all

---

[1] Bradley, 89
[2] M285
[3] Jowett, letter to CMS, quoted by Miller, 151. See also Miller, 32, 84, 95. On Groves's possible pietist influences, see PEANG, 78ff.
[4] M295

things well, but they are certainly, in every respect, as far above those who censure them, as the blue vault of heaven is above the clouds.[1]

It would be interesting to know more about the "prejudices" picked up with evident reluctance by Groves. His reference to Carey's personal poverty may provide a clue, for the critics of Carey, Marshman and Ward had pointed to the substantial expenditure and extensive properties of the mission as a sign of worldly materialism. In this regard, Groves's relations with the Baptists at Serampore is a subject worthy of investigation.

For the previous twenty years, the Baptist institutions, despite their Nonconformist origins, had enjoyed a privileged status as part of the foreign establishment in Bengal. And yet, as Christopher Smith observes, "The Trio admitted in private that they found themselves in a 'predicament'. They felt torn between the need to live *simply* among the *hoi polloi* in keeping with a dynamic, apostolic type of spirituality, and a competing desire to so co-operate with sympathetic East India Company officials that they would gain acceptance in the corridors of colonial power."[2]

The annual reports from Serampore spoke of the necessity to itinerate freely and cheaply in the manner of the Apostle Paul. But "Their problem was how to integrate a 'primitive' (New Testament) type of spontaneous spirituality with the demands and privileges of a 'professional' lifestyle".[3] Their converts were coming largely from the expatriate community rather than the Indian populace. Their estate, their schools, their printing works, and especially their prestigious college, required a substantial income for their maintenance. "Only with assistance from the affluent British Company could they earn their living and finance their sophisticated mission enterprise."[4] All too clearly, "The Serampore Mission was beginning to get bogged down by institutionalising forces."[5] And yet, "Their financial professional commitments seemed to make it all but impossible for them to develop a more satisfactory or appropriate type of mission strategy for the subcontinent"[6].

The same problems were felt at home. After the death of Andrew Fuller, the Baptist Missionary Society had become an increasingly complicated organisation in Britain, with expectations of authority and accountability. The Trio were aware of the problem, especially after receiving a frank letter from a friendly supporter who hoped, if possible, to dig them out of "the ditch of patronage". He reminded them that they had been warned of the danger long ago, "But no, you would go and play at societies and committees, and see what has come out of it!"[7]

In 1827 Marshman, on furlough in Britain, issued a pamphlet in which he pleaded for a decentralising of administration and a reduction in bureaucracy, proposing that Christian mission should be seen as a movement rather than an institution. This so-called "Serampore manifesto" had a limited circulation and seemed to achieve little apart from the alienation of the Trio from the BMS.

---

[1] M295
[2] Smith, "A Tale of Many Models", 489-90
[3] Smith, Ibid, 483
[4] Ibid, 490
[5] Ibid, 490
[6] Ibid, 490
[7] Christopher Anderson to Marshman, 17 June 1833, cited by Smith, Ibid, 497

It could be argued, nevertheless, that in its attempt to learn from past experience and propose a better strategy, "the Serampore manifesto subconsciously anticipated the rise of Victorian 'faith missions' as well as basic elements of the mission theology and dynamic mission theory developed during the next century."[1] In this case, it might be possible to identify a stronger link between Serampore and the "faith missions" than a mere "subconscious anticipation" – a link, indeed, provided by Anthony Norris Groves. Smith suggests that "What Marshman and Carey did between 1825 and 1827 was map out the way in which they felt Christian missions needed to develop, even though they were unable to disengage themselves from many burdensome institutional ventures in which they had invested so much."[2] It was Groves, appearing fresh on the scene in 1833, and profiting from the experience of Serampore, who perceived a better way of working, and shared it widely with others.

The problem was evident. The Serampore missionaries with their college and their estates had become alienated from the people they aspired to reach. They had discovered "how difficult it was to be both a *sahib* and a *sadhu*."[3] Indeed,

> India was unmoved by such expatriate grandeur (based on large supplies of secular earnings), because spirituality, for her people, was achieved by much humbler means... Indigenous church life needed to spring up using all sorts of resources that God had imparted to Asian people, *without* their being bemused by the beguiling wonders of Western technology and finance. But that was a tall order, and it took Westerners and others a century or more to begin to appreciate the need for such awareness.[4]

Perhaps so, for most Westerners, but for Groves this was obvious from his earliest days in India. We might be led to wonder why.

Early in 1822, Joshua Marshman, representing the Serampore trio, had been invited to meet the BMS committee in England. The intention was to resolve a dispute concerning properties in India whose ownership was claimed by the home committee on the grounds that they had paid for them. Marshman's biographer describes the occasion. For the committee, "Mr Gutteridge... maintained, with all the tenacity of a fundamental principle, that all missionary agencies must labour in the strictest subordination to the will of the parent institution. The Serampore missionaries were equally inflexible in the maintenance of their independence." The eventual outcome was an agreement that the missionaries were to act freely in their daily activities, and in the acceptance and deployment of missionary colleagues, but "that the freehold property at Serampore should be vested in the society."[5]

---

[1] Smith, Ibid, 492

[2] Ibid, 492. Smith suggests that the missiology of the Serampore trio developed piecemeal as a pragmatic response to circumstances. Closely identified with the colonial culture, they also had little experience of activity outside Bengal, which arguably hindered their aspirations for indigenisation and restricted their wider missiological influence. For a more positive view of their missiology, see Tennent, "William Carey as a Missiologist", and also Oussoren, and also Stanley, *The Bible and the Flag*, 159-60.

[3] Smith, Ibid, 490

[4] Ibid, 495

[5] Marshman, II, 268

The BMS secretary, Mr Dyer, was clearly relieved to have the property, at least, under his control. But in March 1827 further controversy arose over the issue of accountability. Marshman came to England again in an attempt to resolve matters. Despite his protestations that the trio had always rendered the strictest accounts of their expenditure,[1] the committee, influenced by allegations from Eustace Carey (nephew of William Carey), judged that they were misusing the funds sent to them and that accountability required not merely accounts but justification of accounts. Marshman was then informed that his failure to satisfy the committee would necessitate severance of the connection and cessation of the supply. Carey and his colleagues were thus dismissed by the society that he himself had founded in company with Andrew Fuller thirty-five years previously.[2]

The first financial assistance offered to Marshman after the rupture came from the sympathetic secretary of the CMS, Josiah Pratt. At the height of the controversy Marshman received a friendly letter from Wilberforce and an invitation to visit him at his country residence. He had earlier twice been welcomed in the home of the elderly Hannah More and was later pleased to address the annual meeting of the LMS.[3] He subsequently breakfasted with the leading members of the Tract Society. Indeed, "From every denomination, except his own, he received those warm expressions of Christian sympathy and kindness to which he was entitled as one of the pioneers of the missionary enterprise."[4] In these circumstances we are told that he felt himself to be a Christian first and only incidentally a Baptist, and he turned his attention to more positive matters, "advocating the claims of India on the attention of Christians in England."[5]

It was at this point that Marshman crossed to Ireland, reaching Dublin on 1st April (1827). Here he "passed a month in the society of friends of all denominations, who seemed to vie with one another in giving him a cordial reception." Indeed, "the atmosphere of Christian benevolence he now breathed served to sustain and animate his spirits."[6] He "attended meetings of the various Bible, tract, missionary and educational institutions" and wherever he spoke about India, his "enthusiastic addresses" were "welcomed in every circle".[7]

Of the friendships formed at this time in Ireland, his closest was with Thomas Parnell, commonly known as "Tract Parnell", who was secretary of the Irish Tract Society. Parnell spoke everywhere with enthusiasm about the Serampore mission, and a day or two before Marshman's departure, "convened a meeting of more than a hundred ministers of various denominations."[8] Parnell also formed a local committee for the support of the Serampore missionaries. Of particular significance to us is the fact that Parnell's nephew, John Vesey Parnell, was in Ireland at this time and, indeed, had been "breaking bread" informally in a non-denominational setting since 1825. John Parnell was a close friend and subsequently a missionary colleague of Anthony Norris Groves.

---

[1] Ibid, 348
[2] Ibid, 335-51
[3] Ibid, 362
[4] Ibid, 362
[5] Ibid, 360
[6] Ibid, 360
[7] Ibid, 360
[8] Ibid, 360

The date of Marshman's major public meeting in Dublin must have been 29th April (1827) or thereabouts. We know that Groves was in Dublin during the spring of that year,[1] so it is probable that he personally heard and even met Marshman. Returning to England in the summer of 1827, Marshman visited Sir John Kennaway in Devon,[2] and it is likely that Groves met him again there. He will certainly have heard about the controversy from John Parnell and from friends in Devonshire, and the sad story will have given him early cause to question a system whereby missions in other lands are directed by committees in London.

Seven years later, both Marshman and Groves were in India, the latter on his initial tour of the subcontinent. We know from other sources that Marshman had suffered from severe depression for some months at the beginning of 1834, in consequence of the long sustained hostility of the younger Baptist missionaries and the London BMS committee. Happily, "in the beginning of March he recovered his spirits."[3] Indeed, on 15th April (1834), Groves received "a most kind note" from Marshman inviting him to visit Serampore: "Indeed, so kindly was it expressed that it quite overwhelmed me."[4] Was Marshman's particular kindness inspired by a memory of Groves's support and affection expressed in Dublin and Devonshire at the time of his earlier profound sorrow and distress? It is not unlikely. When Groves reached Serampore the following day (16th April 1834), he will have found Marshman in good spirits, sixty-four years of age and supporting the aged Carey through the final months of his life.

The friendship of Marshman in Serampore may go some way towards explaining why Groves, two months later (in June 1834), considered Bengal such a good base, not just for evangelistic outreach but also for encouraging Christian fellowship across denominational lines. He declared, "My first great object is to promote the publication of the testimony of Jesus, far and near. And that which I feel to be of the next importance, is contending against sectarianism in the East. For the attainment of these ends, I could not be better situated than at Calcutta."[5]

Marshman died in 1837, but his significance for our study extends after this date. In 1840, a paper attributed to Groves in *The Christian Witness*[6] warmly approved an article in *The Friend of India*, a monthly magazine founded and published by Marshman with assistance from his Serampore colleagues. The article, quoted by Groves, was highly critical of the custom whereby missionary societies were controlled from London and wielded power in India. We will discuss this paper in due course, and do no more here than suggest that in Groves's most extended missiological writing we may identify the cause of the Serampore trio taken up, defended and advanced. Elsewhere in Groves's writings we might see reflected the Serampore realisation that mission should be simpler, cheaper and more mobile than hitherto, and with more interdenominational sympathy and co-operation.

---

[1] M39

[2] Marshman, II, 362

[3] Ibid, 474

[4] M294

[5] M321. In this region he would also enjoy fellowship with his friend William Start of Patna (FOFM 220-1) and the ecumenical John Weitbrecht of the CMS in Burdwan (BDEB; FOFM 221).

[6] *The Christian Witness*, Vol.VII (April 1840), 127-41. On the content of this paper and its attribution to Groves, see FOFM 446-7; 467.

2. Contemporary Intellectual Currents

Missionary Motivations

Johannes Van den Berg identified ten motives that combined to inspire early nineteenth-century missionary initiatives. In his view, individuals were moved to propagate Christianity by interests that could be described as political, humanitarian, ascetic, romantic, by a sense of personal compassion or of communal guilt, a jealousy for the glory of God or for the interests of a church denomination, by eschatological excitement or by a wish to obey biblical commands.[1]

For Groves the greatest motive for missionary service was none of these. For him, it was personal devotion to Christ that inspired his willingness to follow his Master wherever his Master might lead. Contemplating a call to overseas missionary service, Groves declaimed, "Oh, for a heart to love as He loved! Oh, for such meekness, gentleness, and devotion, as shone in everything He did, who is our Great Exemplar... O, for more and more of that vital acquaintance with the love of Christ to a perishing world, which enables the soul in *truth* to say, 'the love of Christ constraineth me!'"[2] Three years later, as a pioneer missionary beset by difficulties and sorrows, "All my desire is to love thee better and serve thee more singly, who art infinitely worthy of all love and all service."[3]

Groves's motivation was distinctly pietistic. He wished to be, as expressed in the title of Van den Berg's book, "constrained by Jesus' love". But he was also frankly motivated by a desire for God's blessing – that is, blessing for himself and especially for others. Indeed, he observed, "The doctrine of rewards, as an incentive to the saints, prevails from one end to the other of the sacred volume."[4]

David Bosch has more recently identified four epochs in the history of Protestant missions typified by four successive forms of missionary motivation.[5] He suggests that the earliest cross-cultural initiatives, owing much to the Puritanistic teachings of Jonathan Edwards, were inspired primarily by an eighteenth-century desire to manifest the glory of God.[6] A second more pietistic current was moved by perceptions of the constraining love of Christ. A third phase, represented by Hudson Taylor and the "faith missions", was concerned especially to rescue the perishing.[7] Then, finally, in the 20th century came an emphasis on the

---

[1] Van den Berg, *Constrained by Jesus' Love*, 144-64. Stuart Piggin has analysed missionary motivations in early nineteenth-century India. In his sample of British missionaries, compassion for the "lost" is paramount, embracing a concern for them to repent and accept Christ as Redeemer and thus find salvation from the eternal consequences of sin. Eschatological expectations also encouraged the missionaries in their task, as did the hope of heavenly rewards, a sense of duty, and a desire to glorify God (Piggin, *Making Evangelical Missionaries*, 124-55).

[2] M43

[3] R166

[4] R283. For further discussion of this idea see FOFM 431.

[5] Bosch, 286

[6] Groves criticised Jonathan Edwards's view that the service of God should be motivated by a mental appreciation of his "abstract perfections". He considered this "all very fine and very philosophical, but in my humble apprehension, most unscriptural" (R282).

[7] An urgent emotional concern to save the "lost" was naturally most evident in Arminian circles. Groves's Calvinism was neither a particular spur to mission nor, if we may judge

social aspects of the gospel, attending to the material and physical needs of the suffering.[1]

In Bosch's scheme, we should certainly place Groves in the second phase. His greatest motivation was always his desire to express his love to the saviour who had first loved him. And he might easily echo the sentiment of Zinzendorf, who said, "Wherever at the moment there is most to do for the Saviour, that is our home."[2] As Groves himself expressed it, "How true it is, in natural love, that labour loses its character when the object is beloved... I feel what we want is *personal attachment* to our dear Lord, and all thoughts of trouble in His service would fly like the mists upon the mountaintops, before the rising sun."[3]

With reference to America, R Pierce Beaver confirms Bosch's historical analysis in part, observing, "The major motive in American missions from the seventeenth century until the rise of overseas missions was *gloria Dei*. But, most strangely, the giving of glory to God then lost influence and was replaced by the motives of obedience and pity for the perishing souls of the heathen." Beaver's words suggest that in America the second of Bosch's historic phases might be perceived more in terms of obedience and duty than constraining love. Groves advocated both, but the emotional intensity of his character probably placed love before duty, a position that might be reversed in a person of more dispassionate temperament. One such was Groves's contemporary Rufus Anderson: "For him Christian obedience is the prime motive... Seeking the salvation of souls because of love of Christ is his second motive, and the opportunity of meeting the greatest need of mankind is the third."[4]

Anderson also drew encouragement from his conviction that Christian civilisation must inevitably spread throughout the world, culminating in a thousand years of millennial bliss. This view was famously epitomised by William Wilberforce in his exhortation, "Let us endeavour to strike our roots into the soil by the gradual introduction and establishment of our own principles and opinions; of our laws, institutions and manners; above all, as the source of every other improvement, of our religion, and consequently of our morals."[5]

Postmillennialist theory of this nature assumed that Christianity and civilisation together would gradually transform the world in preparation for the second coming of Christ. Opinions differed, however, concerning whether the introduction of Christianity to "the heathen" should precede that of civilisation, or vice versa.[6] Henry Venn argued that civilisation will always be a *consequence* of embracing the gospel, not a necessary *precursor* to it.[7] Many hoped they would be simultaneous.

---

from his surviving writings, a particular impediment. It may nevertheless account for his relative equanimity concerning the condition of the unconverted.

[1] Bosch, 287
[2] quoted by Bosch, 287, from Warneck (1906), 59
[3] M235
[4] Beaver, *To Advance*, 17
[5] Edwardes M, *British India 1772-1947* (Rupa, New Delhi 1967), 53-4, quoting Wilberforce from a speech to the House of Commons, 22nd June 1813.
[6] Ingleby, 52-5
[7] Shenk, *Venn*, 26. This was the official line of the CMS, as expressed jointly by D Coates and J Beecham, with W Ellis of the LMS, in their aptly titled *Christianity, the Means of Civilisation: Shown in the Evidence Given Before a Committee of the House of Commons* (London, 1837).

In 1810 "civilizing and christianising" went hand in hand for the American Board of Commissioners for Foreign Missions, and in 1816 the Basel Mission declared its purpose to promote both the "gospel of peace" and a "beneficent civilization".[1] David Livingstone was concerned both to suppress the slave-trade and to Christianise the Africans. Indeed, Brian Stanley has pointed out that "'Commerce and Christianity' was an anti-slavery ideology" buttressed by the belief that an expanding trade in useful goods would prove more profitable and more beneficial to all parties than trade in human flesh.[2] But "In practice, and despite the missionary rhetoric, the argument that civilising precedes evangelising won the day, certainly for those involved in the higher reaches of education."[3]

Ultimately, of course, the Gospel mattered for all these men more than civilisation. Alexander Duff established his English schools to "emanate and diverge the rays of quickening truth" and the Bible was prominent in his curriculum.[4] Livingstone, too, would insist, "You will see I appreciate the effects of commerce much, but those of Christianity much more."[5] Andrew Porter notes that "'Empire', like 'civilisation', was at best something to be turned to missionary advantage, a means to an end but equally something to be ignored or rejected out of hand if it failed to serve the missionary's main purpose."[6]

Indeed, as a motivating force, the vision for spreading "Christian civilisation" could be applied in various ways. Stephen Chilcraft summarizes: "Wilberforce emphasised the ethical and moral dimension, Duff the educational, and Livingstone the economic, but all accepted the link between mission and western civilisation."[7] Then, most pertinently, "Groves stands against all three emphases, because he believed that his heavenly citizenship supplanted his earthly citizenship rather than complemented it."[8]

As a premillennialist, Groves had no expectation that Christianity and Western civilisation would combine to save mankind. This was not among his personal missionary motivations. Indeed, his experience of the slow and painfully contested advance of Christian civilisation into a largely suspicious and resistant world was evidence enough to him that its missionary proponents were on the wrong track: "I am much led to think on those of my dear missionary brethren who look for the kingdom of Christ to come in by a gradual extension of the exertions now making. This view seems to me very discouraging; for surely after labouring for years and so little having been done, we may all naturally be led to doubt if we are in our places."[9]

And yet his eschatological views, though pessimistic about the state of the world, offered a very positive motivation for mission. In his view, although the whole world will not be converted before Christ comes, the whole world will certainly hear the *testimony* concerning him:

---

[1] Bosch, 296
[2] Stanley, *The Bible and the Flag*, 71
[3] Ingleby, 63
[4] Piggin & Roxborogh, 109
[5] Schapera I, 301-2, cited by Stanley, *The Bible and the Flag*, 73
[6] Porter, *Religion versus Empire?*, 116
[7] Chilcraft, Ch.7
[8] Chilcraft, Ch.7
[9] R20; M88

Those who know it is their place to preach Jesus and to publish the New Testament in His blood, whether men will hear or whether they will forbear, have nothing to discourage them, knowing they are a sweet savour of Christ. I daily feel more and more that, till the Lord come, our service will be chiefly to gather out the few grapes that belong to the Lord's vine, and publish His testimony in all nations; there may be here and there a fruitful field on some pleasant hill, but as a whole the cry will be, 'Who hath believed our report? And to whom is the arm of the Lord revealed?'[1]

This encouraged Groves in his missionary task: "I consider the *testimony* of Jesus is to be published through every land before the Bridegroom comes. This makes my heart feel an interest in heathens, that we may hasten the coming of the Lord."[2] He considered one of the "two great objects of the church in the latter days" to be "the publication of the testimony of Jesus in all lands."[3]

In this regard, Groves's premillennialism motivated him to Christian mission in a way that J N Darby's could never do.[4] Whilst Groves expected his generation to "publish His testimony in all nations" before the return of Christ,[5] Darby anticipated a "secret rapture" of individual Christians from a still unevangelised world prior to the Great Tribulation and the inauguration of a Jewish kingdom of God.[6] This eschatological divergence within the evolving Brethren movement is reflected in the far larger number of missionaries sent out by the Open Brethren than by the Darbyite Exclusives.[7]

In conclusion, it is evident that as a motive to mission, Groves's eschatology draws its power from his perceived personal relationship with the coming Christ. His desire to please, to love, and to be rewarded by Christ himself is what moves him to testify as widely and as quickly as possible, and thus to hasten the day of his appearing.

The Romantic Movement

The first decades of the nineteenth century marked, in art, literature and music, the beginning of the Romantic Movement in Europe and Britain.[8] During Groves's formative years the emphasis in educated and cultured circles was shifting from

---

[1] R21; M89

[2] M258. Groves frequently spoke about the second coming of Christ when preaching in India or England. Although he was "a forward thinker" with great "powers of persuasion", he cannot easily be classed as an eschatological story-teller of the type identified by Richard Lee Rogers as one inspiring fervent missionary vision ("A Bright and New Constellation", 60). His millennialism offered personal comfort and hope for individuals rather than an optimistic program of improvement for the world, simply because it was pre- rather than postmillennialist in orientation.

[3] R56; M91. The other great object was "growing up herself into the stature of the fulness of Christ".

[4] Stuart Piggin, in his sample of several hundred British missionaries to India in the first half of the nineteenth century, found both post- and premillennialism a positive motivation to mission, whilst "pure dispensationalism of the Darbyite sort" was an inhibiting factor (Taber, 59-60, citing Piggin, *Making Evangelical Missionaries*, 142-5).

[5] R20

[6] For a comparison of Darby's and Groves's dispensationalism, see PEANG, 136ff.

[7] Grass, *Gathering*, 12.1.1. On the effect of eschatology in the development of diverse views of mission, see below, 117ff and 192ff.

[8] On religious dimensions of Romanticism, see Prickett, 115-63 and Reardon, *passim*.

"reason" to "sentiment", from "thinking" to "feeling", from the head to the heart, from the real to the ideal. One could suppose that Groves, as a sensitive and idealistic man, would be drawn to art, music and poetry, and would express some interest in the creativity of the Romantics. Such does not seem to be the case. His surviving writings (after his evangelical conversion in 1816) do not show him reading secular literature at all. As he travelled down the course of the Volga and through the Caucasus mountains, a "deep romantic chasm" was to him no more than a hazard from which the providence of God had saved his family when a wheel on their carriage threatened to detach itself.[1]

Groves, as an Evangelical of his period, was not alone in this. In her old age, Hannah More, though honoured with a visit from Coleridge, was not greatly impressed by the Romantic poets, except belatedly (in 1814) by Wordsworth.[2] Several reasons might be suggested for this. Moral values found little place in their thoughts. Their politics, in some cases, smacked of republicanism. But their greatest weakness from an evangelical perspective lay in what would appear a very vague and subjective concept of the Deity, placing more emphasis on mystical perceptions than on the absolute truth of divinely inspired Scripture. The philosophers among the Romantics, and especially the continentals such as Friedrich E D Schleiermacher and G W F Hegel, were moving in a direction somewhat distant from the biblicism of British Evangelicals.[3]

Despite this, the yearnings of radical Evangelicals for a more "personal" religious experience, and a purer and more "apostolic" missionary vision, owed much to sensibilities aroused by the Romantic Movement. Edward Irving, as minister of the Scottish Presbyterian Church in London, became a great Romantic preacher. His sermons were intended to move the emotions as much as to impart information, and it is no coincidence that his so-called Missionary Orations were dedicated to the poet Samuel Taylor Coleridge. It was as a Romantic that Irving declared his vision for missionaries after the apostolical school, craved a restoration of supernatural powers, and proclaimed Christ's imminent return in majesty.[4]

There is no doubt that Groves himself was drawn to "romantic" doctrines – the primitivist ideals of the apostolic age, the bold challenge to forsake all and live by faith, the stirring call to the uttermost parts, the dramatic return of Christ in person. Bebbington attributes the success of millennarian ideas largely to the spirit of the age: "It was part of the Romantic inflow into Evangelicalism. Christ the coming king could readily be pictured by poetic imaginations fascinated by the strange, the awesome and the supernatural."[5]

We should note that the aspects of this "Romantic inflow" which appealed to Groves's intensely sensitive and emotional character were rooted in the perceived "Romanticism" of Scripture rather than that of literature, art, or the natural world. And unlike some Romantics, Groves did not manifest any tendency to dwell nostalgically and passively on an idealised past. His diligent study of New Testament Christianity was motivated by the need for guidance in present action

---

[1] J73
[2] Jones, *Hannah More, passim*
[3] Reardon, 10, 46, 56
[4] Prickett, 134; Bebbington, *Evangelicalism*, 84
[5] Bebbington, Ibid

rather than a mystical desire to recapture the feelings of a former age. This made him, in his generation, an unusually practical and obdurate Romantic.[1]

Evangelical Primitivism

Granted that the Romantic movement of the early nineteenth century provided a fresh stimulus to popular religious primitivism, there had been "back-to-the-Bible" movements well before this.[2] Bozeman identifies in the Puritanism of the seventeenth and eighteenth centuries a pronounced belief in the Bible as a divinely-inspired authority and guide for every age, along with a perception that, since New Testament times, the Church had lost much of its original purity, simplicity and truth.[3] Hughes and Allen describe the ethos of this early Protestant primitivism:

> The pattern of Puritan primitivism is characterised chiefly by an elemental belief in the power and exemplary authority of an ancient "first time", a time when supernatural power and presence had transformed ordinary history into an extraordinary time full of precedential authority. This ancient primordium – dramatically reported in the Old and New Testament scriptures – was the 'great time' when God intervened at will, transporting his chosen actors far beyond the realm of the commonplace and giving their lives unparalleled force and significance. It was the time when truth was fullest and clearest, when humankind could be seen at its highest and best. The primordium, in short, was the time of unmatched purity and simplicity. Postprimordial time, in sharp contrast, had brought nothing but an ever-increasing decline from the original standards and a mounting loss of supernatural power.[4]

There is no doubt that Groves belonged to what Bellah describes as "that part of Reformed thought which saw the major task to be the weeding out of centuries of distorted tradition and a return to the condition of the earliest Christian church."[5] Models drawn from the Patristic or Tudor periods or from Calvin's Geneva held no interest for him. And although the Anglican evangelicalism that claimed his allegiance during the period 1816-27 "held the restorationist's goal of Christian unity", it was clear that "they wanted it under Evangelical Episcopal banners."[6] As Groves subsequently drifted away from the Anglican Establishment towards an individualistic form of Dissent, he became increasingly intent on taking the New Testament alone as his ecclesiological model. Thus, "We wish you to read the New Testament that you may learn to judge of God's truth, not by what you see in the churches around you, but by the word of God itself."[7]

As a philosophical system, "The notion of 'primitivism' suggests that 'first times' are in some sense normative or jurisdictional for contemporary belief or

---

[1] The varied currents within the Romantic Movement and Groves's affinity with them are discussed more fully in PEANG, 34.

[2] Among early primitivists we may identify the Paulicians, Bogomils, Waldenses, Lollards and the Unitas Fratrum, with notable leaders such as Wycliffe, Hus, Erasmus and Lefèvre, and then, from the age of the Reformation, Zwingli, the Anabaptists, Bullinger, Bucer, and Calvin (Broadbent, *passim*; Hawley, 29-66).

[3] Bozeman, 13-19

[4] Hughes and Allen, 28

[5] Bellah, in Hughes and Allen, x

[6] Holmes, 155

[7] M69 (J95-96)

behaviour."[1] Although Hughes and Allen claim to employ the terms "primitivism" and "restorationism" interchangeably,[2] other scholars discern a significant difference between them. A primitivist may be passive whereas, by definition, a restorationist must be active. Whereas primitivist perspectives "have enshrined first times as an ideal to be approximated and even as a kind of transcendent norm that stands in judgment on the present age,"[3] we will find that "a restorationist movement not only claims to know what original Christianity is but also tries to reproduce it in the present."[4] Groves was both a primitivist and a restorationist.

It was his reading of the New Testament that led Groves in 1825 to contrast the teaching of Jesus with the current practice of Christians, and to write his *Christian Devotedness* advocating literal obedience to the Sermon on the Mount. But we may wonder what had led him to think this way.

Methodism may be discounted as a direct influence, for two reasons. Firstly, there is no evidence that Groves had any personal acquaintance with Methodists or with Wesley's writings during his formative years. Secondly, Wesley's form of primitivism, with its special clubs, its rules, fasts and disciplines drew on traditions postdating the apostolic age in a manner quite untypical of Groves.[5]

The fact that Groves turned to primitivist ideals shortly after his conversion to Calvinism around 1824 suggests a connection between the two. There were undoubtedly primitivist tendencies in the Anglican circles that Groves now entered, with their long Puritan heritage. But the Puritans had restricted their primitivism essentially to doctrine. Indeed, their representatives, both Anglican and Nonconformist, continued to conduct their religion with ordained ministers in vestments, pulpits and pews, with sacramental ceremonies and massive church buildings, all owing far more to ecclesiastical tradition than apostolic precedent. Within these circles, however, there existed individuals, and loose networks of individuals, whose contact with continental Pietism added fresh facets to their system of beliefs and practices, and some of these were notable for Jewish sympathies. It may be that the developing primitivism in Groves's thought owes much to pietist and especially Jewish pietist thought.[6]

Judaism is a religion arising from God's supposed dealings with humankind in history. In Jewish theology, principles are customarily thought to have been revealed through events. A defining experience is thus given by God on a single occasion, so that all generations may learn from it and act in the light of it. "Things did not merely *happen* to the ancient Israelites. Events were shaped, reformed, and interpreted by them, made into the raw materials for a renewal of the life of the

---

[1] Hughes, in Hughes, *American Quest*, 1
[2] Hughes and Allen, 4; also Hughes, *American Quest*, 4
[3] Hughes and Allen, xiii
[4] Holmes, "Restoration Ideology", 155. Like many others, Mark Noll has questioned whether it is possible for any of us to step outside our own culture sufficiently to understand a former age and to read scripture in a way that does not impose upon it our own cultural assumptions (Noll, "Primitivism", 124). The point is a fair one, but hardly invalidates the distinction we may draw between those who attempt this and those who do not. The question will be considered in more detail below, 261ff.
[5] Carter, Kelly D, "The High Church Roots of John Wesley's Appeal to Primitive Christianity", *Restoration Quarterly*, Vol. 37 no. 2
[6] On Groves's possible early contact with Pietists and Moravians, see above, 21ff, and for a fuller treatment, PEANG, 78ff.

group. The reason is that the ancient Israelites regarded their history as important and significant, as teaching lessons."[1] In consequence, "Great events called forth, and continue to call forth, a singular two-part response among Jews: first, to provide a written record of those events; second, to reflect in a religious spirit on their meaning."[2] And for this reason, "Loyalty to the norms and thoughts conveyed in the event is as essential as the reality of the event."[3] In short, the event sets the precedent, and the precedent establishes the principle.

A Christian with this Jewish heritage will be likely to consider events recorded in the New Testament as precedents establishing principles. And on this basis, the experiences of the early church, in its meetings and missions, would be considered normative for the Christian in the same way that the Passover and the giving of the Law would be for the Jew. Such a belief was held and taught by Groves throughout his mature years, and it may be attributable, at least in part, to his friendship with several Jewish converts to Christianity during the years 1824-6, and to his contact during the same period with a circle of radical Evangelicals (represented especially by Irving, Drummond, Wolff and Way) who had a marked interest in the prophetic prospects of the Jews.[4]

---

[1] Neusner, *Time and Eternity*, 16
[2] Neusner, *The Way of the Torah*, 3
[3] Heschel, 217
[4] For a fuller discussion of primitivist thought and Groves's engagement with it, see PEANG, 38ff.

3. Groves's Missionary Experiences

Groves's Experience in Eastern Europe and Baghdad (1829-33; aged 34-38)

At the time of his departure from England in June 1829, Groves was very much a novice in missionary matters. He was, however, a man with strong ecclesiological convictions, an enquiring mind and a willingness to learn, both from his own experience and from the imparted wisdom of others. Travelling overland from St Petersburg to Baghdad, he found he could enjoy happy fellowship with any Protestant Christians he met along the way, whatever their racial or denominational background – Anglican chaplains, Moravian colonists, Lutheran evangelists, and the occasional Congregationalist, Presbyterian or Quaker. He saw his concept of Christian unity fully confirmed.[1]

Groves's contact with the expatriate community in St Petersburg quickly showed him that a missionary with a clear calling from God and no visible means of support may arouse the interest and the sympathy of Christian people, and find them generous in seeking to supply his needs. He recorded in his journal, "I cannot but rejoice in the sensation which the coming of this little yacht on such an errand has excited in the minds of many! It has stirred them up to desires and, I trust, actions of which they had not thought before… I think it may prove a stimulus to many others who hitherto have been satisfied in contributing a yearly guinea to the cause of God among the heathen."[2] When the missionary party moved on three weeks later, they went fortified with many prayers and laden with offerings – a bag of biscuits, sugar, coffee, cakes and a quantity of lemons. The cost of their accommodation and their onward transport had all been paid by the friends they had made in St Petersburg, and Groves reflected, "I trust this will make us doubly careful to spend all for his glory and as little as possible for ourselves."[3]

The party initially comprised about ten persons, including Groves's two sons and their tutor, John Kitto. Throughout their long journey Groves found that, although the money brought from England failed to cover all their expenses, unforeseen provision along the way repeatedly supplied the lack. He was learning to live "by faith": "I cannot help being overwhelmed with the Lord's goodness in this respect. Instead of being in want, we have always had more than enough."[4] On arrival at their final destination, they could look back on the experiences of the past months: "We can now say, having finished our long and perilous journey, that from St Petersburg to Baghdad we have not lost from a thread to a shoe-latchet, but have all, with all our goods, been brought hither in safety."[5]

In Baghdad itself, Groves rapidly discovered the practical impediments to pioneer mission in a hostile environment. He began to research the possibilities and to experiment. During his first year, as we have seen, he learned from Karl Pfander how to start and run a mission school. He also started to give away copies of the Protestant scriptures in various languages, and witnessed Pfander's frequent discussions with Jews, Muslims and members of the various eastern churches. By

---

[1] On Groves's view of Christian unity, see PEANG, 98ff. For a narrative of his journey, see FOFM 110-20.
[2] M55
[3] J28; M55
[4] J98; M69
[5] J111; M74

locating in a city known to his generation as "the headquarters of Islamism",[1] Groves's intention was to establish a base for wider outreach. He anticipated teams of workers itinerating throughout the region and then settling further afield in other promising centres. With this in mind he questioned travellers who arrived from distant parts, and wrote careful notes in his journal about the possibilities of evangelistic work in each place and with each religious faction.[2]

Through the visit of a doctor by the name of Montefiore on his way to Bombay, Groves realised the potential for medical missions, and shortly afterwards opened an ophthalmic clinic.[3] Launched in April 1830, this medico-evangelistic outreach in Baghdad should be recognised as the first Protestant mission to Muslims in the Arab world.[4] As Groves's knowledge of colloquial Arabic increased, he was able to converse quite well with his many visitors, and distributed scriptures to enquirers. The medical work was expanded with the arrival of Edward Cronin the following year. Although no Muslim converts were evident at the time, the team was encouraged by the conversion and rapid spiritual growth of an Armenian youth, Serkies Davids, and some months later by that of a young Chaldean woman, Harnie Thomas.[5]

Groves had originally hoped to accompany Pfander on an exploratory trip into the Persian highlands.[6] Once settled in Mesopotamia, however, with responsibility for a wife and young family in addition to his school and medical ministry, he decided to remain where he was. Pfander undertook the trip alone, leaving Baghdad permanently in March 1831. The city then entered upon two years of devastation through plague, cholera, famine, floods and civil war. Groves remained throughout this time, suffering the death of his wife and baby daughter.[7] During his three brief and troubled years in Baghdad, Groves learned a great deal. But he would learn more in India.

Groves's Experience in India (1833-52; aged 38-57)

Initial Impressions

In 1813 a revised charter to the East India Company had allowed Protestant missionaries free access to the subcontinent. Under increasingly effective British control, India might seem to offer more immediate scope for evangelistic outreach than the Middle East with its Muslim power structures and embattled religious minorities. Indeed, in his second volume of *The History of the Church Missionary Society*, covering the period 1849-1872, Eugene Stock devotes a full 232 pages to

---

[1] Eadie, 191; Stern, 34, 40
[2] R24-5
[3] J112, 117; M76
[4] The American Presbyterians, located in Beirut intermittently from 1823 onwards, spoke Arabic but confined their ministry to nominal Christians and Jews. Elsewhere, the attention of men such as Henry Martyn, William Glen and Pfander's colleagues of the Basel Mission had been directed to Muslims who spoke languages other than Arabic, although Martyn himself attempted a preliminary draft for an Arabic translation of the New Testament (Richter, 93-100, 186-9; Vander Werff, 31-2, 100-8, 118-9).
[5] On Serkies and Harnie, see FOFM *passim*.
[6] J84, 92
[7] A narrative of these events appears in FOFM 157-202.

the work of the gospel in India and Ceylon, and the remaining 217 pages to all the other countries of the world.

Accompanying Colonel Arthur Cotton, Groves disembarked at Bombay (Mumbai) in July 1833. During the next fourteen months he would travel almost three thousand miles – from Bombay down the west coast almost to the southern tip of the subcontinent, then inland to Tinnevelly (Tirunelveli), then further inland to Trichinopoly (Tiruchchirappalli) and across to the south-east coast; then a brief visit to Ceylon (Sri Lanka), up the east coast to Madras (Chennai) and on towards the Ganges Delta, then inland to Benares (Varanasi) and neighbouring towns before finally reaching the great eastern capital of Calcutta. Travelling in short stages, he set out to survey the entire spectrum of Protestant missions on the subcontinent, deliberately introducing himself to representatives of every denomination and society in every place he came to, and enquiring in detail about their work. Wherever possible, he participated in their open-air preaching, their teaching of converts, and in their schools.[1] We are probably justified in believing that he acquired a wider and more ecumenical knowledge of Indian missions at this period than anyone among his contemporaries.

His journal and letters show that his intention was not to settle permanently in India, but rather to establish links between his base in Mesopotamia and the more established Christian communities on the subcontinent.[2] Though suffering from bouts of depression, he was willing to preach in English wherever he was invited. His unordained status, however, meant that in Anglican circles few doors were open to him, and he noted, "In Bombay I generally met with kindness, but there was evidently a fear that prevented their wishing me to minister."[3]

The expatriate community in Bombay spoke of problems at a mission in the far south. A disagreement had arisen between the local CMS committee and some of its own German agents, led by the Lutheran Karl Rhenius, which threatened to bring to a halt a remarkable work in the area of Tinnevelly (Tirunelveli, Tamil Nadu). At their "earnest solicitations", Groves decided he should go and see if he, as an impartial outsider, could do anything to help.[4]

Moving in stages down the coast, accompanied by a young Lebanese, Mokayel Trad,[5] Groves found Christians occupying military and administrative positions in many places. Everywhere he saw an urgent need for missionaries. In Cannanore he spoke at length with members of the British garrison bemused by a recent visit from Joseph Wolff. The apocalyptic excitement aroused by Wolff's dramatic portrayal of the imminent and cataclysmic second coming of Christ had led to the conversion of some but the estrangement of others. For a time Groves the peacemaker despaired of any reconciliation. Later, however, one of the officers wrote warmly of Groves's intervention, saying, "He found all in confusion and left all in peace."[6]

---

[1] For a documented narrative of his travels, see FOFM 205-23.
[2] Groves's intentions are discussed in FOFM 200-1, 212-3.
[3] M230. William Carey and his Baptist colleagues were similarly forbidden to preach to British soldiers because they were "not episcopally ordained" (Smith G, *Carey*, 161).
[4] M228
[5] For Mokayel's background and subsequent career, see FOFM 205-7, 209, 212-3, 238.
[6] M240

Continuing south Groves shared his thoughts informally in many places, especially concerning "the liberty and love of the church."[1] Eventually he struck inland on horseback towards Tinnevelly, where he hoped to find Karl Rhenius.

Indian Roman Catholicism

In order to appreciate the roles of Groves, Rhenius and the CMS in the so-called Rhenius affair, we must have some understanding of the religious context in which they found themselves, and the history that lay behind it. The far south of India was unusual in possessing a substantial number of Indians who had traditionally for many generations considered themselves Christians. Since the mid-sixteenth century there had been Roman Catholic missionaries here, and their method was to draw people into the Catholic fold and then attempt to teach them the dogmas and practices of the Church. The result was a sizeable population that considered itself Roman Catholic, without possessing, according to Protestant observers, much understanding of the gospel or aspiring to any high degree of Christian holiness. The Roman Catholics themselves had built upon a foundation laid by the traditional Mar Thoma Church, started, according to common belief, by the apostle Thomas in the first century. It was among these Indian Roman Catholics that Protestant preaching of the gospel had met with its greatest success.[2]

To Protestant observers, Indian Catholicism appeared syncretistic and corrupt. It had certainly adapted itself to the traditional Hindu caste system, and in many places displayed large religious paintings, especially of the Madonna and Child, which often made it hard to distinguish at first sight between a Catholic chapel and a Hindu temple. It offered regular sacramental sacrifices and made full use of processions, images, statues, holy water, fasts, feasts, invocation of the saints and prayers for the dead, all of which resembled familiar Hindu practices. In 1815 a French Roman Catholic missionary Abbé J A Dubois described his embarrassment at how closely the popular processions of his own Catholic communion resembled the religious festivals of the Hindus:

> Their processions in the streets, always performed in the night time, have indeed been to me at all times a subject of shame. Accompanied with hundreds of tom-toms, (small drums), trumpets and all the discordant noisy music of the country; with numberless torches, and fireworks: the statue of the saint placed on a car is charged with garlands of flowers and other gaudy ornaments according to the taste of the country – the car slowly dragged by a multitude shouting all along the march – the congregation surrounding the car all in confusion, several among them dancing or playing with small sticks or with naked swords: some wrestling, some playing the fool; all shouting or conversing with each other, without anyone exhibiting the least sign of respect or devotion... They are all exceedingly pleased with such a mode of worship.[3]

There is no doubt that the early Catholic missionaries had succeeded in gaining the allegiance of a large number of Indians. Less certain was the extent to which they had succeeded in inculcating Catholic dogma. The Catholic catechism would be

---

[1] M243
[2] See Frykenberg, "Impact of Conversion", 189-97, and "Christians in India", 40-6.
[3] Hudson, 97. Dubois himself doubted that genuine conversion of Hindus was possible, and he disapproved in general of proselytism. His personal views tended towards a detached non-dogmatic theism (Frykenberg, "Impact of Conversion", 199, 227).

studied under the supervision of trained teachers, but direct access to the Bible was denied to the Indians on the ground that it could not be understood until properly explained according to the traditions of the Church. In consequence it could seem that the majority of Roman Catholics possessed little knowledge of biblical history or doctrine.

A people accustomed to such a sensual form of religion might well find Protestant worship cold, stark and unimpressive. Yet Indians who already considered themselves Christians responded in significant numbers when Protestants undertook to teach them more intelligibly about the faith they had long accepted. A succession of Protestant missionaries, located in diverse places, encouraged them to read the Bible for themselves, providing translations as simple as possible for them to understand, and during the course of the eighteenth and early nineteenth centuries many thousands were converted to the evangelical faith of these Protestant pioneers.[1]

Earliest Protestant Missions

The first to arrive were the Lutherans Bartholomaeus Ziegenbalg and Heinrich Plütschau, sent out from Halle in 1706. Commissioned and financed by the King of Denmark, as head of the Danish state church, they landed in the Danish colony of Tranquebar on the south-eastern Malabar coast.[2] As Pietists, the emphasis of Ziegenbalg and Plütschau lay not in church ceremony but in evangelism, and in small-group Bible study, informal fellowship and the inculcation of spiritual disciplines. They also began to train promising young men with a view to ordination. They established schools for boys and girls, and engaged in frequent scholarly discussions with Hindus and Muslims.[3]

Prior to this, books had always followed the Tamil literary conventions preferred by the educated elite, but the Lutherans translated scripture and Luther's shorter and longer catechisms (with Spener's pietistic amplifications) into colloquial Tamil. The Catholic method, using a catechism to teach converts by means of memorised questions and answers, was thus adopted by the Protestants and became a feature of their work. In 1713 the slow process of copying manuscripts by hand was superseded by the introduction of a Tamil printing press.[4]

Ziegenbalg and Plütschau made no attempt to confront the issue of caste. In the services of their New Jerusalem Church, Europeans and Indians in European dress sat on benches or stools. High-caste Indians, traditionally dressed, sat on mats. Low-caste Indians sat directly on the paved floor.[5] This represented for them a cultic unity combined with a social pluralism: "At the Lord's Table they sat together separately."[6] Likewise, in the mission school, the high caste and low caste

---

[1] Frykenberg, "Impact of Conversion", 197, 200-1 etc.
[2] Hudson, 1
[3] Hudson, 37
[4] Hudson, 40-1
[5] Hudson, 50
[6] Hudson, 108. The Lutheran missionaries built an additional church in Porayar, completed in 1746, to the same design as that in Tranquebar. They "again designed it as a cross, to facilitate the social pluralism of Christian unity. In the south wing behind the altar sat the Velalan ('sudra') women. Opposite them in the north wing sat the Velalan men. In the east wing sat the 'pariah' women. And in the west wing sat the 'pariah' men" (Hudson, 108-9, citing Lehmann A, 129).

children sat, learned, ate and slept separately.[1] Although the missionaries might privately regret the caste system, they felt obliged to conform to the local culture until such time as the Indians themselves saw fit to change it. In the meantime they would simply teach the Bible.

Sixty miles from the Danish colony of Tranquebar was another town, Tanjore (Thanjavur) with its own territory under the control of an Indian prince. Protestant work was launched here by another gifted Lutheran Pietist, Christian Schwartz, under the auspices of the Anglican missionary agency, the Society for Promoting Christian Knowledge. Like Ziegenbalg and Plütschau, Schwartz employed only high caste servants in his kitchens, so that the boys in his school could be faithful to their caste requirements whilst under his care.[2] As early as 1787 he had ordained Indian catechists at Tranquebar, and from 1810 in Tanjore,[3] and his disciple Sathianathan (Satyanathan) became a figure of great influence in his own right. Significant in the light of future developments is the fact that the SPCK expressed its approval of these Lutheran ordinations by printing the sermon preached by Sathianathan on the occasion of his ordination by Schwartz in 1790.[4]

Christian Schwartz served in India for forty-eight years without a break, and wielded such influence in Tranquebar, Trichinopoly and Tanjore that the churches, numbering thousands of believers, are said to have fallen into a "state of considerable disarray" within a few years of his death in 1798.[5] This was the situation facing Karl Rhenius in 1819 when sent by the CMS, at the request of the military chaplain James Hough, to restore some order to the Protestant community in southern India.[6]

Karl Gottlieb Ewald Rhenius (1790-1838)

Rhenius had been ordained in the Established Church of Prussia, "commonly denominated the 'Lutheran Church'".[7] Impressed by his early experience of the Moravians, he had visited their headquarters at Herrnhut in 1811. After some preparation at Johannes Jänicke's short-lived missionary training institute in Berlin,[8] he spent the summer of 1813 in England with Thomas Scott, an Anglican clergyman who at that time assisted the CMS by preparing their candidates for work overseas.[9] In July of that year (1813), the British parliament sanctioned free access of missionaries to India, which encouraged Rhenius to accept an immediate appointment there.[10]

---

[1] Hudson, 109, citing Lehmann A, 128
[2] Hudson, 114. Ward W R (p.302) notes how both Schwartz and the SPCK had been influenced by Auguste Francke at Halle. Another directly influenced by Francke was Groves's brother-in-law George Müller (Müller, *Narrative*, I, 100, 129, 143 etc.).
[3] Neill, *Christianity in India*, 117; Rhenius, *Memoir*, 197
[4] *Christianity in India*, 117
[5] Neill, *Christian Missions*, 233-5, 272
[6] *Christian Missions*, 272
[7] Rhenius, *Memoir*, 10, 497. His forenames were sometimes anglicised as Charles Theophilus. Groves was evidently mistaken in his belief that "Neither Mr Rhenius nor Schmid are Lutherans at all… but they were ordained on the Bible in the Reformed Church" (Groves, *Tinnevelly Mission*, 14).
[8] On the Berlin institute, see Jenkins, "The CMS and the Basel Mission", 48, 59.
[9] On the role of Thomas Scott in missionary preparation, see Warren, *Social History*, 48.
[10] Rhenius, *Memoir*, 9-11

Due to a shortage of English recruits, the CMS were accustomed to enlist trained Lutheran and Reformed (Calvinist) ministers – Germans, Swiss and Danes – despite the fact that these followed their own Protestant traditions, taking no account of the Thirty-nine Articles or the Book of Common Prayer of the Church of England.[1] This had already been a cause of periodic difficulties between the missionaries and the local Corresponding Committees appointed to oversee them.[2]

Based initially in Madras, Rhenius had there expressed to the CMS committee his opinion that the Anglican Prayer Book was unsuited to Indian meetings, that British bishops and government officials should not expect to exercise authority over Indian churches, that Indian evangelists should not be obliged to travel hundreds of miles to receive ordination, and that no restriction should prevent fellowship with Dissenters in public acts of worship.[3] In his role as official chaplain to the expatriate community, Rhenius received a request to baptise the illegitimate child of an army officer. Although the Archdeacon of Madras insisted that the Canons of the Church of England would allow this, Rhenius himself considered it would set an unhealthy precedent by condoning the sexual laxity of many British soldiers and administrators. Rhenius resigned the chaplaincy, though not his missionary connection with the CMS.

In November 1814, a bishop was appointed to Calcutta, the first of a succession.[4] His name was Thomas Middleton. Five years later, a resolution was passed by the Madras committee of the CMS: "That the English Episcopal Establishment being now erected in India, the Committee feel themselves bound, as well by their attachment to the Church of England as for the maintenance of their own consistency, to require that the form of worship adopted therein, whether by English or Lutheran missionaries, shall be exclusively that of the United Church of England and Ireland."[5] This meant that Anglican forms must now be adopted by Lutheran missionaries.

Tensions between Rhenius and the CMS committee worsened. There were several points of disagreement, including his strong objection to the Anglican doctrine of baptismal regeneration and the indiscriminate baptising of infants, but when the CMS dismissed him from his post in Madras, he believed the reason was

---

[1] After its first ten years of activity, the CMS had sent only five missionaries overseas, all of them Germans (Hylson-Smith, 213). As late as 1850, the great majority of CMS workers were still German. The LMS also recruited heavily from continental Europe (Walls, "The Eighteenth Century Protestant Missionary Awakening", 36-9).

[2] Chilcraft describes the activity of the local CMS committee: "The Madras Corresponding Committee was formed in 1814 and consisted of chaplains and officials from government and the services. Its task was to advise and assist the London headquarters, to act as the medium of correspondence between the missionaries and London, and to raise funds. As with other Corresponding Committees in India it had almost autonomous power. The committee met monthly and dealt with every aspect of the administration of the mission" (Chilcraft, Ch.4).

[3] Rhenius, *Memoir*, 193; Strachan J M, 36

[4] The first Anglican bishops in India (Calcutta) were:
 i) Thomas Fanshaw Middleton (Nov. 1814 – died July 1822)
 ii) Reginald Heber (1823 – died April 1826)
 iii) John Thomas James (died shortly after appointment in 1828).
 iv) John Matthias Turner (Dec. 1829 – died 7th July 1831).
 v) Daniel Wilson (1832 – died Jan. 1858).

[5] Strachan J M, 11-12

"solely because we had too catholic a spirit and desired to embrace all as Christian brethren who hold the Head".[1] He was relocated to Palamcottah (Palayankottai) in Tinnevelly, where, from 1820 onwards, he oversaw what could be described as a people movement, involving extended groups and families from the *nadar* community (known in the nineteenth century as *shanar*), whose distinctive work in the palmyra forests distanced them from the normal social obligations and constraints of Hindu village life.[2] The social context no doubt played a part in the success of the mission, but so did the remarkable character of Rhenius himself. Joseph Wolff, who visited Tinnevelly in 1833, considered him "the greatest missionary that has ever appeared in the Protestant Church", and calculated that "the number of Hindoos to whose conversion he has been instrumental amounts to 12,000."[3] By that date he had established 111 local schools, in which 2,553 boys and 146 girls received Christian instruction.[4]

Rhenius spoke fluent Tamil and in addition to translating the New Testament he composed a full historical catechism, and shorter doctrinal catechism, comprising a series of written questions and answers with appropriate Bible references. Both were intended in the first instance for children but found wide acceptance with adults. His strategy was to send out trained Indian catechists to preach, distribute literature and teach the basic doctrines of the faith using these catechisms.

The catechising itself took the form of questions asked publicly by the catechist and answers given by those present, with free discussion of matters raised.[5] The task of leading such informal discussions was a far more demanding one than simply preaching to a passive audience or coaching them in the memorisation of written texts, but it proved highly effective. Indeed, it awakened intense interest, and engaged the attention of both participants and bystanders. Rhenius emphasized the value of this method: "Catechising the natives, both children and adults, is at present our most important engagement; for by it alone are we enabled, humanly speaking, to touch their minds. Mere preaching to them, as to Europeans, will generally be of little effect."[6] And again, "Causing the children or adults merely, or for the most part, to repeat what we have said before them, can be of little use to them; they become mere parrots."[7]

In each village where there was a significant response, a small elementary school would be established. As the schools prospered, conversions followed, and the converts were gathered into local fellowships where meetings were largely informal, allowing much free participation. Simple meeting places were freely constructed by the Indians themselves, "being principally mud with palmyra leaf roofs", and many were large enough for two hundred people.[8] Each congregation

---

[1] Rhenius to Jowett, 18th July 1835, in Groves, *Tinnevelly Mission*, 36
[2] Oddie, 242-4; Rhenius, *Memoir*, 312. Rhenius was assisted by a succession of capable colleagues. These were L B E Schmid (1820-33), J Winckler (1827-34) P Schaffter (1827-61), J Devasahayam (an ordained Tamil Indian, 1830-61), P Fjellstedt (1832-35), J Müller (1832-43) and J Lechler (1833-37) (see Frykenberg, "Impact of Conversion", 200, 227-8).
[3] Wolff, II, 207
[4] Wolff, II, 211
[5] Rhenius, *Memoir*, 135-6
[6] Ibid, 202
[7] Ibid, 202
[8] Groves, *Tinnevelly Mission*, 11. See also Rhenius, *Memoir*, 458-60.

was governed by a group comprising the catechist, the schoolmaster and one or more village elders. Together these resolved conflicts, maintained suitable standards of behaviour and exercised discipline.[1]

The majority of Indian Protestants, here as elsewhere, lived in social communities of mixed religion. But even before the time of Rhenius, the severe social dislocation suffered by converts from Hinduism had led to the creation of a number of Christian villages where they could live and work in peace.[2] Rhenius himself developed the concept of the "Christian Village" as a strategy for mission, and introduced administrative structures that would formalise it. In 1830 he established a "Native Philanthropic Society", whose object was "the settling of native Christians in villages, the building of schools etc., the acquisition of grounds etc. for these purposes, and the rendering of other assistance to the native Christians in their external affairs."[3] He introduced a regular custom of "morning prayer" before work, and "evening prayer" after work, in which the whole village would participate.[4] He established a permanent fund for the poor, from which two to three hundred needy Christians received an allocation every week, along with special assistance for cases of temporary hardship.[5] A widows' fund also existed for the widows of catechists and schoolmasters.[6] Rhenius himself was often called upon to settle disputes in the administration of these matters, and his judgment was widely and generally respected.

As early as 1819 he had started itinerating in the surrounding region with one or two Indians, encouraging them to take a leading part in the catechising and the ensuing public discussions.[7] By 1823 some catechists were being sent out on their own, and two years later he was encouraging experienced Indian Christians such as David Pillei to establish congregations and take on considerable local responsibility.[8] By 1831 there were nine experienced men in distant "stations", who would return regularly to Palamcottah to discuss progress, study Matthew's Gospel and learn how to prepare sermons.[9] A "Native Missionary Society" was formed for the financial support of men itinerating further afield, especially in Madura, and contributions were received for this from Indian believers.[10]

Rhenius himself appointed the catechists and decided where they should go. Some proved to be of limited spiritual quality, and discipline or dismissal was

---

[1] Frykenberg, "Impact of Conversion", 202

[2] The difficulties encountered at this period by Indian Christian converts trying to earn their own living are vividly portrayed by Clark, *Robert Clark*, 259-63. On the caste system in general see Flood, 58-61; also Klostermaier, 334ff.

[3] Rhenius, *Memoir*, 459

[4] Ibid, 458-60. This was a significant innovation (Caldwell, *Lectures*, 27, cited by Frykenberg, "Impact of Conversion", 201).

[5] Rhenius, *Memoir*, 462

[6] Ibid, 465

[7] Rhenius, *Memoir*, 192. Rhenius's method was to chat with any individuals and small groups that gathered round him whilst out walking, and then ask leading questions. This often stimulated a discussion, and sometimes, if a crowd gathered, led on to spontaneous preaching (Ibid, 365). He also asked questions as a means of encouraging Christians, even questioning one old Indian believer on his deathbed (Ibid, 414).

[8] Ibid, 277-8, 331-3

[9] Ibid, 334, 391, 467-8, 495

[10] Ibid, 471

occasionally necessary.[1] Collectively, however, they were accomplishing a highly significant work, establishing local schools and congregations over a wide area. By the time of Groves's visit to Palamcottah in 1833, the number of catechists associated with Rhenius had risen to a hundred and fifteen.[2]

Before the arrival of Rhenius there had been no significant controversy concerning caste in the Protestant missions to India. The Lutherans had defended their tolerance of it on the grounds that rigid social divisions also existed in the churches of Europe, where rich and poor, noble and serf would not think of sitting or eating together or of sharing a common cup at Holy Communion.[3] In the early 1820s Bishop Heber of Calcutta had maintained that missionaries should not interfere in such social customs.[4] By 1835 his successor, Daniel Wilson, though forbidding the observation of caste at communion in the Anglican Church, "still followed the 'natural' order that Europeans were served first, followed by the respectable Indians and finally their servants."[5]

But caste was an issue that Christians elsewhere in India were beginning address seriously. As early as 1803, Carey and his colleagues had rejected caste distinctions in their Christian communities and schools,[6] as did Alexander Duff from 1830 in his educational establishments.[7] By 1819 Rhenius was intent on eradicating caste distinctions from the churches under his oversight.[8] His task was rendered more difficult by the long Christian tradition of caste observance established by his Catholic and Lutheran predecessors. It was a cause to which Groves had probably not given much thought before arriving on the subcontinent, but one which immediately attracted his interest. Hastening south to offer encouragement to Rhenius, he confided,

> I have often desired to go to Tinnevelly, but circumstances directed my course elsewhere; how strange that, without any design or thought about it when I left Bagdad, I should find myself most deeply engaged in seeking to help on the spiritual prosperity of this country. And as I desire to break down caste among the Hindus, to pave the way for the reception of truth, so do I desire to break down caste in the Christian Church, to prepare the way for publishing it.[9]

A few months later, his convictions had deepened: "When I think of this subject of caste, in connection with the humiliation of the Son of God, I see in it something

---

[1] Ibid, 468, 476-7, 549-55, 561
[2] M255
[3] Hollis, 10
[4] Hudson, 156
[5] Hollis, 49-50, citing *Diary of Daniel Wilson* (Nisbet), 53. See also Bateman, *Life of Daniel Wilson*. It was not till 1847 that an Anglican mission agency, the SPG, would formally resolve to employ only such Indians as had renounced caste (Ingleby, *Education and India*, 222).
[6] Smith, "A Tale of Many Models", 479-500; Oussoren, 85
[7] Ingleby, *Education and India*, 220-1n.
[8] Rhenius, *Memoir*, 174. Newbigin suggests that the egalitarian ethos of a new generation of missionaries owed as much to the French Revolution and the Enlightenment as to a fresh understanding of the Bible (Newbigin, *Pluralist Society*, 186-7).
[9] M242

most unseemly, most peculiarly unlike Christ... It is truly hateful that one worm should refuse to eat with, or touch another worm, lest he become polluted."[1]

The Rhenius Affair

Having successfully resolved the doctrinal and emotional conflicts resulting from Wolff's recent visit to Cannanore, Groves no doubt felt optimistic that he could act as peacemaker in the dispute between Rhenius and the CMS. On arrival at Palamcottah in November 1833, he was hugely impressed with the opportunities for outreach and with the Christian groups he found there: "The other evening, when we had a little meeting at a village, eight families of the *Maravers* or thief caste came desiring Christian instruction, and in the village which sent for a teacher there were twenty-five families ready to submit to Christian instruction. In fact, in every direction, they are anxious to hear."[2]

His subsequent travels only confirmed his conviction that Tinnevelly was "a field of usefulness nowhere to be equalled in India."[3] He visited a number of the congregations in various villages and found the meetings to be lively and interesting, with extempore prayer, discussion of Bible passages and the opportunity for all "to give an answer or to say what they feel."[4] He confessed, "My heart was truly delighted at the sweet simplicity which prevailed in their religious exercises."[5] Rhenius might be a Lutheran working with an Anglican society, but it would be hard to identify these congregations as either Lutheran or Anglican. Western forms of worship were far from evident. Indeed, Groves remarked, "I do not believe that one Tamil Common Prayer Book will be found *in use* among them all."[6]

Groves enquired about the present controversy. Rhenius, like his Lutheran predecessors, had long enjoyed the privilege of "ordaining" Indian catechists.

Unlike some of his German colleagues, Rhenius himself had never requested Anglican orders, and he simply ordained his catechists after Lutheran practice, without the significant political requirement that they declare allegiance to the

---

[1] M271. There were Indian Christians who disagreed with Rhenius on the question of caste. Under Schwartz, high caste men (Velalans and Valangamattars) had been leaders of congregations, elders, and in a few cases ministers, whilst low caste men (Pallars and Parayers) were catechists and schoolteachers and servants. Vedanayagam Pillai (1774-1864), known as the Sastri, was a poet and musician who had grown up with Schwartz and became a great Christian writer in Tamil. Between 1824 and 1829, a major conflict arose between the middle aged Sastri and the "junior missionaries", led by Rhenius, who wanted to ban caste distinctions in the church. Eventually Sastri was expelled. In 1824 he wrote a "Dialogue on the Difference of Caste", which in 1829 was followed by a collection of anonymous texts in Tamil from the congregation in Tanjore under the title "The Foolishness of Amending Caste". Sastri and his supporters believed they were simply defending Schwartz's position that the custom of the country should be respected (1 Cor 10:32), that Christianity is not a matter of meat or drink (Rom 14:15) and that every man should remain as he was when converted to Christ (1 Cor 7:20). Hudson provides the information for this brief analysis. On Hindu perceptions of caste, see Brockington, 118-24.
[2] M256
[3] M362
[4] Groves, *Tinnevelly Mission*, 25
[5] M256
[6] *Tinnevelly Mission*, 25

British crown.[1] He had recently been informed, however, that his present practice in Tinnevelly was "irregular". Bishop John M Turner in Calcutta, overriding the CMS committee in Madras, felt led to insist that in future all catechists must receive Anglican ordination from him rather than Lutheran ordination from Rhenius.[2] Rhenius replied that, at that date (1829), more than ten years had passed since an Anglican bishop had been seen in Palamcottah and many years more seemed likely to pass before one came that way again; hence his determination to ordain them himself.[3] He was informed that Bishop Turner would shortly visit Madras, so he and his colleagues must "send thither such Catechists as they deemed eligible to present to his Lordship for Holy Orders in order that they might be prepared by suitable instruction."[4] Rhenius insisted that Indians were not accustomed to travelling four hundred miles and preferred to be commissioned among their own people by their own teachers. The bishop, in conference with the CMS committee, replied "that it was necessary to the existence of the Society, as a Church of England institution, and as pledged to propagate Christianity agreeably to its doctrine and discipline, that no other than Episcopal ordination should be allowed."[5] Higher authority was sought from the "parent committee" in London, who reminded all concerned that the CMS was "composed of members of the Church of England and to such the management of its affairs is exclusively limited." For this good reason they did not feel at liberty to make arrangements for Indian converts "on any other principles than those of the Church of England."[6] The catechists remained in Tinnevelly, without ordination.

Following the death of Bishop Turner, his successor, in 1832, was Daniel Wilson. A High Church Evangelical, formerly a member of the CMS committee in London, Wilson was vehemently opposed to any form of ministerial "irregularity", and he was resolved to exercise his full authority as bishop over all India.[7] Considerable tensions ensued between him and another CMS committee, located in his own city of Calcutta, involving what amounted to a temporary severance of relations between them.[8] The extreme position taken by Wilson is evident from his "charge to the clergy" at this time, in which he declared, "I discovered a system at work in the extreme south – province of Tinnevelly – in direct opposition to our Protestant Episcopal Church, a system so ruinous in my judgment to the holiness and peace of the new converts as to threaten a subversion among them of Christianity itself."[9] Rhenius was informed that ordinations were now the bishop's prerogative and that if he wished to dispute this he should go to England and there consult a higher authority.

Groves heard the story with interest and a degree of indignation. On no account should he go to England, Groves advised, lest his converts be led astray in his absence, and lest by doing so he lent credence to the idea that Indian churches must

---

[1] *Tinnevelly Mission*, 8
[2] This idea had first been proposed by Bishop Heber some five years earlier.
[3] Strachan J M, 19
[4] Ibid, 20
[5] Ibid, 21. Ongoing tensions between Rhenius and Turner are noted by Groves, *Tinnevelly Mission*, 20, and by Rhenius, *Memoir*, 400.
[6] letter dated 2nd Aug. 1831; Strachan J M, 25
[7] Yates, *Venn*, 26-7; Rhenius, *Memoir*, 475, 478, 510
[8] Neill, *Christianity in India*, 409
[9] Rhenius, *Memoir*, 475

be subject to English authority. In his journal he recorded, "There is a deeply interesting work going on here, one that I would strain my last nerve to prevent falling to the ground."[1] He suggested that Rhenius write a paper, stating the position from his point of view, so that supporters of the CMS might understand the facts of the matter. Encouraged by Groves, Rhenius, for the time being, stayed at his post.[2]

Groves himself travelled on, eventually reaching Calcutta in the spring of 1834. Here he enjoyed meeting Archdeacon Daniel Corrie, who persuaded him to call personally on Bishop Wilson. There seems to have been no particular tension between Wilson and his visitor, and perhaps no reference made to Rhenius. Groves simply reported, "he received me most kindly."[3]

The salaried secretary of the CMS Committee in Madras at this time (September 1833 to January 1847) was Rev John T Tucker. He had been sent from the London headquarters to negotiate the delicate relationship between the CMS and this uncomfortably assertive bishop.[4] On his arrival, Tucker expressed satisfaction with the work in Tinnevelly, which he considered to fall under his jurisdiction.[5] But he confirmed that Lutheranism was now no longer appropriate on Anglican territory. Following Groves's advice, Rhenius wrote two reports, "which I think," said Groves, "are calculated to do much good. They are written in a nice spirit, exposing many objectionable things in the Church of England… I feel he is appointed of the Lord for the propagation and upholding of the truth and liberty of the Church of Christ."[6]

In defence of Rhenius, Groves himself had published *A Brief Account of the Present Circumstances of the Tinnevelly Mission* in 1835. A reply to this came immediately from a member of the Madras committee, James Morgan Strachan. He wished to state the case for a more clearly defined Anglicanism:

> On every reference upon the subject from the earliest time, the Society's sentiments and directions were uniform. The Book of Common Prayer was to be used for the Public Service of the churches, open to such modifications as should be sanctioned on the spot by competent authority or usage… Their missionaries, while cultivating all friendly sentiments toward and uniting with ministers of other denominations in all common objects are urged for the sake of order to confine their regular public ministrations to their own churches"[7]

---

[1] M254

[2] On 1st December 1833 Groves reported, "I set out from this place (Palamcottah) on the 27th [November], after having brought the great object of my coming to a happy issue, that of preventing my dear brother Rhenius from going to England, which would, I fear, occasion the separating, or, at least as far as we can see, the scattering of this most affectingly interesting mission. I think he will now stand by the work, should the Lord preserve him, let the Society decide as it may, relative to those points in which they differ. He has the most unsectarian spirit I have met with for many days" (M255).

[3] M294

[4] Rhenius, *Memoir*, 448, 516; Yates, *Venn*, 30

[5] Rhenius, *Memoir*, 476

[6] M331

[7] Strachan J M, 58.

Strachan concluded that "from the very nature of the case and of the Society, only episcopal ordination could be sanctioned.[1] Under pressure from the bishop, the CMS offered Rhenius and his three colleagues the choice of submission or resignation. Seeing no alternative, they resigned.

The Indian converts and co-workers were dismayed; they begged Rhenius to change his mind. Leaving Tinnevelly, he set out to visit a young missionary by the name of John Bilderbeck in the town of Chittoor, some four hundred miles to the north.[2]

Bilderbeck was associated with the London Missionary Society. Two senior missionaries of this society, William Hoyles Drew and Edmund Crisp, had already received a visit from Rhenius in Madras, where he had discussed with them the possibility of transferring from the CMS to the LMS. They considered it likely that he would do so.[3] Bilderbeck himself was perfectly willing for Rhenius to take over "two or three schools which he had established near and at Arcot".[4] So in August 1835 Rhenius moved to Arcot, where thirty people began to meet for Christian fellowship. Plans were made to "erect a place of worship of a humble description".[5]

Barely a month later Rhenius had returned to Tinnevelly. Without joining the LMS, he had decided to continue working in his former sphere, under his own auspices. As the CMS claimed the churches previously in his care, he built new meeting rooms in close proximity, with walls of compacted mud, and roofs of palmyra leaves.[6] He conceded to the CMS that "the property is theirs", but the Christians he considered his.[7] A period of tension ensued as the Indians were

---

[1] Ibid, 58. Replying to Strachan, Groves issued a second and somewhat expanded edition of his *Brief Account*, under the title, *The Present State of the Tinnevelly Mission*. With Rhenius's second letter appended, this was printed in Britain in 1836. The CMS archives contain much correspondence about the controversy in addition to records of numerous meetings between missionaries, committee members, ecclesiastical dignitaries, Rhenius and his colleagues, and Groves. Most of these make for tedious and unedifying reading, and their chief interest lies, as Chilcraft notes, in the way they reveal the diverse spiritual characters of the protagonists. None manifest a more gracious attitude than Groves himself (Chilcraft, Ch.4).

[2] Rhenius, *Memoir*, 487

[3] Drew to Ellis, 10th July 1835; Bilderbeck to Ellis, 20th Aug. 1835

[4] Rhenius, *Memoir*, 487

[5] Ibid, 487

[6] Ibid, 542

[7] Rhenius to Tucker, 30th May, 1835, in Rhenius, *Memoir*, 482. Rhenius complained to the CMS, "You maintain that the whole Mission is yours, because in the first instance you sent me to Tinnevelly, gave me the temporal support which I needed, and defrayed other expenses of the Mission... You say that *we* have no right whatever – what monstrous doctrine is this!... Henceforth money is to be deemed the principle consideration... The sweat of the missionary's brow, his anxious labours, are nothing to be accounted of in the matter!" (Rhenius to Jowett, 18th July 1835, quoted by Groves, *Tinnevelly Mission*, 33; Rhenius, *Memoir*, 513).

Groves shrewdly remarked that financial support for the CMS had increased in consequence of the publicity given to Rhenius's success, and added that if Rhenius's connection with the CMS were to be severed, the support would, and indeed should, be directed to him rather than the Society: "In fact, as regards money, Tinnevelly has conferred on the Society more than it has received... I scruple not to say that the Society has increased its funds vastly beyond the disbursements for that Mission [i.e. Tinnevelly]

obliged to decide whether their loyalties lay with the English society or the German missionaries. No one seems to have considered the possibility that they might be capable of continuing on their own as Indian fellowships, without any supervision, either from the Germans or the English.

Groves had, by this time, left India to recruit new workers in Britain and Europe. He arrived back in Madras in July 1836. With him was a young German, Hermann Gundert, who was despatched immediately to see how Rhenius was faring in Palamcottah.[1] Groves, from his base in Madras, urged the Lutherans to look directly to God for their daily bread, and he encouraged others to send provision. Gifts came from friends in Bombay and Calicut,[2] and from Germany,[3] and a few weeks later Groves declared, "God has hitherto wonderfully supported them. And now the Lord will decide where and with whom his blessing shall abide... I trust they will show that Societies are not needed to carry on very extensive missionary work any more than to begin it."[4]

Rhenius and his colleagues, with Groves's encouragement, were now "living by faith" in the same manner as Groves himself, and George Müller, and Hudson Taylor twenty years later. In May 1838 Groves wrote to a friend, "We heard from dear Rhenius last night; he is reduced to a fortnight's provision of bread; but has in hand a good stock of faith and trust. I am daily more and more resolved to share my last crust with the brethren at Tinnevelly."[5]

Whilst taking Rhenius's part, Groves was nevertheless still endeavouring to act as peacemaker between him and the CMS. Chilcraft quotes a remarkable observation by Tucker, in response to a letter from Groves, intimating their agreement "that the true Christian course to pursue was for both parties to hold to their principles without concealing or compromising them and that each should carefully avoid placing the other in such a position, as to make it necessary for him to act in opposition to the principles of the other party, and both to occupy the large common ground of Christian love and zeal."[6] Emphasizing points held in common, Groves wrote to Rev J F Thomas, one of the CMS missionaries appointed to replace Rhenius: "All I desire is that my Lord will be well served, and his image brightly reflected and I care not by whom, and I trust when this brilliancy and manifestation of moral power begins to burst forth in Tinnevelly, all that surrounds

---

by telling at its various meetings all over England the tidings of success at Tinnevelly." What is more, the schools, churches and villages in Tinnevelly had been financed largely by Rhenius's personal friends, "many of whom, to my certain knowledge would never have given the same to the general funds of the Society" (*Tinnevelly Mission*, 20).

[1] M363. Gundert's perspective on the so-called Rhenius Affair was eventually (in 1991) published in German as *Hermann Gundert: Quellen zu seinem Leben und Werk*, pp.321-36.

[2] Rhenius, *Memoir*, 543, 590-1

[3] M363

[4] M363

[5] M389

[6] Tucker, "Notes on Mr Groves' letter, received 23rd July 1836", cited by Chilcraft, Ch.4. Tucker's evident respect for Groves may date back to a brief meeting two years earlier in Madras (Aug. 1834). At that time Groves noted, "Dear Mr Tucker, who has the charge of the Church Missions, asked me before we parted to join him in prayer, and we spent a holy parting moment near our uniting Lord, the savour of which so remains on my heart that I feel how impossible it is for anything to divide when love reigns and rules" (M332).

will be animated by such an example to press forward in the same course till it spreads from Cape Comorin to Delhi."[1]

But ideals and practicalities were two different things. Still optimistic and still, one might think, considerably naïve in matters touching on ecclesiastical politics, Groves could hardly fail to emerge from this experience a sadder and wiser man, and one, almost inevitably, with a more sceptical and negative view of missionary societies and church authorities.

During Groves's furlough in England in 1835, the suggestion was made that Edward Cronin and John Parnell, his old colleagues from Baghdad, might join the work in Tinnevelly. There was a furious reaction from Tucker. Tinnevelly, in his view, belonged to the CMS and would accept no interlopers.[2] Despite the fair words, the battle lines were drawn. As Chilcraft notes, the question was clear but the answers conflicting: "The Anglican community in India was embroiled in a protracted dispute about authority and who should have control over the emerging native congregations; was it the missionaries (Rhenius), the local committee (Tucker), the London committee (Coates and Venn) or the bishop (Wilson)? Groves' simple, farsighted response was the converts themselves."[3] With hindsight we might expect Groves to take this line. Yet it is unclear how fully, at this stage, he would have advocated a purely indigenous leadership. He was still in the process of translating his ecclesiology into a coherent missiology. He was, after all, still learning from experience, and learning, in particular, from Rhenius.

Groves and Rhenius

Groves had found the German, in many respects, a man after his own heart. Firstly, they shared a personal dislike for paperwork and administration, preferring informal discussion of plans, problems and policies.[4] And like Groves, in matters relating to Christian ministry, Rhenius deliberately took Scripture as his authority, rather than culture or church tradition. On one occasion, for example, "In the Holy Scriptures it is nowhere said that the administration of the Lord's Supper is confined to a minister" so that Christians thrown together by circumstances with no officially appointed pastor "possess the liberty of breaking bread together."[5] Groves will also have appreciated Rhenius's determination to ignore caste, providing just one mat in the meetings so all must sit on it together.[6]

The influence of Groves himself might be discernable when, shortly after his visit, Rhenius advised an enquiring missionary, "'Sell that thou hast' and devote it to the poor Heathen. Lay all at the feet of Jesus Christ and spend it for him, fully confident that he will care for you and yours. Thus honouring him, he will honour you and will make you a light that shineth."[7]

---

[1] Groves to Thomas, 2nd Sep 1836. Chilcraft (ch.4) notes, "The CMS committee in Madras rejected Groves' two proposals for a compromise solution, which he believed had the support of Thomas. The German and British missionaries continued to operate separately in the same area although both parties felt deeply aggrieved by the other" (see Groves to Tucker, recd. 16th Oct.1836).
[2] Tucker to Nelson, 23rd July 1835
[3] Chilcraft, Ch.4
[4] Rhenius, *Memoir*, 439
[5] Ibid, 544
[6] Hudson, 157
[7] Rhenius, *Memoir*, 584-5

But above all, Groves strongly approved his belief in the spiritual unity that transcends denominational identities. Rhenius encouraged his friends to "embrace every servant of Christ, of whatever denomination, as our fellow-labourer, and mutually exchange our services according to the spirit of the gospel, allowing others to differ without putting them, either privately or publicly at a distance from us."[1] He warned against "the party-spirit from which, and in which, much missionary labour is performed in India," and he complained, "See what a spectacle the Heathen have of Christianity in its Ministers! The one is of Paul, another is of Apollos, another of Cephas etc., and not only are such distinctions made, but they are made so as to make people believe that we are *opposed* to one another. It arises, no doubt, from the fact that other masters than Christ are set up."[2] And again, "India is becoming full of missionaries... Let them all come only in his name, and his blessing will not fail them. I fear there is too much of coming in other names."[3]

Rhenius denied that, in resisting Anglican control, he wished to create congregations "on the Lutheran model". Indeed, "I assure you that I am as much and as little affected towards the English as towards the Lutheran Church. In both, I love that which is scriptural and tending to real edification; but, whatever others may think, I dare not touch that which to the best of my judgment is not scriptural and does not tend to edification; and I feel it my bounden duty to teach and uphold the truth, in whatever connexion I may be placed."[4] When, in April 1837, gifts and enquiries arrived from certain friends in Europe, Rhenius remarked that they "seem to be staunch Lutherans and wish to find out whether we also are such." Another potential supporter was "wishing first to know whether we are genuine Lutherans." His reply will have pleased Groves: "I have answered... that we are not Lutherans but *Christian* missionaries and I have given them a faithful account of our views respecting baptism and the Lord's Supper."[5]

But there were certain quirks of character and custom in his Lutheran friends that Groves could hardly fail to notice. In 1836 he confided, "Things in Tinnevelly may have been very defective, but there is freedom for the truth there... They are, with all their faults, *dear* brethren; open to truth and capable of improvement."[6] We can only guess what was so "defective" and what these "faults" might have been. Among them may have been the infrequency of the Lord's Supper, celebrated, in practice, only when one of the ordained missionaries happened to be present. Many outlying congregations received the ordinance only two or three times a year.[7] Groves might also have observed that some of Rhenius's catechists were not Christians of such quality as might be wished for, and many of his

---

[1] Rhenius, *Memoir*, 296
[2] Ibid, 585
[3] Ibid, 599
[4] Ibid, 427-8
[5] Ibid, 571-2. Rhenius would only baptise adults who professed sincere faith, and also the children of such adults. Groves noted that Rhenius made no spiritual distinction between the Anglican and Lutheran forms of baptism or ordination, wishing merely to avoid imposing on Indian converts the particular principles, doctrines and vows of obedience required by the Anglican ordinance (Groves, *Tinnevelly Mission*, 20).
[6] M362
[7] Groves, *Tinnevelly Mission*, 26.

schoolmasters were not Christians at all.[1] Rhenius, moreover, was proving to be a rather abrasive personality, inclined perhaps to manifest more pious rectitude than Christian love.

As time went on, Groves grew increasingly uncomfortable with the combative stance adopted by Rhenius, and perhaps began to regret becoming so irretrievably identified in the public mind with his cause. Dandeson Coates of the CMS committee in London was of the opinion that Groves, though not intending to encourage a permanent estrangement between Rhenius and the CMS, had nevertheless, by offering him an alternative means of support, naïvely sustained and perpetuated a conflict he now regretted.[2] Groves himself was certainly having second thoughts. On 24th July 1836, "My own impression, relative to the affair of Rhenius, is far less comfortable than when I first undertook to care for it... Every day my soul feels more and more that the way of strife and contention is the way of moral weakness, even as the way of returning blessing for cursing is one of power."[3]

Longer experience of Tinnevelly had shown that the immense spiritual stature and reputation of Rhenius himself tended to inhibit initiatives that were not of his own instigation. If Groves had quickly seen good reason to condemn the basic ethos of the traditional missionary societies, he had also discerned some disconcerting deficiencies in Rhenius's uncompromising and somewhat authoritarian style of leadership.[4] It was all part of the learning process for Groves and no doubt contributed to the view he subsequently took of the missionary task of the church and the role of the foreign worker in it.

Nevertheless, by 1838 as many as 11,000 Indian Christians were once more under the care of Rhenius and his colleagues. Groves had played no small part in strengthening the German missionary's hand at a crucial time, and the CMS historian states baldly and rather inaccurately that his "breach with the Church was due to Mr Groves's influence."[5] In fact Groves had made repeated attempts to reconcile Rhenius with the CMS at a time when the rather more judgmental Gundert was encouraging him to act independently.[6]

Groves himself willingly admitted, "I do feel great thankfulness for having been the instrument of keeping Rhenius in his work."[7] But he could not have foreseen that Rhenius, exhausted by the stresses of the past months, would die

---

[1] Rhenius justified the employment of non-Christian schoolteachers by suggesting that parents preferred their children to be taught by such. So long as the curriculum and textbooks were thoroughly Christian, he thought both teacher and pupils would benefit (Rhenius, *Memoir*, 404-5, 549-55, 561).

[2] Coates was a layman, who had been Venn's predecessor as CMS secretary in London. Described as business-like, astringent and legalistic, he was less amenable than Venn to episcopal interference (Yates, *Venn*, 13, 22).

[3] M359

[4] Rhenius's biographer considered this a positive quality: "Few could so well as Mr Rhenius unite authority in directing and ruling with familiar intercourse and friendly counsel" (Rhenius, *Memoir*, 192).

[5] Stock, *Hist CMS*, I, 283

[6] Brecht, 139-40

[7] M331

shortly afterwards, in 1838, at the age of only forty-seven. He left Christian groups in nearly three hundred villages over an area of about two thousand square miles.[1]

Groves's Later Missionary Career

After his initial visit to Rhenius in 1833, Groves had travelled south to Jaffna in Ceylon (Sri Lanka), probably on Rhenius's recommendation,[2] where he was delighted to find missionaries of several societies and denominations meeting regularly together for prayer. Then, sailing north, he paused briefly in Madras, receiving a warm welcome from the expatriate community and an encouraging response to his exhortations about Christian devotedness.[3] Continuing to Calcutta, he made contact with missionaries of various societies and, as we have noted, some Anglican clergy. He also went to see the Baptists at Serampore. Among his more memorable visits was that to the English school in Calcutta started by Alexander Duff, with whom he then sailed back to England in the summer of 1834.[4]

The following year Groves visited Basel and Geneva, with George Müller acting as interpreter, where he recruited several Swiss and German missionaries, among them Hermann Gundert. He was then joined in England by William and Elizabeth Bowden, and George and Elizabeth Beer, and after his remarriage (to Harriet Groves of Malvern), returned with his party to India, arriving in Madras, as we have noted, in July 1836.

Here he found the expatriate community embittered against him on account of his support for Rhenius against the CMS. There was now little opportunity for ministry amongst them despite the fact that overworked LMS missionaries were pleading for a Minister to be sent to Madras in order to relieve them of pastoral responsibility for the Nonconformists in the expatriate community.[5] Also in Madras at this time were John Parnell and Edward Cronin, who having earlier joined him in Baghdad, then followed him to India. They both returned to Britain in 1837.

With doors closing to him in Madras, and needing to feed and clothe himself and his team, Groves bought a house with a small area of farmland in Chittoor, about a hundred miles to the west, in July 1837. Less than two years had passed since Rhenius's abortive plans to settle in this region. Groves evidently had in mind to take on the task Rhenius had briefly accepted and then relinquished, and thus to work, more or less closely, with John Bilderbeck. The area of particular interest to him extended beyond Chittoor to include the towns of Vellore, and

---

[1] M389. For two years the future of the churches remained uncertain, but all were ultimately taken over by the CMS. The Anglican Church eventually paid Rhenius a generous but rather paradoxical tribute: "To him we owe the practice that in 700 villages in the Tirunelveli diocese the bell rings every evening to call the Christians together for Evensong" (Neill, *India and Pakistan*, 70). The bell might justifiably be credited to Rhenius, but not the Evensong.
[2] Rhenius, *Memoir*, 254-5; M277-8
[3] M285
[4] Duff was extremely ill at the time. For a documented narrative of these events, see FOFM 213-4 and 219-27.
[5] Drew to Ellis, 10th July 1835. For additional documentation see FOFM 231-41.

Arcot (where two cavalry regiments were stationed),[1] and many villages throughout the region.[2]

The relations between Groves and Bilderbeck have not hitherto been the subject of detailed research. One reason for this is that Groves's *Memoir* makes no reference to Bilderbeck at all, leading us to suppose that, in moving to Chittoor, Groves was pioneering virgin territory. Indeed, his widow Harriet, who was there at the time, states unequivocally, "Hearing that Chittoor, a civil station, ninety-six miles from the Presidency, had no missionary, Mr. Groves purchased a house there on reasonable terms."[3] This is, to say the least, misleading. Gundert hardly sheds much additional light on the matter, for the entries in his diary (in German, English and Tamil) are brief and tantalisingly enigmatic. The question must therefore be asked, why Groves went to a place where another missionary was already labouring, and having done so, why he found such evident difficulty in working harmoniously with him. The answer must be sought in the surviving correspondence of Bilderbeck himself.

The earliest record we have of Protestant mission in Chittoor dates from 1818, when about twenty Indian Christians were understood to be there, through the personal influence of a Mr Dacre of the East India Company. Dacre continued to devote himself, his time and money to these converts till his death in 1829, at which point, according to Rhenius's editor, their interest seems to have faded.[4]

In 1818 or 1819 Rhenius had found a number of expatriate Christians resident in Chittoor, including a Mr and Mrs Harper, Mrs Harris and Dr and Mrs Macauley, and in 1819 he assisted "at the ceremony of laying the foundation of a mission church", probably the building later known as Bilderbeck's chapel. There seems to have been no resident clergyman in the vicinity at the time of Rhenius's visit, and about six Indians received the Lord's Supper from Rhenius himself. He advised, "It is extremely desirable to have a missionary stationed here as soon as possible."[5] It was not till April 1833 that the post was filled by Bilderbeck, aged at that time only twenty-four and newly married.[6]

---

[1] M370

[2] As early as 1818 Rhenius had found in Vellore a certain Mr and Mrs Jackson who had a schoolroom (Rhenius, *Memoir*, 128), and in 1819 he spoke in that town to thirty Indians. Although "some of them seem to love the Bible," his overall impression was that they "are in a very desolate condition. They have none to care for them" (Ibid, 182-3). In 1837 Gundert heard of some LMS catechists in Vellore whose evangelistic efforts extended only to Roman Catholics, not to Hindus (Gundert, *Tagebuch*, 16). There was evidently plenty of scope for missionary activity in the district.

[3] M370

[4] Rhenius, *Memoir*, 128

[5] Ibid, 182-3

[6] An East India Company agent by the name of Nimmo was resident in Chittoor from 1831 to 1835, but his ordination and appointment as an LMS missionary did not take place until 1837, after he had left Chittoor (Lovett, II, 67). Lovett traces the history of LMS work in the town: "A church of native converts was formed here about 1825 by Mr E Crisp of Madras. From 1831 to 1835 Mr Nimmo was the resident missionary; from 1833 to 1840 Mr Bilderbeck laboured here, and at Arni and at one or two other outstations of Madras; and from 1840 to 1842 it was under the charge of Mr Alexander Leitch." Then he adds, "Work at Chittoor appears to have been carried on in a somewhat intermittent fashion, and after this period it ceases to appear as a head station in the Society's reports" (II, 68).

John Bilderbeck was the son of a landowner with indigo plantations near Nayoor. Having grown up in Madras as a Roman Catholic, he studied for a year in England before his ordination as a Congregationalist minister and acceptance by the LMS for work in India. Early in his missionary career (1833-4), Bilderbeck had some unspecified disagreement with an LMS colleague, William Taylor, leading to Taylor's resignation and to Bilderbeck's continued apprehension lest this might prejudice the LMS directorate against him. Indeed, he feared it might account for the fact that, despite his urgent and repeated pleas, they had never sent a missionary colleague to assist in his large area of responsibility embracing a long line of towns and villages between Madras and Bangalore.[1]

In July 1837 he informed the LMS Directors of his plans to move his base away from Chittoor to a neighbouring town and he reiterated his continued need for additional manpower:

> Walajapettah, the largest of the District and the most central of the whole will soon, I trust, be occupied; but then what is to become of Chittoor? A missionary does not possess *ubiquity*, and therefore if the Directors do not send or appoint an additional Missionary soon, how am I, a single soul, to answer the wants of so many? I really cannot see the degradation and condition of the many unoccupied stations about me and continue stationary only at Chittoor. My soul is ready to fly to all about me and do what I can for the whole. I cannot forget that I am a Missionary and not a Pastor. But this is *killing* work if I am to do both these duties alone. Is there none to come over and help me? Or rather to devote for God?[2]

This was exactly the kind of appeal to interest Groves. With his pastoral and Bible-teaching abilities, he might feel capable of complementing Bilderbeck's more evangelistic inclinations and thus free the younger man for the wider ministry he so obviously desired.

Nothing in our knowledge of Groves's character would lead us to suppose he intended to compete with Bilderbeck. On the contrary, his wish would be to demonstrate the benefits of working together without denominational distinction, combining their varied gifts for the progress of the Gospel. He would be encouraged in such expectations by Bilderbeck's earlier willingness to co-operate with Rhenius,[3] and even more so by the welcome accorded to Groves's colleague

---

[1] Bilderbeck to Ellis, 30th Dec. 1835. Bilderbeck finds no place in Horne's brief survey of LMS work prior to 1904, and receives only a brief mention in Lovett's larger work, with no such glowing tribute as is offered to Crisp, Drew and other LMS contemporaries. He is said to have served initially in Madras for a year or two under the leadership of John Smith (brother of Mary Moffat) before moving to Chiltoon [i.e. Chittoor] in 1833 (Lovett, II, 56). Groves, on his initial tour of India (in 1834), met the Smiths and found them very responsive to his view of Christian devotedness (M285). In the course of fifteen years their Davidson Street Independent Chapel in Black Town, Madras, sent out at least eight European missionaries to other parts of India, one of whom was Bilderbeck (Bromley, 26). It is uncertain whether Groves's earlier contact with Smith affected Bilderbeck's opinion of him.

[2] Bilderbeck to Ellis, 28th July 1837. An edited version of this letter appeared in the *Annual Report* of the LMS for 1838.

[3] A year after Groves's arrival in Chittoor, Bilderbeck referred warmly to "that Great Missionary of Southern India, the late C T Rhenius", praising "his eminently valuable and useful life" (Bilderbeck to Ellis, 10th July 1838, 8).

Edward Cronin on a recent visit to Bilderbeck (in late 1836 or early 1837), during which Cronin preached from his pulpit and itinerated with him to a number of his "out-stations".[1]

Six months before Groves's arrival in Chittoor, Bilderbeck had printed a leaflet announcing the formation of what he called an "Indian Missionary Society", with himself as Acting Clerical Secretary. Its regulations stated, "The Fundamental Principle of this Society is to call into unison and co-operation all Protestant Christians who profess the great principles of the Reformation, without regard to any tenets they may hold on Church Government."[2] Groves would surely have warmed to the prospect of Indian missionaries carrying the Gospel to their own people, especially as the non-denominational basis of the enterprise was so strongly emphasized. If, as seems likely, Groves was aware of this initiative, he must have looked forward with keen anticipation to supporting and encouraging it.[3]

We may thus assume that Groves had heard about Bilderbeck's long-felt desire for missionary reinforcements, about the recent success of Cronin's visit to him, about his Indian mission initiative, and about his plans to leave Chittoor in order to make his "head station" in Walajapettah. Always optimistic and inclined to think the best of others, Groves may not have appreciated that Bilderbeck actually had no intention of abandoning his Chittoor congregation or of letting anyone else assume leadership of it without his personal approval. He was also unaware that Cronin's view of his visit was rather more favourable than that of Bilderbeck himself, who later observed that his guest had preached heresy in Bangalore and unsettled the mind of one of his best catechists in Arnee.[4] Groves was also not to know that the Indian Missionary Society would fail to progress beyond its earliest description on paper.[5]

Bilderbeck was twenty-eight years of age and had been in Chittoor barely four years when Groves (aged forty-two) arrived in July 1837 with his family and co-workers. In addition to Norris and Harriet Groves and the boys Henry, Frank and Edward, the team consisted of Hermann Gundert, George Baynes, Julie Dubois, Emma Groves, Harnie Thomas and the two ex-soldiers MacCarthy and

---

[1] Bilderbeck to Ellis, 10th July 1838, 4

[2] It was constituted as a typical "voluntary society" after the fashion of the LMS, with a committee, trustees and an Annual General Meeting. It appealed for candidates, proposed a salary for its agents, and made provision for the widows and orphans of deceased missionaries. Any supporter who agreed to pay one rupee per month would become a "member". Bilderbeck's initiative should not be confused with the later "Indian Missionary Society" created by V S Azariah in Tirunelveli in 1903.

[3] We might think Groves would question the foreign institutional nature of the society, but at this stage he had no experience of an alternative, that is, of indigenous initiatives without foreign leadership.

[4] Groves's cause in India was seriously compromised by Cronin's efforts to introduce to the expatriate communities certain tracts on "the sinful humanity of Christ" (an Irvingite doctrine) and to preach "Universal Pardon" (Bilderbeck to Ellis, 10th July 1838, 2, 4-5). There is no evidence that Groves himself held these doctrines, or that Cronin continued to do so after leaving India. Cronin returned to Britain about a month before Groves arrived in Chittoor. Among early Brethren, the evangelist Thomas Dowglass of Salcombe was teaching "universal salvation" by 1834-5, and around the same time shifted his allegiance to the Irvingites (Grass, "Thomas Dowglass").

[5] No further reference to this initiative is evident in the LMS archives, and Bilderbeck's idea seems to have been quickly abandoned.

MacFarlane, along with John Christian Arulappan (who as a boy had attended one of Rhenius's schools) and another Indian Christian named Andrew. This represented a sizeable addition both to the expatriate community and to the incipient circle of Indian Christians. It would substantially alter the balance of spiritual influence.

The decision to move to this locality from Madras may initially have owed more to Gundert than Groves, for the editor of Gundert's journal notes that after Gundert's initial visit to Rhenius in Tinnevelly, "on his return to Madras, he formed the resolve to found a mission station, which Groves agreed to after some hesitation."[1] Two months later, in September 1837, Gundert (aged only twenty-three) attended "Bilderbeck's Chapel". He was apprehensive of Bilderbeck's attitude towards him, referring in his journal to "my great fear of quarrels with Bilderbeck".[2]

Bilderbeck himself, despite his earlier disagreement with an LMS colleague, does not seem to have been a quarrelsome person. His letters demonstrate a humble and generally amenable spirit, and he appears to have been a diligent and effective missionary in the role of a youthful Congregationalist Minister overseeing his widely scattered companies of Indian converts. But the natural defensiveness of a young man facing the prospect of losing his beloved flock to a mature newcomer of strong character will have been exacerbated by the bitter personal prejudice against Groves and his colleagues communicated to him by supporters of the CMS. Indeed, Gundert tells us that at this particular time Archdeacon Harper "in open company had called Groves without specification a preacher of blasphemous doctrines."[3] Feeling that Cronin had betrayed his trust and abused his goodwill, Bilderbeck was determined not to make the same mistake again. In July 1838 he reluctantly and belatedly informed his London directors concerning the newcomer:

> It is very generally known that he has imbibed many peculiar views of Doctrine and practice and is doing his utmost to spread them in every possible way to the discomfort of many private Christians and the disorder of Churches. He has published a Tract against the Moral Law as the Rule of Life, another on "the liberty of the Christian Ministry" opposed alike to the views of the Establishment as to those of Dissenters... His main object seem[s], to all appearance, to be that of getting converts to his own particular opinions among the higher classes of European Society by unhinging the minds of the good, thereby to give solidity and respectability to a particular system now I believe rising to notice at some quarter in *Plymouth*.[4]

In fact Groves's visit to Plymouth three years earlier had shown how fundamentally he differed from the prevailing ecclesiological views of the Brethren under Darby's influence there. He was unfortunate to be tarred with that brush.

Bilderbeck saw a number of his converts yielding to the "interference" of Groves and his colleagues, and in particular rejecting the idea of infant baptism and Sabbath observance. He found the changed circumstances "truly painful" and reported, "Since then my people have become very much divided and I have had

---

[1] Gundert, *Tagebuch*, ix
[2] *Tagebuch*, 13
[3] *Tagebuch*, 9
[4] Bilderbeck to Ellis, 10th July 1838, 3-4. On the content of these writings, see PEANG, 115ff and 136ff.

various difficulties to encounter."[1] Despite this (or perhaps because of it), Bilderbeck registered more conversions that year (1838) than any previously.

A far warmer welcome was accorded to the missionary team from a family living in Chittoor by the name of Lascelles. In his journal Gundert recorded his first impressions of a school run by Mrs Lascelles: "Examination in the Lascelles school. The old [i.e. older] girls answer very well. It is a great mercy to see at least so much of Christian knowledge spread through the rising generation of Chittoor in consequence of the efforts of dear d'Aere [i.e. Dacre] and his successors."[2]

Lascelles himself was engaged in some secular activity, possibly in government service, which enabled the couple to provide generous support for Christian work, including, in due course, the work of Groves himself. But the expatriate community in Chittoor was divided in its opinion of the newcomer. Mr Cassamajor, the "first provincial judge in Chittoor", decided, on the strength of Groves's view of the Decalogue,[3] that he "shall not support any Mission connected with Groves", to which observation Gundert added the comment, "great loss".[4] But others seem to have been freshly converted and greatly encouraged through attending the "evening reading at Groves's" and through meetings he addressed in the town, including some at the provincial courthouse.[5] Groves also initiated a weekly celebration of the Lord's Supper for believers, which soon had a larger attendance than his previous similar meetings in Madras.[6]

At the time of Groves's arrival in 1837 there were about forty to sixty persons (excluding children) attending public worship in "Bilderbeck's chapel", and the total number of professing Christians associated with the LMS mission was said to be 113 expatriates and seven "native Christians".[7] The following year (1838), Bilderbeck reported that "the exposition of the Scriptures is continued every morning on the mission premises, when nearly 20 adults attend." The "native church" now numbered ten.[8] Then in 1839 he complained of a decrease in numbers as a consequence of "other places of worship having been opened in the vicinity."[9] Throughout this time Bilderbeck was still pleading and praying for new workers to be sent out for the extension of his mission, and he clearly did not consider Groves or Gundert an answer to his prayer.

In fact Gundert's journal reveals continuous tensions in the relationship. In September 1837, shortly after the arrival of Groves's team in Chittoor, we find an Indian Christian worker threatening to leave them and join Bilderbeck if conditions did not improve. We are left to guess what the conditions in question might have been; perhaps they related to finance.[10] In the same month Gundert noted that Dean W H Drew of the LMS preached in Bilderbeck's chapel whilst staying with his

---

[1] Bilderbeck to Ellis, 10th July 1838, 2
[2] *Tagebuch*, 4
[3] For Groves's view of the Decalogue, see PEANG, 145ff.
[4] *Tagebuch*, 12. Groves evidently bore no resentment towards Cassamajor, and in 1847 was welcomed by him to a mission he had founded "among the natives on the Hills" at Katy (M433; 437).
[5] *Tagebuch*, 14
[6] M375
[7] *Annual Report of LMS*, 1837, 61
[8] *Annual Report of LMS*, 1838, 55
[9] *Annual Report of LMS*, 1839, 53-4
[10] Gundert, *Tagebuch*, 8

wife in "the London Society bungalow", a considerably grander house than the "humble dwelling" occupied by himself and Groves, and he observed that Drew had many servants.[1] Throughout his journal Gundert refers bluntly to "Mr B" and to "Drew", whilst other expatriate Christians receive from him the epithet "dear" and "Br." [i.e. brother]. In October of that year (1837) Gundert recorded his own arrival in a particular village, adding "Mr Bilderbeck seems to have been here before." He heard that Bilderbeck's catechist was encouraging Bilderbeck to think that he (Gundert) and Groves were giving rupees to Bilderbeck's converts and contacts as an incentive to join them, and he commented, "Bilderbeck seems to be afraid of losing his church."[2] During another itineration, in December, an innkeeper remarked that Bilderbeck had been there before him and had "inquired after my transactions here and in the villages about."[3] Bilderbeck had evidently made a point of telling Indians and expatriates that Groves's doctrines were heretical, and Gundert, often inclined to exaggerate in his critical judgments, spoke of Bilderbeck "lying according to the spirit that is in him". A little later he noted "the miserable consequences of Bilderbeck's loveless calumnies".[4] In February 1838 there was "much talk about missionary interference" and later that year some parents transferred their children from Groves's school to Bilderbeck's, whilst Bilderbeck's schoolmaster desired to leave him and join Groves.[5] It was evidently an unhappy state of affairs, and one that could not fail to distress and perplex a man of Groves's sensitive temperament with his strong belief that Christians should be able to co-operate in the service of their common Lord.

Bilderbeck's repeated and increasingly desperate requests for reinforcements were finally rewarded in February 1840 with the arrival in Chittoor of a young Scots recruit to the LMS by the name of Alexander Leitch. From the start this was considered a temporary appointment, and the following August Leitch left, to be replaced by a "native pastor".[6] This meant that in July 1841 Bilderbeck could report, "Revd. Isaac David is now in entire charge at Chittoor."[7]

Leitch seems to have been on rather better terms with Groves than was Bilderbeck, perhaps because he had invested less personal time and energy in establishing an LMS mission at Chittoor. Indeed, shortly after his arrival he reported to his superiors in London, "As you may desire to know my position with

---

[1] *Tagebuch*, 8. Groves seems to have enjoyed relatively good relations with Drew, and in June 1847 visited him in Madras: "I called on Drew (of the London Missionary Society). He is truly rejoicing in the Lord, and spoke most sweetly of the Lord's ways" (*Memoir* 1st edn., 304).

[2] *Tagebuch*, 13

[3] *Tagebuch*, 14

[4] *Tagebuch*, 13, 27. Speaking a foreign language, one often sounds more dogmatic than intended, and this no doubt compounded the harsh effect of Gundert's pietistic tendency to hold other Christians spiritually accountable to himself. Groves contented himself with observing, "At Arcot, Gundert found every effort had been made to cast doubts into the minds of men, relative to my soundness in the faith; especially, because I consider *Christ's life* and *words* our *only rule* of *life*; but this evil speaking has less and less effect; so many have heard me now, that they practically reject the accusation, though they may understand too little to disprove it verbally; but I feel such peace in leaving my cause with the Lord" (M378).

[5] *Tagebuch*, 22, 27, 32

[6] Bilderbeck to Directors of LMS, 22nd March 1841

[7] Bilderbeck to Directors of LMS, 8th July 1841

respect to Mr Groves, I may state that we are on amicable terms, it having been my object to avoid *intimacy* that we might avoid *collision*. Judging from his large silk manufactory he is not likely to leave this place soon."[1] The following year, as Leitch moved away, he remarked, "We parted from Mr and Mrs Groves on the very best terms. They very kindly entertained us for two days previous to our departure. Mr Groves very materially assisted in making arrangements for our journey and saved the Society some expense."[2]

This is typical of Groves's attitude towards other missionaries and we must assume that the same open-hearted fellowship was offered to Bilderbeck and was refused by him. Groves's failure to win Bilderbeck's confidence will have saddened him, especially as he and Bilderbeck might have found themselves entirely of one mind on a number of issues, especially on the importance of frugal living. In 1840 Bilderbeck expressed his view to the LMS that no distinction, financial or otherwise, should be made between Indian and European missionaries, and that no distinction should be allowed between clergy and laity such as would reinforce class differences in the minds of the "heathen". He advised, moreover, that several Indian Christian workers would "cheerfully resign one half of their salary if their European Brethren would but set them an example."[3] This line of thought would certainly have impressed Groves. Bilderbeck, however, had clearly decided that he and Groves were incompatible, and after the latter's arrival he preferred to work separately and for the most part at a distance from his former sphere in Chittoor. In September 1841 Bilderbeck resigned from the LMS, after nine years' service, and moved out of the region.[4]

The subsequent course of Groves's missionary career is described in my *Father of Faith Missions* and will not be discussed in detail here. In brief, we should note that his farm settlement in Chittoor flourished for about five years, then met with a sequence of crushing misfortunes. Initially he and Gundert itinerated separately throughout the region on "monthly mission tours", accompanied by Indian believers who translated, preached and engaged in spontaneous discussions with bystanders along the way. The method they used was very similar to that which Groves had seen successfully employed by Rhenius, and like him they offered to

---

[1] Leitch to Foreign Secretary of the LMS, 19th Sep. 1840
[2] Leitch to Foreign Secretary of the LMS, 21st Aug. 1841
[3] Bilderbeck to Directors of LMS, 8th Dec. 1840
[4] Bilderbeck gave several reasons for his resignation. Notable among them was his frustration with the tendency of his more ecumenical colleagues to jeopardise what he considered the interests of the LMS, exposing his converts to alternative views concerning baptism and church government: "The practice and conduct of several of my Brethren in connexion with the Society is so compromising that I have really found it difficult to maintain and preserve a *separate* interest for the Society. While I am endeavouring to exercise a jealous care over the people and interests of the Society at my stations and by a watchful and cautious oversight to guard them against the inroads of error and of schism and of party influence, my brethren, by mixing freely with sects who would be glad to see our missions supplanted to make room for theirs, and by getting such even to preach in their Pulpits, do what they can to break down my fences and bulwarks and to weaken my hands by giving my people a sort of practical licence to mix themselves up with other parties. So that all I do for the London Mission as a Mission, by studiously raising up a community of interests for them, comes to nothing" (Bilderbeck to Tidman and Freeman, 23rd Sep. 1841). After his resignation he attempted to oversee his stations independently. Later he so far overcame his aversion to Anglican forms as to join the CMS (see Sibree).

establish elementary schools wherever the local villagers desired them, for the instruction of their children in reading, writing and Scripture.[1] Groves threw much responsibility on his young Indian assistants, Arulappan and Andrew. Visiting small groups of Indian Christians in many places, especially those related to Arulappan's extensive family, Groves encouraged the Indians to share together in the Lord's Supper.[2] At this time Arulappan received a modest salary as a schoolteacher and translator of Christian literature, until, embarrassed by the taunts of an onlooker, he declared that, in order for his motives to be free of suspicion, he no longer desired wages and would prefer to live "by faith".

In 1838 Gundert married another of Groves's recruits, Julie Dubois, and the couple left the area. In 1840 John Christian Arulappan also left Chittoor, to establish an indigenous work under his own leadership in the Madurai district, south of Trichinopoly (Tiruchchirappalli). Groves commented, "When he left me, I wished to settle something upon him monthly, as remuneration for his labour in translating for us; but, unlike a native, he refused any stipulated sum."[3] Two years later Arulappan had succeeded in establishing a Christian village with its own meetings for worship, and its own agricultural projects enabling it to be largely self-supporting. It went by the name of Christianpettah, meaning "Christian village".

A large proportion of Groves's time and energy from this point onward was expended in teaching Indian school-children to read the English Bible, and in the management of his agricultural and cottage industries, but he also took particular interest in visiting and teaching the groups of expatriate Christians in Arcot, Vellore and in Chittoor itself, and sometimes further afield, especially in the British military camps.

As Groves never learnt to speak an Indian language, he was restricted to English as a medium of communication with Indians. Accompanied by a capable translator, this was probably no great handicap,[4] and in his ministry to the growing number who wished to learn English, it would be a positive advantage. In his native tongue, Groves was "peculiarly gifted with the power of language",[5] and many testified to spiritual help received from him.[6]

Conclusion: The Development of Groves's Missiological Thought

The early missionary interest of Anthony Norris Groves was awakened through John Owen of the BFBS, and was stimulated by continued contact with representatives of the CMS such as Edward Bickersteth. Despite the pietistic elements of Groves's thought, evidence is lacking for direct Pietist influence in his

---

[1] Gundert, *Tagebuch*, 3ff.
[2] See M393, and additional comment in FOFM 238-40.
[3] M392
[4] In a missionary context, a genuine love for others and an ability to speak with imagination and enthusiasm can count for more than linguistic excellence. Groves's son Edward noted how effective an evangelist among both British and Indians was Samuel Hebich, a German possessing no more than five hundred and fifty words of English (M520; Groves E K, *Successors*, 46). The extent of Hebich's vocabulary was calculated by Hermann Gundert (Neill, *Christian Missions*, 277).
[5] Bilderbeck to Ellis, 10th July 1838, 4
[6] See FOFM 372-84.

early years. He was probably aware of the primitivist vision proposed in Edward Irving's *Missionary Orations*, and he was certainly aware of Henry Drummond's enthusiastic support for independent missionaries in Europe, and also of Joseph Wolff, whose itinerations he followed with interest. His contact with Joshua Marshman will have deepened his distaste for the authoritarian aspects of mission society administration.

Groves's early desire to serve overseas as a missionary was fulfilled only after many years of frustration and delay. His motivation from the start was essentially pietistic, "constrained by Jesus' love", but as a missionary he drew particular encouragement from the prospect of eternal rewards for faithfulness. The primitivist ethos of his early ecclesiology resurfaces in his missiological thought as he moves into a cross-cultural context. His preaching and teaching continued to reflect his early emphasis on personal devotion to Christ, with a strong eschatological element, testifying to what he considered a doomed and desolate world concerning the redeemer's imminent return to judge and to save.

On his journey from London to St Petersburg and thence to Baghdad, Groves sought fellowship with Protestant Christians of diverse racial and denominational backgrounds. His positive experiences confirmed his appreciation of spiritual unity transcending organisational identities.

In Bagdad itself he suffered both intense anxiety and personal loss, but during his three years there he learned colloquial Arabic and had the opportunity to distribute many scriptures and engage in religious discussion with people from diverse backgrounds. He experimented with both medical and educational ministry. His happy working relationship with Karl Pfander will have stimulated an interest in the Basel Mission and the German Pietist tradition from which its recruits were drawn.

Relocating to India, Groves was impressed with the opportunities he observed there for direct evangelistic outreach among Hindus and Indian Roman Catholics, far exceeding what could safely be done in the Muslim context of Baghdad. Throughout the subcontinent, he again sought fellowship with expatriate Christians from diverse denominations and nationalities. His involvement in the so-called Rhenius Affair confirmed his early conviction that foreign church denominations had no valid place in India and that Indian churches should not be subject to foreign administrative hierarchies. His experience of working with young Indian Christians, especially John Christian Arulappan, confirmed his conviction that Indian Christians were capable of undertaking initiatives and bearing responsibility, and indeed should be encouraged to do so without waiting for foreign training, authorisation and payment.

These, then, were the missionary experiences of Groves's early and middle years, experiences which will have contributed to the progress of his missiological thought. They served to confirm his primitivist convictions and to shape the application of his ecclesiological ideas, developed largely before leaving England, to a very different cultural and religious context overseas. We will now look in detail at the missiological principles he defined and advocated.

Part 2. The Missiology of A N Groves

Introduction: An Ecclesiologist Overseas

The missiology of Anthony Norris Groves may be considered a practical application of the primitivist ecclesiology he developed before leaving England in 1829. His basic principles are reiterated in his writings during the course of his first exploratory tour of India, from Bombay via Ceylon to Calcutta, in 1833-4. To this very different cultural context he extrapolated his concepts of spiritual unity, liberty of ministry and Christian influence.[1] These we will recapitulate:

1) *Spiritual unity*. With no formal church or society connection, Groves felt able to relate to every Christian he met simply as a fellow-believer in Christ. And he could speak of Christ to the Muslim or Hindu without having to defend or justify the transgressions of churches ancient or modern. He hoped to see increasing co-operation between Christians reflecting their spiritual unity. On his way to Baghdad in November 1829, he rejoiced in representing no denomination or society: "I feel I am happy in having no system to support in moving among either professing Christians or Mahomedans. To the one, a person so situated can truly say, 'I do not desire to bring you over to any church, but to the simple truth of God's word.' And to the others, 'We wish you to read the New Testament that you may learn to judge of God's truth, not by what you see in the churches around you, but by the word of God itself.'"[2]

2) *Liberty of ministry*. Groves encouraged individual Christians to take their own initiatives, never attempting to recruit them to a society or a denomination or even a local fellowship. He simply ministered wherever he had the opportunity, and he encouraged others to do likewise. His purpose was not to organise churches, but to make disciples. And he was delighted when he saw disciples become apostles. In southern India in early December 1833, he declared his wish for Christians to engage freely in service to others: "Daily my desire is strengthening to see the Church free in the use of God's word and in his modes of ministry, every one being free to exercise the gift the Spirit has given."[3]

3) *Christian influence*. Groves rejected the common view that influence for good should be exerted in the world through access to the corridors of power. He believed it better to "follow Christ" simply and wholeheartedly and thus to show the world an alternative lifestyle, a genuinely Christian way of living. He lived frugally and sacrificially as a mentor and friend to everyone he met. In a tract dated 1833 he spoke of exerting a positive spiritual influence: "Simply do as Christ *did*, and as he *taught*, and in *his Spirit*. There is your maximum of Christian influence."[4]

As our study proceeds, we will see how Groves applied these ecclesiological principles to the missiological issues of his day, and we will do so under three headings: Missions and Churches, Civilization and Education, and Finance and Providence. In particular, we will consider his views concerning the relations

---

[1] For a detailed discussion of Groves's ecclesiology, see PEANG, 97ff.
[2] M69 (J95-6)
[3] M256
[4] Groves, *Influence*, 54

between local churches and missionary agencies, the development of congregations with indigenous leadership, the appointment and financial support of missionaries, the merits of local culture and Western civilisation, missionary co-operation, Christian industries and Christian schools. We will also discuss his understanding of "living by faith" and of "accountability".

On arrival in India, Groves quickly discovered his principles to be radically different from the assumptions and methods of his missionary contemporaries. His journals, as he travelled throughout the subcontinent, are full of comments concerning the work and the workers, many of whom received his warm approval for their personal devotion, their discipline, and their zeal in preaching the Gospel. He commended the early vision of such agencies as the CMS, LMS and BMS in recruiting the missionaries he met, and he clearly had no desire to be unduly critical. Nevertheless, he perceived certain tendencies in the work, and certain assumptions among the workers, that he felt seriously hampered their effectiveness. He said, "I do not desire for one moment to set myself in opposition to those blessed institutions whose labours roused us from our lethargy; but this I may say, that I do not think their plan is the best, or the only good one."[1] Some months later, "I long to see some one mission carried on in unison with the principles I feel to be right."[2] And again, "From my arrival in Bombay to the day I reached Jaffna, I had been continually hoping to find missionary institutions carried on with that simplicity which I think so highly becomes us, but I have been deeply disappointed."[3]

The conclusion that Groves drew from his exploratory tour was a sweeping and, perhaps to some minds, a presumptuous one. He declared, "My earnest desire is to re-model the whole plan of missionary operations so as to bring them to the simple standard of God's word."[4] It is this uncompromising statement, in the spring of 1834, which most clearly marks Groves as an early primitivist among mission thinkers.[5] Indeed, he insisted, "Much will not be done till we go back again to *primitive principles* and let the nameless poor and their unrecorded and unsung labours be those on which our hopes, under God, are fixed."[6]

As we compare the methods of Groves with those of his contemporaries, and with those of missionaries and missiologists in subsequent generations, we will trace the course of these primitivist ideas from his own time, through the following century, and into the modern age. But first we must turn our attention to the existing "plan of missionary operations", as conducted by the "blessed institutions" to which he referred. What, we might wonder, was so seriously wrong with them?

---

[1] R95-6; M118
[2] M274
[3] M274
[4] M285-6
[5] Groves considered events in the New Testament to be precedents establishing principles of permanent validity for every age and every culture. For analysis of Groves's primitivism, see PEANG, 38ff. It could be argued that he was more a restorationalist than a primitivist, but in fact he was both (see PEANG, 195ff).
[6] R22 (italics added)

1. Missions and Churches

Missionary Societies

Historians have commonly regarded the Protestant missionary societies of the nineteenth century as examples of a social phenomenon typical of that age. They were "voluntary societies". Indeed, Henry Venn, in 1871, willingly described the CMS as such:

> The constitution of the Church Missionary Society has been from its very cradle that of a *voluntary society*, receiving in its early years no support from persons of high position in the Church, that its supporters were attracted to it by the declaration of the principles on which it was to be conducted, that its Committees have been annually elected on the faith of their adherence to these principles – and must therefore regard themselves as trustees of a fund which is to be disbursed with scrupulous regard to the terms of their trust.[1]

The same is true in the Nonconformist sphere for Carey's Baptist Missionary Society. In his famous *Enquiry* he made the proposal, "Suppose a company of serious Christians, ministers and private persons, were to form themselves into a *society*, and make a number of rules respecting the regulation of the plan and the persons who are to be employed as missionaries, the means of defraying the expenses etc…"[2] David Bosch comments,

> There was something businesslike, something distinctly modern, about the launching of the new societies, whether denominational or not. Carey took his analogy neither from Scripture nor from theological tradition, but from the contemporary commercial world – the organisation of an overseas trading company, which carefully studied all the relevant information, selected its stock, ships and crews, and was willing to brave dangerous seas and unfriendly climates in order to achieve its objective. It should be an "instrumental" society, that is, a society established with a clearly defined purpose along explicitly formulated lines. So the organising of such a society was something like floating a mercantile company.[3]

Rufus Anderson, Congregationalist secretary of the American Board of Commissioners for Foreign Missions, was optimistic about the newly discovered potential of these "voluntary associations for religious purposes"[4]. He remarked, "Our age is singular and remarkable for its disposition to associate in action. It associates for the accomplishment of almost every object." Indeed, Anderson believed "this Protestant form of association" to be "among the great results of the

---

[1] Venn to the Archbishop of York, Oct. 1871, in Warren, *To Apply the Gospel*, 134. The voluntary societies of the Church of England were often viewed with suspicion by strict churchmen, who considered their independent operations subversive of ecclesiastical authority. The voluntary society ethos did not sit well with an establishment ecclesiology (See especially Yates, *Venn*, 17-20, 195 etc.).
[2] Carey, *An Enquiry into the Obligations of Christians to use Means for the Conversion of the Heathens*, in George, App.E, 55. For an appreciation of Carey as an initiator of the "business model for mission", with an analysis of the strengths and weaknesses of the model, see Baker, 174-202.
[3] Bosch, 330
[4] Anderson, *The Time for the World's Conversion Come*, in Beaver, *To Advance*, 64

progress of Christian civilization in this 'fulness of time' for the world's conversion... Never until now did the social condition of mankind render it possible to organise the armies requisite for the world's spiritual conquest."[1]

The "voluntary associations", in Anderson's view, depended for their success, firstly, on the personal interest of individual investors, and, secondly, on the efficiency with which those entrusted with the administration of their investment worked towards the fulfilment of their agreed goals. He advised, "It is *the contributors of the funds* who are the real association; not the American Board, not the General Assemblies Board, nor any other, but the individuals' churches, congregations, who freely act together *through such agencies* for an object of common interest."[2] Harold Rowdon describes what commonly took place:

> The missionary society (like other "voluntary societies") was modelled on the structure of a contemporary trading company. It called for a number of individuals committed to promoting the enterprise, a board of directors to assume responsibility and exercise authoritative direction, a number of agents to do the actual work (under the control of the directors) and a body of supporters (roughly corresponding to the shareholders of a trading company) whose role was to provide prayer and financial support for the enterprise, and who would need to be provided with information and other forms of stimulus to help produce such support. In practice, and in view of the enormous distances between the home board and the scenes of operation abroad, it was found to be necessary for the work of missionaries to be directed by leaders drawn from their ranks, and often described as constituting a "field council".[3]

Andrew Walls suggests that the creation of these societies was an essential prerequisite for the fulfilment of the Great Commission in the circumstances of the day. When Carey, for example, proposes the formation of a Baptist Missionary Society, "he is looking for the appropriate means to accomplish a task which cannot be accomplished through the usual machinery of the church... The simple fact was that the Church as then organised, whether episcopal, or presbyterian, or congregational, *could* not effectively operate mission overseas."[4] The societies represent, therefore, in Walls' memorable phrase, "the fortunate subversion of the church".[5]

There were, however, serious drawbacks in the system of voluntary societies. Firstly, it was all too easy for the supporters of the society, or of a missionary appointed by the society, to regard themselves quite frankly as investors, and as such they would tend to compare the work being done by various agencies and individuals, and to invest in whichever seemed likely to offer the best immediate return on their investment. Support, on this basis, could become extremely erratic. Secondly, it meant that "overseas mission" could easily be seen as a hobby of interest only to those with funds to invest, or with particular colonial interests. Thirdly, it burdened the missionaries and the societies with administrative duties. They had to justify to their investors a proposed course of action, excusing failures,

---

[1] Ibid, 65-6
[2] Ibid, 65
[3] Rowdon, "The Brethren Contribution to World Mission" in Rowdon, *The Brethren Contribution to the Worldwide Mission of the Church*, 42.
[4] Walls, "Fortunate Subversion", 146
[5] Frank Severn has recently defended the view that the "voluntary society" method is both more scriptural and more effective than other models (Severn, "Mission Societies").

quantifying successes, and this generated a particular concern with issues of accountability. Fourthly, the expense of maintaining a home office with a salaried secretary almost inevitably reduced the proportion of funds actually sent overseas.[1] Fifthly, a missionary who found himself under pressure to prove his work worthy of investment was almost inevitably tempted to colour his reports, add emotion to his appeals, and to think perhaps more than is healthy about his need to raise financial support. And finally, it added enormously to the stresses of life when a missionary felt called of God to undertake a task or ministry and met with disapproval, or an outright veto, from his superiors on the field or at home. Society agents generally had to accept and conform to a set of rules, and follow the directions of their superiors in decisions relating to the type and location of their work and the expenses they incurred. Most could not get married, for example, without the official approval of the mission authorities.[2]

The historical fact that Protestant missions almost all started as voluntary societies may lie behind the emphasis in modern missions on financial and operational accountability, manifested in meetings directed to defining job descriptions and terms of reference, undertaking feasibility studies, outlining five-year plans, composing white papers, creating project proposals and vision statements. An awareness of how these societies were launched may help us understand the commercial ethos that still dominates many of their procedures.

In his study of mission history, Bosch compares missionary societies to Nonconformist churches. Both, he suggests, are seeking to attract voluntary support for spiritual initiatives. Both feel a need to justify their activities in order to retain that support. Both are, in essence, "voluntary associations".[3] Now, if Groves saw good reason to deny the validity of the one, it is entirely logical that he would do so for the other. Just as the Nonconformist church finds no place in Groves's ecclesiology, so the voluntary society finds no place in Groves's missiology.[4] And if Scripture describes a single, universal, spiritual and mystical church which is itself committed to mission, then this would be the logical basis of the alternative he proposes.

To Groves's mind, the true church cannot be a voluntary society seeking volunteers: it is, in its very essence, an organic body to which every member is already joined, and in which every true Christian is already playing a part, whether passively or actively, badly or well. And as the church proclaims the Gospel in all

---

[1] In March 1831 the Plymouth auxiliary of the CMS found its support dwindling through disenchantment with the fact that almost one third of the society's income was devoted to home expenses (Stunt, *Awakening*, 301n).

[2] John Kitto's proposed marriage in 1827 was contingent upon the approval of the CMS committee in London (Eadie, 146). In 1853 the young Hudson Taylor observed how the rules of the CES stipulated, "Every missionary shall be subject to the Board of Management; and also he shall abide by the instructions given him... Every person... shall hold himself ready to go to such a place and at such a time as the Board shall decide upon" (Broomhall, *Treaty Wall*, 88; see also Taylor, *Growth of a Soul*, 175). Elizabeth Goldsmith has recently written of the frustration faced by two Presbyterian ladies desiring to start a "village settlement" in India: "The scheme took some time to get off the ground because although the Board approved, the Mission did not. Oh the heartache of being answerable to several managers!" (Goldsmith, *Roots and Wings*, 36).

[3] Bosch, 329

[4] For Groves's view of Nonconformity, see PEANG, 88ff.

the world, so every true Christian is already engaged in that work, albeit in some cases weakly, and in some, far more strongly.

This means that Christian mission is not a task for salaried agents contracted by subscribers to accomplish a defined task in a specified place. It is not a work to be left by default in the hands of voluntary societies. On the contrary, Groves saw Christian mission as a task to be accomplished by the whole church, and every member of every congregation in it – some to go and the rest to support those who have gone.

Groves argued that there is no need for the progress of the Gospel to be hindered, as it so often seems to be, by want of funds. As early as 1825 he had questioned the methods adopted by "the Agents of our Societies... who travel from one end of the land to the other to gather a scanty pittance from half-reluctant Christians – nay who are often led to sharpen their goads at the Philistines' grindstones to the dishonour of the cause of God."[1] The CMS practice of collecting funds by penny subscriptions seemed altogether inadequate to the needs of the situation.[2] And the practice of begging the patronage of aristocrats and industrialists whose Christianity was nominal at best, seemed even more so. Groves believed that the resources to complete the task of the Great Commission were already in the Church's possession. Her inordinate wealth must simply be released from its worldly fetters and put to work for the cause she claimed to uphold. This would be done, not by societies labouring painfully to attract investors or raise funds, but rather by deepening the spiritual life of the Church as a whole and thus transforming the attitude of Christians in general towards stewardship. And this would be achieved primarily by setting them a powerful example, showing how stewardship could and should work in practice. Groves declared,

> My brother, the Church has infinite resources. The only thing you want is to find the way to her heart, and that is by loving her and trusting her, and living yourselves as she must live if her energies are to be brought to bear on the world with power, either as a blessing or a witness. Then you would see the ponderous bags that now weigh down the Church disgorged, on holy principles – a spirit would be stirred that could not stop, till the Spirit which set it in motion itself was stopped.[3]

But there is another aspect to the scenario. The missionaries themselves, once they had arrived on the mission field, would need, in Groves's view, to reassess their loyalties. His experience confirmed that the salaried agents of a voluntary society will naturally feel a particular loyalty to the agency that pays and directs them, a greater loyalty indeed than they will feel towards the infant church coming slowly and painfully into existence through their labours. He found that many missionaries in pioneer situations hardly thought about "church" at all, and he remarked, "Very many of us have felt the utter want of Church character and authority in all existing societies."[4] The time had come, so he believed, to look for a better way of working:

---

[1] D8
[2] Jones, 210
[3] Groves, *Influence*, 60. For Groves's view of missionary support, see below, 131ff.
[4] Groves, "A Letter on Missions", 129. Three generations later, in 1917, the great-grandson of William Carey (bearing the same name) regretted that some promising young Indian leaders were being taken from their churches to become Indian agents of the Baptist

"The grand point to be arrived at is that the Church act so as to prove that the work societies endeavour to accomplish with the world's help can be done better, because more scripturally, by the Church herself."[1]

His vision was for mission to be conducted simply in the name of Christ and by the church of Christ. Following this principle, converts and groups of converts would not belong to any society, or any denomination, but, as he would view it, to Christ alone.

Rivalry and Comity

Groves arrived in India at a moment in history when the missionary societies were shifting from their initial attitude of tolerantly ignoring one another to an altogether more competitive view of their mutual relations.[2] He saw the danger ahead as existing societies opened additional stations, and newer agencies began to move in and compete for influence. He remarked,

> Never was there a more important moment than the present for India. Up to this time everything in the Church has been as free as our hearts could wish. Persons have been converted, either by reading God's word or through one another, and have drank [sic] the living waters, wherever they could find them, full and clear. But now the Church of England is seeking to extend its power, and the Independents and Methodists are seeking to enclose their little flocks.[3]

The Baptists, too, were acquiring "members".[4] Indians were rapidly absorbing all the prejudices that divided Christian from Christian in Europe and America.

We have noted that Groves, though sceptical about mission conducted through the agency of voluntary societies, nevertheless felt obliged to co-operate with such societies as already existed. Indeed, his concept of Christian unity gave him special pleasure in moments of happy fellowship spent with Christians whose views he knew to differ substantially from his own. Timothy Stunt observes his friendly dealings with the CMS during the period after he had resigned his formal connection with the Society: "Groves was earnestly encouraging the Committee of the Society (in a letter of October 1832) to send someone to Ispahan to whom 'we

---

Missionary Society. He observed, "The Mission educates, employs, pays and controls this agency without reference to the Church. This method should cease. It withdraws the very men from the Church who would naturally be its leaders, and forms them into a separate body of professional evangelists under a foreign organisation" (Carey, "The Indian Church", BMSA minutes 1911-7, cited by Stanley, "Planting Self-Governing Churches", 384.)

[1] Groves, "A Letter on Missions", 141

[2] Beaver has pointed out that, despite their diverse denominational origins, the earliest pioneers of Protestant mission were drawn together by the common difficulties they faced and the lack of alternative opportunities for Christian fellowship. As their numbers increased and their missionary status became more securely recognised, they could become more selective in their choice of friends and ecumenical activities (Beaver, *Ecumenical Beginnings*, 22).

[3] M285

[4] Having baptised an Englishman a year after his arrival in India, William Carey cheerfully reported, "A Baptist church is formed in this distant quarter of the globe." A charter had just been drawn up, with four "members", and Carey, for the first time in India, presided at a celebration of the Lord's Supper (Letter dated 1795, quoted by George, 113-4).

would be delighted to give… a brotherly help by the way in the language or one of us would go with him till he got a little accustomed to his work.'[1] But Groves took a particular interest in the Basel Mission:

> Of all the missionary societies, however, for Groves the Basel Mission Institute was in a special category of its own and increasingly he began to look in the direction of Switzerland for reinforcements who would share his own concern for a simple life-style and his disregard for social status. After his meeting with Pfander we find Groves writing to Admiral Pearson of the need to establish an Armenian female school: "I wish Mr [Joseph] Greaves and [his wife] your daughter could come here from Basle… or at all events stir up the Basle Committee to send them some one or two faithful men to encourage and strengthen them."[2]

In 1834 Groves expressed his hope to the Mission director, Christian Gottlieb Blumhardt, that ten or twenty young recruits would be sent from Basel to places where Groves thought they would be useful in India. He even offered to make provision for their basic support. In fact, there was regular correspondence between Groves and the Basel headquarters, both before and after his visit there in 1835. Stunt observes,

> Indeed for a while Groves's thinking in missionary matters had a discernable impact on the policies of the Basel Mission. In his account of the missionary Samuel Hebich, Gundert indicates that it was Groves's plea for a simpler life style that led to Blumhardt's proposal that the Basel missionaries should receive no stated income, but simply draw what was necessary for their subsistence from the society, it being understood that their mode of life was to be as simple as possible, conforming, whenever they could do it, to the habits of the natives of the country.[3]

In April 1835, when representatives of the CMS were preparing to meet their Basel counterparts in order to discuss matters relating to Rhenius, the views expressed by Groves to Blumhardt were extensively reported in their own minutes.[4] But Groves clearly saw no need to join the Basel Mission himself, and in fact he would have fretted intolerably under its authoritarian structure of command.[5]

In our study of Groves's ecclesiology we have noted that the Christian unity he envisaged was a spiritual, mystical unity rather than an organisational unity.[6] It was a unity of individuals, each individual walking with God, and each individual free to follow the guidance of his or her conscience. But far from absolving the individual of responsibility for others, it increased that responsibility, extending it beyond the limits of one's own church or mission or denomination to embrace all true Christians everywhere. The believer was part of the spiritual body of Christ

---

[1] Groves to Woodroffe, 25th Oct.1832
[2] Stunt, "International Context," The Basel Connection, citing Groves to Pearson, 14th Oct. 1829.
[3] Stunt, Ibid, citing Gundert, *The life of Samuel Hebich*, 55-6. Stunt notes that in another account Gundert considers the Basel Mission's leaders somewhat less enthusiastic about Groves's proposals for fully autonomous missionaries (Gundert, *Hermann Mögling*, 75,77).
[4] Chilcraft, Ch.8
[5] See above, 32ff.
[6] See PEANG, 104ff.

comprising all who belonged to Christ, wherever and however they might worship, and he must play his part for the well-being of the body as a whole.

We have seen that Groves never attempted to draw Christians away from other groups to a circle of his own. He had no desire to start a new church denomination. Even less attractive was the idea of founding his own missionary society. Had he wished to do so – perhaps an India Inland Mission – there was ample opportunity, but his journals and letters show no trace of such an idea. He knew how to recruit workers, but when he did he sent almost all to assist Anglican and Nonconformist pioneers in other places. Indeed, the twelve young missionaries he recruited for India, during his fourteen months in Britain and Europe (1835-6), went on to five different centres and served with four different denominations or missions.[1] Perhaps he lacked the toughness, the thick skin, the air of authority required for a successful church or mission director. Perhaps he remembered that those who joined him in Baghdad and Madras did not long follow his lead. Perhaps he sensed a personal lack of administrative ability (although a capable assistant could have met that deficiency). But overriding all these personal considerations stood his belief that the fulfilment of the Great Commission required not the establishment of a new denomination or organisation but a simple obedience of individual Christians to the teachings of the New Testament.

In modern terms Groves was what we might call a "facilitator". He would be an advocate of "partnership", drawing together workers from existing agencies rather than creating a new agency of his own. In May 1834 he confided, "I have realized one hope, which, on entering India, I only indulged as a possibility, viz. that there is no insurmountable barrier to a most extensive union among all who love the Lord Jesus in sincerity."[2]

He was, of course, by no means the first to approve of fellowship between missionaries attached to various agencies. Visiting Jaffna, Ceylon, earlier that year, he discovered already in existence "a meeting of all the missionaries of all denominations for prayer and general communication which takes place every month." He found it "a very delightful meeting... The subjects of discussion were most interesting."[3] Indeed, as early as 1806, Carey had dreamed of a missionary conference "of all denominations of Christians from the four corners of the world."[4] But Groves would carry this idea beyond occasional conferences of denominational delegates, into the realm of ongoing missionary co-operation ignoring denominational identities altogether. He confided, "I have every reason to

---

[1] Kälberer, a German tailor, and Brice, a Devonshire schoolteacher, joined the independent Baptist William Start in Patna. Rodolphe De Rodt and Ferdinand Gros from Switzerland joined a German Lutheran couple by the name of Weitbrecht in Sonamukhi. Harriet Baynes became Groves's second wife and settled with him in Madras, assisted by two young Swiss women, Marie Monnard and Julie Dubois. Hermann Gundert, having completed his theology studies at Tübingen, spent a year with Rhenius in Tinnevelly before rejoining Groves at Madras. William and Elizabeth Bowden and George and Elizabeth Beer pioneered a work of their own in the Godavari Delta.

[2] M306

[3] M277-8

[4] George, 163. It was not till June 1888 that the first major inter-mission conference actually took place. This Centenary Conference on the Protestant Missions of the World (in Exeter Hall, London) was followed by the celebrated International Missionary Conference at Edinburgh in 1910.

hope that the elements of union, which the Lord allows to exist among us, will lead to a missionary combination and service that, to some extent at least, will resemble what there was in the days of the apostles."[1]

In this regard, Groves was of one mind with Rhenius. There is a distinctly Grovesian flavour to the reply Rhenius gave when approached in 1833 by a group of Indian Christians who were translating a book from German into Tamil, and who sent him a statement of their principles. He responded,

> I tell you candidly that I did not like one clause in your rules, viz., that by which you restrict your Society to members of one Church only [i.e. one denomination]... Some sections of the Church of Christ differ from us in certain forms, but we need not, on that account, exclude them from our communion. If they but hold the *head*, viz., the Lord Jesus, and follow his blessed word, we should embrace them as brethren, and not thrust them from us by a sectarian spirit... You would do well to revise that regulation and to form your Society on a more liberal plan.[2]

Before Groves arrived in India, the year 1830 had seen the start of a monthly meeting in Madras for any Protestant missionaries who might wish to attend.[3] Rhenius wholeheartedly approved such an initiative and he remarked, "We endeavour to be free from all party spirit and to embrace every one as a brother who loves the Lord Jesus in sincerity. It is also our fervent prayer that this apostolic spirit of universal love and union may spread more and more."[4]

That same year Rhenius took issue with an anonymous writer who argued that there should be a single "form" of church in India – that is, one according to Anglican tradition – to which all should conform. Rhenius preferred to recognise a variety of "forms", so long as there was unity of spirit. This would constitute no stumbling block to the "heathen", he believed, if they saw affection, fellowship and love between Christians who differed on points of doctrine and practice.[5] His anonymous opponent, conceding that a monolithical Anglicanism was an ideal incapable of realisation, accepted that a variety of "forms" was inevitable.[6]

In the mid-nineteenth century the idea of actually working together was regarded as unrealistic by most Protestants, and vigorously opposed by some. Despite his desire for consultation and prayer with "all denominations", Carey himself would take the Lord's Supper only with believers baptised as adults; many Anglicans in their turn would refuse to take it with him. Andrew Fuller for the Baptist Missionary Society discouraged Carey's "pleasing dream", believing it could do more harm than good.[7] Likewise for the Church of England, Henry Venn

---

[1] M270

[2] Rhenius, *Memoir*, 442-3

[3] Ibid, 378

[4] Ibid, 379. Rhenius did not include Roman Catholics among Christians with whom he would willingly have fellowship. Indeed, he was unhappy that some British residents in India considered there was no great harm in "Popery", and in consequence he prepared a lecture for them on the Antichrist, based on 2 Thess 1:11 (Ibid, 464).

[5] Ibid, 410-1

[6] Ibid, 412-3

[7] Carey, *William Carey*, 249. Carey himself had earlier advised, "In the present divided state of Christendom it would be more likely for good to be done by each denomination engaging separately in the work than if they were to embark in it together... If all were

might say, "God grant that unity of spirit may ever exist," but warned nevertheless that "unity of operations we are not prepared for, except where the object is so definite as in the Bible Society."[1] As corresponding Secretary of the Church Missionary Society, Venn would not even contemplate combining CMS activity with the other Anglican agencies, the SPG and SPCK, far less with denominations outside the Established Church. He advised, "In the constitution and management of missionary societies each section of the Church must conduct its operations upon its own distinctive denominational principles."[2] In general, Groves found British missionaries more divisive than others: "In the whole extent of my missionary tours, Germans and Americans have been the most to my taste; the most laborious, most simple, and least sectarian by far."[3]

The closest that most nineteenth-century voluntary societies would approach to "missionary combination" was a system later identified by the term "comity".[4] A given area would be parcelled out between two or more missions or denominations so that each took responsibility for a defined district or language group. Where a mission agency had already occupied a territory, other agencies agreed not to intrude unless invited.[5] The aim was to avoid unnecessary competition and duplication of effort, but the system caused serious difficulties, especially when a mission was thought to be failing to fulfil its commitment or when agencies not party to the original agreement subsequently arrived on the scene.

Indeed, comity was not an idea universally accepted by Groves's contemporaries. A supporter of the religious Establishment, such as Henry Venn, would consider the whole land (comprising parishes, districts and dioceses) to be the spiritual responsibility of the Church of England. One might anticipate in a Congregationalist, such as Rufus Anderson, a greater willingness to divide a nation into spheres of influence, and indeed, Beaver notes that "The American Board's foreign secretary was one of the chief architects of the pan-Protestant system of comity."[6] Groves himself was aware of incipient problems associated with this system even in his own day. He noted how the practice was directly attacked by an Indian periodical which stated, "They [i.e. missionary societies] have made a territorial division of the heathen world among themselves, with a view doubtless of preventing collision among their missionaries; but the division serves all the

---

intermingled, it is likely their private discords might throw a damp on their spirits and much retard their public usefulness" (Carey, "Enquiry", in George, App.E, 56).

[1] Letter dated 1845, quoted by Shenk, *Venn*, 32

[2] Statement dated 1867, quoted by Shenk, *Venn*, 57. Robert Noble, an Anglican whose generous ecumenicity is evident in his praise and financial support for Groves's Nonconformist colleagues, Bowden and Beer (Noble, 180, 194, 196, 202; M426), nevertheless confided, "Being mindful of the dispersion of Judson's little band, I should not like to engage with anyone (as a fellow-missionary) who is not, after patient enquiry, thoroughly attached to our Church" (Noble, 109-10). Judson had been appointed to Burma as a Congregationalist by the ABCFM, but then, having changed his views on baptism, opted to launch a Baptist mission there instead.

[3] M288

[4] The term "comity" was first heard in the 1880s, but Beaver notes, "The practice of comity in foreign missions antedated the use of the term by more than sixty years" (*Ecumenical Beginnings*, 15).

[5] For details of an early and influential comity agreement for southern India in 1858, see Beaver, *Ecumenical Beginnings*, 82-5.

[6] Beaver, *To Advance*, 24

purpose of consolidating and perpetuating their power by making it the *common* interest to keep out interlopers."[1] Klaus Fiedler, writing in an African context, remarks,

> As a reason for such a concept of comity, the pious intention was often given of saving the Africans from the "unfortunate divisions" of western Christianity, which were so meaningless for Africans. In fact the result of comity was not to wipe out the divisions for Africans but to cement them. The pattern had already been employed after the Thirty Years' War, when the Augsburg Peace Treaty ruled : *cuius regio, eius religio* ('whose the land, his the religion'). For the Africans, of course,... their denomination was not decided upon by a territorial prince, but by the territorial agreements of the various missions, although these were backed up by the worldly rulers of the country.[2]

In 1900 Groves's third son Edward attended a joint mission conference in Madras where he found Anglicans, Nonconformists and Open Brethren, each working in distinct districts of southern India. He called it "a considerable advance in the way of 'comity' from the condition of former years."[3] But it fell far short of his father's ideal. Carey's successors were setting up Baptist churches in one district, Venn's establishing Anglican congregations in another, Methodists and Congregationalists elsewhere, but Groves had hoped for missionaries everywhere to work in partnership for the creation of local Christian fellowships quite independent of the foreign denominations. His view was uncompromising: "Inasmuch as any one glories either in being of the Church of England, Scotland, Baptist, Independent, Wesleyan, etc., his glory is his shame."[4]

Subsequent years saw a measure of formal and informal missionary co-operation in many parts of the world, but the development of "partnerships" and "consultations" to support the growth of independent indigenous churches only became a major emphasis towards the very end of the twentieth century, through the influence of non-denominational agencies such as Interdev[5] and the Billy Graham Organisation. But the idea may be traced back to the vision of Anthony Norris Groves in January 1834 for "missionary combination and service that, to some extent at least, will resemble what there was in the days of the apostles."[6]

Western missiologists have long tended to focus their attention on the failures and successes of Western agencies, and thus to overlook the significant contribution to the missionary task, and to its ecumenical initiatives, made by indigenous Christians throughout the world. T V Philip has recently noted the positive and often decisive role played by indigenous church leaders in efforts for spiritual unity, manifesting a greater desire for it, in many cases, than Western

---

[1] "A Letter on Mission to the Heathen", 128
[2] Fiedler, 190. On the history of "comity" as a missionary practice, see Beaver, *Ecumenical Beginnings*.
[3] Groves E K, *Successors*, 194; Newton, *Mysore State*, 12-15
[4] M49
[5] Interdev was founded in 1974 by Phill Butler as a communications consulting agency to missions organizations, and went on to advocate and facilitate inter-mission co-operation. "Interdev's vision is that every people group and city of the world might have its own nationally led, reproducing church. Our mission is to serve the Church by developing effective, self-sustaining ministry partnerships" <http://www.interdev.org> (accessed 25th Feb. 2005).
[6] Journal entry for 13th Jan. 1834 (M270).

colleagues long accustomed to the divided state of the Church in their home countries. He comments, "The missionary conferences in the mission field were concerned mainly with the co-operation in mission for the sake of evangelistic efficiency and not with unity as such. The real impetus for unity came from the Asian Christians who, under the inspiration of the national movement, took the initiative for Christian unity and for the building up of indigenous churches."[1]

Evidence in support of this is not lacking. The Edinburgh Conference of 1910 noted that in China, "the sense of a common national life and a common Christianity is stronger than the appreciation of the differences which had their origin in controversies remote from the circumstances of the Church in mission lands."[2] The same was true elsewhere, as Philip remarks,

> The extent to which the tragedy of Western denominationalism occupied the minds of the Indian Christians was shown in 1879 when the Synods of the Church Missionary Society and the American Presbyterian Church in India met in Amritsar and Lahore respectively. At both these Synods, the Indian clergy frankly expressed the opinion that the difficulties which stood in the way of the establishment of a national church, were caused solely by Western missionaries.[3]

The issue is addressed by the Danish theologian Kaj Baago:

> Transplanted to another soil outside Europe, the denominational differences suddenly seemed not only absurd, but harmful. Generally the missionaries at the end of the 19th century have been given credit for seeing this and having started the discussion which led to the Ecumenical Movement. It is a question, however, whether the credit should not go to the Indian, Chinese, and Japanese Christians who started the protest movements against western denominationalism.[4]

In refusing to adopt a denominational identity, Groves was surely attuned to the best interests of an indigenous Christianity. If his ideals had prevailed upon his generation, then perhaps no occasion would have arisen for protest against circumstances that became both "harmful" and "absurd".

Church Organisation

An appreciation of Groves as a innovative thinker will owe much to the contrast that is evident between his thought and that of his contemporaries, and in particular that of Henry Venn and Rufus Anderson.

Henry Venn (1796-1873): An Introduction

Henry Venn had spent his childhood in the High Church evangelical circles of Clapham, where his father, John, was rector.[5] He served as corresponding Secretary of the Church Missionary Society between the years 1841 and 1872. Both he and Rufus Anderson were exact contemporaries of Groves, born just a

---

[1] Philip, *Edinburgh to Salvador*, Ch.1
[2] *Commission VIII on Co-operation and Promotion of Unity*, Published for the World Missionary Conference (Oliphant, Anderson & Ferrier, 1910), 84
[3] Philip, Ibid, Ch.1
[4] Kaj Baago, "First Independence Movements", 78. For a perceptive analysis of Baago's thought, with a useful bibliography, see Jorgensen, "Among the Ruins".
[5] Yates, *Venn*, 11

year after him, although they outlived him by twenty and twenty-seven years respectively and produced the bulk of their missiological writing after his death.

Chilcraft has searched for possible connections between the two Englishmen, Groves and Venn, noting that they did indeed have at least one acquaintance in common. When visiting Devon, around 1821, in order to acquire information for a biography of his grandfather, Venn stayed with Sir John Kennaway, who was a friend of Groves.[1] They all shared a common interest in the CMS. Indeed, Venn's father John had been one of the founders, along with Charles Simeon, of the society, whose London committee Henry joined in 1822, the year after his visit to Kennaway. As early as 1816 Groves had expressed to the CMS his interest in serving under their auspices overseas. He was involved in local activities of the society at the time of Venn's visit, and may indeed have met him. He later read Venn's book with interest.[2]

It is unlikely, however, that Groves and Venn met at any other time, and evidence for personal correspondence between them is lacking. Venn was not a member of the CMS London committee which approved Groves's candidature in 1825 (having resigned temporarily in order to pursue other activities).[3] By the time Venn rejoined the committee in 1834, Groves was in India and embroiled in the Rhenius Affair. The copious reports and correspondence concerning that controversy no doubt kept Venn informed of events and aware of the general displeasure aroused by Groves's attempts to intervene. Although Venn was willing to learn what he could from the Serampore Baptists and other Nonconformists,[4] there is no evidence that he attached any value to the opinions of Groves.

Our study of Venn and Anderson will remind us how profoundly the missiology of an individual will be shaped by his ecclesiology. Venn was, by conviction, an Anglican, strongly committed to the English establishment as a guarantor of law and order in the religious as in the secular sphere.[5]

Venn was aware that the English establishment had initially introduced itself to India, and to other parts of the world, without reference to the CMS or any other missionary society. Chaplains of the East India Company had long represented the Church of England on the subcontinent, and whilst serving the expatriate communities, were subject to episcopal supervision (albeit initially from a distance). Anglican Missionaries working among the Indians were almost an embarrassment to the first bishop resident there, Thomas Middleton (in Calcutta), who wished to be responsible simply for the chaplains and the expatriate community.[6] His successor, Reginald Heber, allowed the missions considerable freedom. Those who followed him, John James and John Turner, both died shortly after their appointment. Daniel Wilson became Bishop of Calcutta in 1832, and

---

[1] See PEANG, 45. Sir John Kennaway's son, John, was an "intimate college friend" of Venn, and an "influential supporter" of the CMS (Knight, 30; Stock, *Hist CMS*, III, 43).
[2] M450
[3] See Chilcraft, Ch.8.
[4] Williams, *Self-Governing Church*, 25-6
[5] Yates, *Venn*, 15; also 192. A generation earlier, Claudius Buchanan had advocated the securing of an Anglican establishment in India, which, once it had provided for the religious needs of the Christian populace, including the members of non-Protestant Churches, could turn its attention at some future date to the "heathen" (Buchanan, *Memoir of the Expediency*, 22).
[6] Yates, *Venn*, 17, 24

immediately showed the high value he placed on "church order", as we have seen in the Rhenius affair. After extensive correspondence and discussion, Venn and his CMS colleagues acquiesced to his demand that every ordained missionary must henceforth seek a personal licence from the bishop in India before starting to "exercise his spiritual functions", and they accepted (with great reluctance) that "a Missionary cannot be removed from one district to another without the sanction of the bishop."[1]

In such circumstances Venn was concerned to define the role of the CMS (and its agents, employees and converts) within the English establishment, and much of his administrative effort was devoted to making precise definitions of principles, rights and obligations. He was seeking to establish a legal form of liberty that would prevent religious authority (and especially episcopal authority) exceeding its proper bounds, and which would guarantee the freedoms within the Established Church, firstly, of the CMS committees, and then of the individual missionaries and of the local churches.[2] The latter two sometimes had to be protected from the CMS itself.

Venn was considerably less authoritarian than many of his Anglican contemporaries. Indeed, he was often concerned to resist the exercise of authority and to simplify the forms of organisation. He wished the "native congregations" to be self-supporting, self-governing and self-propagating. Max Warren remarks,

> Venn, we must remember, was deeply committed to the goal of a genuinely native church. His great ambition was to see a native church become self-governing under a native bishop. This, so it seemed to him, was much more likely to happen if the church grew naturally with only a very simple organisation to begin with than if there was foisted upon it from the start the complex structure that in Venn's time seemed likely to be necessary once a foreigner was appointed as a bishop.[3]

And again, "The organisation of a native church should, according to Venn's thinking, grow from the bottom up. The bishop, and Venn always envisaged the due appointment of a bishop, would be the crown of a development and not its foundation."[4]

This scheme met with opposition from other Anglicans, and especially from the High Church wing of his communion represented by the missionary agencies SPCK and SPG, who considered his approach "inconsistent with church principles."[5] Thus, in a debate in the House of Lords in 1846, we find Samuel Wilberforce declaring, "The bishops must *first* be sent to plan and guide the work, instead of the pastors going first like a scattered army, and then, if indeed at all, for the leader to follow after."[6] There were those among the Tractarians who held that where there was no bishop there could be no church.[7] Venn could not agree: "It cannot be said that Tartary, Persia or Arabia need an extension of the episcopate.

---

[1] Thirty-ninth Report of the CMS (1838-9), in Warren, *To Apply the Gospel*, 153; Yates, *Venn*, 41.
[2] Warren, *To Apply the Gospel*, 143-73; Yates, *Venn*, 17
[3] Warren, Ibid, 25
[4] Ibid
[5] Ibid
[6] Yates, *Venn*, 99-109
[7] Ibid, 20

The first need of such countries is of missionaries and evangelists... The office of evangelist necessarily preceded the episcopate."[1] Indeed, without a missionary society to provide missionaries, and in due course converts, there would be very little in such countries for a bishop to do: "A bishop among the heathen is dependent upon the voluntary agency of missionary societies at a distance to supply the means and the men for the work of the ministry."[2]

Nevertheless, there was essential agreement between the Anglican factions on their ultimate goal: "native churches" administered under the territorial jurisdiction of a "native bishop". Thus would the English establishment exercise its constitutional and benevolent control over the colonies. At this point we might pause to identify three alternative models for the creation of an indigenous church in a pioneer situation: (1) Venn's preference was to start with a simple organisation and become more complex; (2) Wilberforce's preference was to start complex and remain complex; (3) Groves's preference, as we shall see, was to start simple and remain simple.

Venn's ecclesiological presuppositions envisaged the extension of the ecclesiastical establishment into new territories. This would be a gradual process, and indeed a process in two phases, the first evangelistic and the second pastoral. Indeed, he drew a clear distinction between the initial evangelistic task of the foreign missionaries and the subsequent pastoral task of the ordained "natives". As Chilcraft describes it, "Crucial to Venn's strategy was the clear distinction he made between missionaries and pastors. He defined a missionary as one 'who preaches to the heathen, and instructs inquirers or recent converts' and a pastor as one 'who ministers in holy things to a congregation of native Christians.' He did not want missionaries to act as pastors once a local church was viable. At that point, a national should be its pastor."[3]

Venn's scheme had significant geographical implications. It meant a distinction between unevangelised areas where the work must be done by the mission, and evangelised areas where the "native church" must take over responsibility for the converts. This, as Chilcraft notes, was "a complication that Groves did not have to face."[4]

Like many other commentators, Warren commends Venn's perceptiveness: "Where Venn was far ahead of almost all his contemporaries, and of all too many of the men who came after him, was in seeing the danger for the native church of domination by the foreign missionary."[5] Yet having seen the danger, he was seriously hindered in his efforts to overcome it by the ecclesiological constraints under which he was working. He could not encourage a newly converted Indian simply to take his own initiatives in evangelism, teaching, pastoral care and in the gathering of groups for worship and fellowship. Such a man must be made part of the Establishment that had been introduced by the colonial power, and must be trained to uphold the legal liberties that the Establishment allowed him.

---

[1] Venn, letter dated 13th April 1857
[2] Venn, letter dated 12th April 1858, in Warren, *To Apply the Gospel*, 165. See also Williams, "Not Transplanting", 154-6.
[3] Chilcraft, Ch.8. See CMS Pamphlet, *The Native Pastorate and Organisation of Native Churches*, 1866 (reproduced by Shenk, *Venn*, App.I, 118-29).
[4] Chilcraft, Ch.8
[5] Warren, *To Apply the Gospel*, 86

Appointment to spiritual leadership required submission to a long course of academic instruction from a foreigner, and indeed, "Stringent requirements for the priesthood, including an English-medium theology course, Greek, and Hebrew, [were] an effective barrier to most Indians interested in the ordained ministry."[1] Indian Christians in such circumstances could hardly avoid a feeling of "domination by the foreign missionary", the very trap from which Venn had hoped to rescue them.

Rufus Anderson (1796-1880): An Introduction

Rufus Anderson is described by R Pierce Beaver as the "Grand Strategist of American Missions".[2] In 1832 he was elected one of three corresponding secretaries of the American Board of Commissioners for Foreign Missions, and shortly afterwards received appointment to the society's Prudential Committee in the role of "foreign secretary".[3] He retained this post until 1866, at which point he continued as an ordinary though still highly influential member of the Committee until his retirement in 1875. He kept on writing and advising until his death five years later.

Anderson took a remarkably similar line to Venn on most issues. He proposed the same "three-self" formula: "the planting and fostering of churches which would become self-governing, self-supporting and self-propagating."[4] As a Congregationalist, his ecclesiology required the creation of independent local congregations rather than a politico-religious establishment with an ecclesiastical hierarchy, and whereas Venn's three-self ideal was applied to parishes, districts, dioceses and ultimately "national churches", Anderson's was restricted to individual congregations.

Both Venn and Anderson drew encouragement in their task of mission administration from their postmillennialist eschatology, although Venn tactfully says far less about it than Anderson, in deference perhaps to premillennialist colleagues such as Edward Bickersteth.[5] As early as 1813 the American Board had stressed the importance of "the preaching of the gospel in every part of the earth" as "indispensable to the general conversion of mankind".[6] And Anderson himself declared, "The true follower of Christ rejoices to anticipate the triumphs of his King, the universal extension of his reign, and the clearing off from the face of the whole earth of the ruins of the fall."[7] He went so far as to estimate the workforce that must be mobilised in order to secure "the universal triumph of the gospel on earth."[8] It would require that

> a million of preachers be furnished every twenty years for the pulpit and more than six millions of teachers every five years for the schoolroom. And to bring the world under such a holy and blessed influence as the word of God predicts, even within the space of a century, the Church must hear of not less than twenty millions of souls brought into

---

[1] Harper, "Ironies", 13-20
[2] Beaver, *To Advance*, 9
[3] Ibid, 11
[4] Ibid, 10
[5] On Bickersteth's premillennialism, see PEANG, 28ff.
[6] Anderson, *The Missions*, Ch.3, in Beaver, Ibid, 91
[7] Anderson, *The Promised Advent of the Spirit*, in Beaver, Ibid, 49
[8] Ibid, 52

the kingdom of Christ every year... All this and far more would take place if the Spirit were to be poured out upon all flesh; for the great body of these teachers both for the schoolroom and the pulpit, are not to be sent from Christian lands; they are to be raised up on the spot; they are to be of native growth.[1]

Such beliefs undoubtedly shaped Anderson's missiological perspective. In a pioneering situation, the firm conviction that small beginnings will be followed by massive spiritual growth must affect the decisions made by a missionary or mission administrator. In particular, the expectation that a village currently possessing a mere handful of believers will, in the course of time, be entirely converted must tend to encourage the construction of substantial church buildings in the confidence that before Christ returns they will be filled to overflowing. It will also arouse hopes that many outstanding "native ministers" will be forthcoming. A contrasting (premillennialist) eschatology, such as that held by Groves, anticipating not the gradual extension of millennial blessing but rather the imminent onset of persecution, apostasy, earthly cataclysm and the return of Christ to redeem a faithful remnant, will logically lead its exponents to be satisfied with more modest structures for their meetings and simpler forms of spiritual leadership. Here we see the influence of eschatology on ecclesiology, and in turn on missiology.[2]

One theme in particular stands out in Anderson's writings. He, like Venn, felt obliged to emphasize repeatedly and urgently the need for missionaries to hand over responsibility to suitably trained "native pastors".[3] The evidence is that missionaries, both Congregationalist and Anglican, found it very difficult to trust the "native pastors" they were attempting to train. Indeed it seems to have surprised them when Indian Christians proved trustworthy. Looking back over the period 1845 to 1865, Venn declared himself pleasantly surprised to see how well the local Christians in various parts of the world had progressed, manifesting capabilities that the supporters of the CMS might consider rather remarkable: "At the commencement of the period now under review, a native ministry was regarded as an experiment, to be cautiously entered upon, with a long diaconate and an European superintendent." In the event, the men appointed as "ordained native teachers" had proved to be, in some cases, "powerful preachers" and, in others, "skilful and wise pastors of the flock". This was cause for encouragement. Nevertheless, Venn cautioned, their full conformity to Anglican expectations must be secured by further training: "Their efficiency will increase in proportion as they are instructed in biblical knowledge and accustomed to co-operate in council and in the ecclesiastical administration."[4]

Anderson, for his part, was impressed by "the remarkable steadfastness of native Christians in the great India rebellion of 1857." He admitted, "This was wholly unexpected."[5] In fact, the experience of fending for themselves during the Mutiny seemed to do them a great deal of good. In Calcutta, Dr Mullens of the LMS knew of Indian Christians previously "weak in character" (fed, lodged,

---

[1] Ibid, 51-2
[2] For a discussion of this, see PEANG, 158ff.
[3] See, for example, ABCFM, *Outline of Missionary Policy*, 18, in Beaver, Ibid, 28; Anderson, *ABCFM Annual Report 1848*, in Beaver, Ibid, 139
[4] Venn, "An Address at the Islington Clerical Meeting", 10th Jan 1865, in Warren, *To Apply the Gospel*, 125
[5] Anderson, *Foreign Missions*, Ch.8, in Beaver, Ibid, 111

educated and employed by missionaries), who during the Mutiny suddenly "gained health and vigour".[1] Anderson reiterated that such men should have been given responsibility much sooner, and he bewailed "the excessive caution of early missionaries in putting native converts into the ministry". He noted the case of "a Karen preacher, pastor and missionary named Quala, a convert of the Baptist mission in Burmah." "His labours and fatigue were truly apostolical" although he "did not receive ordination until fourteen years after his reception into the church."[2] Elsewhere, John Thomas of the CMS spoke in glowing terms of "a native preacher among the Shanars of Southern India". who preached "the greatest sermon I ever heard."[3] These stirring examples were offered as encouragement for the ABCFM missionaries to place more trust in the capabilities of their "native ministers" and to be more eager to relinquish responsibility into their hands. The missionaries remained largely unconvinced.

Moreover, despite their exhortations, we find a paradoxical reluctance in both Venn and Anderson to allow either recent converts or mature indigenous Christians to undertake evangelistic initiatives. Venn specifically advised that evangelism should always be conducted under the supervision of a foreign missionary. In 1848, his CMS committee issued a series of "Resolutions on the subject of Native Ministers" which restricted such "ministers" to a specified district under missionary supervision:

> The first Resolution provides that a Native should only be ordained when there is some body of native Christians to whom he may act as a native Pastor – so that he may have a Church or District assigned to him, in which he may minister, under the general superintendence and direction of a Missionary, until he is proved to be qualified for a more independent position. It is assumed by the Regulation that the work of evangelising the heathen is best carried out by European Missionaries and Native Catechists – and that it is not advisable to employ Native Ministers in this department but that ordination should only be connected with the Pastorate.[4]

The reason for this is not clearly stated, but one suspects a fear of allowing Indians the opportunity for independent action. Venn went so far as to insist that if a local Christian progressed so far as to receive ordination, he must of necessity be given a settled pastorate and no longer preach in public. The reason given is an extraordinary one: "If Native Ministers were associated in the work of evangelisation they must necessarily assume too much of the European status. As Clergymen of the Church of England they would appear before their countrymen as belonging to a different class and as the well-paid agents of a foreign Society."[5] Indeed, one Brahman catechist, to Venn's knowledge, had refused ordination because it would compromise his position as an evangelist. This was an ecclesiastical system that seemed, almost intentionally, to restrain the most gifted

---

[1] Anderson, Ibid, 111
[2] Ibid, 113-4
[3] Ibid, 115
[4] Venn, memorandum dated 4th Aug. 1856, in Warren, Ibid, 65. Venn emphasizes the distinction between ordained Ministers and catechists, who bore much less responsibility (and whose appointment was also sometimes termed "ordination").
[5] "Memorandum on the views of the Committee upon presenting for ordination native catechists in their employment", 4th Aug. 1856, in Warren, Ibid, 65

indigenous Christians from preaching the gospel to their own people. Here we see the influence of ecclesiology upon missiology, determining the nature of mission and, we might think, seriously inhibiting it.

On his exploratory tour of India, Groves came across many British and American missionaries ministering to Indians. But his journal contains little or no reference to Indians preaching and teaching among their own people. Only in association with Rhenius did Groves see indigenous Christians taking a significant part in evangelistic outreach, and this was one reason for his particular concern to support Rhenius.

The Three-Self Principle

The question that exercised Venn, Anderson, and Groves himself, was a simple one: How might an English or American missionary establish churches in a foreign country – churches that would be thoroughly indigenous, flourishing under the leadership of people native to that country? It was, admittedly, a question far more easily asked than answered.

In 1854 Venn proposed his "three-self" vision for an emerging national church. Established initially by the missionary society, the church would gradually acquire a capability for self-government, self-support and self-propagation. Though started by Church of England missionary agencies such as the CMS or the SPCK, it would become a Church of India, for example, administered by Indians, or a Church of Nigeria led by Nigerians. Along with this went Venn's concept of the foreign mission as a *scaffolding* which must remain until the national church has been firmly built, and then *removed* once it is able to stand alone. Venn saw the missionary society as a temporary necessity. It would buy land, construct buildings, and train and ordain local ministers to lead services and administer the sacraments, and then "once the mission has brought a church into being, it may die out in that area."[1] Venn summarised his proposal:

> It is important ever to keep in view what has been happily termed "the euthanasia of a mission", where the missionary is surrounded by well-trained native congregations under native pastors, when he gradually and wisely abridges his own labours and relaxes his superintendence over the pastors till they are able to sustain their own Christian ordinances, and the district ceases to be a missionary field and passes into Christian parishes under the constituted ecclesiastical authorities.[2]

Simultaneously, and perhaps coincidentally, Rufus Anderson in America proposed a similar scheme, whereby his Congregationalist *mission* would establish Indian or African Congregationalist *churches*.

Fourteen years earlier, Groves had suggested a very different approach. He would make no distinction between *church* and *mission*. Indeed, the mission was the church, and the church was the mission. He believed that "the work societies endeavour to accomplish… can be done better, because more scripturally, *by the Church herself.*"[3] There was no question in his mind of a foreign scaffolding to be erected and then dismantled, no extension and then "euthanasia" of a Western organisation.

---

[1] Neill, *Christian Missions*, 260
[2] CMS Minute 71, [1853/4?], in Warren, *To Apply the Gospel*, 63
[3] Groves, "A Letter on Missions", 141

Henry Venn argued that, "the proper position of a missionary is one external to the native church"[1]; he would plant and water it, but not see himself as part of it. Groves, in contrast, saw himself as part of the body of Christ wherever he happened to be.[2] To Venn's mind, "The missionary was essentially the evangelist, and the native leaders would be increasingly the pastors within the newly formed church."[3] Groves, in contrast, sought to share the diverse tasks of evangelism, Bible teaching and pastoral care with his Indian friends, drawing no distinction in ministry between himself and them. He had been only four months in India when he begged, "Pray for *all* who love the Lord in India, and for me especially, that I may be the instrument in the Lord's hand to promote the *liberty and love of the church*."[4]

The "Native Pastorate"

In order to appreciate the radical nature of Groves's thought, we must give some further attention to the assumptions and objectives of his contemporaries. A belief in the "White Man's Burden" was deeply rooted in the missionary psyche of the day – the benevolent responsibility of the favoured nations to labour for the improvement of "native peoples" in less fortunate parts of the globe.[5] Rufus Anderson, as Secretary of the American Board of Commissioners for Foreign Missions, rejoiced that "the civilisation which the gospel has conferred upon our New England is the highest and best, in a religious point of view, the world has yet seen."[6] His generation perceived an enormous contrast between the developed West and the "primitive" societies found elsewhere, and his biographer simply observes that he "had no respect for Oriental, Pacific and African cultures and religions."[7] Anderson's ambition was to introduce Christian principles to foreign lands and thus raise them gradually to the spiritual level of New England. The more that "native peoples" became "Christianised and civilised" the more closely they would, in the very nature of things, come to resemble the cultured citizens of Boston or London. Such was his hope.

Henry Venn likewise believed that undeveloped nations particularly needed the "European mind and intelligence to regulate, mature and discipline the congregations of native converts." He counselled his colleagues, "Let it be remembered that the great principle of Protestant missions is *native agency under European superintendence*. Hence our large and expensive educational establishments to raise up an educated class."[8] In the Nonconformist sphere, the Serampore trio advised that time must elapse before the Indian churches could become independent, but "These churches will be in no immediate danger of

---

[1] Williams, "Not Transplanting", 165
[2] See PEANG, 115ff.
[3] Ibid, 157
[4] M243
[5] On the high ideals professed by leading British imperialists at this and a slightly later period – their compassion for the perceived miseries of the "uncivilised", and their aspirations to establish justice, security and a measure of good health in the colonies, see Morris, *Pax Britannica*, 122-7.
[6] Anderson, *The Theory of Missions to the Heathen*, sermon dated 1845, in Beaver, Ibid, 73
[7] Beaver, Ibid, 35-6, 73-4
[8] Letter dated 1846, quoted by Shenk, *Venn*, 81

falling into errors or disorders because the whole of their affairs will be constantly superintended by a European missionary."[1]

To mission secretaries with this background, the "scaffolding" was absolutely essential, for as yet only the Americans and Europeans really knew how a proper church or community or civilisation might be established and maintained!

To his credit Venn believed "that the new church ought to be left as free as possible to adapt ecclesiastical forms inherited from the missions."[2] We might think this an improvement on the view that the national church should *retain* the ecclesiastical forms inherited from the missions, but it nevertheless assumed that the mission must introduce "ecclesiastical forms" in the first place.

Ten years later, to Venn's frustration, little had changed. The CMS was still paying the salaries; the missionaries were still looking after the churches; and a "mission station" mentality was still stifling *mission*.[3] As Groves observed, "The native naturally loves a provision and ease, and thereby he is kept in dependence on the creature [i.e. rather than the Creator]. The European, on the other hand, loves to keep the native in subjection and himself in the place of rule."[4]

Venn bemoaned the fact that Anglican agencies were less successful in producing indigenous churches than the Baptists in Burma, the Congregationalists in Armenia and the "native Christians" (after the expulsion of the foreign missionaries) in Madagascar. He suggested,

> The unfavourable contrast may be explained by the fact that other denominations are accustomed to take part in the elementary organisation of their churches at home, and therefore more readily carry out that organisation in the missions. Whereas, in our Church, the clergy find everything relating to elementary organisation settled by the Law of the Land – as in the provision of tithes, of church rates, of other customary payments, in the constitution of parishes, and in parish officers. Our clergy are not prepared for the question of Church organisation, and therefore in the Missions they exercise the ministry of the word without reference to the non-existence of the organisation by which it is supported at home.

Venn proposed a method to remedy "this imperfection in Church Missions". He would start by "introducing into the Native Church that elementary organisation which may give it 'corporate life' and prepare it for its full development under a native ministry and an indigenous episcopate."[5] He stated, "It will be seen that the proposed scheme or organisation will prepare the Native Church for ultimately exhibiting in its Congregational and District Conferences, the counterpart of the Parish, and the Archdeaconry, under the Diocesan Episcopacy of our own Church system."[6] This, Venn hoped, would enable Anglicanism to become Indian.

Across the Atlantic, Rufus Anderson was following the same line of reasoning. His biographer asserts that by the end of his life he had been "acclaimed as the restorer of the apostolic model for mission, and all North American overseas

---

[1] "The Bond of the Missionary Brotherhood of Serampore," 1805, reproduced by Oussoren, 281
[2] Shenk, *Venn*, 54
[3] Shenk, *Venn*, 43-5, 110
[4] M393
[5] CMS Minute 116, 9th July 1861, in Warren, *To Apply the Gospel*, 67-8.
[6] CMS Minute 116, Ibid, 70

missionary agencies professed to follow his teaching and to act on his principles."[1] Impressive as this eulogy may sound, its warrant is simply his insistence on establishing churches rather than educational or medical institutions.[2] But Anderson himself argued that the Congregationalist missions under his control differed substantially from those of apostolic times, and were, he believed, in most respects superior! Firstly, the missionaries themselves were sent out by "churches of long standing and experience", from a land of "freedom and high religious intelligence", which gave them "a great advantage over the primitive missions". Secondly, modern missionaries, though lacking the apostles' miraculous powers, possessed the entire New Testament in printed form. But thirdly, and most significantly, Anderson observed that "the pastorate in modern missions differs from that of the apostolic age, in that it ordinarily has but one pastor for each church, whereas the New Testament always uses the plural in speaking of the pastorate in the churches planted by the apostle Paul." He quotes, indeed, from the Acts of the Apostles, noting that "they appointed elders for them in each church."[3] But then he comments,

> This practice seems to have been lost, with the very idea of the apostolic church, in the great decline of the Early and Middle Ages; and when that idea was recovered, as it was at the Reformation, and put in practice, the usage of having but one pastor in each church was adopted by all evangelical denominations as being more conformed to the demands of the age. And this is now the general usage in all the evangelical churches; and it has thence been transferred to the mission churches among the heathen. The apostolic principle is retained, but the form is changed.[4]

The change is undeniable, but we might wonder whether Anderson's justification of it as "more conformed to the demands of the age" would make it something to be imposed automatically on every culture in every age. In reality, the "apostolic principle" had been lost, and the "form" he advocated was, by his own admission, that of the Middle Ages.

The implication was very clear. For Anderson, the ordination of a "native pastor" was the key to creating a local church:

> I now enquire what should be the nature of the mission church? It should be composed only of hopeful converts, and should have, as soon as possible, a native pastor, and of the same race, who has been trained cheerfully to take the oversight of what will generally be a small, poor, ignorant people, and mingle with them familiarly and sympathetically. And by a native pastor I mean one recognised as having the pastoral care of a local church, with the right to administer the ordinances of baptism and the Lord's Supper.

In short, the foreign missionary (paid by the mission) should hand over his responsibilities as soon as possible to a "native pastor" (paid by the church): "As soon as the mission church has a native pastor, the responsibilities of self-government should be devolved upon it…The salary of the native pastor should be

---

[1] Beaver, *To Advance*, 11
[2] Anderson, *Foreign Missions*, Ch.7, in Beaver, Ibid, 97
[3] Acts 14:23
[4] Anderson, Ibid, in Beaver, 100-1

based on the Christianised ideas of living acquired by his people, and the church should become self-supporting at the very earliest possible day."[1]

But where were these pastors to come from? Anderson urged the establishment of a seminary at each major mission station, where suitable young men could, in his own words, "pursue their theological studies" before being "set apart for the sacred ministry". He elaborates his scheme: "It is an essential feature of the plan that the pupils be taken young, board in the mission, be kept separate from heathenism, under Christian superintendence night and day. In general, the course of study should embrace a period of from eight to ten or twelve years, and an even longer time in special cases... In due time they may be licensed to preach, and after proper trial, receive ordination as evangelists or pastors."[2]

Anderson admitted that the education of such pastors was a difficult process, especially as they must be "trained to system and order".[3] He advised against "requiring too much of the native converts before we are willing to entrust them with the ministry of the word." In fact he judged that, "Generations must pass before a community emerging from the depths of heathenism can be expected to furnish a body of ministers equal to that in our country."[4]

Indeed, there were inevitable dangers to forestall, one of them being the ordination ceremony itself, which could "inflame the self-conceit and ambition remaining in the heart of the heathen convert." He warned that,

> The native pastors themselves are, for a season, but 'babes in Christ', children in experience, knowledge and character. And hence missionaries who entertain the idea that ordination must have the effect to place the native pastors at once on a perfect equality with themselves are often backward in intrusting [*sic*] the responsibilities of the pastoral office to natives. They fear, and justly, the effects of this sudden comparative exaltation.[5]

But he reassured his apprehensive missionary colleagues that they would still retain a powerful means of control over the churches, since "a wise disbursement of funds will provide all the checks which are necessary or proper."[6]

Here then was Anderson's implementation of his vision for self-governing, self-supporting and self-propagating churches. It was well-intentioned, benevolent

---

[1] Ibid, 98

[2] ABCFM, *Annual Report*, 1841, 44-7, in Beaver, Ibid, 103-4. William Carey and his colleagues also had high hopes for their Serampore College as an institution capable of training Indians for the Baptist pastorate (Potts, *British Baptist Missionaries*, 129-35). And they too struggled with the perceived necessity to cut off financial support for Indian churches in order to compel them to provide for themselves (Stanley, *History of the BMS*, 148-56).

[3] ABCFM, *Annual Report*, 1848, 62-80, in Beaver, Ibid, 124

[4] ABCFM, *Annual Report*, 1841, 44-7, in Beaver, Ibid, 104-5. In 1843 the Congregationalist seminary in Jaffna was rocked by the discovery in its dormitory that "the teacher and many of the students were practising sodomites," including "almost the entire select class of students who were being specially trained as native preachers." Fifty-seven were then dismissed. The blame was placed on the worldliness of the trainee pastors rather than the method chosen for their training (Harris, *Nothing but Christ*, 71; "Denominationalism and Democracy", 78).

[5] ABCFM, *Annual Report*, 1848, 62-80, in Beaver, Ibid, 123-4

[6] ABCFM, *Outline of Missionary Policy*, 1856, 15-16

and optimistic. He cheerfully pointed out that in India "native pastors" should cost a lot less to support than American missionaries. They might be expected to "travel on foot", to "live... upon rice alone, with a piece of cotton cloth wrapped about their bodies for clothing, and a mud-walled grass covered cottage without furniture for a dwelling."[1] But Anderson evidently failed to foresee that an Indian pastor, ordained after ten years' theological study, might consider himself entitled to the same living standards as an American missionary. Such a pastor would need a large wealthy church to assure his salary. Failing that, he must be added to the payroll of the American Board, which was not Anderson's intention at all! And having been "kept separate from heathenism" for ten years, would such a pastor still remember how to communicate anything useful to the Hindus and Muslims outside?[2]

Both Anderson and Venn faced continuous opposition from members of their own societies who wanted to pastor churches, teach in boarding schools and oversee mission stations. Both became increasingly desperate to dismantle the mission scaffolding, but the missionaries knew better than they did that without the scaffolding the building would simply collapse.[3]

John Nevius added a number of useful and perceptive refinements to the "three-self" formula. He proposed that a Mission should only introduce programmes and institutions which the national churches desired and could support, that "native" evangelists should be given intensive Bible training, and that local Christians should choose their own pastors and erect their own buildings using local materials.[4] But though Nevius wished to simplify things, and to make it as easy as possible for local Christians to take responsibility, he too, like Venn and Anderson, was the salaried agent of a Western denomination, in his case the American Presbyterian Mission Board. Even as he wrote, a *Presbyterian* synod existed in China to oversee the *Presbyterian* churches that he and his colleagues hoped to establish. Rufus Anderson, for his part, confidently declared that *Congregationalism* was the system "best adapted to our day". Henry Venn fully expected his CMS missionaries to translate the *Anglican* Prayer Book into every language so that the "native churches" could follow the order of service with its designated Lessons and Collects, morning and evening, every Sunday of the

---

[1] ABCFM, *Annual Report*, 1841, 15-16, in Beaver, Ibid, 105. See also Harris, "Denominationalism and Democracy", 66.

[2] Anderson's biographer remarks, "From his point of view, the chief obstacle to self-support came from native pastors who expected higher salaries than their congregations could afford – pastors, in other words, who expected to live more like the missionaries than like their own impoverished flocks. He therefore urged missionaries to maintain a clear hierarchical division between themselves and their native assistants to guard against the danger that the natives might come to see themselves as the missionaries' equals" (Harris, *Nothing but Christ*, 114; see also "Denominationalism and Democracy", 77).

[3] In 1847 Daniel Poor bemoaned the fact that, after more than thirty years of Congregationalist activity in Jaffna, their only congregations were composed of the mission's own "beneficiaries and dependants", who preferred services to be led by the missionary - especially if the appointment of an ordained "native preacher" would mean they must pay him (Harris, *Nothing but Christ*, 136).

[4] *The Planting and Development of Missionary Churches* by John Nevius was first published in 1886.

Church calendar. Venn's biographer remarks, "Few men have done more to promote episcopacy as a form of church government all over the world."[1]

For Venn, Anderson and Nevius, "indigenisation" simply meant appointing "native Christians" to do what foreign missionaries had previously done, according to the requirements of their particular denomination. But it is clear that for each of them the real key to indigenisation lay in the management of money. Of the "three-selfs" which they advocated, it was "self-support" that really concerned them. Anderson frankly admitted that among the missionaries themselves, "most of the questions that arise have more or less connection with finance."[2] For Venn the priority was the establishment in each locality of a "Native Church Fund" to which the local believers would contribute. Indeed, as soon as there were a few converts, they must be instructed about "making the weekly collections".[3] He advised, "The first step in the organization of the Native Church will be taken when any company, or one or more neighbouring companies unitedly, shall be formed into a congregation having a *Schoolmaster*, or Native Teacher, located among them, whose salary is paid out of the Native Church Fund." The missionary in charge would judge when enough money had been contributed. Then, "the second step in the organisation of the Native Church will be taken when one or more congregations are formed into a *Native Pastorate*, under an ordained native, paid by the Native Church Fund... This step may be taken as soon as the congregations are sufficiently advanced and the payments to the Native Church Fund shall be sufficient to authorise the same."[4]

---

[1] Warren, *To Apply the Gospel*, 29. Venn's conversion to the idea of "missionary bishops" was a gradual one. In his early years as CMS secretary he had resisted high-church pressure to appoint bishops as overseers of pioneer missions, believing that their presence would hinder the emergence of national leaders (Williams, "Not Transplanting", 154-60). It was Venn himself who secured the ordination of the first African bishop in 1864, although the role of Bishop Samuel Crowther was to lead a mission in another part of Africa rather than govern a circle of churches in his own. Crowther was, by this time, an old man who had lived away from Africa for many years and considered himself a "black Englishman". He was a gifted and godly man, but as he depended on interpreters for communication with those under his charge he could hardly be considered an indigenous church leader. His successor was an Englishman (Shenk, *Venn*, 107-9; Neill, *Christian Missions*, 377; Warren, *To Apply the Gospel*, 30).

[2] Anderson, *Foreign Missions*, Ch.9, in Beaver, *To Advance*, 204. Williams comments, "It is a very proper question whether self-support did not assume quite an exaggerated importance and whether it is not therefore evidence of a major weakness in Venn's thinking" (Williams, *Self-Governing Church*, 24)

[3] CMS Minute 116, 9th July 1861, in Warren, *To Apply the Gospel*, 71. In the Punjab, Robert Clark of the CMS also regarded finance as the key to creation of an indigenous church. He declared, "The first condition of any independence that was not a sham must lie in financial self-support." In 1877 a Punjab Native Church Council was established under his chairmanship with the purpose of collecting money from Indian believers. This Council, however, met with "suspicion, jealousy and opposition" from among the CMS missionaries themselves and their converts, who preferred the local churches to be governed and financed by the Church of England. Clark endeavoured, without success in his own lifetime, to free the Indian Church from its official subjection to the authority of the Church of England and of the bishops and archbishops appointed by the British government. In fact, freedom from such subjection came only with the political independence of India (Clark, 305-10; Vander Werff, 52-4).

[4] CMS Minute 116, 9th July 1861, in Warren, *To Apply the Gospel*, 69-70.

The third step involved the establishment of a District Conference consisting of clergy and laymen, nationals and missionaries. Then when the "Native Church Funds" were finally able to afford an episcopal stipend, a bishop would be enthroned for them, with mitre and crosier and coloured robes brought out from England. What it meant was that the church could progress through the stages of increasing organisational complexity just as far as the congregations paid money into the "Native Church Fund". This was the meaning of "self-support". On the same basis, "self-propagation" meant the congregations paying the wages of the evangelists; "self-government" meant the congregations paying for the upkeep of the properties.

This was Venn's ideal. In practice the local catechists, teachers and pastors were already receiving salaries from the CMS and were reluctant to lose them. They naturally raised the question: If the wealthy patrons of the CMS are able to finance the church, why should the poor Indian believers be asked to do so? Venn was forced to concede, "In older missions the change of system should be very gradual. For when a mission has grown up in dependence upon European missionaries and upon native agency salaried by European funds, the attempt to curtail summarily its pecuniary aid, before the introduction of a proper organisation, will be like casting a person overboard before he has been taught to swim."[1]

Despite Venn's optimism it became evident that indigenous churches could not be created by well-meaning London secretaries imposing "a proper organisation". His whole scheme suffered from a basic flaw. To follow his own analogy, if a mission has put up the organisational scaffolding then the mission has already designed the building. And the design is a foreign one.

Groves suggested an alternative. In the New Testament he did not see wealthy missions establishing complex organisations and then charging others with their maintenance; he saw poor apostles preaching the gospel, teaching those who respond, and letting them develop their own fellowships in their own premises. He saw clearly enough the dire consequences of foreign denominations making everything far too complicated, far too static, and far too expensive. Rather than projecting an eventual shift from foreign government, support and propagation to self-government, support and propagation, Groves would start with no organised government, support or propagation at all, expecting these to develop naturally as local believers prayerfully considered the needs and possibilities before them in the light of New Testament principles and precedents. He spoke frequently on this theme, "endeavouring to show them the beauty and glory of being contented with Christ as a *Head* and his word as a *guide*."[2] He confessed, "Daily my desire is

---

[1] CMS Minute 116, Ibid, 70. To Venn's pleasure, in 1854 the Anglican missionary Thomas G Ragland proposed that the Indian congregations in each district of North Tinnevelly "should bear the expense of one native catechist to labour for a month." Ragland reckoned this was a financial burden even they could bear (Warren, *To Apply the Gospel*, 64; Stock, II, 186-9). The CMS missionaries themselves eventually scrapped the scheme, preferring to supervise, rather than work alongside, the Indian evangelists (Williams, *Self-Governing Church*, 23).

[2] M307. On Groves's ecclesiological principles, see above, 12f, and for a much fuller treatment, PEANG, 115ff.

strengthening to see the Church free in the use of God's word and in his modes of ministry, every one being free to exercise the gift the Spirit has given."[1]

As an administrator, Groves cannot compare with Henry Venn or Rufus Anderson, but as a practical missiologist he is arguably their superior. His experience of missions in India led him to a simple conclusion: "It must be obvious to all, if the native churches be not strengthened by learning to lean on the Lord instead of man, the political changes of an hour may sweep away the present form of things, so far as it depends on Europeans, and leave not a trace behind."[2]

To be fair to both Venn and Anderson, we must recognise that they were responsible for the administration of things as they were, having inherited a system not of their making. They were never free to imagine the ideal and pursue it. Indeed, they were forced to compromise in almost every situation, and often had great difficulty persuading missionaries to allow indigenous converts any responsibility at all. In fact, after Venn's death, the CMS abandoned his policies altogether and built up an ever more elaborate, expensive and intimidating organisational structure under European control.[3]

Subsequent missionary leaders have added a multiplicity of suggestions and propositions in their attempts to put the "three-self" scheme into effect. But almost all appear to be starting from a position of weakness. Their first assumption is that one institution (a mission board) must create a separate institution (an indigenous church). Their second is that both must be staffed and supervised by salaried employees. Their third is that denominational identities and authority structures, hallowed by long usage in the homeland, should be imposed on the rest of the world. Groves considered these assumptions seriously flawed.

Missionary Appointment

The most important single source for Groves's missiological thought is "A Letter on Missions to the Heathen" reproduced in *The Christian Witness* of April 1840.[4] Here he sets out what he calls his "plan for carrying out missions". He starts by quoting extensively from a recent article in a periodical called *The Friend of India* which was highly critical of the missionary societies currently at work on the subcontinent. "In consequence of the monopoly of all power and influence in London, a vast machinery has gradually been constructed, in the management of which the spirit of the missionary cause is deteriorated and runs every risk of

---

[1] M256
[2] M393
[3] Peter Williams argues that, contrary to common supposition, Venn, far from being a missiological innovator whose ideas were quickly forgotten, was a somewhat conservative spokesman for a CMS consensus that survived well into the 1890s. According to Williams, it was Eugene Stock, early in the following century, who pushed for a more racially integrated Anglican (episcopalian) Church in India, in contrast to Venn's preference for keeping the races distinct and thus producing a purely Indian Church (Williams, *Self-Governing Church*, xiii-xv, 45).
[4] The editorial policy of *The Christian Witness* was to publish all contributions anonymously, but this particular article is attributed to A N Groves by a contemporary who carefully noted the identities of the contributors in his copy (now held in the Christian Brethren Archive, Manchester). The attributions made by this reader were based on information derived from the editor, J L Harris, and show every indication of being accurate. The style and content are typical of Groves.

becoming eventually extinct." The writer noted that "the affairs of these bodies are managed by an oligarchy, endowed with the dispensation of large sums... Through their affiliated societies they have acquired a paramount influence in the country, and by means of their salaried agents they wield that influence at will." Even the Indian newspapers must toe the establishment line "so that nothing can reach the public ear but with their permission." The cost of religious buildings and salaries required such an enormous income that "they are obliged to use the most strenuous efforts to maintain their pecuniary position, and these efforts are not always in scrupulous accordance with the sacredness of the object." The tendency was all too clear: "The support of the *Society* becomes the primary object; that of the *cause* one of secondary importance."

So what is to be done? Groves suggests, "The important question is not so much to know what is *wrong* as to learn from the Lord what is *right*."[1] And as always he asks, "What does scripture teach?" He observed that the earliest Christians, meeting as "households of the faithful", were concerned for two things: firstly for the progress of their own family in the faith, and then, secondly, for the "spiritual welfare of others... For exactly in the same proportion in which any church realizes [i.e. fulfils] what it has found in Jesus will its *desire* be that others may be similarly enriched."

How, then, did the early Christians set about sharing their spiritual riches with others? "I believe the offspring of this sympathy and love were the 'messengers of the churches'."[2] These "messengers" went sometimes to help other churches, but more often to preach the gospel to the unconverted.

And how were they supported? Taking nothing from the "heathen", "they were entitled to the support of that church from whence they came out, to the extent of their reasonable wants, as also to the hospitality and love of those to whom they might come on their way."[3]

This was a plan, Groves thought, easily adapted to any age. Some churches might be able to provide for several "messengers"; some might need to pool their resources together to support just one. But the missionary must always be considered the "messenger" of his own home fellowship: "Should it happen, as is very possible, that among the *poorest* churches there may be many whom the Lord had fitted and made free, it should be the *glory* of the richer churches to give them help, but never attempt on *that account* to transfer the *church* connection of the poorer church to themselves, because that would be breaking a spiritual connection which God has formed." In practice, just as the Lord will guide the missionary in his service, so the Lord will guide the churches in their support of him – through a sense of the Spirit's leading and in answer to prayer. Nevertheless, "whatever support was given to help on any brother should be without any pledge of continuance or amount." There would be no arrangement that might put the missionary under obligation to those who supply his needs, or compel him to

---

[1] Groves, "A Letter on Missions", 130

[2] In 2 Cor 8:23, the word "messengers" (AV) or "representatives" (NIV) translates Gk. *apostoloi* (apostles). Epaphroditus was one such "messenger" (*apostolos*), sent from the church in Philippi to help Paul (Phil 2:25). Groves later, in 1840, expressed a preference for the term "messengers of Christ" (rather than "messengers of the churches"), as representing more clearly the source of their authority and nature of their work (*Remarks*, 32; see 1 Thess 2:6; Jude 17).

[3] Groves, "A Letter on Missions", 130 (3 Jn 5-8; 2 Cor 11:7-9)

conform to their wishes. He must be free to obey God without desire for man's approval or fear of man's displeasure.

In the book of Acts Groves saw how the earliest missionaries were appointed. The local leaders at Antioch, through fasting and prayer, were led by the Spirit to set apart Barnabas and Saul for the work to which God had called them. With the blessing of the church, they were "sent on their way by the Holy Spirit."[1] This simple scheme bore no resemblance to the current custom of missionaries obtaining salaried appointments from official committees meeting in city offices, and financed through public appeals, subscriptions and the gracious patronage of prominent figures and men of the world. Groves took pains to emphasize that the missionary should be *sent* from the local church and *supported* by the local church, and he concluded, "The grand point therefore to be ever kept in view, in the union between the church and the evangelist going forth, is that it should be *as close as possible*, and this beyond all doubt will be when the messenger is sent by those who know him."[2]

In fact, as Groves pointed out, the apostolic method has a number of significant advantages. Firstly, it is "calculated to draw out the strongest and best affections as well as the sympathies of the church from which the missionary proceeds." He himself has been an active participant in the fellowship; they all know and love him. His friends and family will thus "seek for themselves a spirit to care for and sympathise with those who do thus go, and of whom they are the divinely appointed guardians on earth."

Secondly, it ensures that suitable people will be sent. "Christians in the midst of whom an individual has been walking would, as a general principle, be far better able to estimate both his excellencies and weaknesses, appreciating the one and making allowances for the other." The mischief caused by worldly men taking missionary appointments for the sake of salary and status would be ended, for the church would refuse to send or support them, and "few such, without the expectation of sympathy or support would be induced to undertake so profitless a service."

Thirdly, it will encourage cheerful giving. A church that has confidence in its "messenger" will be glad to support him generously, without any need for appeals, publicity or other forms of fund-raising. Once overseas, the missionary will write regularly with news of his progress, and the church will reply with encouragement, assurance of prayer and with whatever financial help they can send. "There would

---

[1] Acts 13:4

[2] Groves, "A Letter on Missions", 132. These ideas had been maturing in Groves's mind for at least four years. In his report dated 1836 on *The Present State of the Tinnevelly Mission* (p.31), he had declared, "My grand object in England or in India is to promote the principle of *Congregational Missions*; the design of which is to make the connexion as close as possible between those who go forth and those who send; so that as far as possible they may be personally acquainted, and at least acquainted by intimate personal interest; and that the Missionary may stand in the liberty wherewith Christ has made him free, and not be entangled in the bondage of any home system." Referring to the withdrawal of Rhenius and his colleagues from the CMS, and hinting perhaps at his own financial support for them, he added, "Control over his Mission I would not take, and he would not give; both of us believing it to be an odious abuse, that he who ministers to the Lord's servants in mere carnal things should hereby become vested with authority in spiritual things."

therefore be no need of that ensnaring evil, the publication of reports to excite the liberality of the public, as it is called."

Fourthly, it will allow the missionary complete freedom to do what he believes to be God's will. He will not be restricted by the resolutions of a committee, the decrees of a superintendent, or by a book of "principles and practice" that might take no account of the complex circumstances facing him. Although a home church will willingly offer counsel or advice to its "messenger", it will trust his own judgment concerning what he should do, without seeking either to direct or to obstruct his activity.

Fifthly, it will enable every fresh opportunity to be taken without deliberation or delay. If a need arises, the missionary can go immediately to meet it, without waiting for approval from a finance committee or a board of control.

Sixthly and lastly, it will greatly reduce the cost of taking the gospel into all the world. Indeed, Groves estimated, "it would enable us to carry out missions at one third the expense." The "messenger", without the social standing of an ordained clergyman, would have no need of a fine house, a carriage, servants, banquets and entertainments. He will choose to live as cheaply as he can, so that funds may provide for additional workers to join him or to pioneer in other places. And unlike a clergyman, he will quickly look for ways to provide for himself and for his co-workers. If he can become self-supporting, he may soon need no financial help at all.

This was what Groves called his "plan of missions", at least with regard to the sending and support of the missionaries themselves. What made it so radical was its focus on the local church. On biblical grounds Groves argued that a missionary should be sent by a church to create churches, not appointed by a committee to promote a society. And when a local church feels itself responsible to set apart and send its own "messengers", there will soon be "a real deep missionary spirit" in the church – a desire to send out more workers and as many workers as possible.

As always, Groves was propounding an ideal, and he would never turn an ideal into a law. Although he considered the support of a home church to be a great benefit, especially in the early stages of missionary service, it was by no means an essential requirement for a servant of God willing to live "by faith". He himself was not formally commended or sent by any local church in Britain, and neither, so far as we know, were his co-workers Baynes, MacCarthy, Walhouse or Henry and Frank Groves in India. Like the evangelists in the New Testament (Barnabas, Silas, Timothy, Mark and many others) such missionaries belonged to the whole body of Christ without claiming a special *permanent* relationship to a particular "sending church".

In fact, he was particularly aware of the problem faced by potential missionaries in congregations that, in consequence of extreme Calvinistic or dispensational teaching, disapproved in principle of overseas missionary work.[1] He advised that, in such a case, if called by God, the missionary should simply trust and obey, "going forth where he feels the Spirit leading him, without any prospect of sympathy or support from man." His condition, "whilst on the one hand it is the most deeply trying to which the soul which is faithful can be subjected, yet it is one which in a peculiar degree fits the missionary to direct the eyes of those to whom he preaches to the living God as their only object of trust, while he is to them a

---

[1] On the inhibiting effect of hyper-Calvinism on overseas mission, see Cracknell, 20-7.

living witness of the faithfulness of God... a God who never fails, never disappoints those who put their trust in him."[1]

Spiritual Leadership

Groves had personal experience of the difficulties caused by mission boards and committees, especially when their members were secular men who misunderstood the issues. The high-handed decision of the CMS to dismiss Rhenius was a striking example. Another was the extraordinary demand by the home committee of the Baptist Missionary Society that the Serampore trio submit to their direct control from England.[2] There were many other tensions. Missionaries obliged to follow instructions sent by a committee would be compelled at times to stifle their own sense of calling, and such men could not easily teach their converts to be guided by the scriptures or the leading of the Holy Spirit.[3] Legal conflicts arose periodically over property and work contracts, and there were racial tensions too, as foreign clergymen enjoyed homes and incomes appropriate for British colonials whilst their Indian assistants had hardly enough to eat. The committees no doubt meant well, but their efficiency and authority, and their ability to pull strings with the government, overawed the poor Indians. Opening a new "station", the land would be acquired by the committee. A massive stone or brick "church" would be designed by a foreign architect appointed by the committee. The steeple, altar and bells would be paid for by the committee; the salaries of the Indian staff and the clergy would be assured by the committee. No one had the slightest doubt that the church belonged to the committee.[4]

On his first visit to India in 1834 Groves observed, "From my arrival in Bombay to the day I reached Jaffna, I had been continually hoping to find

---

[1] "A Letter on Missions", 131

[2] George, 164-5; Smith G, *Carey*, 359-76; Tucker, 120-1. Hudson Taylor, too, had great difficulty throughout 1891-2 in persuading the London council of the CIM to agree that control of the mission should be retained by the leadership in China once he himself had retired (Taylor, *Growth of a Work of God*, 506-7).

[3] Anderson claimed that his own Mission adhered to "the great Protestant maxim" that "the Scriptures are the *only* and the *sufficient* rule of faith and practice" (Anderson, *ABCFM Annual Report 1848*, in Beaver, *To Advance*, 129). This did not prevent him from insisting that, "The missionary engages, on accepting his appointment, to conform to the rules and regulations of the Board... He thus pledges himself, among other things, to be governed by the majority of votes in his mission, in regard to all questions that arise in their proceedings; the proceedings being subject to the revision of the Prudential Committee. He comes, moreover, under certain other distinct and well-understood pledges." Among these is the obligation with regard to "ecclesiastical usages; to which he must conform substantially as they prevail among the churches operating through the Board" (Anderson, Ibid, in Beaver, 127-8). In practice, then, the authority of Scripture could be superseded, at any time, by that of a vote, or of the Prudential Committee, or of "ecclesiastical usages". A missionary so constrained would surely find it difficult to teach potential church leaders that "the Scriptures are the *only* and the *sufficient* rule of faith and practice."

[4] Oddie notes that "Tirunelveli, even to this day, is dotted with parish churches which look remarkably like Anglican parish churches in Victorian England" (Oddie, 253). Indeed, "The Gothic-style steeples visible in villages throughout Tirunelveli today attest to the enduringly Western character of much of nineteenth- and even twentieth-century church life, its aesthetic expressions, liturgy, and ritual" (Harper, "Ironies", 13-20). For a further consideration of buildings, see Neill, *Christianity in India*, 410-1.

missionary institutions carried on with that simplicity which I think so highly becomes us, but I have been deeply disappointed. Wherever I have been, the system of the world and its character of influence have been adopted instead of the moral power of the self-denial of the gospel."[1] Though Groves might wish with all his heart to work in harmony with existing agencies, he could see great benefit in starting from scratch wherever possible, not building on another man's foundation. "I do hope the Lord will allow us," he said, "to gather a holy little band who will unite in defending the liberty of the Church of God from the supremacy, pride and control of man."[2] His particular concern was "to try and impress upon every member of Christ's body that he has some ministry given him for the body's edification – and instead of depressing, encouraging each one to come forward and serve the Lord." And he added, "I have it much at heart, should the Lord spare me, to form a church on these principles."[3] And again, "We may not all have the appointments of apostles or pastors or teachers, yet we have some gift, and this we should exercise in love for the edification of the church"[4]

Above all, it was Indian evangelists he longed to see at work: "My heart has particularly brought before it today the importance of the office of an evangelist. I long to see immense additions to the blessed little band. I shall be very thankful to be the servant of such the remainder of my worthless life."[5] He wondered what would be the best way to train such national believers. Rufus Anderson hoped that eight or ten years in a seminary might make a man suitable for ordination (though still by no means the equal of a regular New England "minister"). Henry Venn proposed theological training for suitable "natives", but all too rarely could a candidate be found with the required moral and intellectual stature.[6] In 1834 Groves wrote home,

---

[1] M274
[2] M331
[3] M285
[4] *Liberty*, 76, referring to 1 Pet 4:10-11
[5] M280. As early as 1805 Carey had advised that foreign missionaries were too few and too expensive to offer a realistic means of evangelising the whole Indian sub-continent. The work must be placed in the hands of suitably trained Indian evangelists (Marshman, I, 228-9). He arranged for them to go out "two by two, without any European brother" (Carey, minutes of meeting, 8th Aug 1806, quoted by Oussoren, 214).
[6] Anglican missionaries in India were long frustrated by the preference of the Indians themselves for the appointment of foreigners to positions of authority. In 1912, when V S Azariah was proposed as the first ever Indian bishop, "there was strong resistance among Indian Christians... Petitions sent to protest Azariah's consecration were signed by a wide range of Tamil and Telugu Christians, criticizing him for lack of experience and education, for low social position, for Nonconformist associations with the YMCA, and for Tamil origins" (Harper, "Ironies"). In his role as bishop, Azariah's preferred style was not really as "indigenous" as some of his missionary friends would wish. Then, "As appointment procedures were opened to greater democratic participation after the 1930 disestablishment of the Anglican church in India, it became harder rather than easier to appoint Indians to high posts in the church. After Azariah's death in 1945, a similarly vehement campaign was launched by Indian Christians against the appointment of an Indian successor... Some congregations were so opposed to native bishops that they threatened to desert to Catholicism, and most petitions ended with a call for the election of a European or English bishop." Eventually, "an Irish CMS missionary, A B Elliot, was elected by a vast majority of the diocesan synod": he accepted the post with reluctance (Harper, "Ironies").

> I have been greatly exercised relative to the best way of bringing forward the native ministers of Christ in these countries, and I have finally rested on our dear Lord's plan: that is, to get from two to twelve, and to go about constantly with them, eating what they eat and sleeping where they sleep and labouring, whether in a *choultry* at night or by the way, to impress on their souls a living exhibition of Jesus.[1]

But was this not too difficult, too much to ask of a Western missionary? The simple fact is that Groves himself by this method trained two highly effective Christian leaders, Andrew and Arulappan (three if we include Mokayel;[2] four if we add Serkies[3]). And they in turn trained dozens. He advised,

> One great object will be to break down the odious barriers that pride has raised between natives and Europeans; to this end, it would be desirable for every evangelist [i.e. missionary] to take with him wherever he went from two to six native catechists, with whom he might eat, drink and sleep on his journeys, and to whom he might speak of the things of the kingdom as he sat down and as he rose up, that they might be, in short, prepared for ministry in the way that our dear Master prepared his disciples, by line upon line, precept upon precept, here a little and there a little, as they could bear it, feeling from beginning to end that our place is not to set others to do what we cannot do ourselves… but that we are rather to be ensamples of every thing we wish to see in our dear brethren. And I do not yet despair of seeing in India a church arise that shall be a little sanctuary in the cloudy and dark day that is coming on Christendom.[4]

Before setting out for the East in 1829, Groves had held a rather heroic view of the pioneer missionary – a tough, self-sufficient ambassador for the gospel, preaching the Word in season and out of season, doing the work of an evangelist, able to accomplish all things through Christ who strengthens him.[5] After the traumas of the plague in Baghdad, and despite his longing for spiritual fellowship amongst a settled group of co-workers, Groves declared "I therefore now purpose, the Lord enabling me, after nearly six months interruption, to return to the studies preparatory to my future duties as an itinerating missionary. To this service I ever thought the Lord had called me."[6] He never lost this vision, but his chastening

---

[1] M280. Choultry: a caravanserai or inn where animals occupy a central courtyard (from Telugu: *chawadi*).
[2] Mokayel is mentioned above, 50.
[3] Serkies is mentioned above, 48.
[4] M287
[5] R301
[6] R240. Missionaries have often been torn between a desire to follow the apostolic method and the opportunities presented to them for a more sedentary ministry. The fact is that itinerant preaching requires arduous travel; it causes offence and sometimes danger; and it brings no financial reward; whilst schools, clinics and orphanages offer congenial surroundings, with the appreciation of rulers and people, and sometimes a significant income. Andrew Porter suggests that missionaries preferring an itinerant ministry may have chosen an "easy option". Restless and independent, they opt out of the more stressful and tedious task of discipling new converts, teaching local fellowships, and staffing schools, clinics and other beneficial institutions (Porter, *Religion versus Empire*, 184). To be fair, one might think that a choice of ministry will depend greatly on the personal gifts and calling of the missionary. One person's stress is another person's stimulus, and vice versa.

experiences in Baghdad, and his discovery that his own gifts lay more in the area of teaching and pastoral care, brought him a deeper awareness of the spiritual body of which the evangelist is a part. In fact, his conception of the missionary evangelist expanded to embrace that of the missionary church. And though the work of an itinerant preacher was always, to Groves, the highest of all callings, he recognised the need of the evangelist for the support, the prayer, the teaching, and the encouragement of other mature Christians – and the necessity for the evangelist's gifts to be complemented by the gifts of others.[1]

It was, of course, in the New Testament that he sought guidance about evangelistic methods. An evangelist, as we have seen, should be sent out by his local church and prayerfully supported by its members.[2] But once the evangelist, labouring in some distant place, has secured a number of conversions and gathered a small group together, he faces a dilemma. Should he remain in that place and feed the new flock? Or should he press on to further unreached fields? The apostles generally stayed only a matter of weeks or, at most, a few months before leaving their converts to fend for themselves. For this reason, Groves thought, "missionaries ought to go from place to place, preaching the gospel, and only become stationary when they have gathered a church. And rather than remain so, if called to the office of an evangelist, they should do as the apostle did: set some over the church and go on."[3] The temptation to settle and become the permanent pastor of the fellowship was hard to resist, but "I think that missionaries would not only be more useful but in much better health if they were to move about more."[4] Subsequent experience in India confirmed this. At Allissic, near Quilon, he found an excellent Church of England missionary, overwhelmed by the amount of work required to keep his station going. "He is here alone, and what with translating, schools, and a hundred other things, his hands are so full that though he seems most anxious to go about preaching among the people, he is not able to do it. I do think the plan of locating missionaries singly is most pernicious. The American plan of sending three or four together is far, far better."[5]

It was, indeed, more scriptural. Christ sent out his disciples two by two; Paul worked with Barnabas and then Silas, and he established missionary teams with the help of Mark, Luke, Timothy, Aristarchus and others mentioned in his letters. If that was the best plan then, why not now? The presence of co-workers will not only provide fellowship and encouragement for the missionary; it will also enable him to leave church, school and clinic in the hands of capable colleagues whilst absent for days or weeks on preaching tours. It was with this in mind that Groves himself established a team in Madras and Chittoor, and recruited help for solitary missionaries in several locations.

---

[1] R303.

[2] See above, 102ff. In Groves's experience, itinerant evangelists were normally male, though not necessarily bachelors. Married couples might find it convenient to establish a family home in a population centre, from which the husband would itinerate, often in company with other men.

[3] M308-9

[4] M254

[5] M247

Indigenous Initiatives

The greatest practical contribution of Groves to the Protestant Church in India was undoubtedly the encouragement he gave to Arulappan and others in taking initiatives of their own. He enjoyed close fellowship with these Indian Christians. To him they were friends and equals, and he respected the skills they brought to the work of the gospel in their own culture.[1] He would never expect greater frugality or stronger faith from an Indian than he would require of himself and his English colleagues. In 1840 he wrote of the British ex-soldier MacCarthy and a newly converted Indian bookbinder called James. Both, in their evangelistic itinerations, were trusting God to provide by means of casual labour, or through things they might sell, or in other unexpected ways.[2] Groves commented, "Those who know the natives will, I am sure, feel with me that this plan of missions, whereby the native himself is thrown on God, is calculated to develop that individuality of character, the absence of which has been so deeply deplored, and the remedy for which has so seldom been sought."[3]

Groves was a humble man, and humility marked his dealings with people of other races. He advised, "The office of a missionary in these countries is to *live* the gospel before them in the power of the Holy Ghost, and to drop like the dew, line upon line, and precept upon precept, here a little and there a little, till God give the increase of his labours. But it must be by patient continuance in well-doing against every discouraging circumstance, from the remembrance of what we ourselves once were."[4] Groves himself had no official position, no title, no authority over anyone. He could influence others only through qualities of personal character – a godly example, wise advice, sound teaching, and of course through effective prayer. At the Edinburgh Missionary Conference of 1910, Bishop Azariah remarked, "Missionaries, except for a few of the very best, seem to me to fail very largely in getting rid of an air of patronage and condescension, and in establishing a genuinely brotherly and happy relation as between equals with their Indian flocks… You have given your goods to feed the poor. You have given your bodies to be burned. We also ask for *love. Give us friends.*"[5] Groves was remarkable in the warmth of his love for the people amongst whom he lived and his willingness to live as they did on terms of equality.

---

[1] By way of comparison, Henry Venn only ever met an indigenous leader when one sufficiently educated to speak English, and sufficiently wealthy to book a sea passage, happened to come to London and make an appointment with him. In theory, of course, Venn advocated indigenous leadership, but his efforts to ordain the African bishop, Samuel Crowther, and his subsequent failure to support him against missionary opposition, contributed to the years of conflict that ensued between local West African leaders and the CMS. The evidence suggests that Venn simply failed to comprehend the difficulties faced by indigenous church leaders (Warren, *To Apply the Gospel*, 30).

[2] M392

[3] M393

[4] R19; M88

[5] *World Missionary Conference, 1910*, Vol. IX, 309, quoted in Bonk, *Missions and Money*, 49. As the nineteenth century progressed and the number of missionaries and other expatriates increased, their social activities developed and their leisure time was increasingly spent in English-speaking circles. "At times it was possible for Indians, both Christian and non-Christian, to feel that they were no longer the primary concern of the missionary" (Neill, *Christianity in India*, 410).

Not surprisingly, there was considerable agitation when he expressed his view that Indians were perfectly capable of creating and leading their own churches, and even more when he encouraged them actually to do so. In a letter home, dated 1840, he confided,

> The fact that our position here puts pastoral work and fellowship on a simple Christian footing among the natives is by no means the least important feature of our work. Until we came, no one but an *ordained* native was allowed to celebrate the Lord's Supper or to baptise; and when our Christian brethren Arulappan and Andrew partook of the Lord's Supper with the native Christians it caused more stir and enquiry than you can imagine. The constant reference to God's word has brought and is bringing the questions connected with ministry and church government into a perfectly new position in the minds of many.[1]

The method Groves advocated was remarkably successful. As Arulappan and others travelled round southern India, preaching, baptising, teaching, and breaking bread in remembrance of Christ, assemblies came together in many places, and local leaders began to emerge among them. Before long the Indian churches were writing their own hymns, their own tracts and teaching materials.

In his day, as in ours, Groves stands out as a most unusual kind of missionary. He belonged to no denomination; he was subject to no mission board. No one could claim the right to oversee his work or to discipline his converts. There was little reason for Arabs or Indians to think he might provide them with status or a salary, or a church building, for he was obviously as poor as they were themselves, and he had no official status in the colonial administration. What he had to offer was essentially spiritual – comfort, encouragement, teaching from the Bible and prayer. It was this that drew people to him, and through him to his Lord about whom he spoke with such heartfelt warmth and conviction.[2] By helping local Christians *spiritually* he prepared *them* to take the initiatives that would give rise to a genuinely indigenous church.

This is surely the most striking aspect of Groves's vision – the potential it has for stimulating vigorous indigenous initiatives. Anglican missionaries were astonished to see Indian believers setting out from their villages and preaching to their own people. The *Church Missionary Intelligencer* for August 1860 declared, "It is indeed a new era in Indian missions – that of lay converts going forth, without purse or scrip, to preach the gospel of Christ to their fellow-countrymen, and that with a zeal and life we had hardly thought them capable of." Here, the writer believed, was "the first entirely indigenous effort of the native church at self-extension."[3] Perhaps he was led to wonder why he had never seen such things among his own converts.

What he saw was, in fact, the fulfilment of Groves's vision. In 1840 Groves had encouraged John Arulappan and his Indian friends in their desire to establish a completely Indian fellowship at Christianpettah in Madurai province. Sunday

---

[1] Letter dated 1840 (M393).

[2] Groves "was one of those men who exercise an immediate and deep personal influence on others" (Eadie, 162). Many examples of this are cited in FOFM 371ff.

[3] M622. The writer admitted that "Church of England clergy are backward in accepting such movements as these".

meetings there followed a simple, informal and largely spontaneous pattern. As Arulappan himself describes it,

> Some read with me in the New Testament, on the morning of every Sunday... men as well as women, and they listen to exhortations on the subjects. After 12 o'clock some of the church members will come from surrounding villages within 10 miles distance. We have preaching with singing hymns and reading a chapter from the Bible. We divide a text into several heads and ask questions and they give answers as much as they can. After the service is over we collect alms for the poor. The church breaks bread every Sunday afternoon with prayer and exhortation, and thanksgivings. There is liberty to feed the flock of Christ from the nourishing words of God according to the ability of their gifts by the Holy Ghost.[1]

This assembly was an Indian initiative from first to last, and the simple building in which three hundred regularly met had been erected by them at their own expense. Arulappan's biographer asks why it is that other churches – those connected with foreign denominations – seem unable to provide for themselves like this, and he remarks, "The fact is that they can and will... if Arulappan's plan, that is the apostolic plan, be followed, of first building the spiritual house, the company of really converted people, and then training and leaving them to build the material things needed."[2]

From Christianpettah, bands of Indian evangelists travelled continuously to preach throughout the region.[3] Arulappan himself had relatives scattered widely over southern India, and his visits to preach and teach among them spread his influence over an area extending far beyond his base in Christianpettah and his original home in Tinnevelly. He took teams to preach and distribute tracts at the great Hindu festivals and he trekked high into the mountains among the tribal peoples.

This Gospel preaching by Indians to Indians was remarkably successful, and families were converted in many villages both nearby and further afield. By 1853, congregations had been established in 16 places, comprising nearly 200 believers. By 1856, there were 25 villages with 300 believers; and in 1859, 33 villages and 800 believers including children.[4] Despite their poverty these Indian fellowships erected their own buildings, paid their own schoolteachers and supported their widows and orphans. From time to time the believers came in from these villages to conferences held at Christianpettah.

Arulappan's diaries are filled with experiences familiar to those who "live by faith". In 1847 Groves commented, "I think dear George Müller would be comforted in hearing an Indian speak that language of faith to which his own heart would so fully respond."[5] Thirteen years later, Arulappan's principles were

---

[1] Lang, *Aroolappen*, 96
[2] *Aroolappen*, 219
[3] Arulappan's letters were published in *The Missionary Reporter* (1853 and 1856-8) and *The Indian Watchman* (July 1860 to October 1861). Extracts from these and other sources appear in Harriet Groves's *Memoir* (M571-640) and in Lang's *Aroolappen*.
[4] Lang, *Aroolappen*, 90-1. These were villages with a sizeable Roman Catholic population, where converts were not subject to such severe social exclusion as in purely Hindu villages.
[5] M447

unchanged when he confided, "I never ask my friends for money, but leave it altogether in my Lord's hand."[1]

The Indian evangelists associated with Arulappan had no contract or salary. They were not trained in a theological college or invested with authority by a church or mission agency. They looked directly to God in prayer for their daily needs. A proportion of their support came from gifts sent for distribution at Arulappan's discretion but they were also expected to work with their hands for the benefit of the community. Only the schoolteachers were paid a modest wage for what was considered secular rather than spiritual work. This arrangement was not always popular. Arulappan himself admitted, "Some may not like to work with their own hands, because they see other mission servants live well without any hand's work and receive a monthly salary, but I advise them to see our fore-runner St Paul and other saints even in this time. May the Lord keep them steadfast in faith."[2]

One who cheerfully supported himself as an evangelist was Aquillah. He had been offered a salaried post as a Church of England catechist, but Arulappan tells us "he had no mind to receive a salary for the preaching of the gospel." Aquillah trekked from village to village, selling sugar and salt fish. "When he entered a village he used to read the gospel and preach on the subject and distribute tracts, and sell his sugar and salt fish for a livelihood."[3]

As Arulappan was a mentor to many, so, for almost twenty years was Groves himself to the Indian apostle. Shortly before his death Groves remarked, "In writing to dear Arulappan, I tell him not to lay too much stress on the mere question of baptism, or the Lord's return, or unpaid ministry. They all have their place, but the important thing is Jesus Christ and him crucified: the grace, the fullness and freeness of the gospel."[4]

Men like this might be considered the legacy of Groves to India and to the world. From him they had learned to live frugally and "by faith", ignoring foreign denominational distinctives, without complex church structures and organisations, looking directly to God for guidance, undertaking their own indigenous initiatives and developing their own local leadership. They demonstrated his missiology, not as an academic theory urged upon unwilling subordinates (as was the case with Venn and Anderson), but as a highly effective method for spontaneous church growth that actually worked in the real world.

Conclusion: Missions and Churches

When Groves first set foot in India in July 1833, he found Protestant mission conducted by a number of "voluntary societies", both Anglican and Nonconformist, and each with its own supporters, salaried agents and converts. These societies were shifting from an earlier attitude of mutual tolerance towards a more competitive view of their conflicting ambitions.

Groves, as an independent observer, feared that the effect on the Indians of this incipient denominational discord could only be disastrous. He considered it both

---

[1] M609

[2] *Aroolappen*, 132

[3] *Aroolappen*, 107-8

[4] Letter dated Nov. 1852 (M481-2). The subsequent progress of Arulappan's work is discussed in FOFM 357-61.

unscriptural and unnecessary, and just as his ecclesiology denied the validity of a church denomination, so his missiology had no room for a missionary society. To his mind, the people of God should be considered a single spiritual body, and the whole body called to mission. He hoped that the existing periodic conferences for prayer and communication that he found in some places would lead in time to a much fuller "missionary combination".

In theory Groves believed mission should be conducted simply in the name of Christ and by the church of Christ. Following this principle, converts and groups of converts should not belong to any society, or any denomination, but to Christ alone. And missionaries should feel free to serve on their own initiative, with the support of other Christians but without requiring authorization or a salary from a society. Though he felt obliged to co-operate with societies that already existed, he mistrusted the implications of early comity agreements, fearing they would perpetuate foreign rivalries and inhibit the ministry of Indians among their own people.

Groves's ecclesiological emphasis on "liberty of ministry" found expression in the encouragement he gave to indigenous and expatriate Christians in taking personal initiatives. He stimulated the development of local fellowships, where ministry could be largely informal and where the Lord's Supper could be taken without the presence of an ordained minister. He encouraged foreign and indigenous evangelists to itinerate widely, preaching, baptising converts, teaching and gathering believers into new fellowships where gifts might be developed for ministry to their own circle and beyond it. In these fellowships, the Bible, and especially the New Testament, were considered the sole authority in determining doctrine and practice.

This approach stands in striking contrast to that of Henry Venn and Rufus Anderson who anticipated the creation by one institution (the foreign mission) of another institution (the native church), seeing the former as a scaffolding to be removed once responsibility had been transferred to the latter. Rather than projecting an eventual shift from foreign government, support and propagation to self-government, support and propagation, Groves would start with no organised government, support or propagation at all, expecting these to develop naturally as local believers prayerfully considered the needs and possibilities before them in the light of New Testament principles and precedents.

In refusing to adopt a denominational identity, and in urging the growth of indigenous congregations independent of foreign control, Groves desired to simplify the task of mission so that indigenous Christians might engage in it without waiting for foreign training, authorisation or finance. Rather than separating young men from their friends and families in order to educate them for formal church leadership, he would simply encourage local believers to develop their abilities through ongoing service to their own people. This simple method of practical "on-the-job training" contrasts with the far more formal system of theological education for "native pastors" developed during the following decades by the majority of denominational missions. In Groves's own lifetime, its practical outworking is most evident in the remarkable indigenous movement associated with his Indian disciple John Christian Arulappan.

2. Civilisation and Education

Cultural Identification

The mid-nineteenth century was a patriotic age, and as he left the shores of England, Groves was moved by patriotic sentiment, despite himself, on hearing the National Anthem: "When we passed under the stern of the Admiral's ship her band on board struck up 'God save the King', a circumstance which gave that sort of national pleasure which will steal through the heart even of one who wishes to become a citizen of the world, as far as national attachment goes."[1]

To Groves's mind, the ideal was clearly to become "a citizen of the world", and like Irving's "apostolical" missionary, he would aspire to represent Christ alone: "to be of no country, that he may remove political hindrances out of the way."[2] His task was to propagate New Testament Christianity, not British Christianity, and this implied turning his back, as far as possible, on his British heritage.

Once he reached India, it is evident from his journals that the culture of the East held as little interest for Groves as that of his homeland.[3] He makes no reference to local customs or beliefs, or to indigenous architecture, music or literature, and he shows no sign of adapting Christian teaching to the cultural context around him. In his generation, he was by no means alone in this. But he differed from contemporaries such as Rufus Anderson, in that his disinterest extended equally to Eastern and Western cultures. His declared purpose was to teach the truth as he found it written in his Bible. He was not consciously seeking to export British civilisation to the colonies any more than he was seeking to conform the Gospel to other cultures. Culture and Christianity were, to his mind, two entirely different things. He declared, "I do feel so sure that we have lost our true power by decking ourselves out and prosecuting our plans according to the spirit and principles of the world, whereas I am sure we ought to stand in *contrast* with it at *every point*. Wherever I can literally follow scripture, I feel easy as to the act. Where I cannot, or fancy I cannot, I feel weak in proportion to my distance from it."[4]

---

[1] J16

[2] Irving, *Missionary Orations*, 96

[3] On Groves's disinterest in culture, see PEANG, 175ff.

[4] M229. Chilcraft suggests that, following Niebuhr's fivefold classification, Groves stands in the category of "Christ against culture" (Chilcraft, Ch.7, citing Niebuhr, *Christ and Culture*, 39-44). But Groves, in his surviving writings, shows little or no interest in culture (beyond his obvious antipathy to the religious systems of his homeland), and he was certainly not a great critic of "the world". He might therefore be better placed in the category "Christ and culture in paradox", seeking to be both a good citizen and a radical Christian. Alternatively, and more convincingly, we might find for him, in Niebuhr's preface, a sixth category, to be labelled, "Christ ignoring culture" (*Christ and Culture*, 3). Niebuhr here admits the influence of Rabbi Joseph Klausner stimulating him to consider the relation between Jesus and the Jewish culture of his day, and to suggest that, "instead of reforming culture he ignored it". This view would argue that Jesus sought neither to use, nor to challenge, nor to transform, the culture of his generation, but rather to create a disparate and other-worldly culture for his own disciples. In their personal lives, this would simply replace, rather than continuously conflict with, the ways of world. For Klausner, then, Jesus "imperilled Jewish civilisation" by extracting individuals from their culture and focusing their attention on a kingdom "not of this world", a kingdom to be established by divine rather than human power (Klausner, 369-76). This manner of thinking frequently reappears in Groves's writings.

As an educated Englishman in India, a medical man with a professional standing, Groves might be expected to move in a privileged stratum of society, and to enjoy the comforts and prerogatives available to him.[1] In reality, he was shocked, on his arrival in Bombay, at the astonishing luxury in which expatriate Christians appeared to live. The fact that he had just emerged from months of famine, poverty and squalor in Baghdad no doubt made the present contrast all the more striking, but it was an issue that had long occupied his mind. Three years earlier (in 1830), he had remarked,

> I am sometimes led, in contemplating the gentlemanly and imposing aspect which our present missionary institutions bear, and contrasting them with the early days of the church, when apostolic fishermen and tent-makers published the testimony, to think that much will not be done till we go back again to primitive principles and let the nameless poor and their unrecorded and unsung labours be those on which our hopes, under God, are fixed.[2]

Now he found Christians, and even missionaries, concerned to maintain the respect of the local people by a display of gracious affluence demonstrating the supremacy of Western ways. He noted,

> During my stay at Bombay, I ventured to suggest to some of the missionaries privately, that certain expensive, and apparently self-indulgent habits might be avoided, but all resisted the idea. If even good and devoted servants of God are deceived as to what constitutes their true influence in the Church of Christ, namely, *being like Christ*, can we be surprised that the world at large go altogether wrong?[3]

A little later he was dismayed to hear one missionary declare that he himself would never live *among* the people, for "nothing was to be done with [them], without keeping them at a distance and not making yourself too cheap, and keeping a certain degree of external respectability."[4] As he continued his journey, he remarked, "The farther I go the more I am convinced that the missionary labour of India, as carried on by Europeans, is altogether above the natives; nor do I see how any abiding impression can possibly be made till they mix with them in a way that is not now attempted."[5] When, eventually, he was able to initiate a mission on his own terms, he offered a model that many of his contemporaries would consider dangerously radical: "We purpose that our domestic arrangements should all be very simple and *very inexpensive* and our plan strictly evangelical. One great

---

Furthermore, as Newbigin points out, Niebuhr "deals with the relation of church and culture within a single culture and does not raise the difficult and complicated questions that arise in the communication of the gospel from one culture to another" (Newbigin, *The Open Secret*, 145). In a missionary context, Groves consistently attached more importance to the norms he identified in New Testament scripture than to those of any culture (either Western or Eastern), and for this reason developed a missiology significantly different from that of many other strategists in his day and in ours.

[1] On Indian perceptions of the British at this period, see Edwardes, 242-58.
[2] R22
[3] M230
[4] M282
[5] M271

object will be to break down the odious barriers that pride has raised between natives and Europeans."[1]

By ignoring cultural expectations, Groves hoped that primitivist Christian principles (derived from the New Testament) might be more easily communicated and accepted. The value of this approach was confirmed in his mind by a letter received from a lady missionary in Burma. She had recently spoken to some "native sisters" about "the importance of modesty, cleanliness etc." and they had replied "that they should very much like to live as we did if they had money enough to do so."[2] The need was obviously to demonstrate a Christian lifestyle with an income no greater than theirs.

But living like the Indians at the level of bare subsistence, giving away any surplus, trusting God to supply one's *daily* bread; this was something that no reputable missionary society would allow. Groves concluded, "It must be some who, like us, are free to act thus. Those who act under societies are in so many ways fettered."[3] And it would not be easy: "I feel assured, without inconceivable crucifixion of self the work that is to be done in these lands cannot be accomplished; for the material you have to work on is so very low that close and real contact, so as to leave a lively impression, involves an abasement so great that none have yet had the heart to attempt it."[4] The deliberately frugal lifestyle he had advocated almost ten years earlier in his *Christian Devotedness* would now be a positive advantage, Groves believed, for a missionary in India. So, whether one's income be small or great, "However the Lord may dispose of you, let this be your firm abiding purpose: to share in the humiliations of the gospel."[5]

Commerce, Civilisation and Christianity

Jonathan Bonk has described the idealistic basis for the Christian imperialism that underlay much nineteenth-century missionary endeavour:

> Missionaries were from nations which, having sought God's kingdom and righteousness first, could now point to all the things which had accrued as a result; and since, furthermore, these things had been bestowed by a beneficent God upon the righteousness-seeking West, it followed that these things were – at their root – Christian things! Western civilization, with its evident political, ideological, material, social, technological, and racial superiority, was but the simple effect of a search for God's Kingdom and righteousness.[6]

Following this line of thought, the West would not wish to keep these benefits selfishly for her own enjoyment. The "search" and the rewards were to be urged upon other races and peoples, for Christian civilization was a blessing intended for any nation that would seek first the kingdom of God and his righteousness. Indeed, the West had paved a way for the whole world to follow:

---

[1] M287
[2] M278. The letter was from Mrs Ward, associated with Judson's Baptist mission.
[3] M280
[4] M279
[5] M275
[6] Bonk, *Missionary Identification*, 264

Among the ideas which influenced missionary theory and practice from the beginning of the modern era, probably none can match the pervasiveness or the power of Western belief in the inevitability of progress... Not only did missionaries believe in the inevitability of progress, they regarded themselves as its true emissaries. The indolent temperaments or the stubborn conservatism of non-Western peoples might, it is true, *delay* progress, but there could be no doubt about its ultimate triumph.[1]

In 1853 Earl Grey declared, "The authority of the British crown is at this moment the most powerful instrument, under Providence, of maintaining peace and order in many extensive regions of the earth, and thereby assists in diffusing among millions of the human race the blessings of Christianity and civilisation."[2]

All this stands in contrast to the position held by Groves. His premillennialism inclined him to anticipate not so much the inevitability of Western advancement as the imminence of Eastern disintegration, and Western disintegration too. In particular, he expected a general disillusionment with non-Christian religions and a collapse of traditional societies and authorities, accompanied by divine judgments and devastations preceding the coming of Christ as redeemer of a fallen world. In 1831, as Baghdad groaned under her multiplied afflictions, "Surely every principle of dissolution is operating in the midst of the Ottoman and Persian empires. Plagues, earthquakes, and civil wars, all mark that the days of the Lord's coming are at hand; and this is our hope; on this our eyes and hearts rest as the time of repose, when all these trials shall cease, and the saints shall possess the kingdom."[3] And again, "If the wrath of God is pouring out on the mystical Babylon, as it is on this province of the literal Babylon, the two antichrists are beginning to draw near their end."[4]

Brian Stanley has attempted to locate the earliest origins of this new way of thinking. He suggests that

> The first signs of missionary scepticism towards the values of Western civilisation had appeared... in a context where Western identity was a distinct evangelistic liability – in imperial China. James Hudson Taylor horrified the foreign community in Shanghai in 1855 when he shaved his head, apart from the obligatory pigtail, and adopted Chinese dress. Taylor's decision was primarily a strategic one, but it may also have reflected the influence upon him of a theological tradition (that of the early Brethren movement) which had little room for notions of the advance of Christian civilisation. Taylor's missionary approach significantly became most popular amongst missionaries influenced by the holiness movement, which emphasized personal consecration rather than social regeneration.[5]

---

[1] Bonk, *Missions and Money*, 18-19
[2] Earl Grey, *Colonial Policy of Lord John Russell's Administration*, London, 1853, II, 13-14, quoted by Bowen, xii, and by Warren, *Church Militant*, 60.
[3] R115
[4] R122. The two antichrists were Roman Catholicism and Islam. Bowen notes that premillennialists saw the humbling of the Papacy by Bonaparte and the French Revolution as the "deadly wound" which Antichrist was to receive according to Revelation 13. The prophecies of Daniel 7 and Revelation 13 seemed to be unfolding before their eyes, leading them to suppose that in their own lifetime the "vials of wrath" described in Revelation 16 would be poured out and Christ return to commence his thousand-year reign on earth (Bowen, 64-5).
[5] Stanley, *The Bible and the Flag*, 165

Yet Groves in India was twenty years ahead of this, and he was operating in a place where Western civilisation was regarded with considerably more veneration than in China. He was perceptive enough to argue that such respect was a hindrance rather than a help to the Gospel, and that a disciple of Christ should deliberately shun it, seeking not social influence but spiritual influence. We might indeed feel justified in tracing back to Groves rather than Taylor "the first signs of missionary scepticism towards the values of Western civilisation".

There is no evidence that Groves adopted Indian clothing, despite the fact that some East India Company officials and government agents were in the habit of doing so for the exotic novelty it afforded in their moments of leisure.[1] But Groves identified with the local people at a far more fundamental level. He shared their poverty, living as they lived, eating what they ate, sleeping where they slept. His decision to do so was certainly as deliberate and as "strategic" as Taylor's, and, coming twenty years earlier, might be said to have *launched* the "tradition". The emphasis on "personal consecration rather than social regeneration" was very typical of Groves.

Among Groves's own contemporaries, Henry Venn held that civilisation was an inevitable *consequence* of embracing the gospel, not a necessary *precursor* to it. He argued, "The principle that men must be civilised in order to embrace Christianity is untenable; for civilisation, though favourable to the development of Christianity, so far from being essential for its initiation, is, on the contrary, the consequence, not the forerunner of the gospel."[2] But Venn considered mission schools and colleges necessary for imparting the essence of civilisation to families that had already accepted the gospel: "Extension without these (institutions) is like extending military lines without men to man them. The Committee ... are anxious to press upon every missionary the duty of regarding such educational institutions ... as of prime and essential importance to their own work. They must be ready, if required, to take part in them."[3]

Groves himself valued the evident "civilising" effect that the gospel had produced in India. The contrast between Hindu and Christian villages in Tinnevelly was a striking one:

> I have seen so much of the blessing Christianity brings with it, that my whole heart desires to spend its little remaining strength in publishing or promoting the publication of its precious hopes. The heathen women fly before one like a flock of sheep, running anywhere to hide themselves; if you speak they will not answer, and they give no salutation; but, in the Christian villages, you see cleanliness and quiet, the mother with her little children, and the grandmother standing at the wicket gate of their little hut, to bid you welcome.[4]

But Groves did not share the feelings of racial superiority apparent in some of his colonial contemporaries. Thirty years later David Livingstone would say, "We

---

[1] On one occasion, visiting the Nilgherries, Groves noted, "On arriving at the summit, I was so cold that I laid aside my white clothing, and I am now clothed from head to foot as in England, and not at all too warm" (M263). But the nature of the "white clothing" is not evident.
[2] Shenk, *Venn*, 26
[3] Address to departing missionaries, 1st June 1855, cited by Knight, 430
[4] M256

come among them as members of a superior race and servants of a government that desires to elevate the more degraded portions of the human family."[1] Groves considered himself neither a member of a superior race nor the servant of a government. He spoke of Indian Christians simply as "our dear brethren".[2] He was as warmly attached to "dear Hannai" and "dear Serkies", and to "this dear youth, Mokayel", as to any European or English friend.[3] In 1833 he remarked, "I take with me from hence a dear Christian youth [Arulappan]."[4] A little later "a dear native minister of Christ, as black as jet, offered ten rupees" towards an Indian printing of *Christian Devotedness*, and Groves noted, "he is a poor man".[5] Most striking of all, "I have just been spending an hour or two with a most dear native brother, and the account he has given me of the simple faith and the prayers of the poor people in these congregations is wonderful, and puts me to shame."[6] This is not the comment of a man intent on "civilising the natives", but rather of one willing to learn from them and follow their Christian example. Indeed, he respected and admired their spiritual character: "That dear young native, by name Aroolappen, who went from us some months since, has, amidst many discouragements and many allurements, remained faithful to his purpose."[7]

Groves, with his sceptical view of the religious establishment, would stand apart from the condescending type of missionary or colonial official who acted in "the role of trustee and tutor to native peoples".[8] He consistently treated Indian Christians as equals, as brothers and sons. They were as capable as himself of taking responsibility, and in many cases more so. From 1835 onwards, as his relations with the Establishment grew increasingly strained, Groves would find it easy to sympathise with Indians suffering in a similar fashion from the high-handed dealings of British officialdom. Unlike the agents of the CMS and SPCK, he had no line of communication via committees and home secretaries to powerful evangelical politicians and administrators in Bombay, Calcutta or London. Although he could count among his personal friends several judges and colonial families, he could hardly be mistaken for an Establishment man.

Groves's early experience of schools

A large part of Groves's missionary life was spent teaching children in the schools he established in Baghdad and Chittoor. This might seem surprising in view of the early doubts he expressed about the value of education for missionary purposes. In 1829, on his way through eastern Europe, he declared, "Education is one thing, which may or may not be a blessing; the knowledge of God's word is another. To forward the one, separated from the other, I would not put forth my little finger; to the latter, all my strength."[9] Educating the labouring classes, he

---

[1] Warren, *Church Militant*, 65, citing Wallis, J P R (ed.), *The Zambesi Expedition of David Livingstone, 1858-1863*, Vol. 2 (London, Chatto & Windus, 1956), 416.
[2] M287
[3] On Hannai (Harnie), Serkies and Mokayel, see FOFM *passim*.
[4] M257
[5] *Memoir* 1st edn., 177 (modified in both subsequent editions)
[6] M257
[7] M392
[8] Bradley, 89
[9] J44-5; M59

thought, would tend merely to "pride, rebellion, infidelity and discontent".[1] But in St Petersburg he saw Sarah Kilham's school for girls, and later in Shushi he visited the school run by Zaremba, Pfander and their Basel mission colleagues. In Baghdad, where direct public preaching was hardly possible, Groves was persuaded that elementary schools might prove to be an effective means of evangelism.

The purpose of Groves's first elementary school, opened on 19th April 1830, was not to civilise Mesopotamia but rather to teach boys and girls how to "translate God's word with understanding."[2] He found some Armenian families interested, the Roman Catholics less so.[3] Groves and Pfander decided to use a colloquial Armenian translation of the Bible as their textbook, and they appointed an Armenian teacher. Seeing a demand for a similar school in Arabic, an Arab teacher was also appointed. The teachers, though not themselves evangelical Christians, were willing to give lessons in literacy using the vernacular scriptures given to them by the missionaries. In addition, requests soon came for English lessons from families who saw this as a means of entrance into the commercial and political sphere of British influence in the East. Groves realised that the English language might be a particularly effective medium for the gospel, "for people will bear opposition to their own views more easily in another language than in their own… and thus truth may slide gently in."[4] He started his own English classes, with the Bible (the Authorised Version) as his text.

The Baghdad school, using these various languages, was an undoubted success. Numbers of pupils rose and, having established a method that would "bring God's word before them in a form intelligible and clear," Groves was confirmed in his conviction that the spoken idiom reached the heart, and that books and tracts in the vernacular could revolutionize the reading habits of a people too long cowed by a literary and ecclesiastical elite:

> I believe I have many times mentioned the deep-rooted opposition which exists among the clergy and literary men in the East to having anything translated into the vulgar dialects. They are worse than the literati of Europe used to be with their Latin, many among whom but lately came to see that it was no disgrace to communicate their ideas in a vernacular dress. As the common sense of mankind has triumphed over the literary pride of the learned [in Europe], so we shall find that babes will one day overthrow the literary pride of these Orientals.[5]

---

[1] M59

[2] R169

[3] M83. For details of the school see FOFM 130-5.

[4] M85 (R5)

[5] R98; M119; also R211. Groves observed that the Armenian clergy "obstinately resist the scriptures being translated into the modern languages, because, say they, the ancient language was spoken in Paradise and will be the language of heaven, and that therefore translating the sacred book into that which is modern is a desecration. How wonderfully does Satan blind men, and how by one contrivance or another does he endeavour to keep God's word from them as a real intelligible book which the Spirit of God makes plain even to the most unlettered. But the more we discover him endeavouring to pervert God's word from becoming intelligible, the more we should strive to let every soul have the testimony of God concerning his life in Christ in a language he understands. In this point of view I look to the schools with comfort" (R28-9).

The school was forced to close with the onset of plague in 1831, following which Groves and his colleagues abandoned the work in Baghdad. In retrospect he advised that when it was impossible to preach openly (in an Islamic context for example), and when the people seem hardened against the gospel, the pioneer missionary should not be "discouraged from attempting schools, for although they may not stand above a year or two, you may by the Lord's blessing be the instrument of stirring up their minds to think and examine for themselves, and without violence lead them to question the truth of some of their dogmas. And when you have once dislodged the principle of implicit faith you have at last opened the door for truth."[1]

On his arrival in India in July 1833, Groves found mission schools flourishing in many places, both day-schools and boarding schools, generally for younger children, with teaching by both missionaries and Indians. Many such schools used the vernacular language, with the Bible as a reading text. Some had proved more successful than others in securing conversions among the pupils. Rhenius was not alone in employing non-Christian teachers, owing to the scarcity of suitable believers, and his preference for a sincere Hindu teacher over one claiming hypocritically to be a Christian, was probably shared by others.[2] Among the earliest and most successful efforts were those initiated by the Baptists of Serampore, and by 1817 William Carey and his colleagues had opened 103 Bengali schools, with an average attendance of 6703 boys and girls.[3]

Alexander Duff (1806-78) and English Language Schools

As his initial tour of India drew towards its close in July 1834, the value of educational institutions for the progress of the Gospel was confirmed in Groves's mind when he saw Alexander Duff's far more ambitious work in Calcutta. Indeed, the responsiveness of Duff's older students to his words about the Gospel led him to remark, "This is what I have been in quest of ever since I left old England... I feel that every word is finding its way within. I could empty the whole of my own soul into theirs."[4] Duff answered by opening the door into the large hall where the infants' class was learning the English alphabet; it was here, he said, that the work of conversion began.

Eleven years younger than Groves, Duff was an Edinburgh man of ardent temperament, trained as a Presbyterian minister in the Church of Scotland.[5] Arriving in India in 1830, he had suggested that, in order to transform the country as a whole, the Indian elite must be reached, and to do this they should be offered something they desire – a British education, starting with an infant's class and progressing up to and beyond secondary level. This education would naturally include the principles of Christianity, the religion of Britain. The idea was a timely one. The expanding influence of British trade was stirring an intellectual interest in the outside world, whilst traditional Hinduism faced growing discontent through its failure to meet the appalling social and spiritual needs of the country. The East India Company had introduced remarkable scientific and technological advances

---

[1] R192. The progress of the Baghdad school is discussed in FOFM 130-5.
[2] Rhenius, *Memoir*, 404-5; Ingleby, *Education and India*, 75-6
[3] George, 145.
[4] Smith G, *Duff*, I, 267-268; M323
[5] On Duff's character and early training, see Piggin & Roxborogh, 14, 36 etc.

(roads, medicine and steam power), and the developing markets of the Empire had conferred new and unexpected prosperity on the producers of Indian tea, cotton, and jute (for making sacks). Along with this, the British military posts and colonial service had brought to the country a substantial measure of law and order, with efficient administration and genuine justice in the law courts. The boys who came to Duff's school were boys whose parents had seen benefits for themselves in British civilisation.[1]

Duff was convinced that Hinduism and all other non-Christian religions would inevitably yield when forced to come to terms with rational thought and modern knowledge. He declared, "Once let the foundation be undermined and the whole fabric must crumble into fragments."[2] Ingleby comments,

> He was convinced that Western (Christian) culture was an inestimable boon which could be conferred through education on Indian society. The way forward was the replacement of Indian ways of thinking, based on "Hinduism" and steeped, as he believed, in error and superstition, by European culture based, again in his view, on the sure foundation of a Christian heritage. So he steadfastly insisted that in higher education, at least, the medium of instruction should be English and the subjects taught should be, for example, English literature and "modern" science.[3]

Duff had little respect for local culture, and his desire to undermine traditional beliefs led him close to "a condemnation of all things Indian."[4] The first conversions that he saw through his efforts were mostly students from the Hindu College who attended his extra-curricular lectures rather than students at his own school.[5] But Christian schools following his pattern were soon established with Church of Scotland sponsorship in Bombay, Madras and Nagpur, and his methods were adopted elsewhere in India by the CMS, SPG, LMS, American Presbyterians, American Methodists and others.[6]

At Chittoor, the schools established by Groves extended no higher than a primary level. Lessons in his boarding school were conducted by the missionaries in English, lessons in the day-school by an Indian in the vernacular (Telugu). Whilst in Baghdad, Groves had laboured to use colloquial Arabic with his pupils in addition to English, but in Chittoor, of necessity, for a period of ten years he taught

---

[1] On Duff's educational initiatives, see Millar, *Alexander Duff of India*, and the earlier biography, Smith G, *Duff*.
[2] Duff, *India and Indian Missions*, 593-4. For an excellent summary of Duff's theory, see Maxwell, 138-40.
[3] Ingleby, *Education and India*, 19-20n.
[4] Ibid, 47
[5] Ibid, 56
[6] Ibid, 57. For a positive assessment of Duff's significance and influence see Warren, *Social History*, 100-3. We should not forget that Duff, as a young man at university in Scotland, owed his "first glow of devotedness" to reading Groves's *Christian Devotedness* in 1826-7 (M295). Later in Calcutta he probably owed his life to Groves when suddenly afflicted by a "terrible attack of Bengal dysentery which," he recalled, "brought me soon to the very edge of the grave" (M323). Seeing the gravity of the illness, Groves immediately changed his plans, found berths on a ship for Duff and his wife (who had just given birth to a little boy), and nursed them throughout the voyage, accompanying them as far as their native Scotland. In tribute to him, the baby was christened Alexander Groves Duff.

in English. Having passed the age of forty, and lacking any conspicuous linguistic ability, the task of learning an Indian language was evidently beyond him.

In 1847, thirteen years after his visit to Duff's school, Groves could look back on his own experience, and that of others, and remark, "The more I see of an English school among natives, the more sure I am it is the way of real access to their minds. Only think, eight little girls in Anderson's school have professed their determination to be baptized, and have left father, mother, caste, and everything, and are now living with Mrs. Anderson."[1] And later the same year, referring to his own establishment in Chittoor, "You will be glad to hear the English school is going on very nicely; there are today twenty-seven boys in attendance. Two of them are quite clever, others very intelligent. I could be very happy in labouring among them."[2] In 1851 Harriet Groves records, "he was able to give much personal labour to the English school, and was greatly encouraged with the progress of the boys."[3]

The influence of Pfander, Duff and others may be seen in Groves's educational initiatives. But the evidence from his surviving writings is that he considered his own educational work a means of teaching the Bible and little more. It was not, for him, an aspect of Western civilisation or a way of extending British influence. Its success would be judged solely on the conversion of pupils to the Christian faith. This was a view that some other mission strategists, though by no means all, would come to share in the following decades.

Educational Mission

Groves's initial resistance to the idea of missionary schools stemmed from the fact that the New Testament gives no instance of apostles or evangelists acquiring properties or setting up educational or other institutions. Granted that the gospel has inspired Christian compassion and many forms of Christian service throughout the centuries, its earliest pioneers were preachers pure and simple, devoting themselves to prayer and ministry of the Word.[4] The essence of Groves's ecclesiology lay in his desire to imitate the apostolic example and none other. Nevertheless, following his visit to Alexander Duff in Calcutta he confided, "My interest in boarding schools is very much increasing, not because I think it was the way in which the apostles propagated Christianity, but because I see the Lord now blessing it."[5] Groves observed that the apostles, in their day, had the advantage that their preaching was confirmed by signs and miracles of the Spirit, and yet their message and their aim were the same as that of the modern Christian educator: "I think direct preaching to the natives a much higher and more noble work," he affirmed, yet the work of conversion, which "in the days of the Spirit's energy, was done by a single sentence brought home and sealed," may even now be accomplished, he believed, through the slower process of teaching children in school the truths of the gospel.[6]

---

[1] *Memoir* 1st edn., 299-300 (omitted from subsequent editions). These Andersons were presumably no relation to Rufus Anderson.
[2] M441
[3] M470
[4] Acts 6:4
[5] M326
[6] M326-7

Here Groves clearly felt himself under some pressure to justify the adoption of a method lacking apostolic precedent. Rufus Anderson felt no such obligation when he declared,

> Nothing can be more illogical than the objection brought against missionary schools because the Apostles established none. How many things the Apostles omitted to do, which they would have done if they could. And how absurd to restrict the Church of the nineteenth century to the means that were at its command in the first. Must no use be made of the numberless providential gifts to the Church since then? Must no notice be taken of the subsequent changes in her circumstances? Must no regard be had for the very different attitude of the pagan world towards her?[1]

Anderson considered that, in their circumscribed and largely urban ministry, the apostles were preaching to people as educated as themselves, whereas the modern missionary has to address a relatively ignorant and illiterate populace:

> The heathen to whom the Church then sent her missions were as well instructed in human science as she was herself; now, the heathen are as much lower on the scale of intelligence as the Church is higher; and does this fact create no additional obligation? Besides, where is the divine command to restrict ourselves to *one mode* of propagating the Christian religion? The Apostles certainly had *two*. They preached; and then, by the laying on of hands they instrumentally conferred extraordinary gifts of teaching, prophecy, government, tongues and miracles on certain of the converts. The first we do as they did; the second, in the only manner within our power, viz., by a course of instruction.[2]

Duff promoted his vision for Christian education as a missionary method of worldwide application. He urged the establishment of English secondary schools and colleges, which he believed would create an enlightened elite in every nation, capable of promoting Christian values among their own people. This was not a strategy that Groves, in his surviving writings, either approves or disapproves. It is likely that he would commend it, along with any other effort in Christian service, for he was always willing to recognise the blessing of God in the work of others. It was not, however, the way he chose to work himself.

Anderson and Venn both questioned the value of Duff's top-downwards approach. "Anderson approached every people in evangelism at the bottom of the social scale, among the masses and would work up towards the elite. Alexander Duff took the opposite approach, hoping to win the elite and through them eventually capture the masses"[3] Some missionary societies attempted both: "American agencies increasingly added Duff's emphasis to that of Anderson, and gave institutions a place which the latter would have thought unwise."[4] In fact, Anderson and Venn both became increasingly uneasy about the vast amount of missionary money, time and effort poured into Anglophone secondary schools, where the lessons seemed merely to prepare pupils for careers in law or commerce, and led relatively few to profess faith in Christ.[5]

---

[1] Anderson, *Missionary Schools*, in Beaver, *To Advance*, 160
[2] Anderson, Ibid, in Beaver, 160-1
[3] Beaver, Ibid, 38
[4] Ibid, 38
[5] See Beaver, Ibid, 26-7.

The year 1851, in particular, marked a turning point for Venn. For twenty years he had approved the extensive education of indigenous peoples by missionary teachers, but financial pressures meant that the CMS could no longer afford to pay the salaries of the vast body of workers associated with the Society. He suggested turning over all the schools in India to the secular government. The missionaries protested that they would be deprived of a valuable teaching role and argued that placing the schools in the hands of the government would identify the Christian religion with the British Empire, which would be disastrous for the cause of the gospel.

In fact the role of education in Christian mission became a matter of considerable controversy to nineteenth-century mission administrators. The earliest generation of Protestant missionaries had found the "heathen" slow to understand the gospel, and so advised a long preparatory course of education to raise their level of intelligence to the point where the gospel could finally be understood. Subsequent experience had shown that if presented in their own language, the "heathen" could understand a great deal concerning these matters before receiving any education. Anderson argued that the task of evangelism belonged not to the school teacher but to the gospel preacher. Those who responded positively to the preaching would then be educated in the schools. The value of a school, in his view, was not to prepare the "heathen" for the gospel but "more especially for converts and for such as are being trained for the gospel ministry."[1]

Anderson concluded, "The rule is this: that the system of education, in all its parts, so far as it is supported by the funds of the mission, should have a direct reference to the training up of native teachers and preachers."[2] Thirty years later, in retirement, Anderson's views on this point were unchanged: "Without education it is not possible for mission churches to be in any proper sense self-governed; nor, without it, will they be self-supported, and much less self-propagating."[3]

Vernacular Schools

Commentators are agreed that the thousands of vernacular schools scattered over the face of India became a major means of Christian influence. By the end of the nineteenth century every denomination had its own network of educational institutions, often following principles of comity which avoided unnecessary competition.[4] The schools were, in general, greatly appreciated by the Indians, although the reasons for this may not have been fully realised by the missionaries themselves. In the Tinnevelly District, for example, the Nadars probably anticipated that through education they might raise their status *within* the caste hierarchy, whilst the missionaries were hoping that conversion to Christ would lead them to reject the caste system altogether.[5]

Jonathan Ingleby's study of early educational initiatives in India has identified three different strategies, followed by those he respectively terms Anglicists,

---

[1] Anderson, *Foreign Missions*, Ch.9, in Beaver, Ibid, 204-5
[2] Anderson, *Missionary Schools*, 164, in Beaver, Ibid, 26
[3] Anderson, *Foreign Missions*, Ch.7, in Beaver, Ibid, 26. On the relative merits of English and vernacular schools, in the opinion of Venn and Anderson, see also Porter, *Religion versus Empire?*, 170-4.
[4] Ingleby, *Education and India*, 361
[5] Ibid, 334

Orientalists and Vernacularists.[1] Anglicists held the view that the Christian civilisation of the West must replace traditional beliefs and customs. Orientalists looked to the earliest and highest ideals of eastern cultural traditions and attempted to weave Christian truth and technological progress into this existing framework. Vernacularists were concerned with contemporary culture and local dialects, not as matters of inherent interest in themselves but as necessary means to individual conversions. Described in these terms, we might judge Groves by temperament and disposition a Vernacularist, though somewhat handicapped by his ignorance of Indian languages. He was not by conviction an Anglicist or by inclination an Orientalist.

Ingleby argues that Duff's Anglicist vision proved to be an expensive and largely fruitless "diversion" in the history of Protestant missions in India. He suggests that the vernacular system, running parallel to the English system was far more effective in producing conversions and in launching young men and women along the path to church leadership.[2] Duff was too confident in his belief that his young scholars, once extracted from their families, would abandon the values and beliefs of their home and risk ostracism and isolation for the sake of a foreign religion. Village conversions, on the other hand, generally involved the whole family adopting a path they perceived to offer communal prospects of social and financial advancement. Ingleby concludes, "The evidence is that, in terms of missionary strategy, it was the lower class vernacular education which was the most effective educational tool, and which contributed most to the building of the Indian church."[3]

The experience of a century and a half since then has failed to answer the question of whether the finance, time and effort invested in educational institutions have brought a commensurate spiritual benefit. Duff and his contemporaries saw some conversions at the Christian colleges, but the number decreased in the following generation.[4] In fact, the urban and the rural churches of India have tended to develop somewhat separately. The English colleges and the vernacular colleges (which increasingly adopted English) both failed to prepare committed Christians for work in the villages, and the village churches became reluctant to send talented young people to the colleges.[5] Direct evangelistic work has undoubtedly been more productive in terms of conversions, and yet the fact remains that significant Christian leaders in successive generations are graduates of Anglophone mission schools and colleges. One such was John Arulappan; another

---

[1] Ibid, 14-29

[2] Ibid, 372-3. In Bengal, for example, following their primary education in a local vernacular school, they would progress to Serampore College (BMS, Baptist), or the Bishop's College (SPG, Anglican) to complete their education. But both these institutions were grand in appearance, Western in style, and became largely English in language. Ingleby judges that neither of them succeeded in creating an effective and educated Indian leadership for the churches (Ibid, 47). Stanley remarks, "Serampore fostered in its students a grand lifestyle ill suited to pastoral ministry among the rural poor and fatal to the development of self-supporting churches… Serampore never became the training institution for indigenous missionaries which was at the heart of its original vision" (Stanley, "Planting Self-Governing Churches", 380).

[3] Ibid, 375

[4] Ibid, 365

[5] Ibid, 357

was Bakht Singh, and in a different cultural context, Watchman Nee. And we should note that there were conversions through the elementary schools launched by Groves himself, in both Baghdad and Chittoor.[1]

Social and Medical Mission

Groves spoke warmly of other types of Christian institution, although he never established any of his own. In offering ophthalmic care in Baghdad and dental care in India, his intention was primarily to gain acceptance with the local populace for the spiritual teaching he wished to give them. In Baghdad he reported, "There is this one value in medical practice which I never so fully felt before – that it affords to Mohammedans an unsuspected excuse for coming to us."[2] In India his professional income also served for the support of himself and his colleagues, but he noted, "My profession gives me access to many I should not otherwise see; and the Lord blesses me by allowing me to bring very many of the people of God to contemplate subjection to Jesus as a very different thing to attachment to a system."[3] His chief interest was spiritual, and once he had moved on, he left behind him no permanent medical work in either place.

He valued the literature produced by the CMS printshop in Malta, and he even arranged for a small portable press to be sent to Baghdad with a view to producing Sunday school materials and scriptures in the spoken dialects of Mesopotamia.[4] But Groves himself was more comfortable talking than writing, and though he composed a number of controversial tracts and books in English, he seems to have given no thought to establishing a publishing house, and he never undertook major writing or translation projects for India or the Arab world.

Of greater interest to him was the plight of abandoned and endangered children. Orphans never failed to find him a protector and provider, and he went to great lengths to help with the creation of the orphanage at Sonamukhi. He valued Müller's foundation in Bristol as much for its practical provision for the physical needs of destitute children as for its effectiveness in leading them to faith in Christ.[5] On at least one occasion he urged his fellow Christians to establish hospitals and hostels where believers and others who had fallen on hard times could find healing for body and soul and enjoy wholesome Christian fellowship.[6] In fact, wherever Groves himself established a home for his wife and children it became a place of refuge for people in need. In Baghdad he welcomed both Serkies and Harnie into the family when they were homeless and bereaved, and as members of the Groves household they both experienced an evangelical

---

[1] M214, 520. Among them were Serkies Davids, first known to Groves as a pupil in his Baghdad school, and Kistname, a Brahman pupil at Chittoor, who continued his education in Madras where he professed faith in Christ, "forsaking all earthly prospects and advantages for our Redeemer's sake" (See FOFM 351).

[2] M82

[3] M368; also M364

[4] R76

[5] Visiting the Müllers in 1852 he wrote, "You would be greatly delighted with the orphan house, and the untiring devotion to it of dear George, and Mary, and Lydia, walking there and back every day, and working there all day long. They seem so to love the children" (M482).

[6] Groves, *Influence*, 52

conversion.[1] In Chittoor, of course, he attempted to establish a farm colony providing homes and incomes for Indian Christians, and this could be considered a major social ministry. Throughout his life Groves simply cared for people. This was not a matter of missiological theory; it was the natural response of a loving heart to human need.

Conclusion: Civilisation and Education

Groves was an Englishman and therefore easily identifiable in India as a member of the ruling elite. What made him unusual was the extent to which he attempted to ignore this fact and to deny himself any advantages that might accrue from it.

In particular, he chose to live at an economic level below that of his colonial compatriots in order to relate better to the Indians around him. The deliberately frugal and sacrificial lifestyle he had advocated as a young man in England would prove a positive advantage for the middle-aged missionary in India as he sought to make the Gospel accessible to the poor who formed the majority of the population.

Groves's premillennialist views inclined him to take a far less sanguine view of British civilisation than many of his contemporaries. He never felt called to introduce "commerce, civilisation and Christianity" in preparation for a golden age of millennial bliss. On the contrary, he anticipated hard times ahead before the coming of Christ to rescue a persecuted remnant. In this regard he stood in the vanguard of a new generation of missionaries identifying with the indigenous people rather than the colonial establishment.

Though impressed with Duff's English educational establishments in Calcutta, Groves was less overtly critical of Indian culture than he was, and in contrast to Duff's urban work for the rich, his own ministry was essentially among the rural poor. He opened an elementary day school in Chittoor, where Indian teachers used the vernacular, and an elementary boarding school where he and others taught in English.

Although he practised ophthalmics in Baghdad and dentistry in Madras, Groves's greater concern was to convey a spiritual message to the people around him. His desire was to offer neither health nor civilisation, but Christian teaching leading to personal salvation and devotion to Christ. In these various ways, we can see his ecclesiological roots bearing missiological fruit.

---

[1] On Serkies and Harnie, see FOFM *passim*.

3. Finance and Providence

Missionary Support

The subject of missionary support has been introduced in our discussion of "voluntary societies". It was a matter to which Groves gave much thought, from his earliest account of Christian devotedness in 1825 to his final exhortations at Hackney and Tottenham in the year of his death, 1853. Elsewhere we have looked in some detail at Groves's concept of Christian stewardship as an aspect of his ecclesiology.[1] We must now consider its implications for mission. We should enquire how this practice differed from the customary method of raising subscriptions for the investment of limited sums in voluntary societies. How, in Groves's mind, for example, would potential donors become aware of needs? How would missionaries obtain the funds required for fresh and potentially expensive initiatives? What would it mean to seek provision from God rather than man? How would it work in practice?

Firstly, we should note that the idea of Christian devotedness was a challenge given to committed Christians alone. Groves never asked non-Christians to contribute money for what he considered the work of God. On this point, as always, the New Testament was his guide. He noted that the apostle Paul resolved that no one should have grounds to question his missionary motives.[2] Though willing to receive gifts from the established Christians of Philippi, he would accept nothing from the pagans or Jews who heard him in Corinth or Thessalonica.[3] Committed to "preaching the gospel... free of charge," he would prefer to support himself, working with his own hands if necessary, "in order not to be a burden to anyone."[4] The apostle John, too, commended evangelists who "have set out for [God's] sake and have accepted nothing from the heathen." And John advised his Christian friends, "We ought to support such men."[5] These verses convinced Groves that God's work is the responsibility of God's people; the unconverted should not be asked to finance it.[6]

Secondly, we may observe how the outworking of Christian devotedness brought Christian families in Britain and India into a practical and personal relationship with the poor around them and with evangelists and missionaries trusting God to provide for their daily needs. After a conversation with Groves in India, two Christian men offered each to finance the passage out and ongoing support of a missionary for the new orphanage at Sonamukhi; others provided food and clothing for the forty little girls in their care.[7] A little later, as the Bowdens and Beers set off for India, a young woman sold her gold watch to help with the cost of their passage.[8] This, indeed, was a vision that appealed to Groves's generation – the thought that the sacrifice made by the clerk or engineer or housewife might correspond with that made by the missionary, enabling them to be partners in

---

[1] PEANG, 172ff
[2] 2 Cor 2:17
[3] Phil 4:15-18
[4] 2 Cor 11:7-9; 1 Thess 2:9
[5] 3 Jn 7-8 RSV
[6] See especially D11.
[7] M312
[8] Bromley, 14

reaching the world for Christ. From his earliest days in India, Groves shared this idea with the expatriate families who welcomed him into their homes. Some, to his delight, responded wholeheartedly; they "adopted the simple manner of living I approve." A number cheerfully "began to alter their expensive style of living." One couple "parted with their superfluities in a very sweet spirit."[1]

The Great Commission, as conceived by Groves, must be a united effort, engaging the two essential social strata of British society, that is, the rich and the poor. In general, the former will provide the finance, and the latter the labour, for the missionary task, and both will have the opportunity for genuine personal sacrifice:

> The influence of the rich is manifested in being willing to become poor...The influence of the poor in refusing to be richer himself... the one by his example leads the rich saints to relinquish, the other the poor saints to labour, for the cause of God. I am absolutely at a loss to know which is most beautiful, or which would be most influential. The one would pour into the *treasury* more perhaps, the other provide the *soldiers* for the warfare of truth against error. And then those who abode at home would be fellow helpers to the truth with those who went to minister the things of the kingdom; for they would supply their wants.[2]

But the rich will not be restricted to *financing* mission. They will have the freedom to become missionaries and thus join the ranks of the poor. He himself had chosen this course. And, similarly, the poor, if unable to serve overseas, will not be denied the privilege of providing financially for others. In this regard, Groves noted how highly appreciated is a reliable servant in any well-to-do family in Britain, and how hard it is for such a family to find servants it can depend upon. He proposed a novel idea. Why should not a hundred Christians of modest means apply for posts as servants, and then through their diligence win the appreciation of their masters? And why should they not save, from their resulting income, whatever might prove surplus to their requirements? Collectively, he calculated, the hundred would be able to raise more than £4000 a year for Christian mission. His conclusion was a bold and exciting one: "Then these hundred servants might support one hundred single evangelists to go through the length and breadth of the land."[3]

These ideas were offered constantly to the expatriates he met on his travels after leaving Britain in 1829. In St Petersburg the coming of the missionary party on their way to Baghdad stimulated a remarkable spirit of generosity that helped them on their way.[4] Then arriving in India in 1833 Groves observed, "I have just met another gentleman, a civilian, who seemed quite delighted at the thought of supporting a missionary at his own expense."[5] The following year he met a certain Mr Pearce who owned "an enormous printing establishment, the whole profits of which he bestows on the promotion of God's cause."[6] As time went on, many missionaries and many Indian evangelists were fully supported by expatriate Christians who had dedicated to Christ their entire salary or the proceeds of their

---

[1] M285
[2] Groves, *Influence*, 57-8
[3] *Influence*, 59
[4] M55. See above, 47ff.
[5] *Memoir* 1st edn., 183 (omitted from subsequent editions)
[6] *Memoir* 1st edn., 224; M319

business. It was evidently possible for a government official and an itinerant preacher to live quite comfortably off a single income shared between them, and a number did so.[1]

But missionaries will not merely be the recipients of gifts. They have the privilege of offering them too. Indeed, any funds they possess surplus to their immediate requirements may be prayerfully passed on to those around them in greater need. Groves himself contributed largely to the support of Bowden, Beer, Arulappan, and other workers. He noted the apostle's observation, "God is able to make *all* grace abound to you, so that in *all* things at *all* times, having *all* that you need, you will abound in every good work."[2] He commented, "This has been *my experience*. Never had I so much in my hands to give as at this moment, when I have not a shilling in the world of my own."[3]

An additional motive for frugality on the part of the missionary will, of course, be the desire to identify with the people around them, who are, in general, poor. In Baghdad Groves found a habit of frugal living a positive advantage for the missionary in other respects too. Possessing little, he had little to worry about, and little to lose to thieves and extortioners. He remarked, "What a mercy it is to us to have the world, with its honours, its pleasures and its hopes, crucified with Christ; how it takes away the edge from the Enemy's weapons. When he thinks to make a deadly thrust at us he finds he can only touch that which we have ceased to value, because we have a better inheritance: one incorruptible, undefiled and that fadeth not away."[4]

Nevertheless, there were occasions when living economically actually made it more difficult to serve Christ. Once, travelling by sea, Groves admitted, "I miss very much the retirement of a closet [i.e. small room] which I enjoyed on shore. To avoid expense I allowed a Christian brother to have a third of my cabin, and I have up to this time slept on the floor of the cuddy. Sometimes I have felt the spiritual loss to be greater than the value of a few hundred rupees, yet I think again it is right."[5]

In principle, it was "right", for Groves believed poverty to be, in its very nature, a stimulus to faith. It compels the missionary to depend on God rather than on his own resources or other human agencies, and places him in circumstances where he will pray and see answers to prayer. Only then will the missionary have a genuine testimony of God's faithfulness. He learns to live "by faith", and his living "by faith" becomes an example to those he is seeking to influence.[6]

Groves's Life of Faith

To their admirers, Norris and Mary Groves would hardly look out of place among the heroes of faith depicted in the eleventh chapter of Hebrews. "By faith," they gave up all they possessed in order to carry the gospel to the heart of the Muslim world. And they did it gladly, believing this to be among the toughest of all possible assignments. Groves declared,

---

[1] M229; M422
[2] 2 Cor 9:8
[3] M244
[4] M9 (1 Pet 1:4 AV)
[5] M328
[6] M469. Despite the similarities, there is no evidence that Groves had any contact with Franciscan influences.

> Whilst I should not hesitate to go to the farthest corner of the habitable earth, were my dear Lord to send me, yet I feel much pleasure in having my post appointed here, though perhaps the most unsettled and insecure country beneath the sun. Without, are lawless robbers, and within, unprincipled extortioners; but it is in the midst of these that the almighty arm of our Father delights to display his preserving mercy. And while the flesh would shrink, the spirit desires to wing its way to the very foremost ranks of danger in the battles of the Lord.[1]

Here, it would appear, was a faith of heroic proportions – a faith that expected to deal directly with God – and subsequent events would test that faith to the utmost. Cut off from the outside world by flood, plague and civil war, with no mission board or home committee to support them, there might seem every human likelihood that the Baghdad mission would sink without trace. It was in such a setting that Norris and Mary Groves would depend upon their Father's "preserving mercy", and where their testimony to his faithfulness would encourage others to exercise the same faith. Groves describes the great object, not merely of their mission, but of their lives: "The Lord gives us great peace and quietness of mind in resting under his most gracious and loving care, and *as the great object of our lives is to illustrate his love to us*, we believe that in the midst of these awful circumstances he will fill our tongues with praise, as he now fills our hearts with peace."[2]

Facing the prospect of siege and bloodshed, Groves recorded, "August 19th [1830]. Things here seem most unsettled, and require us to live in very simple faith as to what a day may bring forth. It is stated, that between twenty and thirty thousand Arabs are close to the gates of the city... What will be the result of all this we are not careful to know, for the Lord will be to us a hiding-place from the storm, when the blast of the terrible ones is as a storm against the wall."[3]

For a husband and wife to trust God to provide and protect in such conditions would seem hardly sensible. But to take two small boys with them might be considered positively irresponsible. Some might feel that looking literally to God for food in a place of famine, for health in a place of disease, and for safety in a place of danger, would be to display "presumptuous confidence". Indeed, was it not "tempting God"? And was it not written, "Thou shalt not tempt the Lord thy God"?[4] Groves could not agree:

> Many are affrighted and made sad in the ways of the Lord by the erroneous application of this scripture... If they hear of a man selling his property and becoming poor like Barnabas, according to the exhortation of the apostles and the example of our Lord, he is considered as *tempting God*... Again, if he exposes himself to dangers he might avoid, troubles he might escape, for what he believes the Lord's service, far from receiving any comfort or encouragement he is again accused of *tempting God*.[5]

But that, Groves believed, is to misunderstand the scriptures: "Tempting God is the deadly sin of an unregenerate mind and is never charged on any saint, either in the

---
[1] M105
[2] M120 (R97)
[3] R29
[4] Mt 4:7 AV
[5] R217-21

Old or New Testament." When the unfaithful Jews in the wilderness *tempted* God, it was not by depending on his provision, but by doubting it.[1] When the Pharisees and Sadducees *tempted* Christ, their demand sprang not from faith but from disbelief.[2] When Jesus from the pinnacle of the Temple said, "Do not put the Lord your God to the test," he was rebuking not bold faith but craven incredulity.[3] We tempt God by unbelief, by defiance and by sin; never by depending on him to do what he has promised. The Groves family, so very vulnerable, went to Baghdad not tempting God but *trusting* him. "Oh, who would not live a life of faith in preference to one of daily, hourly satiety — I mean as to earthly things; how very many instances of happiness should we have been deprived of, had we not trusted to, and left it to His love to fill us with good things as He pleased, and to spread our table as He has done, year after year, and will do, even here in this wilderness."[4]

Launching a mission to the Muslim world was a step which inspired that great exemplar of faith, George Müller,[5] and it was, in certain respects, a bolder step of faith than his. By the end of his life, Müller had provided through prayer for more than a hundred thousand orphans without asking a soul for a penny. Yet many Christians visited the orphan houses, and many heard Müller preach. His work of faith took place very visibly in the midst of what was still a Christian country with wealthy generous donors among its evangelical aristocrats and industrialists. Norris and Mary Groves proposed to place the same absolute trust in the faithfulness of God where there were no open-days for interested visitors, no supportive churches, no guaranteed communications, no one to turn to if things went wrong except God himself. This, indeed, was part of the attraction. Although his primary reason for going to Baghdad was certainly to proclaim the gospel, Groves wished no less keenly to demonstrate the fact that the life of faith, as taught by Christ, was the most practical and the most joyous way for any Christian to live. "The great object of our lives," he declared, "is to illustrate his love to us." And where better to illustrate it than the hardest place of all?

Though cut off from financial support, and from any place of human safety, the little family was borne up by the prayers of friends at home, as proved by the few letters that did get through. And though their friends could do little but pray for them, the answer to those prayers came in ways that none could have foreseen. Although he did not, like Müller, compile a detailed account of specific gifts received and needs met, he could testify no less clearly of God's perfect provision. A little support arrived erratically by mail in the form of money orders that could be cashed with local merchants. Some came from the kindly British representative of the East India Company, Major Taylor, whose wife Groves had escorted safely to Baghdad. At the beginning of 1831 he looked back on their first year:

---

[1] Deut 6:16; Exod 17:1-7; 1 Cor 10:9
[2] Matt 16:1
[3] The fact that Christ subsequently walked on water was proof to Groves that if he *had* thrown himself down from the Temple he would certainly have been borne up by angels. It was the devil who doubted this, not Christ. Indeed, "the object of Satan was to get our Lord's mind into a condition of doubting God" (R218).
[4] R45
[5] Müller, *Narrative*, I, 52

> I have this day settled all my accounts, and find, after everything is paid, including the expenses of my baggage from Bushire, and of the house and school for another year, that our little stock will last us, with the Lord's blessing, two months longer, and then we know not whence we are to be supplied, but the Lord does not allow us to be anxious; He has so wonderfully provided for us hitherto, that, it would be most ungrateful to have an anxious thought. Even for my baggage, Major Taylor only allowed me to pay half the charge, and he has, moreover, told me, that should I at any time want money, only to let him know and he will lend it me. Now, really to find such kind and generous friends, is more than we could have hoped, but thus the Lord deals with us, and takes away our fears. That we may many times be in straits I have no doubt, but the time of our necessity will be the time for the manifestation of our Lord's providential love and munificence.[1]

On 28th February,

> We received… letters from most of our dearest friends in England, which tell us, at the very moment when our little all was within a month of coming to a conclusion, that the Lord had provided us with supplies for at least four months to come, for which we might draw. Surely the Lord has most graciously seen fit to dry up those sources from whence we anticipated supply, that we might know we depend on Him alone, and see how He can supply us even here; we were ashamed of every little anxious feeling we had ever had, and were much encouraged to trust Him more and more… O! how hard it is to persuade the rebellious will and proud heart, that to depend on our Father's love for our constant support is more for the soul's health than to be clothed in purple and fare sumptuously every day from what we call our own resources; and yet how plain it is to spiritual vision.[2]

The nature of these anticipated "sources" is unclear. Perhaps Groves had hoped for (but not actually agreed) some regular provision in the form of money orders from the wealthy Acland, Kennaway and Drummond in Britain.[3] There is no evidence of their continued interest in him once he had left Britain.

In May of the same year (1831), "Again, the Lord's great care over us in His abundant provision for all our necessities, although every one of those sources failed that we had calculated upon naturally when we left England, enabled us yet further to sing of His goodness."[4] And again, in October (1831),

> He has supplied me, I know not how, in the midst of famine, pestilence and war. And though I have heard from none in England for more than a year, especially from those that supply my wants, the Lord has not suffered me to want, or to be in debt. And though the necessities of life have amounted to almost twenty times their value during our late trials, he has not suffered me personally to be much affected by it. His loving-kindness and care have been wonderful.[5]

---

[1] R74, journal entry dated 14th Feb. 1831
[2] R78-9
[3] See PEANG, 44-5, 65.
[4] R169
[5] R298. Groves must have meant that he had received no communication *sent* more recently than a year ago. He would be aware that he had received on 28th February (seven and a half months earlier) letters written the previous September (more than a year ago), brought out and forwarded by his friends in Aleppo, containing at least one credit note that could be cashed with a local merchant or money changer (R78-9).

After moving to India in 1833, Groves continued to live "by faith", sharing what he had with his missionary colleagues: "We have all things common among us, and when all is gone we shall again be cast simply on God and the love of His Church."[1] Although he often spoke to expatriate friends about Christian stewardship, the evidence is that he rarely, if ever, mentioned needs of his own. In 1834, he remarked, "One dear brother offers me 1000 rupees a year, and I have just received, from another, an offer of 500 more annually, and yet, I never hinted that I wanted; on the contrary, I assured them we had more than enough."[2]

The diaries of his co-worker Hermann Gundert show that Groves was not averse, on occasion, to informing close Christian friends about financial needs for projects such as the erection of buildings.[3] In a preface to his earlier *Journal of a Journey to Baghdad* he detailed several booksellers and other well-known Christians in Britain who would be willing to pass on to him any contributions his readers might wish to make for the support of his schools in Mesopotamia.[4] In his subsequent report on *The Present State of the Tinnevelly Mission*, he indicated how money might be forwarded to him through certain friends in England and in India for the support of Rhenius, adding, "I thus then conclude the case of the claims of the Tinnevelly Mission, and leave them to the prayerful regard and sympathy of my Christian Brethren. I would earnestly solicit from them such help as they feel themselves enabled freely to give, under the sense of having freely received; for the Lord loveth a cheerful giver."[5] He later made a point of speaking to the assemblies in London concerning the need of his colleagues in India for more regular and effective support: "I went to Tottenham and… endeavoured to interest them about missions, spoke of Bowden, Beer and Arulappan, and in the evening brought the subject before the church, and they hope, in union with believers in Hackney, Orchard Street, and other places to form an effectual committee to care for these things. This has been a great comfort to me."[6] Yet neither Groves, nor the magazine *The Missionary Reporter* that was launched in response to his visit, made public appeals for money. In such spiritually sensitive Christian circles the need would be understood without the necessity to spell it out, or to play upon the emotions of potential donors.

Gundert himself was evidently a willing recruit to Groves's "faith principles". Shortly after his arrival in India, he was explaining his financial circumstances to Indians he met in the course of his evangelistic itinerations, and noted in his journal, "I said that of course I have no power, no salary etc. which then was

---

[1] M224
[2] M311
[3] Gundert's journal dated 7th June and 7th July 1838 (Gundert, *Tagebuch*, 32)
[4] They were Mrs Rich and Mr Nisbet of London, three "ministers of the gospel" (Hitchcock of Devizes, Glanville of Sidmouth and Müller of Teignmouth), Mr Fosse of Ilfracombe, and the booksellers Upham of Bath, Bulgin of Bristol, C Upham of Exeter, Kilton of Norwich, Edis of Huntingdon, Tims of Dublin, Waugh and Innes of Edinburgh, Collins of Glasgow, and Lusk of Greenock. The location of these friends may give some idea of the extent to which Groves was known in some (but by no means all) regions of the British Isles. The West Country is well represented, and also London, southern Scotland and Dublin.
[5] Groves, *Tinnevelly Mission*, 14
[6] M481

inquired into by them with much interest."[1]   Groves encouraged others, especially soldiers in the British army, to consider devoting themselves to the missionary task. Receiving a letter from "a young officer in the artillery", Groves observed "It requires great faith to give up a provision, however uncongenial the profession, and to cast oneself in simple dependence on the Lord."[2] Another, by the name of MacCarthy "gives up thirty-five rupees a month, a horse, and a house, that he may do the work of God. He goes through the Tamil and Telegoo country, in a little cart filled with books, tracts, and things for sale, preaching the gospel to the natives in their own tongues... He has already been blessed by the conversion of two natives"[3] This Groves found most encouraging:

> I assure you we all feel that, had we seen no other fruit of our labour than these two or three brethren, acting on these principles of service, we should have said, truly our labour has not been in vain in the Lord. I think, therefore, we may consider that, under God, our residence in India has been the means of setting up this mode of ministry among the native Christians and the heathen, and our continuance will be, I trust, by the grace of God, the means of establishing and extending it.[4]

As a missionary, Groves was by no means unwilling to earn his own living, and to consider this an aspect of living "by faith", especially if other channels of support dried up. After some months in Baghdad, "I often think my dear friends in England will be sadly discouraged at the Lord's dealings with our mission: So difficult is it to act faith [sic] in dark seasons. However, should their faith and hope fail, the Lord will either raise up others, or find me some little occupation by which I may live. His goodness in the way of provision has been so wonderfully manifested, that my heart feels quite easy that He will find a way for the support of His servant."[5] He foresaw circumstances that might prevent a church from sending adequate support to its missionary: "This would naturally lead to the exhibition of another scripture principle, that of uniting, as scripture does, a righteous use of secular occupations with the maintenance of a spiritual ministry."[6]

In Madras, for a period of about a year (1836-7), Groves supported himself and his missionary team through the exercise of his profession as a dentist, although they also received gifts from friends in India and elsewhere. Moving to Chittoor in 1837, he established an agricultural settlement and silk manufactory, hoping to provide a home and an adequate income for Indian converts, and profits which would perhaps support missionary labours further afield. In the event, it was not a financial success, and his subsequent commercial ventures turned out unhappily.[7]

In fact, throughout his missionary life, Groves received most of his finance through unsolicited gifts from Christian friends, the majority being expatriates to whom he ministered in English. He encouraged others to follow this pattern. When Rhenius and his colleagues severed their connection with the CMS, for example,

---

[1] Gundert, *Tagebuch*, 7
[2] *Memoir* 1st edn., 181 (omitted from subsequent editions)
[3] M392
[4] M392
[5] R299
[6] "Missions to the Heathen", 137
[7] For a narrative account, see FOFM 246-54.

Groves was particularly delighted to find Indian Christians offering support to the German missionaries in their time of need:

> I have the strongest conviction of the power of religion among this poor people. When Mr. Schmidt [*sic*] left the mission, owing to some difficulties he had with the Society, and was in great straits, the poor converts, quite unknown to Mr. Rhenius, subscribed among themselves 200 rupees. The value of this testimony can only be estimated by one who knows the extreme poverty of these people, and their fondness, as heathen [i.e. before their conversion], for money.[1]

His other missionary colleagues in India were supported on the same basis. In February 1838, he recorded,

> The Bowdens and Beers seem, by their letters, to be going on nicely, and are quite happy in their work. Each family lives on thirty rupees a month... They tell me they have received from Mr. James Thomas some bread and cakes, from Mr. Jellicoe bread and wine, and from some unknown person thirty rupees: They still have enough for the present, and, I doubt not, will not have finished the old store before the new comes in.[2]

Receiving unexpected gifts from here and there, often from Groves himself, the Bowdens and Beers were furnished with a lifetime's testimony of remarkable coincidences and last minute provisions to match that of Müller himself.[3] Groves himself was also a means of support for Indians living on the same basis, such John Christian Arulappan, whom we will consider in due course.[4]

Living by Faith: Groves's Principles

In light of the above, we may be surprised to find how little Groves actually says about "the life of faith". Compared with the importance this concept had for George Müller and for Hudson Taylor, it is not a prominent theme in his journals or letters or other published writings. What is more, when Groves speaks of walking or living "by faith", it is usually in the context of bearing patiently with trials and sorrows, or undertaking fresh initiatives in Christian service, rather than depending on God for financial provision. Despite this, Harold Rowdon has argued that "his tract on *Christian Devotedness...* was the fountainhead of modern thinking on the subject."[5]

It is certainly in this booklet that the idea of "living by faith" is introduced, and it comes as a practical application of Groves's theme of forsaking all to follow Christ. In his preface to the second edition (1829), he emphasizes, "The principle of God's government is paternal; and therefore its primary object is the development in us of the character of *dear children*, the essential feature of which is unlimited dependence."

By then Groves had abandoned his own lucrative profession, his large house and all his possessions, and was making plans for Baghdad. He asks how a person

---

[1] M257. The name of Rhenius's colleague was Schmid, spelt correctly by Groves in *The Present State of the Tinnevelly Mission*.
[2] M383
[3] Bromley chronicles many such instances.
[4] See below, 213ff.
[5] Rowdon, "The Concept of 'Living by Faith'", 345

in such circumstances can be sure his needs will be met, and he replies by pointing to all the promises of God:

> He knows that the best security for all spiritual blessings and all temporal mercies, both to himself and his friends, lies in doing the will and trusting unreservedly in the promises of that God who hath said, "Can a mother forget her sucking child, that she should not have compassion on the fruit of her womb? Yea, she may forget; yet will not I forget thee." What therefore he has freely received, he freely gives; and trusts for the future the promises of his heavenly Father.[1]

To live like this meant regarding oneself as a servant of God, directly accountable to him, free at all times to follow his direction, seeking first his kingdom and his righteousness, and trusting him to provide for daily needs. Indeed, Groves affirmed, "I can with my whole heart pray for myself and all who are nearest and dearest to me that we be so circumstanced in life as to be compelled to live by faith on the divine promises day by day."[2]

Living this way, indeed, will free a Christian from all manner of human fears and restrictions: "Surely it is a most unspeakable privilege to be allowed to cast all our cares upon God, and to feel that we are thereby delivered from the slavery of earthly expectations."[3] No longer worried lest a benefactor or church or business take offence and cut us off, we can speak the truth in love without fear of man. No longer tempted, when seeking spiritual guidance, by financial considerations; no longer concerned that accident or sickness or commercial failure will leave us destitute; Groves affirmed it was a happy way to live: "What is the 'glorious liberty of the children of God' but to be dependent only upon one 'who giveth liberally and upbraideth not', who says 'Ask and ye shall receive'?"[4]

Though finance was by no means the only thing on his mind, there is undoubtedly a financial element to this scheme. Indeed as a method for financing Christian mission we could describe it as an alternative to that proposed by the voluntary societies, and it was, in Groves's view, the method intended by the Master when he first gave the Great Commission to his disciples.

For Groves, Christian stewardship was, of course, the responsibility of every Christian. He declared, "Whatever the bounty of God may bestow upon *us*, above a sufficiency for our present necessities, is to be esteemed a blessing in proportion as it is *distributed* to relieve the temporal and spiritual wants of others."[5] But this principle of giving was naturally complemented by a principle for receiving. In general the rich will give and the poor receive. If we may encapsulate Groves's view of the normal Christian life in the phrase "trust and obey", then the poor would be called especially to trust, and the rich to obey. When the missionary trusts and the church obeys, then the world may be reached with the Gospel, unhindered by the administration, argumentation and accountancy that afflict the decision-making processes of the voluntary societies. In his own words,

---

[1] D18-19 (referring to Is 49:15 AV)
[2] D22. On the scriptural content of Groves's *Christian Devotedness*, see FOFM 65-76.
[3] D13
[4] D13 (Rom 8:21; Jas 1:5; Jn 16:24 AV)
[5] D8

A church guided by the Spirit of God and freed from the arbitrary laws which encumber a society or a national establishment... will not be hindered by any of those considerations which make societies so cautious how they enlarge their borders. They will feel that their messenger, though refreshed by their love, depends not on them but on their Lord, who never forsakes those who trust him, who commands his children *not* to take thought for the morrow. They would know nothing of those earthly calculations which so often hinder exertion.[1]

To Groves's mind, a missionary living "by faith" was by no means prohibited from engaging in secular employment. Indeed, by devoting an earned income to the needs of his family and his missionary team, he would have all things in common with them as part of a group living together "by faith". This is how the Groves household was run in Baghdad, in Madras and in Chittoor. In Baghdad itself, a young Chaldean woman, Harnie Thomas, begged to join the family as an unpaid servant and remained with them on this basis for thirty-five years, sometimes in positions of great responsibility, whilst refusing to accept any formal wages.[2]

The *idea* of "living by faith" was one that appealed enormously to Groves, yet far from pointing to himself as a man of faith, or seeing his own example as one worthy to be followed, he showed every indication, after the initial excitement surrounding the early stages of his mission to Baghdad, that he felt a degree of disappointment with what he perceived as his personal failure to live up to the ideal. Indeed he often seemed surprised and pleased when others decided to do as he did. In March 1831, a first long-delayed bundle of letters brought some relief from the family's appalling sense of isolation in Baghdad, and Groves confided,

Surely no missionaries with so few pretensions to the love and confidence of the Church of God ever received more solid proofs of deep and hearty interest than we have during these ten months. This is no small point gained, and I think we may go further and add that many may be led, by this weak effort of faith in us, to take steps they might not otherwise have ventured upon... We cannot but feel that the Lord's goodness and care, which our weakness has elicited, may have moved in some small degree the hearts of the little band who are coming to join us; and I hear that their simplicity and faith has yet further stirred up the spiritual affections of others to go and do likewise.[3]

Indeed he was far more willing than some of his "faith mission" successors to admit how difficult he found it to have faith and how severely his faith was tested. For example, in 1830,

Not only did my packets bring me joyful tidings of the Lord's doings among those whom I especially know and love, they also brought me intelligence that He had prepared for me help from among those who had been known and approved, and whom I especially loved. How I felt reproved for every doubt... I am overwhelmed, and feel I can only lay my hand upon my mouth.[4]

---

[1] Groves, "Missions to the Heathen", 137
[2] M532; Groves H, *Faithful Hanie*, 17, 23-6. For Groves's view of secular work, and of stewardship in general, see PEANG,172ff.
[3] R95; M117-8
[4] M105

And three years later, in 1833, "How encouraging is James 1:5-7 to those who can realize God's love and faithfulness, and can indeed ask in faith nothing wavering, which I often feel very difficult."[1]

In later years Groves became increasingly reluctant to refer to his own experience as an example worthy of emulation. This was probably due, in large part, to the long period of financial crisis he suffered from 1842 onwards. This was a consequence of what he later considered a serious error of judgement in borrowing money to finance the expansion of his agricultural settlement at Chittoor. It was an unsolicited loan from a man who offered it as a mark of appreciation for spiritual services rendered whilst making sure that a high level of interest was specified and then obdurately insisting on its payment.[2] To borrow money was against the principles Groves had held since his earliest days as a Christian,[3] and he may have been influenced in his decision by his brother-in-law, George Baynes, who had frequently borrowed money in the past.[4] It was not until February 1853, just three months before his death, that a legacy from his wife's mother enabled him to pay off his outstanding debts and find relief from the crushing sense of oppression they had induced in him. Finally Groves could testify that even his errors had been overruled by providence for good and that God had faithfully, and graciously, provided for all his needs.[5]

The impression we have from his writings is that Groves simply had no great interest in money until he found himself, to his considerable surprise, in financial crisis. Here we might see a contrast between him and George Müller, who always took great interest in money.[6] It is a contrast that reflects their very different characters. Money came and went for Groves quite easily, and he rarely recorded the amounts and the dates. It was, perhaps, his basic disinterest in finance that allowed him to accept the loan in Chittoor. He may simply have felt that if the money could be put to good use then it was his duty to accept it, without considering the practical implications.

A fitting summary to his thought may be found in a brief entry from his journal towards the end of his life. He confided, "I desire to silence all anxieties by the thought 'the Lord will provide.'"[7] Here in a nutshell is his essentially passive attitude towards "the life of faith".

---

[1] *Memoir* 1st edn., 175 (omitted from subsequent editions)

[2] Groves E K, *Successors*, 228

[3] In his *Christian Devotedness*, he had emphasized trusting God in time of need, and giving to others in time of abundance. With Romans 13:8 in mind, he never advocated lending or borrowing. Facing the prospect of famine in Baghdad he had said, "I am determined not to borrow money till my affairs come to the utmost straits, and then only for the simplest necessities" (R305). This attitude contrasts with that of William Carey, who habitually asked for money, and borrowed whenever he was in need (George, 74, 98, 116 etc).

[4] M397; Groves E K, *Successors*, 228; Bromley, 15

[5] M486

[6] Describing "the Lord's dealings" with him throughout his life, Müller's *Narrative* contains more than 6,800 references to specific sums of money defined in terms of pounds, shillings and pence.

[7] M477

Living by Faith: A Critique

For more than a century, the concept of "living by faith" was a distinctive and popular one in evangelical circles. Klaus Fiedler documents the founding of more than thirty missionary societies on this basis in the decades immediately following 1865, and he notes that within a century more than six million converts had been gained in Africa alone by these agencies.[1] In recent years the practice of "living by faith" has been subjected to serious criticism, much of which emanates from within those same evangelical circles.

The historian Andrew Porter has described it as "the art of living constantly on the brink of bankruptcy,"[2] but there is clearly more to the idea than mere poverty. Missionaries or evangelists who "lived by faith" accepted certain ideals and principles. They had no stated salary or secular income, never asked for financial support, and never contracted debts. They would simply pray and wait for God to lead Christians (usually individual Christians rather than churches) to give. The full provision of their daily needs was considered a testimony to the existence of a prayer-hearing God, and was offered as an encouragement for others to put their trust in such a God. Timothy Larsen describes how it worked in practice:

> "Living by faith" was a radical acknowledgment that God alone was the provider for his children. A whole culture developed around stories of missionaries eating their last bowls of rice when a cheque arrived from a mysterious stranger who lived in a distant land. It was always delightful to receive money from a new source because it caused one to picture the secret planning of God which had arranged it. Indeed, many servants of the Lord did find God faithful in the most remarkable ways. The whole tradition was coloured with a deep thirst for the supernatural. Their eyes strained to see the hand of God in their circumstances. Whether or not God was faithful to meet a worker's needs was often construed as an indication of whether or not the Lord wanted that individual in the ministry. God's provision became a sign of God's will. The more exotic the income, the more certain a worker could be of his call.[3]

Larsen's analysis has been corroborated by Harold Rowdon, whose personal experience in Brethren circles of his own and his parents' generation embraces almost the entire twentieth century. He goes on to express a strong element of scepticism concerning the whole concept of "living by faith", in both theory and practice.

In his critique of the idea, Rowdon starts by looking for its biblical origins, suggesting that, "Biblically it means nothing more nor less than a life lived in union with Christ."[4] At the outset, we might consider this a little misleading. In fact, the New Testament passages where the term or its cognates are used all refer back to Habakkuk 2:4, "The righteous shall live by his faith." In every case, the consequence of faith is not "life lived in union with Christ" but justification in the sight of God.[5] Rowdon does not go on to discuss those passages. He does,

---

[1] Fiedler, 36, 102 etc.
[2] Porter, *Religion versus Empire?*, 194
[3] Larsen, "Living by Faith", Ch.2.
[4] Rowdon, "The Concept of Living by Faith", 339
[5] Rom 1:17; Gal 3:11; Heb 10:38 (all citing Hab 2:4), and also Gal 2:20, in which Paul again describes justification by faith (v.17) with the focus of his faith now explicitly fixed on Christ (Hendricksen, *Romans*, 63-4; Bruce, *Galatians*, 144). It is likely that the underlying

however, describe how the term has acquired, in some evangelical circles, and particularly in Brethren circles, a meaning which he considers unwarranted as an extrapolation from any scriptural principle:

> But in some evangelical thinking, particularly in the field of missiology, a concept has arisen which – in practice – restricts the term to a select group of believers who exercise faith not only for their salvation and, some would add for their sanctification, but also for the supply of their material needs. So, instead of relying on any kind of contractual arrangement by which they are guaranteed a regular stipend, or even appealing for voluntary aid, they make known their needs only to God, and look by faith to him to meet them by whatever means he chooses, particularly – some would say only – by moving the hearts of his people to give without otherwise being aware of those needs. This might be described as the "rigorist" concept of "living by faith". Much more common is the less rigorist concept which excludes only specific requests for material help, and does not exclude the giving of information which, directly or indirectly, draws attention to the existence of needs.[1]

There follows a description of how this practice gained wide acceptance from the mid-nineteenth to the mid-twentieth century: "The concept has become well known through its adoption by a plethora of 'faith missions', the most famous of which was the one which did much to disseminate the idea, the China Inland Mission, founded by J Hudson Taylor in 1865."[2] And significantly for our study, "But the concept did not originate with Hudson Taylor. If he was its father, then George Müller was its grandfather and Anthony Norris Groves its great-grandfather."[3]

Our immediate task is to ascertain how far the later practices observed and critiqued by Rowdon and Larsen concord with the principles followed by Groves himself. Attempting to identify Groves's personal view of the matter, Rowdon refers us to *Christian Devotedness*, where "Groves appeals primarily to a literal interpretation of Matthew 6:19-34." Groves does indeed recommend a literal application of Christ's instructions, "Lay not up for yourselves treasures on earth… Seek first the kingdom of God… Take no thought for the morrow," and he does so in full confidence that the accompanying promise will be fulfilled: "all these things shall be added unto you." And Rowdon notes other scriptures used by Groves in his exposition of the subject.[4] He considers Groves's advice influential: "It is significant that both Müller and Hudson Taylor appeal to such scriptural passages, particularly Matthew 6:34 which may be regarded as the key text claimed in support of the concept of 'living by faith'. This is in line with their indebtedness to Groves."[5]

Aramaic *ḥayyē* "means both 'life' and 'salvation'" (Guthrie *et al.*, 1016-7; see also 1098, 1210).

[1] Rowdon, Ibid, 340
[2] Ibid
[3] Ibid
[4] These include Mark 12:41 and Luke 18:22-30; Acts 2:44-45; 4:32, 34, 35 and 2 Cor 8:9, 13-15.
[5] Rowdon cites Müller, *Narrative* (1895 edn.) I:84 and Hudson Taylor, *Retrospect* (Lutterworth, 1951 edn.), 112.

Despite this, we might observe that Groves in his *Christian Devotedness* only once uses the expression "living by faith",[1] and when he does so, he neither quotes nor alludes to Habakkuk 2:4 or its New Testament citations. If others might be thought to have misapplied the biblical text, Groves himself does not.

We may, nevertheless, substitute another biblical term, "walking by faith", and find Groves's principles very much akin to those of the apostle Paul.[2] In Paul's thought, to "walk by faith" simply means to trust and obey God rather than man. In 2 Corinthians 5, Paul links "walking by faith" (v.7) with making it one's aim "to please him [i.e. the Lord]" (v.9). The link is all the more significant when we remember that Groves, Müller and Taylor each withdrew from missionary societies whose requirements conflicted with their personal perception of God's will; they found it impossible both to please the society and "to please him". Faced with this tension they chose to "live by faith". This is the origin of the concept as understood by Groves.

Larsen argues that, in adopting Groves's idea, the Brethren turned it gradually and imperceptibly into a rigid system that differed substantially from his far more flexible practice. They did so, moreover, for reasons which were essentially negative. The reasons were: (1) a concern to avoid creating a salaried ministerial elite; (2) a resistance to a centralised organisation of any sort; (3) a dislike of any system of human authority or accountability. In Larsen's view, the adoption of this new financial *modus operandi* was motivated by a deeply rooted fear of power, and especially the abuse of power, in the church: "The Brethren were afraid of the power of a denominational structure. They were afraid of the power of a missionary society. They were afraid of both the power of a church leader to oppress his congregation and the power of the congregation to manipulate their preacher." "Living by faith", then, was not so much the recovery of a long-lost biblical ideal, but rather a pragmatic reaction to perceived corruptions in the organised churches and missions of the day.

But Larsen then offers a rather misleading assertion: "A remarkable number of the early Brethren leaders were men of wealth. They found it spiritually exhilarating to abandon their favoured position and trust solely in the Living God. This experience was so successful and meaningful for them that they enthusiastically endorsed it for all."[3] We must question this. The fact is that, of the chief exponents of the idea, neither Müller nor Taylor ever possessed wealth, and Groves himself, throughout his missionary career, remained a poor man beset by financial crises. To live this way was no doubt "spiritually exhilarating" but we should not be led to suppose that "living by faith" was an idea proposed by rich Christians who took pleasure in a novel and rather romantic experience of poverty. Most of those who "lived by faith" came from families at the lower end of the social scale, and having gone overseas, suffered "straitened circumstances" often for weeks, months and years on end.[4]

---

[1] As quoted above, "I can with my whole heart pray for myself and all who are nearest and dearest to me that we be so circumstanced in life as to be compelled to live by faith on the divine promises day by day" (D22).

[2] The NIV actually renders 2 Cor 5:7 "We live by faith…".

[3] Larsen, Ch.2

[4] Groves's missionary recruits, Bowden and Beer, were a semi-literate stonemason and shoemaker. "Living by faith" in India, they and their families subsisted on porridge made

Rowdon, nevertheless, develops Larsen's idea that, for missionaries and others "engaged in full-time Christian ministry", there were definite advantages perceived in this method of obtaining financial support. In particular:

1. It will free the missionary from human control. He cannot be forced by his paymasters, or be tempted for the sake of his salary, to teach doctrines or engage in practices contrary to his conscience or his own sense of God's guidance.

2. It will test the missionary's call. If his motives are wrong, or if he has mistaken his guidance, he will find his prayers for God's provision unanswered, and thus he will simply come home.

3. It will provide a testimony to God's faithfulness. He will see people, both at home and on the mission field, drawn to faith by the evidence that God hears and answers prayer.

4. It will deepen the relationship between the missionary and his Lord. He will be compelled to trust and obey God, living in practical holiness, diligent in his work, seeking first the kingdom of God and therefore assured of God's promised provision.

All this is undoubtedly true and, one might think, beneficial. But Rowdon goes on to express serious doubts about the validity of this method of financing mission: "From the perspective of evangelical Christian faith, there is nothing inherently dubious about the concept of trusting an all-powerful, loving and compassionate God to hear and answer the prayers of his people. Far from it. But the point at issue is whether this is the way in which he expects them to meet their financial obligations."[1] Rowdon questions whether advocates of "living by faith" have been justified in claiming scriptural support for their position of asking God alone for financial provision. He denies that the apostle Paul lived "by faith" in the manner of Brethren missionaries. He doubts that the "hard sayings" of Jesus in the Sermon on the Mount should be taken literally. Indeed, he argues that it would be entirely impractical for all Christians to do what Jesus proposes.[2] He remarks, "It could even be said that *some* Christians are able to live by faith only because *others* do not."[3] In fact, Rowdon concludes, "He [Jesus] was not laying down a way of life for his followers (a 'new law') but was teaching principles which could be applied in a variety of ways."[4]

Rowdon then argues that Paul repeatedly claimed the right to financial support from those to whom he ministered (although choosing to forgo that right), which means that modern missionaries can feel justified in *claiming* such a right and receiving such support. Rowdon adds that Paul enjoyed on at least one occasion the hospitality of the unconverted, as did the twelve and the seventy disciples when sent out as itinerant missionaries.[5]

---

from "the commonest coarse black grain", and admitted that "the Lord has brought down our appetites to what he gives us to feed them on" (Bromley, 41-2, 60).

[1] Rowdon, Ibid, 346
[2] A "Minister of the Establishment" made the same point in 1838 (A Minister, *Perpetuity*, 7-8, 17).
[3] Rowdon, Ibid, 346
[4] Ibid, 346. Rowdon suggests that trust in God might thus be expressed quite differently in other circumstances. For example, the twelve and the seventy sent out with no reserves, and the Jerusalem church pooling its resources, are two possible historical applications of principles that could be quite differently applied in other contexts (Ibid, 347).
[5] Acts 28:7; Lk 9:1-4; 10:1-8

How might Groves respond to these assertions? Whatever our view of the matter, he himself undoubtedly considered the Sermon on the Mount a practical "rule of life" for all disciples of Christ.[1] He also regarded Paul as a model missionary, whose methods he would follow as closely as possible.[2] He would be unlikely to concur with Rowdon's advocacy of a practice contrary to that of the apostle (for if the apostle chose to ignore a hypothetical "right", then so would Groves himself). He would also see no necessary conflict between enjoying the hospitality of a non-Christian home and living "by faith", pointing out that when Paul did so, he happened to be under arrest (and amply repaid his host's generosity by healing his father), and that the disciples of Jesus were sent as rabbis to their own people rather than as cross-cultural missionaries to the "heathen". We might assume Groves well capable of answering such objections.

In practical terms, Rowdon's antipathy to the tradition of "living by faith" is intensified by its perceived tendency to create a spiritual elite of "workers" and "missionaries" supposedly living on a higher spiritual plane than ordinary Christians: "Another irony is that a practical result of the concept which, as we have seen, arose in part from a desire to avoid the creation of a salaried elite has been to create an *unsalaried* one! For there can be no doubt that, however loudly it may be denied, those who 'live by faith' in a way that cannot be attained by those who, for example, earn their living, *do* constitute an elite."[3]

Jonathan Ingleby, in a review of Rowdon's paper, agrees that "within the Brethren movement itself... the practice created an elite." His own early experience of Brethren evidently parallels that of Rowdon, for he describes how "he encountered a theoretically egalitarian society ('the priesthood of all believers') rigidly structured in a hierarchical fashion. Missionaries 'living by faith' were at the top of this hierarchical structure, as against, for example, the clergy in some other Christian traditions."[4]

Statements of this nature can, however, be considerably misleading. Evidence abounds that the Brethren ideal of "living by faith" was by no means restricted to their missionaries. Geoffrey T Bull, for example, writes of his father-in-law in the early twentieth century: "In his thirties, in order to support his growing family, he quite daringly opened a poultry farm at Langbank over Milngavie. He was sorely tested but learned to live by faith... How tirelessly he plied his spade to the ground. Yet he was never so busy that he could not stand a while and talk to his Saviour."[5] For this labouring man, and for many like him, "living by faith" meant trusting God to provide for his family through a secular income that was both limited and variable.

Furthermore, a young missionary in his or her early twenties was certainly not considered to be at the top of any hierarchical structure. Even a man with many years of missionary service behind him, though respected and, in some cases, deeply admired, would rarely, if ever, be consulted about matters relating to the leadership of his home church. His missionary wife or sister would be similarly respected and admired, but, as a woman, would certainly not be asked to teach or

---

[1] See PEANG, 136ff.
[2] See above, 131ff.
[3] Rowdon, Ibid, 352
[4] Ingleby, review of Rowdon, 61-2
[5] Bull, *The Rock and the Sand*, 10-11

have authority over any of the men in the assembly. Granted that the "faith missionary" might sometimes have been considered a superior type of Christian, his position lay outside the authority structure of the church that supported him. His role was quite different from that of a paid pastor or clergyman in other Christian traditions.

Ingleby concludes his review of Rowdon's article with the words, "In summary, then, the concept and practice of 'living by faith' had far more to do with issues of control and identity than with the discovery and implementation of a new biblical or theological insight."[1] In reply it could be suggested that these very issues of "control" and "identity" had required and received radical reform in the light of fresh biblical and theological insight. To Groves's mind, the manipulative power of money was a far greater danger than any potential lack of it: "Want of money is, therefore, as I have observed, the least thing to be feared, but [far more to be feared are] unholy inducements to do holy things."[2] Missionaries living "by faith" were freed from the "control" of a denomination and from the "identity" of a voluntary society. This they considered a distinct advantage.

It is sometimes said that those aspiring to "live by faith" went to extremes in following Hudson Taylor's motto of "moving men through God by prayer alone"[3] and refusing to do anything in response to particular needs apart from praying. Rowdon claims to have observed in the Brethren circles of his youth a resistance to anything that might be considered a "use of means", and he goes so far as to contrast this with what he considered to be the practice of Hudson Taylor.

The fact is that Hudson Taylor viewed the founding of the CIM as an act of faith *in contrast to* the raising of ways and means. In his own words, "I saw that the Apostolic plan was not to raise ways and means, but *to go and do the work*, trusting in his sure word who has said, 'Seek ye *first* the Kingdom of God and his righteousness and all these things shall be added unto you.'"[4] Yet, as the mission developed, Rowdon rightly observes that its finances were very carefully organised. Indeed, Taylor later advised, "The use of means ought not to lessen our faith in God; and our faith in God ought not to hinder whatever means he has given us for the accomplishment of his own purposes."[5] We thus find the CIM demonstrating how the practice of "living by faith" could be entirely compatible with the systematic collection and distribution of funds, and with frequent appeals for recruits and for prayer.

Rowdon finds the Brethren, in contrast, too prone to exalt supernatural means above natural means. It is perhaps surprising, then, to find him condemning Brethren missionaries for their very willingness to use natural means: "It is a fact that most missionaries who 'live by faith' spend a considerable proportion of their time (sometimes a third) telling people in their home countries about the work they are doing." As a form of accountability, he admits this type of "missionary report" may be justified, and also as a means of stimulating prayer, "but, unintentionally no doubt, it fulfils a further function – that of drawing attention to the existence of

---

[1] Ingleby, Ibid, 62
[2] Groves, *Influence*, 60
[3] Taylor, *Retrospect*, 21
[4] *Retrospect*, 112
[5] *Retrospect*, 45

material needs. At its worst it can degenerate into subtle hints (e.g. a request to 'pray with me for the provision of [this or that]').[1]

We might wonder how fair it is to condemn the Brethren both for using means and for failing to use means, but their essential error, according to Rowdon, lies in claiming one and practising the other. They use "subtle" means whilst professing the opposite. He suggests that the claim to "live by faith" has become in some cases, perhaps in many cases, a charade – a form of hypocrisy which should be exposed and abandoned. His final sentence presents his recommendation, "Perhaps the time has come to allow the phrase 'living by faith' to fall into disuse."

The evidence, from modern Britain at least, is that the phrase is already in disuse. Evangelical missionaries now rarely speak of "living by faith" and when they do, usually meet with incomprehension. In this regard, Rowdon is surely right to remark that, "In order for it to 'work', it requires not only a highly developed faith on the part of those who live by it (and a prayer-answering God!) but also keen spiritual sensitivity on the part of Christians with the resources to be the channels by which God is to meet their needs."[2]

The system worked best when there were many such Christians in Britain and America, converted initially through the revivals of 1858-9, whose children grew up in the tradition of Keswick and the popular missionary conferences of the "faith missions" and the Brethren in the mid-twentieth century.[3] These generations respected and often admired their missionaries, and believed their work to be important and worthy of wholehearted support. Such feelings are less commonly found in our own day. The system seems largely to have broken down, and the reason may lie not so much in a lack of missionary faith, nor in a divine reluctance to answer prayer, but rather in a progressive dwindling of that "keen spiritual sensitivity" which formerly characterised large numbers of evangelical Christians. The increasingly slick and manipulative "use of means" in wider evangelical circles has surely contributed to the apathy, and perhaps even cynicism, felt by many Evangelicals towards their missionaries. But along with this, and perhaps more importantly, we see in our own day a serious erosion of personal confidence in God, and in the Bible, which could be attributed to the general prevalence of relativistic views of truth and of hedonistic materialism, even among Evangelicals in the churches. The whole system of "living by faith", like that of Christian devotedness, has become anachronistic, a study of passing interest to the occasional historian rather than a way of life admired and approved by large numbers of Christians in Britain.

Living by Faith: Some Early Applications

Groves obviously cannot be blamed for whatever misuse and abuse may have attached itself in later generations to the concept of "living by faith". There are, indeed, discernable differences between his practice and that of subsequent Brethren and "faith missions".

In particular we might think of his willingness to engage in secular employment. Among Open Brethren, George H Lang, in 1939, regarded Groves's

---

[1] Rowdon, Ibid, 354
[2] Ibid, 353
[3] On Keswick, see PEANG, 185ff.

adoption of money-making schemes as a regrettable lapse from the life of faith.[1] The missionaries of Rowdon's acquaintance also seem to have assumed a sharp dichotomy between the practice of praying for funds and that of earning them through gainful employment. In contrast, we shall see how fully Groves advocated the partnership of Christian mission and Christian industry.[2] Indeed, he wished to provide a regular salary for the young Arulappan in his work as a translator, and when the Indian refused it, the reason he gave was not biblical but practical: "Dear Aroolappen has declined any form of salary, because the people, he says, would not cease to tell him that he preached because he was hired. When he left me, I wished to settle something upon him monthly, as remuneration for his labour in translating for us; but, unlike a native, he refused any stipulated sum."[3] Groves maintained this flexible attitude throughout his life. Shortly before his death he confided, "In writing to dear Aroolappen, I tell him not to lay too much stress on… unpaid ministry."[4]

Larsen suggests that for Groves, "living by faith" was "the only available option for him and others like him who came to believe that missionary societies were unbiblical." In fact, there were a number of other options available to him. He could have solicited penny subscriptions, or requested a salary from the expatriates to whom he ministered. He could have advertised his schools publicly as worthy of investment, applied to wealthy and philanthropic benefactors, or appealed to agencies such as the British and Foreign Schools Society (which had already offered him assistance in Baghdad).[5] He could have engaged in all manner of fund-raising activities. The fact that he chose not to do so should be attributed to his concern to follow apostolic methods rather than to any lack of alternative options.

The effect of Groves's example on George Müller has often been noted. Resigning from the LSPCJ, Müller observed,

> I had no anxiety; for I considered, that, as long as I really sought to serve the Lord, that is, as long as I sought the kingdom of God and His righteousness, these my temporal supplies would be added to me. The Lord most mercifully enabled me to take the promises of His word, and rest upon them… In addition to this, the example of brother Groves, the dentist… was a great encouragement to me.[6]

In January 1833 Müller received an invitation from Groves to join his mission in Baghdad. Weighing up the pros and cons, Müller noted one strong reason for going: "The going out without any visible support from a society, simply trusting in the Lord for the supply of our temporal wants, would be a testimony for him."[7]

---

[1] Lang, *Groves*, 314-8
[2] See below, 162ff.
[3] M392
[4] M481-2
[5] R214-5. A number of missionaries known to Groves were supported by individual patrons in Britain. One evangelist to the Jews was "sent out principally by Mr J E of Edinburgh" (M282). Another was working "under the auspices of Mr. Scott and Mrs. Rich" (M531-2). Others, such as William Start of Patna, had private means which they retained, unlike Groves, for their own support (Coates to Blumhardt, 17th Feb. 1835).
[6] Müller, *Narrative*, I, 52
[7] Ibid, I, 99

Larsen places this idea of "testimony" high among Müller's motivations in launching his first orphan house:

> George Müller lived in an age in which many orthodox Christians felt a great deal of anxiety about the rise of popular infidelity and therefore had a deep desire to refute the rationalistic scepticism which was sometimes used to argue against traditional teachings... It did not solve Müller's problem if God gave the individual daily bread through a salary. It did not speak to his point if orphans were provided for by an orchestrated effort of philanthropy. He wanted to find a way to show that God was miraculously at work – the only sphere that seemed to be left for God alone. If people could see a miracle, if they could see a direct response to prayer, it would restore their confidence in a personal, living God. The orphanage was run entirely on the principles of "living by faith". It was undertaken without a commitment from any person or institution to finance it and it never solicited funds or stated its needs. These conditions were necessary in order to prove that it was the Lord, not the schemes of individuals, that was sustaining the work.

This may be a valid analysis in the case of Müller, but there is no evidence that Groves had followed this line of thought. We do not find in Groves's writings any particular "anxiety about the rise of popular infidelity", or any particular concern "to show that God was miraculously at work." Whilst anticipating that God's provision would "illustrate his love", Groves was not motivated by a desire to demonstrate anything new to Christian observers, nor to "restore their confidence in a personal, living God."[1] The benefit he had in mind was not primarily for those who observed it but rather for those who practised it. "Living by faith on the promises" was simply a means of fulfilling the Great Commission in the way that Christ intended.

Rufus Anderson questioned whether Müller's "faith principles" differed at all from those followed at the same period by the American Board. He remarked,

> The enterprise of the celebrated Müller, in England, is often spoken of as if it were peculiarly a work of faith. It does not seem to me to be so very peculiar in this respect. That of the American Board, in appropriating half a million of dollars and more for an expenditure a year before it is received is not less a work of faith. The trust in God is the same in nature, the same in degree; and so, substantially, is the use of means. This is true as to the support of every missionary. The pledge given by the missionary society of a support to its missionaries is nothing more than the expression of an assured faith that the means will be provided. The Board can give no more than it receives. There is no firm footing for the society, or for its missionaries, except in the promise of the great Lord of all. If the missionary feels sure of a support, it is for precisely the reason that is said to animate the celebrated philanthropist just named.[2]

But there were significant differences. Neither Müller nor the "faith missions" who followed his example appealed for funds. Nor did they take out subscriptions or pass round collecting bags. They did not accept "pledges", which donors might subsequently regret or be unable to fulfil. They accepted nothing from the unconverted, and they refused to contract debts. They offered no stated salary to

---

[1] When Groves declared "the great object of our lives is to illustrate his love to us" (R97), the context shows us that his thoughts related far more to protection from danger and disease than to financial provision.
[2] Anderson, *Foreign Missions*, Ch.9, in Beaver, *To Advance*, 201-2

their missionaries and conferred no ordained status or guarantee of future security. These were significant differences.

It was around the time of his marriage to Groves's sister Mary in October 1832 that Müller himself "began to have conscientious objections against any longer receiving a stated salary."[1] His objections, again, were practical rather than directly scriptural. His wages had previously been guaranteed by the payment of pew-rents, a system that discriminated between rich and poor, and by a quarterly collection which might put church members under pressure to contribute, perhaps reluctantly, what they could ill afford. But more significantly, he was unwilling to suffer constraint in his teaching ministry by the possibility of wealthy contributors taking umbrage and publicly refusing to make their agreed contribution. And he admitted that when additional expenses arose, through travel for example, he simply felt uncomfortable asking the church for more money.[2]

The same could probably be said for Groves. Larsen suggests that "Müller's primary concern was for voluntary giving." But we might conjecture that, along with this, went a natural human reluctance to place oneself in a position of vulnerability or of obligation to others. We might even wonder whether the custom of never expressing a need for money actually represents a nineteenth-century upper-middle-class sensibility (a particular concern for good manners, tact and discretion) rather than any identifiable biblical principle. Significant to this may be the fact that the early leaders of the Brethren were drawn largely from upper-middle class and aristocratic circles. Typically they were lawyers, landowners, doctors, schoolmasters, private tutors, businessmen, former military officers or clergymen.[3] Such people, enjoying a genteel upbringing and a cultured education, would not readily mention, let alone ask for, money. To do so would be either a mark of weakness or a sign of dissipation. Indeed, as Embley remarks, "The originators of the Brethren were men of restraint and decorum. The resulting delicacy in worship and social convention among the Brethren probably explains why much later in the nineteenth century well-to-do people often found it easier to pass from Anglicanism to Plymouth Brethrenism than to many longer-established dissenting churches."[4]

Some observers might thus discern, in this rather fastidious attitude towards "filthy lucre", evidence of a dualistic, Platonic world-view, using prayer as a righteous means of obtaining unrighteous mammon – a method well-suited to the social elite of the British Isles.[5] Müller, however, was a Prussian, not an upper-class Englishman, and there is no evidence that he or Groves (or any of the "faith mission" pioneers) considered money an unmentionable evil.[6] On the contrary they regarded its provision as a great blessing, and although Groves rarely writes of his financial dealings, Müller was by no means reluctant to fill his *Narrative of the*

---

[1] Müller, *Narrative*, I, 68
[2] *Narrative*, I, 69
[3] Embley, 215-6
[4] Embley, 216
[5] See Chilcraft, Ch.6.
[6] When Groves writes of "laying up poisonous heaps of gold", he merely condemns the accumulation of excess (*Memoir* 1st edn., 27).

Lord's Dealings with references to money, or to pray for the provision of specific sums.[1]

Neither did Müller have any scruples about offering his assistants a salary. On the contrary, he seemed to consider it eminently desirable. On 29th November 1838, for example, he reported, "I rejoice in the last donation particularly, not because of the largeness of the sum, but because it enabled me to pay my brethren and sisters in the Orphan House the salary which is due them. For though they are willing to labour without any remuneration, nevertheless 'the labourer is worthy of his reward.'"[2] The "masters and governesses" clearly viewed their salaries as a very flexible form of income. When funds were low, they would assemble with the Müllers to pray for God's provision. On 12th December 1840, for example, Müller reported, "The School-Funds are also now again very low. There was only so much money in hand, as that two of the teachers, really in need, could be paid today. Truly, my dear fellow-labourers in the schools need to trust the Lord for their temporal supplies!" Müller himself adds a clarification:

> I notice here, that though the brethren and sisters have a certain remuneration, yet it is understood that, if the Lord should not be pleased to send in the means at the time when their salary is due, I am not considered their debtor. Should the Lord be pleased to send in means afterwards, the remainder of the salary is paid up, and also additional assistance is given in time of sickness or more than usual need, as the Lord may be pleased to grant the means. A brother or sister, in connection with this work, not looking for themselves to the Lord, would be truly uncomfortable; for the position of all of us is of such a character, that it brings heavy trials of faith, in addition to the many precious seasons of joy on account of answers to prayer.[3]

In the course of this study we have seen how Müller and Groves together set the pattern for Brethren financial policy, and in this regard Larsen's conclusion is a fair one:

> The founders of Brethrenism engaged in something like "living by faith", although their understanding of this mode of life was at the same time both more flexible and more radical than what eventually emerged as the Brethren position. It was more radical because it was grounded in a conviction that every Christian should give away all of their possessions and depend on the Lord only for help for the future. To the early leaders, "living by faith" was something for Christians to do, not simply Christian workers. It was more flexible because at least some of them believed a worker could receive a salary and still be depending completely on the Lord.

Here, as in so many spheres of life, we see Groves's idealism adopted and adapted, his spontaneous flexibility turned, over the course of time, into a formal system with unwritten rules and expectations that he could hardly have envisaged. His interest in "living by faith" stemmed from his concern to follow biblical principles, claim biblical promises, and enjoy a close prayerful relationship with his Lord. As applied by George Müller, Hudson Taylor and subsequent generations of "faith

---

[1] Perhaps he was influenced in this by his early admiration for August Hermann Francke, who "knew how to combine faith and calculation, Christian shrewdness and true piety in a masterful fashion" (Danker, *Profit for the Lord*,18).

[2] *Narrative*, II

[3] *Narrative*, III

missions", the practice of "living by faith" became widely accepted and appreciated.

In conclusion, we should remember that the idea of "living by faith" was not the unique property of English-speaking missionaries. The indigenous movements associated with John Arulappan, Watchman Nee and Bakht Singh all deliberately adopted the practice. One example from Arulappan must suffice to illustrate a lifetime's experience of praying for his immediate needs to be met. In 1855 he bought an old printing press, "when I had nothing, except our humble prayers, for a week's time... the Lord helped me through his children who love him."[1] In 1847 Groves remarked, "I think dear George Müller would be comforted in hearing an Indian speak that language of faith to which his own heart would so fully respond."[2] Thirteen years later, Arulappan's principles were unchanged: "I never ask my friends for money, but leave it altogether in my Lord's hand."[3]

Nee, for one, was alert to the dangers that Rowdon identifies, and took care to avoid them. He advised, "There is no need for us to devise means to draw attention to our work. God in his sovereign providence can well bear that responsibility... I feel repelled when I hear God's servants emphasize the fact that they are living by faith... I would counsel my younger brethren to keep silence not only about their personal needs but about their faith in God, so that they may the better be able to prove him. The more faith there is, the less talk there will be about it."[4]

A critic might perceive a measure of hypocrisy in some who have claimed to live by faith, but we would be unwise to tar all with that brush. More serious attention should be given, in particular, to those indigenous movements that deliberately drew their principles from scripture and from the personal example of Groves, Müller and Hudson Taylor.

Accountability

Since earliest times the principle of accountability has figured large in the functioning of "voluntary societies".[5] Groves, in seeking a better way of financing church and mission, ignored traditional ideas of human accountability. He believed that mission should not be managed like a business venture but rather nurtured as a labour of love, driven not by money but by the Spirit of God. As a missionary he would see himself not as a member of a particular society with its headquarters in a specific location, but as a member of the body of Christ in whatever place he happened to be. Indeed, Groves believed that his ideal of "living by faith", looking to God alone for direction and financial support, had this advantage, that it freed the missionary from the bondage to human expectations and human control underlying all contractual relationships. It would make the missionary accountable not to a board or a committee, or even a sending church, but directly and personally to God himself.

Setting out for the East with no promise of financial support from anyone, he wrote to William Caldecott, "I know no state where such close communion with God is necessarily kept up, as where you are almost placed, like the ravens, to be

---

[1] Lang, *Aroolappen*, 120
[2] M447
[3] M609
[4] Kinnear, *A Table in the Wilderness*, entry for 25th March
[5] See above, 77ff.

fed day by day from your Father's hands."[1] Dependant on divine providence for his food and clothing, such a missionary must take great care in his relationship with his divine provider. A moment of sin could cause not merely an hour of regret but a day of hunger, or a year of discomfort and distress. The discipline of God was far more to be feared than that of a committee or a secretary.

Then, just as the missionary must keep short accounts with God, so too must his supporters. The knowledge that the missionary had gone out "by faith" would encourage them to seek continuous guidance from above in the stewardship of their personal resources and in the gifts they sent. Indeed they might feel that the missionary's health, his work and even his life, depended directly on their own sensitivity to divine guidance. This meant that the relationship between the missionary and those who financed him was built on a sense of trust and honour rather than of obligation or accountability, and the primary link between them would be prayer to the God who knew the exact circumstances of each.[2]

Groves's early experiences will have played a part in the development of his thinking on this subject. As a CMS candidate (1825-7), Groves was, according to all the evidence, a model recruit, attentive to every suggestion from the London committee, and almost excessively eager to please. Labouring, whilst maintaining his dental practice, to master Latin, Greek, Hebrew, and to make a start in Arabic and modern Greek as they advised, he wrote, "I trust that in the end I may not disappoint your hopes, yet at times when I contemplate the necessary requisites even of a natural kind in the station to which you have thought it best to direct my thoughts, I am almost overcome with the sense of their magnitude."[3]

The members of the CMS committee were generally drawn, at this time, from social circles considerably superior to those of their paid agents, and were inclined to direct them rather forcefully. Timothy Stunt describes their "authoritarian paternalism", and notes that "more than one of the young continentals who spent time in London has left a record of how insensitive he found the CMS authorities."[4] But Groves was a different kind of recruit, and enjoyed a measure of social equality with the London secretary: "He was well educated and if not yet a graduate, he soon would be; he was older, in his thirties (barely ten years younger than Bickersteth), with almost a dozen years of professional experience; his income was far from negligible; and he was English."[5] He was also headed for a sphere of service (Persia) where he would be on his own, and forced by circumstances to make decisions and arrangements. This might have inclined the committee to view tolerantly his request for some special dispensation, and he was disappointed at its refusal. He recalled, "I went to London, to arrange my going out as a layman, for

---

[1] Letter to William Caldecott, June 1825 (M12), referring to Lk 12:24.
[2] Ted Ward has recently observed that "The habit of insisting on the rights of authorizing the budget and monitoring the expenditures has destroyed many relationships between the mission and the church-on-the-field. As local Western churches are becoming more directly involved in fiscal and personnel support for overseas projects, this budgetary tyranny has become stronger than ever." He concludes, "God is not honoured when control is a stronger value than trust" (Ward, "Repositioning Mission Agencies").
[3] Groves to Bickersteth, 14th March [1826]
[4] Stunt, "International Context", The CMS Connection
[5] Ibid

the Church Missionary Society; but as they would not allow me to celebrate the Lord's Supper, when no other minister was near, it came to nothing."[1]

His CMS candidature was thus terminated, and without any apparent ill-will on either side.[2] It marked a stage in Groves's progress towards secession from the Church of England. The cumulative effect, over eighteen months, of his withdrawal from Trinity College, of his questioning the Thirty-nine Articles, of his decision against seeking Anglican ordination, of the negative response of the CMS to his proposals, all no doubt contributed to a growing disillusionment with denominational requirements and ecclesiastical authorities.[3] It left him considerably perplexed: "My mind was then in great straits; for I saw not yet my liberty of ministry to be from Christ alone."[4]

The public conflict between Joshua Marshman and the BMS in the spring of 1827 may have helped Groves reach a decision which brought him substantial relief. The following year, he realised that he possessed "liberty in Christ to minister the word,"[5] without submitting to such forms of human accountability. Shortly afterwards he remarked, "I cannot tell you how comfortable it is to be independent of everything but the sunshine of the Lord's countenance."[6] And again, "May the Lord grant to us a spirit of simple dependence upon Him, and determination to call no man our master upon earth; for man changes and the Lord remains the same, and all who seek him diligently shall find Him."[7]

Groves has been dubbed "an incurable individualist",[8] and he was pleased to find scriptural justification for his form of individualism. In his Indian journal,

> Today I have been much struck with the stress the apostle, in his epistle to the Galatians, lays on his commission not being in any measure human; and that the way in which the apostles were led to give him and Barnabas the right hand of fellowship was that they saw the grace that was given to them. Perhaps you may think I am proud in not submitting to human authority, but of this, indeed, my heart does not accuse me. In all civil matters I will willingly be subject, but the liberty of the church is not mine to yield.[9]

His concept of spiritual liberty led Groves to argue that a Bible teacher is answerable not to his superiors but to those he teaches. And even to them he is accountable only for godliness of life and soundness of teaching (not for the stewardship of time or money). And if his teaching meets with disapproval in one place, he is free to take it elsewhere if sensing a call from God to do so.[10]

But Groves's reluctance to be under human authority would not make him irresponsible. Indeed, his refusal to be subject to the control of man added enormously to his sense of accountability to God. He insisted,

---

[1] M42
[2] There is no reference in the CMS archives to Groves's resignation, although several earlier letters and minutes relating to his candidature have survived.
[3] Groves's secession is discussed in PEANG, 91ff.
[4] M42
[5] M43
[6] M238
[7] M466
[8] Stunt, *Awakening*, 142
[9] M244-5
[10] See PEANG, 122ff.

> Whilst we profess, my very dear friends, absolute freedom from man's control in the things relating to God, we only acknowledge in a tenfold degree the absoluteness of our subjection to the whole mind and will of Christ in all things. As He is our life, which is hid with Him in God, so let Him be our way and our truth, both in doctrine and conversation. How many, from the neglect of this lovely union, have almost forgotten to care about adorning the doctrine of God their Saviour in all things.[1]

Groves, in fact, chafed against any "system" restricting the freedom of the individual to follow a sense of divine leading. He remarked, "Whatever beauty there may be in natural order for natural purposes, the very moment you apply that kind of order to spiritual purposes, you supersede the order of the Spirit, setting up the external for the internal, confounding that which is natural, and the creation of man, with that which is spiritual, and blows like the wind, 'where it listeth'."[2] He observed that the apostle Paul, on one occasion, abandoned a place of usefulness on account of his personal feelings. Would any missionary society countenance such irregularity from its salaried agents?

> Did it ever strike you that Paul (2 Cor. 2:12), though he had a door opened to him of the Lord at Troas, had no rest because he found not Titus, but took leave of them and went into Macedonia? How few would have sympathy with anyone now in stating a similar reason for quitting a position, where he had work to do. When I read God's word I always feel relief. I see man as he is, a poor, weak being, and have no thought of contemplating him in another point of view. But it seems to me often, that Christians now often endeavour to show their Christianity by the unearthly rules they propose for others, considering a missionary as a mere spiritual existence, rather than by the holiness and devotedness of their own walk.[3]

If he demanded liberty of ministry for himself, he also allowed it to others. In 1826, when his children's tutor, Robert Nesbit, left for missionary service in India, Groves remarked, "In this decision of his I cannot help rejoicing, yet my joy is more mixed than it ought to be, with sorrow for the loss we are about to sustain."[4] It was the first of many such losses. In July 1838, he said farewell to his most promising missionary recruits, Hermann Gundert and Julie Dubois, when they married and joined the Basel Mission.[5] In 1840, he saw John Arulappan and his young wife leaving Chittoor for a new venture in Madurai. Losing friends and co-workers was always a sorrow for Groves, but he refused to stand in the way of their personal guidance from God. His wife Harriet recalled, "He cheerfully gave up his most valued fellow-labourers if they felt the Lord had led them to another sphere of service… He liked all with him to feel themselves the *Lord's servants*."[6]

The Lord's servants they were, and accountable to God, not to him. But the key passage in Groves's writings on this subject comes in his journal during his journey to Baghdad in the autumn of 1830: "The more I see of missions and missionary undertakings, the more I am convinced of the importance of their acting

---

[1] R37
[2] M314. On Groves's view of "systems", see PEANG, 102ff.
[3] M242-3
[4] Groves to Bickersteth, 14th March [1826]
[5] M372, 378
[6] M371

on their individual responsibility before God, and not in bodies, or subject to the control the one of the other, unless of their own freewill."[1] Whilst Groves himself was clearly the leader of the mission in Baghdad, and later in Madras and Chittoor, he had no formal authority over his co-workers. He did not pay them or direct them. His leadership depended on prayer, persuasion and a godly example. He admitted, "This way might seem fraught with many evils, but certainly with much fewer than that which ties men together against their own will. Nothing can be more uncongenial to a Christian than ruling at all, but particularly when there is unwillingness to submit."[2]

Groves hoped that the missionaries and other Christians working with him would all experience the leading of the Holy Spirit and thus (like the early Jerusalem church) be of one mind. Yet he wished no individual to suppress a strong personal leading in order to conform to an official view or an approved policy: "Missionary work is peculiarly difficult for men to labour in together unless the parties are quite of one mind, particularly in the complicated difficulties arising from the best mode of treating fallen churches, Mohammedans and Heathens, in which unity of judgment depends not merely on the truth but on the character of mind of the missionaries"[3]

As always, it was liberty of ministry and *liberty to minister* that Groves valued most highly. Here lay the root of his overriding concern to free the missionary from financial dependence. Only then would the individual be totally available to God and fully able to develop his or her own views on any matter without fear or favour. On this basis, if there should happen to be a disagreement between missionaries, then they could simply part, as did Paul and Barnabas, and work in different places. But how much greater will be the tensions if they have contracted to work together, or if one pays the other: "Now when they are free to go or stay, their little difficulties are more easily arranged; but where there is a dependence for subsistence, the whole changes, and to force a disruption, unless on the ground of Christian unfaithfulness, is not what a Christian could endure to do, even though [financial] support were afforded in the separation."[4]

To Groves then, the ideal would be for missionaries and other Christians to co-operate freely in the work of God, without contractual engagements or financial dependence. Moving here or there, combining for this task or that, they will enjoy a high degree of flexibility. So he concludes, "What I long to see is a number of missionaries come out, one in object but otherwise independent; that they may find companions in labour, now in one, then in another, as Paul did, taking this person for one journey, that for another, as circumstances may suggest."[5] It is interesting that Hudson Taylor enjoyed exactly this form of flexible and informal fellowship in his early preaching itinerations with workers from various societies and denominations in China. We will discuss Taylor's application of Groves's ideas in due course.[6]

---

[1] J77
[2] J77
[3] J77
[4] J78
[5] J78
[6] See below, 192ff.

From his earliest days in India, Groves sought to work along these lines, accompanying missionaries on their preaching excursions in many places, and he recruited others to join him on the same informal basis. In 1834 he expressed to the Basel Mission his hope that they might send him ten or twenty young men, "who would come out simply trusting in God and not man... in their own simple faith willing to cast themselves on Jesus." He offered to find means for their support, "simply as a brother's offer to enable them to carry their own ardent desire into effect." But he disclaimed all desire to control their activities, for they would be directly accountable to God: "I wish them to look on themselves as only His servants and responsible to Him." If they wished, for example, to marry and thus increase their expenses, they must be guided in their decision by God alone: "In fact our whole desire is not to get dependent servants of ours but free servants of Him, whom our desire is to help."[1]

As the Brethren movement expanded throughout the world in the late nineteenth and early twentieth centuries, its missionaries were supported very much as Groves envisaged. To the present day, the 2005 edition of the Echoes *Daily Prayer Guide* states that the individuals mentioned in its pages "look to God for their direction and support, without contractual links with any other group." What is more, they do not have "contractual links" with their home churches, or even with the editors of the magazine.

John Nelson Darby affirmed that, in the early days of the Brethren, a wish to be free from financial control was a prime reason for evangelists to resign from the societies that paid them:

> Other labourers, belonging to societies, believing that they would be happier working under the Lord's immediate direction, and not as subject to committees, gave up their salaries – considering such arrangements to be unknown to the Scripture, both in fact and in principle, since their very existence attributed to money the right to direct the work of the Lord. These began in simple dependence on the Lord, trusting to his faithful care.[2]

George Müller was one such. He described his dilemma: "If I were to stay in England, the Society would not allow me to preach in any place indiscriminately where the Lord might open a door for me... I further had a conscientious objection against being led and directed by *men* in my missionary labours. As a servant of Christ it appeared to me, I ought to be guided by the Spirit, and not by men, as to time and place."[3] Müller gave up his salary in order to be free of the obligations it entailed upon him, and his example was an influential one upon his generation, both within and outside the Brethren movement.

William Carey and his colleagues had earlier protested, "Control originates wholly in Contribution, and is ever commensurate therewith; control indeed follows contribution, as the shadow the substance."[4] Indeed, the control exercised by voluntary societies over their paid agents at this period was particularly oppressive. Rufus Anderson chose to describe each ABCFM mission (mission

---

[1] Groves to Blumhardt, Calcutta, 22nd June 1834
[2] Letter to Dr Tholuck, in Bellett, *Early Days*, 37-8
[3] Müller, *Narrative*, I, 50
[4] Serampore missionaries to BMS Sub-Committee, 4th Sep. 1817, cited by Stanley, "Planting Self-Governing Churches", 382

station) as a political unit, and each missionary as a voter: "In the mission he belongs to a self-governing republic, where every man has an equal vote, and where the majority rules; with the right… of an appeal to the Prudential Committee, and ultimately to the Board."[1] A missionary in such circumstances would find it difficult to seek and follow any personal guidance from God. The problem was intensified by Anderson's insistence that a missionary overseas should be subject to the same degree of accountability as a pastor serving a congregation in America. He should not, for example, "absent himself from his field of labour and his work without the concurrence of the body that furnishes the means of his support." Indeed, "the pastor can no more travel at the expense of his people whether for health or business without their consent than the missionary can do so at the expense of the Board without the consent of the Committee, or, in certain specified cases, of his Mission [i.e. mission station]."[2] Accountability in the ABCFM extended to observing and commenting on the personal behaviour of other missionaries: "As soon as a mission contains three or more missionaries it is expected to organise itself as a self-governing community under the laws, regulations and general superintendence of the Board. Mutual watchfulness thus becomes the official duty of each member."[3] And just as the missionary is accountable to the mission station and to the board which pays him, so are the "native pastors" accountable to the missionary who pays them. In short, as Anderson observes, "a wise disbursement of funds will provide all the checks which are necessary or proper."[4]

In the organisational development of American missionary societies, Anderson's influence has been second to none.[5] By the end of the twentieth century, the absolute necessity for moral and financial "accountability" of the type he envisaged was regularly asserted in missionary circles, and generally accepted without question.[6] Brethren missions, adopting the principles first introduced by Groves, have followed quite a different path. They have been marked by a firm resistance to any hint of hierarchical control and to any form of accountability, preferring to see missionary support and co-operation as a matter of trust rather than obligation.

In the late twentieth-century, however, the tendency of the Brethren in the United Kingdom to engage in lengthy and anguished self-criticism could hardly fail to extend to this issue. In a key article, Ray Cawston, for one, has suggested that Brethren missionaries should consider accepting a much higher level of accountability.[7]

---

[1] Anderson, *Foreign Missions*, Ch.9, in Beaver, *To Advance*, 203. To Anderson's chagrin, European workers had proved awkward in this respect. He proposed that all missionaries should be "trained to feel fully the moral responsibility of a majority vote (as it has been found that Europeans, from a deficiency in their early education, seldom are)."
[2] Anderson, *ABCFM Annual Report 1848*, in Beaver, *To Advance*, 133
[3] Anderson, Ibid, 135
[4] ABCFM, *Outline of Missionary Policy*, 1856, 15-16
[5] Beaver, *To Advance*, 9
[6] Referring to the foremost American missiologist of the twentieth century, Thom S Ranier remarks, "Accountability was McGavran's watchword, and that accountability took place by evaluating numerical results" (in Terry, 488).
[7] Cawston, "Accountability", 39-48

At the outset, Cawston frankly admits that current practices of accountability in wider church and mission circles are derived from secular business management practices rather than from scripture. But he attempts to find in the New Testament some examples of accountability. He asks, "In what sense then can a missionary be *accountable* to his fellow-workers and relate to them in his work?" He proposes, "The biblical answer seems to lie in our understanding of the word 'partnership'."[1]

It is unfortunate for his case that the examples Cawston finds are, by his own admission, examples not of *accountability* but of *fellowship*.

The business practice of accountability differs significantly from the biblical concept of "partnership" or "fellowship" (*koinonia*). It differs, especially, in its connotations of power and authority, with their concomitants of vulnerability and, potentially, of shame and rejection. When one person is *accountable* to another, he joins the ranks of those who are tempted, perhaps even compelled, to offer "eye-service as men-pleasers".[2] This may be considered necessary for industrial and commercial enterprises, where an employee, like the dishonest steward of the parable, must give account of oil and wheat.[3] It seems far removed, however, from the preaching of the Gospel in apostolic times by men who had forsaken all for a task that brought no material reward.[4] Indeed, in many cultures of the world, to require accountability of a Christian friend or colleague will imply that one simply does not trust him, and this can be acutely offensive.[5]

---

[1] Ibid, 41

[2] Eph 6:6

[3] Luke 16:1-8

[4] Taking Acts 13 as a model for church / mission co-operation, Frank Severn suggests that when Paul and Barnabas were sent out from Antioch, "control and accountability were not issues" (Severn, 323). Then when they decided to separate, "the Antioch church did not decide whether this was good or bad." And when other decisions were taken in the course of their mission, "neither Antioch nor Jerusalem determined who should join the Pauline team. Paul and his fellow-workers decided" (p.323). The sending church had thus "released them" to seek guidance directly from God, and although the missionaries subsequently reported back to Antioch, the church there did not in any way control their activities: "This was not a formal organisational linkage but a linkage of mutuality and brotherhood" (p.323). So far, one can hardly dispute his analysis.

Nevertheless, as a professional mission administrator, Severn reverts to type in asserting that Paul was in fact "accountable", if not to Antioch then to Jerusalem, and if not in terms of "control and decision making" then in regard to doctrine (p.324). Thus, "He [i.e. Paul] always felt a strong accountability to Jerusalem" (p.324). Severn then suggests that para-church mission agencies can claim a Biblical precedent in Paul's independent mission agency. He argues that missionaries should be accountable to such a mission agency, that the agency should report to the sending churches concerning those they have sent, "and, if necessary, discipline the missionary" (p.325). Despite his protestation that "the issue should not be one of control but of mutual help" (p.326), Severn's scheme of accountability to the sending church (doctrinally), and to the missionary society (administratively), assumes a marked element of control and institutional authority, beyond anything apparent in the fluid relations between the apostle Paul and the churches and missionaries of his day described in the New Testament.

[5] On this subject, Ted Ward observes, "As the world has polarized into geopolitical camps, the tendency toward secrecy, manipulative cleverness, and distrust has been deeply embedded into intercultural relations. In the interests of truth and trust, it is time for Christians to become more trusting of one another, regardless of ethnicity or nationality, and for Christian organizations, especially mission agencies, to minimize the sort of

Cawston himself describes the "deep sense of comradeship and mutual respect" that can develop between a missionary and the national Christians around him, and he admits, "To use the term accountability here is to run the risk of seriously understating the position."[1] Indeed, we might think "accountability" entirely the wrong word to use in describing this kind of free and happy relationship between brothers and sisters in Christ. And this is presumably the reason why the New Testament describes such relationships in terms of fellowship, service and love, rather than accountability.

Here we may observe the Brethren movement of the United Kingdom, in what appear to be its final phases of disintegration, seeking alternative models in wider Christian circles with which to replace the principles proposed by Anthony Norris Groves at its commencement a century and a half ago.

In reality, Groves's concept of spiritual unity would have led him away from formal identification with the Brethren either at home or overseas. His ideal was "union with the whole circle of God's redeemed family, without exclusive attachment to any section of it."[2] To his mind, every missionary belonged to the whole church of Christ. This meant that every Christian would feel an interest in any missionary he happened to meet, and a missionary would expect to find supportive friends wherever he went. Both missionary and supporters would be accountable to God alone.

Tent-Making

It has been suggested that the most novel contribution of Anthony Norris Groves to mission thinking lies in the sphere of what is now commonly called "tent-making".[3] In fact, he always felt a certain ambivalence towards this subject. During the course of his missionary career he gave much thought to the "tent-making" idea, experimented with it, and eventually abandoned it.[4]

At Sarepta, pausing on his journey to Baghdad, Groves enjoyed fellowship with a Moravian pastor caring for a Christian community of twelve hundred men and women of Calmuc and Russian origin. But political changes meant that the Moravians were no longer permitted to preach the gospel to outsiders, and on this basis they maintained their religious rules and exercises whilst supporting themselves with agriculture and handcrafts. It saddened Groves to find them chiefly concerned with "keeping the young people separate from the Russians",

---

suspicious privacy and secrecy that causes far too many documents to be stamped FYEO [For Your Eyes Only]" (Ward, "Repositioning Mission Agencies"). As a token of mistrust, "accountability" may be one Western value overdue for abandonment if the Great Commission is to be effectively operated in our generation. A recent plea for mission leadership to abandon the authoritarian management practices familiar in most agencies and adopt a more relational and interactive method is offered by Roland Muller, *Missionary Leadership*.

[1] Cawston, "Accountability", 43. Johannes Nissen has recently described Paul's collection for the saints in Jerusalem as a form of "partnership" from which the apostle deliberately excluded any idea of "accountability". The gift had no strings attached. Indeed, he took pains to ensure that the collection and donation of money should not become "an instrument for domination and dependency" (Nissen, *New Testament and Mission*, 121-2).

[2] M433. See PEANG, 104ff.

[3] Newton, *Groves*, 13

[4] See FOFM 486-90.

with the result that "all missionary character is now lost here; they are a simple colony of artificers who, for the sake of the preservation of *this* character, have relinquished that of missionary." And what was to be learned from this? "I see here the great evil of having anything mercantile connected with missionaries, unless as a simple accident [i.e. incidental circumstance] of support and not as an essential part of the constitution."[1]

At this stage of his life, Groves evidently expected the missionary to be an evangelist, not a farmer or an artisan, resorting only in case of necessity to earning his daily bread through secular labour. Shortly after this he discovered that medical and educational services could facilitate contact with the local populace and provide opportunities for spiritual ministry. In Baghdad, he opened a school and offered medical care, especially for diseases of the eye, but saw this as a way of winning the trust and respect of the people rather than as a serious source of income. In his dental work at Madras and Bangalore, he considered the goodwill it engendered to be among its chief benefits, opening doors for the spiritual ministry which he considered of greater importance.[2]

His experience of dental practice in Madras led Groves to consider it "helpful to his spiritual calling to labour with his hands, to show the heathen that it is not for any of man's things for which he labours, but only for their good."[3] It would also silence any who thought missionaries averse to hard work. Harriet Groves commented,

> He had made up his mind that the best way to meet the tendency he had noticed all over India to complain of anything like ease or indulgence enjoyed by a missionary, was at once to follow the apostle's example, and work for his own support, and to encourage those with him to do the same. This led him to practice in Madras, as a dentist, which he did with great success; and one of the Swiss ladies, by employing a few hours a day teaching French, was able to contribute to the Boarding School Department.[4]

At this time, throughout 1837, thoughts of a more ambitious "self-supporting mission" occupied the team in Madras. They had "much correspondence on the subject".[5] It was not only the missionaries who needed to earn their keep. One of their main reasons for moving to Chittoor was to buy farmland which could provide work for Indian converts, "who by embracing Christianity lost their means of support."[6]

Groves's deeply-held belief that no distinction should be made between clergy and laity no doubt encouraged him to think that any working person could exercise a spiritual ministry. And likewise, any man or woman engaged in spiritual ministry could simultaneously be earning their living. Indeed, he actively sought to blur the traditional distinction between professional and amateur in Christian ministry. He proposed, "This plan of service owes its practicability mainly to the absence of all

---

[1] J49; M59
[2] See above, 128ff.
[3] "Missions to the Heathen", 137-8
[4] M358
[5] M370-1
[6] M371

recognition of the distinction between laity and clergy, which prevails not only in the establishment but in the dissenting bodies."[1]

We might consider this a middle course steered between the financially remunerative colonies of the Moravians and the purely spiritual ministries of the contemporary chaplaincies and voluntary societies. Brian Stanley has observed that in these early days "the missionary societies generally took a dim view of any personal participation in trading activity by their missionaries." Indeed, the home committee of the Nonconformist BMS and LMS warned and rebuked their agents on hearing that some were augmenting their meagre income through industry or trade.[2] Anglican chaplains, and agents of the Anglican societies, were similarly barred from paid employment by the terms of their appointment. The CMS, under the guidance of Henry Venn, not only forbade its missionaries to engage in secular employment; it also forbade them to accept support directly from local churches or prayer groups in the homeland.[3]

By 1840 Groves's ideas concerning mission finance had matured.[4] He proposed that missionaries should seek, as soon as possible after arriving on the field, to become self-supporting. Though dependant initially on funds brought with them, "after a while it is more than probable that most of those acting on those enlarged and scripture principles, would be placed in a situation by which they might support not only themselves but those with them."[5] Their financial independence will enable their friends at home to send additional workers, or to sponsor evangelistic outreach in areas hitherto untouched. It would also demonstrate to the missionary's converts the value of honest toil, through which they might provide for their personal upkeep, for travelling evangelists, and for the needy.[6] Groves's advocacy of this "apostolic" method was accepted by recruits to his cause in India. In January 1840, a former soldier, J M Walhouse, described a plan to launch "missionary work" in an unreached area by creating a coffee plantation: "We shall carry on our missionary work among the heathen, according to the apostolic plan, labouring with our own hands that the Lord Jesus may be glorified in us and by us."[7]

On this basis, wherever a missionary team or a Christian farm settlement were established, the labour would be divided; some members might concentrate largely on spiritual ministry, and others on manual labour. But having all things in common, none would lack their necessities and each could develop their gifts. Groves remarked, "I think we all feel an increasing interest in that plan of missions which we are now pursuing: either labouring ourselves, or being associated with those who profess some 'honest trade', that we may have 'lack of no man' and also set an example to others, that by so doing they may support the weak."[8]

---

[1] Groves, "Missions to the Heathen", 138
[2] Stanley, *The Bible and the Flag*, 72
[3] Shenk, *Venn*, 52. Venn's biographer suggests that the society adopted this policy in order to retain complete authority over its agents.
[4] See above, 102ff.
[5] Ibid, 138
[6] Groves, "A Letter on Missions", 136, 140
[7] M548
[8] M391. Whether he knew it or not, Groves was following a pattern advocated by Carey before setting foot in India. In his *Enquiry*, Carey proposed sending with each missionary evangelist "two or more other persons, with their wives and families... who should be

In its earliest form, the farm settlement at Chittoor proved a highly effective means of providing food, accommodation, and other necessities for the support of evangelists engaged in itinerant outreach. Families with agricultural or craft skills did the bulk of the physical work, whilst Groves and Arulappan, Gundert and Andrew, went out preaching the gospel. In addition, "a hundred children were fed, clothed, and instructed, in the boys' and girls' schools."[1] Groves "obtained a little preaching place opposite the Zillah Court,"[2] and when he subsequently planted mulberry trees for the production of silk, a number of "pious pensioners... came as overseers of the work, and thus had the privilege of Christian communion and instruction."[3]

But such a system brought problems to the evangelists themselves. As Arulappan preached and interpreted for him in public, Groves saw the young Indian's motives questioned at every turn; his hearers reckoned he was promoting Christianity only because he was paid to do so. Groves thought of the apostle Paul, who had worked with his own hands during the week and then reasoned with Jews and Greeks in the synagogue every Sabbath.[4] He thought too of a Muslim *mullah* in Baghdad who said, "I know you are devoted men, and give much away, but I know not what your motives are, or what the extent of your riches. If I saw persons labouring from day to day and giving the fruit of their labour to the poor or to missions, I should then see they were making sacrifices for God."[5] It all pointed to the need for the evangelist himself to be a working man, preaching in his spare time at his own expense, and Groves began to feel there was much to be said for an evangelist (whatever his nationality) to be seen working with his own hands and earning his own living from a craft or trade.

This idea was not original to Groves. William Carey, arriving in Calcutta in 1793, had first supported himself by overseeing a number of small indigo plantations.[6] Since the 1820s the Moravians had made it a basic principle that "every Christian is a missionary and should witness through his daily vocation."[7] Karl Pfander's experience among Muslims had led him to favour the concept of the "missionary craftsman". An itinerant watchmaker, he believed, would be more likely to gain the confidence of the local people than would a self-proclaimed

---

wholly employed in providing for them" (George, App.E, 50). The idea probably came from the Moravians (see above, 21ff).

[1] M370
[2] M373
[3] M396
[4] Acts 18:1-4; 1 Thess 2:9; 2 Thess 3:7-8
[5] M371
[6] Carey's employment in this work for three months of the year, by an official of the East India Company, enabled him to live in British India at a time when Christian missionaries were still prohibited by law. He later acquired a more secure and independent income as a teacher of Bengali, as a professor of Sanskrit and Marathi, and as a government translator, and he gave away at least a quarter of what he earned, to further the work of God (George, 105-6). Carey advised that, after an initial stage when charitable help might be received from home, both missionary and converts should expect to provide for their upkeep through secular work. They should also build, maintain and own whatever properties became necessary (Marshman, II, 165). On Carey's views, and on BMS opposition to them, see Oussoren, 164-7; Smith G, *Carey*, 79-80; Stanley, "Planting Self-Governing Churches", 382.
[7] Tucker, 69

propagandist.[1] In Baghdad Groves himself had received a letter from Robert Morrison, the first Protestant missionary to China, "in which he expresses his conviction of the importance of missionaries learning to earn their subsistence by some occupation, however humble, rather than be dependent as they are now on societies." Groves found this persuasive: "I confess my mind so far entirely agrees with him, that if I had to prepare for a missionary course I would not go to a college or an institution but learn medicine or go to a blacksmith's, watchmaker's or carpenter's shop, and there pursue my preparatory studies."[2] But studying the scriptures, Groves found that Paul's work as a tent-maker never tied him to one place; he could pick up his tools or put them down as the Spirit might lead. In case of need, wherever he happened to be, there was work to do with his hands, but his freedom to preach the gospel was never compromised.[3] This would seem to be the ideal.

The ultimate ruin of Groves's increasingly ambitious plans for his silk industry may be attributed partly to his own lack of commercial expertise, partly to some unwise decisions, and partly to economic circumstances beyond his control. But he was not alone in this failure. It might be thought that *indigenous* commercial initiatives would be more sure of success, but Arulappan and others, working independently, were hardly more successful than Groves himself. The skills needed to start a new business were in some cases lacking; in others the business plan was not commercially viable. Drought at times withered the crops in the fields, and the level of government taxation was far too high to enable Arulappan's farm, for example, to be self-supporting. Elsewhere, the entrepreneur for whom Carey worked "found his private indigo enterprise to be disastrous"; he abandoned it and returned to England.[4] In the Punjab, Robert Clark's "Christian agricultural settlement" under Indian leadership was "a melancholy failure".[5]

The Basel Mission likewise attempted and abandoned agricultural projects in India: sugar, food crops, a coffee plantation, small-scale weaving, carpentry, clockmaking – all were tried, and all failed. A printing and bookbinding business proved a little more successful, providing employment for a number of Indians. Real commercial success came to the Basel Mission only with a large weaving factory in Mangalore and with the growth of major tile manufacturing industries in the south.[6] Groves's second son Frank, a man of "mechanical genius", eventually did well with his substantial sugar refinery near Mysore.[7] These many and varied experiences showed that small-scale projects (cottage industries and food crops) could not compete with existing suppliers or create and adequately protect new markets, but that large industries with the latest technology and a dedicated professional management could sometimes do so.

One particular difficulty the "tent-maker" faced in India was the caste system. As a dentist in Madras, Groves had a large European clientele, and his profession

---

[1] Powell, 136
[2] R261
[3] See Groves, *On the Liberty of Ministry*, 50ff, and more briefly "A Letter on Missions", 138.
[4] Smith G, *Carey*, 109
[5] Clark, 264-7
[6] See Danker, *Profit for the Lord*, and also article "The Basel Mission" at <http://www.geocities.com/Athens/2960/basel.htm> (accessed 9th March 2005).
[7] Groves E K, *Successors*, 45

placed him in what had become a respected expatriate caste within Hindu society. But among his missionary recruits, Bowden was a stonemason, and Beer a shoemaker. In India these were low-caste occupations, and there was no mechanism for a foreigner to enter the caste. Indeed, if they attempted to do so, they would exclude themselves from social contact with all higher castes. They never exercised their crafts in India.

Another problem commonly encountered by "tent-makers" is that of commercial and professional jealousy. This may account for the fact that Groves never established a dental practice in Baghdad. He had carried with him his dentist's implements, presumably with some intention of using them, but the local people, for generations, had taken their rotten teeth to "native" dentists who, in return for a few coppers, simply pulled them out. Traditional practitioners would not welcome the encroachment of a foreigner on their domain. In China the young Hudson Taylor found local doctors and druggists resentful of the fact that he was taking away their customers, which almost caused a riot on at least one occasion.[1] Christian commercial projects are always vulnerable to the jealousy of commercial as well as religious rivals, and sabotage may possibly explain the repeated infection of the silkworms at Chittoor, although nothing written at the time suggests it.

Other hard questions have been asked concerning the advisability in general of establishing industries for the support of Christian converts. The plight of those driven out of their families on account of their faith weighed heavily on the first generation of missionaries in India, and where land was available with government approval, Christian villages were established in many parts of the country. Settlements tended to grow up around a mission station, and the missionary often became a well-loved father-figure to the Christian community. But what was originally an emergency solution, providing refuge and sustenance for converts with nowhere else to go, became in the course of time an approved institution – the mission compound. Homes were provided for believers and for interested friends and relations; farms, workshops and schools were built with foreign money. The inhabitants found no further need for contact with their Muslim and Hindu compatriots, and before long Indian Christians had become aliens in their own homeland, separated from all the normal relationships of family, community and caste. The modern tendency is to criticise the early missionaries for this policy, but it is difficult to know what else they could have done in the circumstances.

Groves eventually found from experience just how much time and energy (and capital) can be sunk in commercial ventures, to the detriment of spiritual ministry. He saw John Arulappan distracted with fields and finances, and he began to feel that faithful gifted men like him should be set free to devote their time to the work they did best – the work of the gospel which would endure not for a few years but for eternity. It was through the influence of Groves that *The Missionary Reporter* recommended Arulappan to its British readers as one worthy of support: "Mr Groves considered it would be failure to allow him to spend his strength in ordinary occupations when there is such abundant need for the entire services of men capable of performing the work of an evangelist."[2]

---

[1] Broomhall, *Treaty Wall*, 302; *Survivors' Pact*, 299
[2] *The Missionary Reporter*, No.1 (July 1853), 3

In 1847, at the age of fifty-two, Groves felt a considerable degree of relief in the anticipation of being free at last from commercial responsibilities. He confessed, "It is much my desire, if the Lord clears away difficulties, to give the rest of my short space to an uninterrupted ministry some where or in some form."[1] But the "tent-making" idea refuses to go away. An Indian evangelist is still likely to find his message ignored when his hearers discover he is paid to deliver it. And in some countries where Christian missionaries are not welcome the necessity remains for the evangelist or church planter to establish himself in some secular capacity. The ideal solution is often a part-time job that earns a small amount yet leaves abundant time for Christian service. There are not many such jobs, and not many people willing to take them. And even fewer able to provide them.

This is where the Christian businessman or industrialist may play his part. Colonel Cotton (later General Sir Arthur Cotton) offers a notable example. He never considered himself a missionary, yet it was his standing as a civil engineer in India that enabled him to invite Groves's recruit William Bowden to preach to the labourers on his irrigation schemes in the Godavari delta. It also equipped him to provide financial support for Bowden and his family.[2] In later life Groves's son, Frank, was an industrialist too, rather than an evangelist, and it was through his successful sugar and coffee industries that he was able to provide for others to devote their energies to the work of the gospel. Writing of the sugar refinery which he and his brother Henry had set up in Palhully, Harriet Groves remarked, "Thus, in the providence of God, they illustrate the principle their father so desired to see carried out in India, of uniting spiritual and manual labour, and while availing themselves of the facilities the country affords for their support, they not only seek the blessing of the people among whom they dwell, but strengthen the hands of other missionaries."[3] In the mind of Groves this partnership between Christian industry and Christian mission was an important aspect of his missiological vision, and one radically different from that current in his day. His ideal was "to carry on the work of God independently of help from others."[4] He regretted that his own efforts fell short of the ideal.

In a recent study of modern "tent-making" practices, Dan Gibson suggests that "tentmaking was a natural form of missions in the first century of the church, and only in the last several hundred years has the 'professional ministry' emerged as the approved method of doing missionary work."[5] With reference to the Acts account, Gibson identifies two distinct models for "tent-making", terming one

---

[1] M421
[2] For a biography of Cotton by his daughter, see Hope, *General Sir Arthur Cotton*.
[3] M549
[4] M411
[5] Gibson, 9. The "tent-making" concept has a long history in Protestant missions. It is a subject worthy of more research. In 1923 Roland Allen argued passionately for the appointment of "voluntary clergy", that is, of suitably qualified laymen authorised to exercise all the functions of the Anglican priesthood whilst engaged in secular employment (see Allen, *Voluntary Clergy*). In 1943 Dennis E Clark launched a "tent-maker" enterprise in Afghanistan, the Central Asia Trading Association, a professional import / export business with an openly Christian identity (Gibson, 38). Then the 1980s saw growing interest in the idea of Christian professionals seeking employment for purposes of discreet evangelism in "closed countries", a movement owing much to Christy Wilson, whose book *Today's Tentmakers* first appeared in 1979.

Priscillan and the other Pauline. In the former, a person in remunerative employment will engage in some additional part-time spiritual ministry. In the latter, a dedicated pastor or evangelist will also hold down some kind of secular job. He suggests that the two types of "tent-maker" will naturally complement one another, as indeed they did when Paul joined forces with Priscilla and Aquila.[1] Gibson concludes, "I firmly believe that the teaming up of a Christian evangelist and church planter with Christian business people was the secret of success of the early church."[2] This partnership was exactly what Groves had in mind.

The Rest of Faith

We have observed that when Groves spoke of living "by faith" his meaning extended far further than financial provision. To his mind, it embraced every aspect of God's fatherly care for his children. After the death of his wife Mary, and with the prospect of leaving his young sons as orphans in a city beset by civil war, plague, floods and famine, Groves confided, "Our walking now is altogether by faith; we see not a ray of light for the future, but the Lord will let light spring out of darkness, so that His servants who wait upon Him shall not always mourn."[3]

It is to Hudson Taylor that we tend to turn when seeking for a leading missionary exponent of the evangelical concept of "the rest of faith". It was Taylor who, more than anyone, inspired his generation to live, as he did himself, "trusting in the promises of God". Yet Groves, with his strong view of providence, was, in this, as in much else, a forerunner of Hudson Taylor.

Early in his missionary career Groves declared, "I think it not only a great loss of present comfort but a great sin not to trust God's promises."[4] The repeated difficulties and disappointments he faced throughout his life led him to give much thought to the purposes of God in the suffering of his people. These issues lie outside the scope of our present study and I have addressed them elsewhere,[5] but we should nevertheless note some aspects of Groves's thought that subsequently became characteristic of the "faith missions" and may provide evidence of a link.

He often spoke, for example, of the need and the possibility for the believer to be "at rest in Jesus".[6] Travelling in India in 1834, "I stand now from day to day, and for the future see no rest but on His promises, who has begun and will finish. I feel myself in a waste wilderness here; for nearly seventy miles in any direction there is not one European, yet the Lord reigns, and where He is, there is safety to His children."[7] And again, "How wonderful the Lord's ways are! O, that my soul had faith only to rest on God; and never to think of what is likely, or unlikely, but simply on Him and His promises."[8] "How good is the Lord, who delivers out of every difficulty, truly the Lord has helped me thus far. I do so desire that rest of soul, in all the future, which springs from resting on God, letting Him do what

---

[1] In the words of F F Bruce, "Paul found employment with a tent-making firm" (Bruce, *Paul*, 250).
[2] Gibson, 46. The modern "secular" tent-maker will frequently be a "salaried professional", and Gibson generally designates him or her as such.
[3] R162-3
[4] M17
[5] FOFM, 413-40
[6] M389
[7] M267-8
[8] M296

seemeth Him good, and yet believing and trusting in His love."[1] "When my soul sees the storm again rising among us, I for a moment tremble, but my heart returns and rests on its Lord, who alone abides faithful amidst faithlessness."[2]

We have observed how Groves made it a principle to seek his guidance directly from God. Much of his personal direction he received, in fact, from providential circumstances. Throughout his life he was remarkably adaptable, ready to respond immediately to what would appear a divine ordering of events. It was *en route* to Persia, hearing of Major Taylor's removal to Baghdad, that he decided to make his first base in that city rather than Shushi or Basra. It was on board ship for India, perhaps even after landing, that he found good reason to settle in Madras rather than Calcutta. Seeing providential opportunities at particular times and places, he felt led to establish a clinic or a school or a farm. He welcomed guests when they happened to call; he took up invitations when they were offered. He accepted the departure of old missionary colleagues and the arrival of new. It all meant that his plans could change at any time. A chance meeting, a letter, a verse of scripture; any of these might prove to be God's way of showing him what to do. It meant he was always available, always ready to respond to a need or give his attention to a particular problem.

A similar degree of adaptability is frequently observable in the New Testament narratives. Peter and John, for example, made the most of some quite unexpected encounters. Stephen and Philip, too, took unforeseen opportunities presented to them. Paul preached wherever he found an open door, and moved on when he saw it close. Indeed, one gains the impression from the Gospel records that almost everything Jesus said and did was in response to an interruption. Some would find this degree of flexibility frustrating, others inspiring, but to a greater or lesser degree it was an attitude adopted by those who aspired to live and walk "by faith" in the generations that followed Groves.[3]

This element of spontaneous adaptability stands in striking contrast to the decision-making processes of the older "voluntary societies", where the *fiat* of a director or a bishop, or the consensus of a committee or a mission station, would inexorably determine the course of action to be followed. It was a natural outworking of Groves's great principle of "liberty of ministry", and should be seen as one of the most striking and typical aspects of his missiological scheme.

Conclusion: Finance and Providence

As a means of financing Christian mission, "living by faith" was seen by Groves as an alternative to the contemporary custom of raising subscriptions for investment in voluntary societies. It was, to his mind, the method intended by the Master when he originally entrusted the Great Commission to his disciples.

Regarding the proclamation of the Gospel as a task for the entire church of Christ, Groves expected both rich and poor to participate. In general, the former would provide the finance for the missionary task, and the latter the labour. But the rule allowed for exceptions: a rich person might become a poor missionary, and a

---

[1] M483

[2] M382

[3] Once, at least, in his own experience, it led to disaster. The offer of a loan for the extension of the silk farm had seemed providential, but on this occasion, as Harriet Groves freely admits, he misread the circumstances (M397).

poor one, through hard work, a significant financial supporter of missions. Here we can see a further missiological application of Groves's ecclesiology, and in particular of his concept of sacrificial devotedness as a normal way of living for every Christian.

Nevertheless, in his journals and other surviving writings, Groves actually says very little about his own experience of "the life of faith". Unlike George Müller, he appears reluctant to record details of money received or spent. Though he often spoke to expatriates in India about the privilege of giving oneself and all one has to Christ, he rarely mentioned his personal needs or noted how those needs were met.

This may reflect his general dislike of administration and especially of those aspects of personal control and manipulation that can result from formalised accountability. It may also reflect a fastidious element of upper-middle class Victorian gentility, more comfortable with romantic ideals than sordid practicalities.

But Groves's concept of "living by faith" extended beyond financial considerations to other aspects of missionary life. In particular we may note his custom of looking directly to God for guidance, and his willingness to respond to unexpected providences. In fact, his spiritual adaptability stands in striking contrast to the more ponderous decision-making processes of the contemporary missionary societies, and here we can identify his ecclesiological principle of "liberty of ministry" applied to a missionary context.

Groves drew no sharp distinction between Christian service and secular work. His conviction that no difference should be made between clergy and laity no doubt underlay his view that any working person could exercise a spiritual ministry, and that any man or woman engaged in spiritual ministry could simultaneously be earning their living. Indeed, he considered it a positive advantage for a missionary to be self-supporting, and at certain periods he experimented with the "tent-making" idea and with the establishment of self-supporting Christian agricultural and artisanal settlements. He later encouraged his sons in their industrial enterprises, through which both employment and financial support would be effectively provided for Indian Christians.

Conclusion: The Missiology of A N Groves

The missiology of Anthony Norris Groves can be considered the logical outworking of his ecclesiology applied to a cross-cultural context. His basic ideas were all expressed during his initial tour of India in 1833-4, but his thinking continued to mature during his nineteen years in the south of the subcontinent.

For Groves, the New Testament was always the ultimate authority and the motivating influence. Although Protestant missionaries and church leaders have generally paid lip-service to the principle of biblical authority and motivation, most will, in practice, set other considerations above it: the tradition of a Church or the constitution of a Society or the civilisation of the West or the culture of the East. Groves was unusually single-minded in dismissing all other forms of authority and motivation. The primitivist ecclesiology he drew from the New Testament he applied to the missionary task facing his generation.

His concept of "spiritual unity" inspired a lifelong desire for missionary co-operation, overlooking differences of denomination and society. His hope was for the development of indigenous churches free from foreign causes of division.

His emphasis on "liberty of ministry" led him to encourage individuals to serve Christ without human regulations or restrictions, developing God-given gifts for the benefit of others. He denied the traditional distinction between clergy and laity. He stimulated Christians involved in secular work to engage in preaching, teaching and pastoral care, and he encouraged evangelists and Bible teachers to support themselves through some form of "tent-making". He hoped to see a partnership between full-time evangelists (both Indian and expatriate) and other Christians whose secular income could provide for their support. His purpose was not to organise churches, but to make disciples. And he was delighted when he saw disciples become apostles.

His idea of "Christian influence" is reflected in his personal example of frugality and financial stewardship, in the pastoral care and counsel he offered to individuals, and in his sensitive mentoring of young Indian Christians. His schools were intended to teach the Bible rather than Western civilisation, and his desire was to convert individuals rather than civilise nations.

Groves himself perceived a striking contrast between his views and those of his contemporaries. Though determined to honour all existing missionary agencies for the work they had done, he considered them defective in their authority structures, their financial arrangements and their competitive ambitions. Comity agreements, in his view, served only to perpetuate such difficulties. He disliked the element of control exercised over salaried mission agents by those who paid them. He preferred to "live by faith", responsive to unforeseen circumstances, seeking guidance and provision directly from God. He mistrusted the forms of organisational accountability to be found in missionary societies, preferring accountability to God alone. He observed the complexities involved in foreign leadership of mission churches, and he foresaw the administrative difficulties that would later cause Henry Venn and Rufus Anderson to propose a metaphor of "scaffolding", and a "three-self" model, in their protracted endeavour to transfer the burden of financial and administrative responsibility from the foreign society to the national church.

It can hardly be denied that these were radical ideas. The bitter opposition they aroused, especially from Anglicans of the expatriate community in India, demonstrate the extent to which they were unconventional and largely unwelcome to the generality of Christians around him. The extent to which they were influential is a question we must now address.

Part 3. The Missiological Influence of A N Groves

Researching Groves's formative missionary experiences, and discussing his missiological ideas in detail, we have found good reason to consider him a radical and innovative thinker. Our task is now to discover how influential he might have been – to consider how his ideas were applied in a missionary context in India and elsewhere, and to assess their impact on Brethren missions, on the so-called "faith missions", and on indigenous mission initiatives. We will also consider how far his ideas are reflected in the writings of other missiological thinkers up to the present day.

1. Groves's Missiology Applied

There were aspects of Groves's primitivist ecclesiology that undoubtedly found a place in the Brethren movement of the United Kingdom, and, through Brethren influence, far beyond it. His emphasis on liberty of ministry, active participation in the body, plural unpaid leadership, spiritual unity and co-operation, and his concepts of sacrificial stewardship, holiness, "light", faith and obedience, all became characteristic of the Open Brethren, and eventually found their way, especially through the university Christian Unions, into wider evangelical circles.[1]

From these circles were drawn many nineteenth and twentieth century missionaries, both those identified as Brethren and many who would not claim such an identity. All will owe something to Groves as an early advocate of principles they chose to follow.

Brethren Missions

The influence of Groves on Brethren missions has been both direct and indirect, through the dissemination of his own writings, and through the missiological application of an ecclesiology that owed much to him. It is often difficult at this distance in time to discern whether his influence is, in any given case, direct or indirect.

The Scriptural Knowledge Institution

The direct influence of Groves on George Müller's early thought is well known, thanks to the account of it given to us by Müller himself:

> Soon after my arrival in England [in March 1829], I heard one of the brethren in the seminary speak about a Mr Groves, a dentist in Exeter, who, for the Lord's sake, had given up his profession, which brought him in about fifteen hundred pounds a year, and who intended to go as a missionary to Persia, with his wife and children, simply trusting in the Lord for temporal supplies. This made such an impression on me, and delighted me so, that I not only marked it down in my journal, but also wrote about it to my German friends.[2]

---

[1] On Groves's influence in Britain, see PEANG, 195ff.
[2] Müller, *Narrative*, I, 44

The impact of Groves's *Christian Devotedness* on this impressionable young trainee missionary is described by Müller in his account of his visit in August 1829 to Devonshire, where Groves's former tutor Henry Craik showed him a copy of the booklet:

> It pleased the Lord to lead me to see a higher standard of devotedness than I had seen before. He led me, in a measure, to see what is my true glory in this world, even to be despised, and to be poor and mean with Christ. I saw then, in a measure, though I have seen it more fully since, that it ill becomes the servant to seek to be rich, and great, and honoured in that world, where his Lord was poor, and mean, and despised... My prayer had been, before I left London, that the Lord would be pleased to bless my journey to the benefit of my body and soul. This prayer was answered in both respects; for in the beginning of September I returned to London much better in body; and, as to my soul, the change was so great, that it was like a second conversion.[1]

Müller described his experience as "an entire and full surrender of heart. I gave myself fully to the Lord. Honour, pleasure, money, my physical powers, my mental powers, all was laid down at the feet of Jesus, and I became a great lover of the word of God."[2] A year or two later, Groves's account of God's protection and provision during the course of his journey from St Petersburg to Baghdad was a further stimulus to Müller's faith: "The example of brother Groves, the dentist... who gave up his profession and went out as a missionary, was a great encouragement to me. For the news which by this time had arrived of how the Lord had aided him on his way to Petersburg, and at Petersburg, strengthened my faith"[3]

On 7th October 1830 Müller married Groves's sister, Mary, and a lifetime of personal correspondence between the two men commenced. Groves received copies of Müller's *Narrative* as they were issued, and he no doubt reciprocated by sending Müller copies of his published journals and other writings. Despite their difference of character, they developed a remarkable similarity of view on a wide range of doctrinal and practical matters. It is regrettable that no portion of their correspondence seems to have survived, and that we must infer their mutual influence upon one another by largely circumstantial evidence.[4]

We have already compared Groves and Müller as exemplars of "living by faith".[5] Now we must consider whether other traces of Groves's thinking can be discerned in Müller's missionary activities.

In March 1834, Müller and Henry Craik created their Scriptural Knowledge Institution. At first sight, we might think it a "voluntary society" of the traditional type. But it was not, as Müller sought to explain:

> Some readers may ask why we formed a *new* Institution for the spread of the Gospel, and why we did not unite with some of the religious societies, already in existence,

---

[1] *Narrative*, I, 48
[2] Müller, letter to J G Logan dated 17th July 1895 (referring to July 1829), reproduced in Lang, *Groves*, 39.
[3] Müller, *Narrative*, I, 52
[4] The archives of the Müller Foundation unfortunately contain no surviving correspondence between Müller and Groves.
[5] See above, 133ff. Elsewhere we have argued that the ecclesiology of Groves, mediated through Müller, prevailed over that of J N Darby in the Brethren of the United Kingdom (PEANG, 195).

seeing that there are several Missionary - Bible - Tract - and School Societies. I give, therefore, our reasons, in order to show, that nothing but the desire to maintain a good conscience led us to act as we did. For as, by the grace of God, we acknowledged the word of God as the only rule of action for the disciples of the Lord Jesus, we found, in comparing the then existing religious Societies with the word of God, that they departed so far from it, that we could not be united with them, and yet maintain a good conscience.[1]

The major problems Müller saw in the societies were as follows:

1. They promote the postmillennialist idea "that the world will gradually become better and better, and that at last the whole world will be converted." This Müller considered a delusion.

2. They welcome the support of worldly people, "which is completely contrary to the word of God (2 Cor. vi. 14-18)... for every one who pays a guinea, or, in some societies, half-a-guinea, is considered as a member. Although such an individual may live in sin; although he may manifest to every one that he does not know the Lord Jesus; if only the guinea or the half-guinea be paid, he is considered a member, and has a right as such to vote."

3. They are accustomed "to ask the unconverted for money... How altogether differently the first disciples acted in this respect we learn from 3 John 7."

4. "It is not a rare thing for even Committee Members (the individuals who manage the affairs of the societies) to be manifestly unconverted persons... and this is suffered because they are rich, or of influence, as it is called."

5. They attract the general public to their meetings by asking "persons of rank or wealth" to take the chair. "Never once have I known a case of a POOR, but very devoted, wise, and experienced servant of Christ being invited to fill the chair at such public meetings."

6. "Almost all these societies contract debts, so that it is a comparatively rare case to read a Report of any of them, without finding that they have expended more than they have received, which, however, is contrary both to the spirit and to the letter of the New Testament. (Rom. xiii. 8)."

Müller, like Groves, was quite willing to acknowledge that godly people were involved with such societies, affirming both that he could enjoy warm fellowship with them as individuals and that many were enjoying the blessing of God on their labours. Nevertheless, he and Craik believed they should create a new means of assisting in the support of missionaries, the financing of Christian schools and the large scale distribution of literature, and this for particular reasons. He concluded, "It appeared to us to be His will, that we should be entirely separate from these societies... in order that, by the blessing of God, we might direct the attention of the children of God in these societies to their unscriptural practices; and we would rather be entirely unconnected with these societies than act contrary to the Holy Scriptures."[2]

The significant point for our discussion is that, immediately prior to writing the above, and thus immediately before creating his Scriptural Knowledge Institution, Müller must (almost certainly) have read Groves's *On the Nature of Christian Influence*, published in 1833. In that work, Groves starts by offering an alternative

---

[1] Müller, *Narrative*, I, 107
[2] Ibid, 110

to postmillennialism. He then pleads for the work of God to be done by "devoted" Christians, using scriptural and spiritual methods, rather than through appeals to the world and the exercise of secular influence.[1] The coincidence of view is remarkable, and the circumstantial evidence for Groves's influence on Müller's initiative at this point is almost undeniable. As Müller was particularly concerned to show that his principles were derived directly from Scripture, it is by no means surprising that he made no overt reference to Groves as a source.

For a period of fifty-two years (1834-86) Müller forwarded gifts to missionaries, some independent and some associated with societies. In each case, he affirmed, "We desire to assist those Missionaries whose proceedings appear to be most according to the Scriptures."[2] By the end of his life he had channelled a quarter of a million pounds to missionaries overseas, a vast sum by nineteenth-century values.[3]

In 1883, at the age of seventy eight, Müller travelled to India. This was exactly fifty years after Groves first set foot on the subcontinent, and thirty years after Groves's death. He had particular reasons for wishing to go there:

> My especial object in going to that distant land, was, to encourage the beloved missionary brethren and sisters... I desired also to preach Christ in great simplicity to the many thousands of Europeans, Eurasians, and educated natives with whom I might come into contact, and to set forth the truths of the Gospel before the lower orders of natives likewise... In addition to having these objects before me, I went to India also with a great desire to promote brotherly love amongst all the followers of the Lord Jesus, and tried to stir up His disciples to increased heavenly mindedness. I sought, too, to lead them to love the word of God more and more, and to point out that it alone should be their rule in all spiritual matters; to teach the true character of the present dispensation, namely that the whole world will not be converted, but that God is every where *gathering out* from the unsaved around a people for His name; and to stir up believers to "Look for that blessed hope, the glorious appearing of the great God, our Saviour Jesus Christ."[4]

It is a striking fact that these were exactly the objects which had preoccupied Groves during his time in India. They were matters that Müller had continually mentioned throughout his life in correspondence with the missionaries he supported. Brotherly love and unity, heavenly-mindedness, the "word of God" as "their rule in all spiritual matters", the "true character of the present dispensation" and "the glorious appearing of Christ": these were all thoroughly Grovesian concepts, and Müller promoted them tirelessly. To accompany each money-order sent to missionaries, he wrote a personal letter of encouragement. These letters typically contained exhortations to trust the promises of God and to walk in obedience to his revealed will. They advocated "living by faith" in full confidence of divine providence and provision. Müller sent copies of his *Narrative* to missionaries, and reading it will have encouraged them "to make use of faith and prayer, at all times and under all circumstances".[5] The positive influence of his

---

[1] For a study of Groves's thinking on this subject, see PEANG, 169ff.
[2] Müller, *Narrative*, I, 113 (25th Feb. 1834)
[3] See FOFM, 500.
[4] Müller, *Narrative*, VI (12th July 1884)
[5] Müller, *Narrative*, V (23rd Aug. 1864)

personal correspondence with missionaries, and the sending of his *Narrative* to them, is evident in the case among others of Hudson Taylor.[1]

Müller's official biography by Arthur Tappan Pierson, published shortly after his death, extended his influence to Keswick circles, and for a further half century, as a popular introduction to the concept of "living by faith" and to other "Brethren principles". Indeed Dana Robert has recently suggested that "A T Pierson never received adequate recognition for the importance of the biography in stimulating missionary spirituality."[2] Here we may identify Müller as a mediator of Groves's thought, not merely to a wider sphere but also to a later generation.

The Missionary Magazines

Early Initiatives

Among the earliest Brethren in England and Ireland, Müller was almost alone in maintaining a practical interest in missions. It is perhaps surprising to see how quickly the intense missionary enthusiasm aroused by Groves himself dissipated once he and his circle from Dublin had left for Baghdad in 1829 and 1830. Indeed, during the following fifteen years no record survives of any missionaries sent out by an assembly associated with the Brethren, and Müller alone shows any continued concern for the practical support of overseas mission.

The Barnstaple fellowship, having encouraged the Bowdens and Beers in their missionary resolve, signally failed to provide for them after they had gone. Perhaps there was an assumption that they would earn a sufficient income in India as a stone-mason and a shoemaker.[3] Or perhaps British Christians resident in India were expected to support them. In a similar fashion, the fellowship in Dublin, led by John Bellett and other personal friends of Groves, evidently felt no particular responsibility to send regular sums for the support of Cronin, Parnell or himself once they had departed. Perhaps there was some expectation that Parnell's income from his property in Ireland would meet their needs,[4] or that wealthy patrons (perhaps Lady Powerscourt, Thomas Acland, John Kennaway or Henry Drummond) would sponsor their work.[5]

In contrast to William Carey, Groves had not instructed his friends at home to hold the ropes while he climbed down the mine.[6] His personal disinterest in administration, and his open-handed view of money, meant that he probably neglected to raise the subject. Indeed, living "by faith" would require him to appeal to God alone, and if necessary to labour, like the apostle, with his own hands. No voluntary society had been created, and alternative means of support had simply not been formulated. This may sufficiently account for the neglect of the earliest

---

[1] Broomhall, *Treaty Wall*, 56; *Thousand Lives*, 120

[2] Robert, *Occupy*, 258-9

[3] William Bowden and George Beer did not exercise their crafts in India (see above, 166ff).

[4] Parnell was undoubtedly a financial asset. When he returned to Britain in 1837, Groves confessed, "His departure greatly alters my circumstances; but I must thankfully receive it at the Lord's hands, as obliging me to act simply to Him, and I do feel my soul so much more happy in this state of dependence upon God" (*Memoir* 1st edn., 262).

[5] On Groves's contact with these individuals, see PEANG, 42ff and 51ff.

[6] The need to travel widely soliciting funds greatly preoccupied Carey and his friends prior to his departure for India (George, 73-76).

Brethren to arrange systematic and communal financial provision for their missionaries.

More difficult to explain is their failure, after such a bright start, to send out further missionaries. We might attribute it partly to an increasing preoccupation with doctrinal and disciplinary controversies, partly to a general prejudice against all forms of organisation, partly to an idea newly promulgated by J N Darby that the Great Commission would be fulfilled by the Jews in a coming dispensation, and partly in some cases to an extreme Calvinism that left the conversion of the "heathen" entirely in the hands of God. Indeed, if Groves had been in Britain at the time, he would surely have addressed these issues, writing pamphlets and exhorting assemblies in many places, and had he done so the failure might have been avoided.

When he returned to Britain in the final months of his life, he was troubled to find such a profound lack of missionary interest among the Brethren. Shortly before his death, he several times visited the assemblies at Brook Street (Tottenham) and Orchard Street (Marylebone), and probably in Hackney too,[1] and he took the opportunity to share his thoughts about mission. He noted, "I went to Tottenham and... endeavoured to interest them about missions, spoke of Bowden, Beer and Arulappan, and in the evening brought the subject before the church."[2]

At Orchard Street, Groves met Count Piero Guicciardini from Florence, who had taken refuge in England from a current persecution of Evangelicals in Italy.[3] Guicciardini later returned to his homeland, and established a network of assemblies in northern Italy which continues to the present day. But Groves hoped for more than the recruitment of individual workers to work overseas. He was concerned most urgently about their financial needs. Although some support came from colonial settlers and administrators in India, this was hardly adequate. In fact the Bowdens and Beers in Godavari were almost starving,[4] and indigenous evangelists like Arulappan were labouring with inadequate resources, quite unknown to any Christians in Britain who might wish to help. Groves was delighted to see a positive response to the concerns he raised. After a visit to Brook Street, he confided, in a letter to his wife Harriet, "They hope, in union with believers in Hackney, Orchard Street, and other places to form an effectual committee to care for these things. This has been a great comfort to me... I feel thankful I came home; many things have been accomplished by it."[5]

In July 1853, two months after his death, the first issue of a monthly magazine, *The Missionary Reporter*, came off the press. It was a joint initiative of the assemblies in Tottenham and Hackney, and its fifth issue described its origins:

> This little periodical may be said to have resulted from a few faithful words spoken by Mr Groves this time last year. It was on the 31st Oct. 1852 when Mr Groves, having lately returned to this country on account of his health, gave to one of the churches a statement concerning the work of the Lord in India. With a feeling heart he also spoke of the necessities of some of the Lord's servants there whom he knew to need and to be

---

[1] The Hackney Brethren at this time met in the school room in St Thomas's Square. They did not purchase Providence Chapel in Paragon Road until 1856.
[2] M481
[3] M481
[4] Bromley, 41-2, 60
[5] M481

worthy of help. He stated his views that care for missionaries was one of the duties of a church, and he urged the necessity for activity in its discharge.[1]

The second issue, dated August 1853, included a long letter to the editor from William Bowden in which he suggested,

> The scripture of the New Testament indicates clearly, both by precept and example, that God requires not merely believers in their individual capacity but requires the congregations of the saints as such to take the care of the temporal concerns of its own members who are from any cause incapacitated for caring for themselves, as well as to care for the spread of the gospel and the temporal supply of those who are engaged therein. But it appears to me, dear brother, that most of the churches with which we are connected do not see these matters in this light.

It was exactly this failing which *The Missionary Reporter* sought to rectify.

From the beginning the purpose of the periodical was clear and its principles uncompromisingly Grovesian. No organisational distinction was to be drawn between "church" and "mission". Indeed, the first editorial was headed "Every Church a Missionary Society", and the opening article declared that "the wide world is in truth the mission field, and the one church of Christ on earth is, or should be, the Missionary Society."[2] The editor James Van Sommer (1822-1901) and his associates made clear that they were not creating a "society", or organising missions or appointing missionaries. On the contrary, they encouraged local churches to take initiatives in sending workers overseas. The magazine soon became a channel for gifts sent by individuals and assemblies to missionaries whose letters appeared in its pages.

The Missionary Reporter nowhere claimed to be a "Brethren" publication, and it included reports of missionary meetings and activities conducted by Anglicans and Baptists as well as those without a denominational identity. The majority of letters from the field were sent by missionaries who had gone without any connection to a missionary society – in some cases because there was no society operating in the land to which they were called, in others because they could not subscribe to the doctrinal or practical requirements of a society, or were unable to fulfil the academic requirements for ordination. Bowden and Beer sent regular letters. Issue number four contained a long report from Arulappan and another from Marian, a young man working with him. There was a notice of an interdenominational missionary conference convened by the Evangelical Alliance, an extract from George Müller's current *Narrative*, and a request for prayer for James Hudson Taylor, about to sail for the first time to China. Subsequent issues included further accounts of the work in India, and the thirteenth, in 1854, contained a long letter from Hudson Taylor with news of his arrival in Shanghai and initial impressions of China. By the time it lapsed in 1858, *The Missionary*

---

[1] *The Missionary Reporter*, No.5 (Nov. 1853), 63. An earlier missionary periodical, *The Gleaner in the Missionary Field*, had been in circulation since 1850. In 1853, as the interest of this publication became focused more particularly on China, it was renamed *The Missionary Gleaner*. The need thus arose for a magazine that would include news from other parts of the world.

[2] *The Missionary Reporter*, No.1 (July 1853), 8, 2

Reporter had carried news from forty different countries and more than a hundred missionaries.[1]

It is not clear why the periodical ceased at this point. Its editor hints in his later issues that it had become an expensive and time-consuming operation. Dependent so entirely on the personal correspondence and editorial labours of himself and his wife, it was vulnerable to any change in his personal circumstances, and its demise coincides with his personal removal from London to the south coast. It would not be easy for a solicitor in full-time employment to keep abreast of such a task in his moments of leisure.

Whatever the reason, the cessation of *The Missionary Reporter* marks a further lapse in Brethren missionary interest. But the Brethren were by no means alone in this. There was a similar lack of interest in the interdenominational efforts of the Chinese Evangelisation Society, leading to its humiliating demise in 1860.[2] Neither of these pioneering ventures survived quite long enough to benefit from the massive influx of revival converts that came to invigorate comparable initiatives during the following decade.

It was at this time, around 1866, that Henry Grattan Guinness expressed his frustration with the Brethren at Merrion Hall, Dublin, where he served as an elder. Their attitude towards overseas mission was no better than lukewarm. Despite this, he had a group of ten young men "studying the evidences of Christianity with a view to preparing for home and foreign missionary work."[3] Four went on to join the China Inland Mission. One of these, Charles Fishe, is reported to have said, "The Brethren of Merrion Hall, Dublin, deterred young Christians from going abroad, saying there was enough to be done at home."[4] Guinness himself would soon loosen his ties with the Brethren. Encouraged by Hudson Taylor, he left Ireland to establish his non-denominational East London Missionary Training Institute in the English capital.

Eventually, in 1872, a renewed missionary interest among the Brethren was marked by the launching of a new monthly magazine, *The Missionary Echo*. One of its three founding editors was Henry Groves, son of Anthony Norris. With a change of name to *Echoes of Service* in 1885, its editors continued to publish letters and forward gifts to workers associated with the Open Brethren throughout the world. During the following century, the Open Brethren rapidly became the most active of all British church denominations in sending and supporting cross-cultural missionaries.[5] At present reckoning, Brethren have created assemblies in

---

[1] Early issues of its successor, *The Missionary Echo*, state that *The Missionary Reporter* ceased in 1862, but as no copies from the period 1859-62 are extant, I suggest this may be incorrect. See also Stunt, "James Van Sommer", and Forrest, "The Missionary Reporter".

[2] Broomhall, *Thousand Lives*, 237

[3] Broomhall, *Survivors' Pact*, 114; Fiedler, 37

[4] *Survivors' Pact*, 119

[5] At the present time a total of 380 missionaries are associated with Echoes of Service, a larger body of British workers than any Anglican, Baptist or other denominational mission in the UK. With the extension of the Brethren movement to other parts of the world, magazines similar to *Echoes* have been launched in America, Australia and a number of other countries. The prayer digest *Operation World* currently identifies a worldwide total of 1429 Christian Brethren missionaries working in ninety-seven different nations (Johnstone & Mandryk, 743)

more than a hundred different nations,[1] and there are now approximately two and a half million Christians worldwide identifying themselves as such.[2] Their success owed much to the fact that their home churches functioned without the services of a paid minister. This meant, firstly, that men and women interested in full-time Christian service generally turned their attention overseas, and, secondly, that the home churches, freed from other expenditures, were willing and able to provide for them.

Later Ambiguities

It is not easy to ascertain the extent to which Brethren missionaries have been influenced by Groves in the period since his death. One commentator, in particular, criticised them for failing adequately to follow his example. George H Lang's biography, *Anthony Norris Groves: Saint and Pioneer*, published in 1939, was a deliberate attempt to reconnect the Brethren with Groves, and thus steer them away from paths he considered its subject would disapprove. His intention is clear from his subtitle: "A Combined Study of a Man of God and of the Original Principles and Practices of the Brethren with Application to Present Conditions", but his polemical style of writing, and his rather depressing account of Groves's failures, meant that the book provided little effective stimulus to change.[3]

Somewhat unfortunately for his cause, Lang's tendency to find fault with the editors of *Echoes of Service* also limited the circulation of his book among those associated with magazine.[4] Indeed, the editors at the time, notably W R Lewis, perceived in Lang's various writings an attack on their role as a centralised administration acting somewhat like a "missionary society". One of the magazine's editors, E H Broadbent, was requested to resign on account of his partial sympathy with Lang's view.[5]

Lang was similarly critical of the early-twentieth-century Missionary Study Classes instigated by Arthur Rendle Short. These were effective in stimulating missionary interest and recruitment among young people in the Open Brethren assemblies, but they also tended, in Lang's view, to encourage an unhealthy degree of organisation and administration, which he feared was gradually turning the Brethren into a conventional church denomination.

On his visits overseas, Lang found fault with missionaries who had created Brethren "mission stations", possessing substantial property and registered under

---

[1] Rowdon, "Brethren Contribution", 45

[2] Barrett; also Fiedler, 169.

[3] Many of Lang's books have been reprinted in recent years by Schoettle Publishing Company, including his biographies of Groves and Arulappan, and his autobiography, *An Ordered Life*.

[4] Grass, *Gathering*, 12.1.3 & 17.4. The Brethren similarly ignored the primitivist writings of Alexander R Hay, who in 1947 published *The New Testament Order for Church and Missionary*. Outside his own New Testament Missionary Union, Hay's influence was most evident in the early phases of the New Tribes Mission, but his advocacy of women's participation in church meetings made his book unacceptable to the Brethren of his generation (Fiedler, 282, 290).

[5] Tracing the existence of primitivist groups from the apostolic age to his own day, E H Broadbent (1861-1945) offered an alternative view of church history, thoroughly researched and well written, in *The Pilgrim Church*, first published in 1931. His final chapter provides a fine epitome of missiological primitivism.

the official auspices of the American magazine *Christian Missions in Many Lands*. In his view, these "Brethren missions" and "Brethren churches" bore the marks of a church denomination, having little or no desire to follow New Testament principles.

In subsequent years, occasional references to Groves in magazines such as *Echoes of Service*, along with brief accounts of his life in the histories of Brethren mission by W T Stunt and Frederick Tatford, issued in 1972 and 1982-6,[1] and in Tatford's short booklet about him in 1979,[2] ensured that Brethren missionaries had some general awareness of him as a man of faith with a desire to follow the apostolic pattern. Despite this, very few read anything he wrote, for hardly any of his writings have survived, except in archives inaccessible to the general public. Rarely, if ever, have his own words been quoted by Brethren missionaries. In general, they remain unaware of his views concerning indigenous initiatives, administrative accountability, missionary co-operation, leadership training, Christian industries and schools. There has never been a widely accepted book written by Brethren on the subject of missionary methods. Nor has any consistent or systematic guidance concerning missionary strategy been given to missionaries by the editors of the magazines publishing news of their labours. Brethren missionary writing has typically focused on the dramatic experiences of the pioneer missionary evangelist, with little discussion relating to the development of indigenous fellowships or the encouragement of indigenous leadership.[3] With the exception of Groves himself, there has never been a Brethren missiologist.[4]

Unaware of Groves's missiological thinking, the majority of Brethren missionaries have attempted to apply to their overseas context the "assembly principles" learned at home. In essence, these entailed a plural unpaid leadership, a "Breaking of Bread" every Sunday morning (in which men were allowed free participation whilst women wore a head covering and kept silence), and a "Gospel meeting" every Sunday evening (conducted, if possible, by a different male speaker each week). In general, we find Brethren missionaries directing their attention to spiritual and sometimes medical or educational needs rather than to matters of social or political concern. In this they contrast with many contemporaries. To a greater degree than most Nonconformists, they have made a virtue of "separation from the world", distancing themselves from local officials and secular enterprises.[5] And unlike the early Anglican agents in India, and pioneers such as David Livingstone elsewhere, they have shunned appointments and salaries offered by the politico-religious Establishment; nor have they

---

[1] The first edition of W T Stunt's *Turning the World Upside Down* was published in 1972, appearing in a second edition the following year. Tatford's ten volumes, issued 1982-6, never achieved the popularity of Stunt's work.

[2] Tatford, *A N Groves, the Father of Faith Missions*.

[3] See, for example, Arnot, *Bihe and Garenganze*; Crawford, *Thinking Black*; Marsh, *Too Hard for God?*; Allison, *Leaves from the African Jungle*.

[4] From the Brethren camp, Ken Fleming offers a good brief introduction to Pauline methods in his *Essentials of Missionary Service*, but he does not discuss the application of principles to diverse modern circumstances or address current issues of missiological controversy.

[5] Coad, *History*, 206n

generally been expected by colonial authorities to serve the national interests of their homelands.[1]

Brethren missions have not been consciously or consistently primitivist in orientation, and their success has been mixed. Visiting the Godavari Delta in 1910, seventy years after evangelistic work was launched there by Groves's recruits Bowden and Beer, G H Lang noted that, despite the many conversions, "there was a manifest weakness as regards churches." Indeed, "there were few men ready or fit to shoulder responsibility in the house of God. Practically everything depended on the 'missionary' and his money." Lang's conclusion was typically blunt: "This was sad after so many years. Yet it is scarcely to be avoided where the foreigner who starts the work remains permanently at hand." In particular, "The practice of paying a salary to the native workers in the gospel is baneful. It makes them dependent on him and not on God, prevents a working faith that can surmount difficulties, and keeps the foreigner in the position of being the employer and master."[2] If Lang's judgement is correct, the successors of Bowden and Beer in the Godavari Delta do not seem to have followed the principles for developing indigenous leadership suggested by Groves.

A detailed study of Brethren missions in subsequent generations lies outside the scope of this book, and we can do no more than suggest some lines of enquiry by touching briefly on four case histories, two derived from the experience of missionaries and two from historians of Christian mission.

Dan Crawford (1870-1926)

With reference to Groves's model of frugal living and cultural identification, Chilcraft suggests that "many Brethren missionaries followed Groves' example,"[3] and he points to the case of the twenty-year-old Dan Crawford. In 1892, "he went to central Africa with just one change of underwear and without a spare pair of shoes. When these wore out, he wore native clothing and sandals. His one 'luxury' was an iron camp bed, bought from a trader."[4] Crawford's frugal lifestyle and his sensitive approach to the Africans, along with his ability to communicate in their own languages, contrasted strikingly with the arrogance of Belgian colonial officialdom. His younger colleagues followed his example: "When they approached the natives they did so with empty hands, or with a walking stick; they

---

[1] On Brethren reluctance to engage in politics, see Wilson, "Your Citizenship is in Heaven". Sweetnam notes how novel was the apolitical stance of the early Brethren missionaries: "Caught up in the Belgian and British scramble for Katanga, the missionaries were involved, if only by location, in an issue vital to British national interest. The extent to which these men were defying expected missionary behaviour becomes apparent when we discover that both King Leopold II of Belgium and Cecil Rhodes 'assumed that the British missionaries would do everything in their power to further the territorial ambitions of the agents of Queen Victoria'. However, they had reckoned without the strength of the conviction that motivated the missionaries, and Arnot, Crawford, and the others remained politically peripheral. Crawford's comment on the situation was telling: 'Do not dabble in "high politics," so called; our politics are higher than the high'" (Sweetnam, Para.19, citing Rotberg, "Plymouth Brethren and the occupation of Katanga", 288; and Crawford, *Thinking Black*, 302)
[2] Lang, *An Ordered Life*, 120
[3] Chilcraft, Ch.4
[4] Ibid

shared the native food, and as near as possible entered into native conditions, and consequently the African found he had nothing to fear from them. As they moved from place to place they let it be known they were the friends of all and the enemies of none."[1]

Crawford was, by conviction and inclination, an itinerant evangelist. His nephew and biographer, George Tilsley, records that

> He knew nothing of an organised mission; he had no home committee, no society to whom he looked for his support; he was responsible to God and drew supplies from God. Reports; statistics; constituencies and their clamouring for pictures of visible accomplishments; stipendiary systems – all these commonplaces of missionary-station talk were unfamiliar to him. Indeed he was even a protester against codified creeds; against clerisy and all its ramifications and implications; and even against all forms of federalization of churches. His entire thought and habit were moulded to a wholehearted individualism, which, in principle at least, and largely in practice, he allowed to others equally with himself.[2]

This was unusual. Indeed, "The missionaries whom he met not only did not share such views, but were astonished to discover that anyone held them, and bewildered to conceive how it could be possible to carry them into effect in a pagan land." To his contemporaries "it seemed naïve."[3] Like Groves, he found his relations with other missionaries sometimes tense and strained; in fact he generally enjoyed better relations with Africans than with other Westerners.[4]

Like Groves, Crawford actively encouraged African evangelists to take their own initiatives, to offer the gospel to their own people in their own way, and, if possible, to earn their own living.[5] But again, like Groves, he took pains to make sure the evangelists should not be short of necessities, and even arranged for small regular amounts to be passed on to them by local white traders with whom he settled accounts from time to time.[6] Returning to Britain after twenty-five years, Crawford was not eager to recruit more missionaries, believing that evangelistic outreach would be far better accomplished by the Africans themselves. In his own words, "My life-plan was to work through and only to work by native brethren."[7]

Like Groves, Crawford refused to direct or organise the emerging Christian community.[8] On his itinerations, he frequently left his main congregation in Luanza in the care of its African leaders, without any missionary presence whatsoever. His desire was for local converts to take responsibility from the start, declaring, "We must be hourly on our guard against using our carnal prestige as whites."[9] Although Crawford would not allow local culture more authority than the New Testament in deciding matters of Christian doctrine or practice, he was

---

[1] Hawthorn, 60. In this they contrasted with Bishop Charles F Mackenzie, who took sides in tribal disputes and eventually found himself engaged in violent warfare (Newell, *Not War*).
[2] Tilsley, 473-4
[3] Tilsley, 474
[4] Sweetnam Para. 48n
[5] Crawford, *Thinking Black*, 438-9, 483-4
[6] Tilsley, 486
[7] Tilsley, 489
[8] He memorably described those missionaries who did so as "little Protestant Popes" and "prophets, priests and kings rolled into one" (*Thinking Black*, 324).
[9] Tilsley, 495

remarkably tolerant of indigenous cultural accretions when scripture offered no reason to object to them. He was by no means inclined to inhibit or control his converts or to restrict them to forms of behaviour identifiable in the New Testament.[1] During 1905, several baptisms took place, and Crawford noted, "the local Luanza church has taken these baptisms so definitely into its own hands that we take courage to go forward." Tilsley comments,

> He desired the assembly of Christians to recognise and undertake their responsibilities as a church from the very beginning... He would rarely, if ever, interfere to suggest or to veto any names for baptism; almost never did he himself baptize after the admission of the very first converts had created an assembly; and from the first, ministry in the meetings of the churches was open to any brother, black or white, who was led of the Spirit, whether in prayer or in spiritual song (not always prescribed, but sometimes extempore in true African style), in prophecy or in teaching. The care of all the churches pressed daily upon Mr Crawford. But the way forward, as it seemed to him, was not that he should carry the whole burden, but that the churches should learn, by actually doing it, to carry each its own load of responsibility toward God as a component part of the Body of Christ.[2]

Crawford's biographer concludes, "The manner of Dan's life, coupled with his devotion to the Word of God and the congregational principles which he held and taught, had the effect of building up an indigenous church – though the term became current too late for him to use it."[3]

With his personal ambition to "think black", offering an African gospel to Africa, Crawford stands in contrast to the far more patronising generation of missionaries that preceded him, including Livingstone whom he nevertheless greatly admired. Mark Sweetnam suggests that Crawford's sturdy independence of mind owed much to the habit of anti-establishment thought encouraged by the Open Brethren, and also to his financial independence. Living "by faith", rather than by contract or salary, he felt himself accountable to God alone, and this meant he could freely express his opinions as an individual rather than as the servant of a society or a colonial power.[4]

In fact, Crawford's book *Thinking Black* was the first of a new generation of missionary writings. It sought not so much to document the scientific attributes of a territory with a view to its pacification and administration or its occupation by a missionary society, but rather to "understand", and thus to respect and empathise with, its indigenous inhabitants. His purpose was not simply to derive amusement from African customs, and thus to confirm perceptions of Western superiority, but rather to show how much may be learnt from people of another culture.[5]

There is no doubt that Crawford's individualism, his "naïvety", his independence of mind, his frugal lifestyle and his desire to live like the people to

---

[1] See, for example, Crawford, *Thinking Black*, 55-8.
[2] Tilsley, 496
[3] Tilsley, 497
[4] Sweetnam, Para.21
[5] Sweetnam, Para.13-14. Sweetnam points out that F S Arnot, who preceded Crawford as a Brethren missionary to Africa, wrote what could be considered a very conventional missionary narrative. This might be attributed to his closer personal links with Livingstone and Moffat, and thus his greater identification with the earlier British missionary tradition (Para.21n).

whom he was called, along with his great respect for their personal competence in their own cultural context, mark him out as a missionary of distinctly Grovesian characteristics.

A study of early Brethren mission elsewhere would almost certainly unearth a sensitivity comparable to Crawford's. There is evidence that they had a conscious desire to proclaim a gospel that both harmonised with and challenged every culture. This is confirmed by Pauline Summerton in her account of the Fisher family, younger colleagues of Crawford in central Africa. Although they wished the Christian way of life to replace the pagan way of life, "there was no deliberate attempt to convert the African to the Western way of life, of which they were in many respects critics."[1] Missionaries from this Brethren stable would attempt to respect every culture but reverence none.[2]

Crawford's writings give no indication that he was aware of Groves's missiological thought. Nevertheless, his conversion in 1887, and his early spiritual growth, took place in Brethren circles where George Müller was a household name, and where Robert Chapman, Henry Groves (son of A N Groves) and Hudson Taylor were highly regarded.[3] He was persuaded by F S Arnot to work in Africa in association with *Echoes of Service*, edited still at that time by John Lindsay MacLean and Henry Groves. He was especially affected by a farewell sermon from the latter on the subject "Ye have need of patience."[4] It seems likely that Crawford devised a mission strategy in many respects similar to that of Groves on account of the basic ecclesiological principles they held in common.

Jim Elliot

Brethren missionaries have often warmed to the writings of Roland Allen (which, as we shall see, may owe a certain amount to Groves).[5] Pauline Summerton identifies Walter Fisher as one such.[6] Chilcraft notes another:

> An interesting example of Allen's influence beyond his original target group is in the diary of the Brethren missionary martyr, Jim Elliot. His journal for April 25th 1950 records, "I have been tremendously helped these last two days in the reading of Roland Allen's *Missionary Methods: St. Paul's or Ours...* Such truth if applied to the U.S. in 1950, would revolutionize the entire church. Written by a churchman, it carries that much more weight on the side of simplicity and autonomous assembly development."

Elliot had heard of Groves, and even noted in his journal, "Anthony Norris Groves was a pioneer missionary in India who started work on New Testament lines. I must read his memoirs if I can get them." They were evidently not easily accessible, and as Chilcraft points out, it was Allen, a High Church Anglican, who introduced primitivist missiological ideas to Elliot: "He [Elliot] shows no detailed knowledge of Groves' missiology. The teaching of planting autonomous churches

---

[1] Summerton, 82-3
[2] The distinction is drawn by O'Brien, 354. See below, 252ff.
[3] Tilsley, 32
[4] Tilsley, 37
[5] See below, 223ff.
[6] Summerton, 72-3

had come full circle; from the Brethren it had spread to high Anglicans only to return to a new generation of Brethren missionaries."[1]

In the event, Elliot's early death deprived him of the opportunity both to read Groves's *Memoir* and to plant any "autonomous churches". Interesting comparisons might nevertheless be drawn between the churches that actually were created by Brethren missionaries in many parts of the world and those associated with other mission agencies. We will consider some in Zambia and some in Mysore State, India.

Zambian Assemblies

The Zambian church historian, Kovina Mutenda, observes that "The Brethren are the largest of the evangelical churches in Zambia, with well over a thousand autonomous assemblies."[2]

Mutenda notes that the majority of Brethren missionaries have historically engaged in evangelistic preaching rather than educational or social work, which is relatively unusual in a context where other missions had major educational programmes.[3]

Medical work, on the other hand, early became a major aspect of Brethren activity, involving a number of hospitals and clinics. Colonial governmental authorities required that such work be registered, and the name of the American magazine *Christian Missions in Many Lands* was adopted as an identity for Brethren institutions in Zambia.[4] This has raised many of the same property issues that are faced by other Western mission agencies, and Mutenda identifies difficulties especially when missionaries have wished to retain control of mission stations and medical facilities independently of the Zambian church leaders.[5] Tensions have thus resulted from a perceived attempt to separate "church" from "mission".

Local congregations associated with the Brethren have become known as CMML churches, and are often thought of as a denomination, although they stoutly resist proposals to create a "central governing body" for administration and control at a national level.

The relationship between Brethren missionaries and indigenous Christians appears more generally egalitarian than has been the case in other ecclesiastical traditions. Mutenda remarks that "The New Testament does not speak of 'native helpers' but of partners in the work. Looking at the past and looking to the future in this centenary year [2002], it is clear that the experience of the Brethren assemblies illustrates this relationship abundantly."[6]

The issue of finance has been a delicate one, however, and, with some possible exceptions, Mutenda suggests that,

---

[1] Elliot, *Journals of Jim Elliot*, 183-4, 239
[2] Mutenda, 8
[3] Mutenda comments, "In the 1920s CMML, the biggest Protestant mission, with 54 missionaries in the country, ran only 47 schools. By contrast, the London Missionary Society with 21 missionaries ran 228 schools, and the Dutch Reformed Church Mission with 41 missionaries had 509 schools" (p.16).
[4] Mutenda, 15
[5] Mutenda, 163ff
[6] Mutenda, 1

The Christians in the Zambian Brethren assemblies have never learnt to give, or else they were never taught how to do so... As most, if not all, Brethren missionaries were supported by churches abroad, believers in Zambia never saw in practice how a local assembly goes about supporting a full-time worker. It may well be true that the later generations never heard the teaching, as missionaries avoided the subject, thinking "How can we who appear rich teach those who are poor to give?"[1]

The stewardship of money was a subject avoided not only by missionaries but also by Zambian evangelists, lest they give an impression of begging. In consequence, many seeking to "live by faith" are inadequately supported, and "there are very few assemblies which have learnt to give generously to support their own commended workers."[2] It thus appears that Groves's vision for "Christian devotedness" has been adopted by the evangelists but to a much lesser degree by the generality of Christians. Despite this, Mutenda commends a recent trend for Zambian Christian businessmen to offer significant financial assistance for local evangelistic initiatives.[3] A number of evangelists, or their wives, earn their living through secular work, and if they do so willingly, Groves would approve.

These strengths and weaknesses may be thought to stem from distinctive missionary methods followed by the Brethren in Zambia. In so far as they have formed what is, in effect, a separate denomination, one might think them far from Groves's ideal. And when missionaries claim a distinction between "church" and "mission" that is denied by Zambian Christians, he would hardly approve. But in other respects, the emphasis on indigenous evangelism, congregational autonomy, living "by faith", free participation in meetings, and a weekly Breaking of Bread, are all perhaps elements of a Grovesian heritage in Zambia.

Mysore Assemblies

Turning our attention to an area of southern India not far from the sphere occupied by Groves himself, we can draw upon a useful survey of *Brethren Missionary Activity in Mysore State* covering the century 1876 to 1971 by Kenneth J Newton.[4] In 1969, the Brethren in Mysore State had thirty-eight local assemblies, "a number of which have sprung up through the labours of Indian workers."[5] Most, however, were foreign initiatives from the middle decades of the twentieth century.

From Newton's introduction to his study, we may quickly infer an ethos somewhat alien to Groves's non-denominational and non-societal expectation: "One of the many Missionary Societies which has established and built up churches here is that known as the Brethren." And Newton notes that, in comparison with other parts of India, Mysore State has been "one of the least fruitful" for Brethren missionary activity.[6]

---

[1] Mutenda, 185
[2] Mutenda, 187
[3] Mutenda, 195
[4] Newton's essay was first produced in 1971 at the United Theological College, Bangalore, and then, in 1975, published as a Christian Brethren Research Fellowship Occasional Paper in the UK. References are to the CBRF edition.
[5] *Mysore*, 42
[6] Recent reports speak of more than two thousand assemblies in India identifying themselves as Christian Brethren (Daniel, *Prayer Handbook*, xiv).

His paper was occasioned in 1971 by a matter of urgent concern: "The removal of foreign influence [by government decree] seems likely to be followed by a time of perplexity as these churches assume full self-responsibility." And he observed, "Until recently, foreign influence in the churches in India has been both dominant and essential."[1] This, again, seems to assume a methodology some way removed from the indigenous methods of Groves.

Newton traces the origins of "Brethren" work in Mysore State back to 1876, with the arrival of Miss Louise Anstey "as an independent worker without salary", but he suggests that "the first of the Brethren missionaries to Mysore state" were a Mr and Mrs W A Redwood, who joined her in 1883. Focusing on the Malavalli and Kollegal districts, Newton makes no reference to Groves's sons, Frank and Henry, who had established a sugar refinery in 1847 near Seringapatam, Mysore, assisted later by Edward, who was "able to join his brothers in seeking to make, as his dear father so desired, their employment at Palhully subservient to the work of God."[2] After the sale of this industry in 1862, the company of Indian Christians who remained in the vicinity were evidently not identified as "Brethren".

The Redwoods arrived to find a missionary tradition in India involving the creation of a mission compound, usually on the outskirts of a town or village, with a bungalow and outhouses, dispensary, school and church building, along with the appointment of a salaried Indian helper. Newton observes that "the Brethren Mission followed very closely this pattern."[3] It was, indeed, a pattern that Groves himself had adopted in Chittoor.

As additional Brethren missionaries arrived, their work was co-ordinated by a "Mysore State Brethren Conference" (later known as the "Kanarese Workers' Conference"). Attended by senior and representative missionaries, meeting annually or quarterly, the Conference oversaw the schools, dispensaries, village evangelism initiatives, orphanages and boarding homes. From 1917 onwards it also made comity agreements with other missionary agencies working in the region, thus formalising the good relations which individual Brethren missionaries had generally enjoyed with other expatriate Evangelicals.

But the tendency for the Conference to exercise control over Brethren workers caused evident tensions, and Newton suggests that "the Kanarese Workers' Conference, in its desire for administrative efficiency, contradicted standard Brethren policy."[4] Indeed, "A cardinal Brethren belief is that each worker is a servant of the Lord and responsible to Him alone; but on the mission field there is a necessity to show a common purpose and also to give expression to a spiritual and outward unity among workers." In fact, "The Mission could never blend these two elements."[5] The Conference, indeed, exerted a considerable degree of authority:

> In its chequered career the Conference was responsible for having members recalled to the homeland and excommunicated at least one member (who remained a missionary in the area nevertheless). It refused to endorse several missionary applicants from overseas, in some cases in direct opposition to churches at home who were willing to send the persons concerned. It decided in what ways co-operation could be extended to other

---

[1] Newton, *Mysore*, 9
[2] M520-1. See also Groves, E K, *Successors*, 152-3 etc.
[3] *Mysore*, 15
[4] *Mysore*, 35
[5] *Mysore*, 34

Missions and what policy should be made with regard to ecumenical church movements in the State.[1]

In 1926 the authoritarian stance adopted by the Conference was questioned in a tactful letter from the office of Echoes of Service in Bath.[2] During the course of forty years, Indian Christians were rarely invited to attend the Conference, even as observers.

From the earliest days of this Brethren work, Indian Christians engaging in full-time spiritual ministry were paid a small salary, in some cases supplemented by proceeds from the sale of literature. By 1956, however, there were twelve evangelists who, without a set salary, were living "by faith" on a similar basis to the missionaries. Considerable controversy arose when the Conference decided to extend an invitation to Indian participants, and it stemmed from the question of whether to include only those living "by faith", or some others also – salaried men, who had proved no less diligent in their spiritual labours, and in some cases, perhaps, more so. There was evidently a tendency to consider as second-class workers those who did not "live by faith". The tensions continued for some time unresolved.

Newton discerned a general reluctance among the early missionaries to allow Indians to meet on their own for the Lord's Supper: "There is the example [in 1898] of the missionaries asking the four believers in Talkad (one the evangelist and another the Mission School teacher) to go to Kollegal for the 'breaking of bread' meeting rather than arrange their own service."[3] The reason for this was plain: "The main question was not how many believers were required to be present to allow a 'breaking of bread' meeting, but what spiritual gift was necessary before they could thus meet."[4] Also significant was the problem of illiteracy, which was felt to inhibit free participation and the development of spiritual gift, and tended to give the educated evangelist an unfortunately exalted status in each local group. As most Indian Christians were drawn from the "depressed classes", they were thought to lack sufficient confidence to take responsibility, and therefore remained merely passive observers in small local congregations.

Newton suggests that, for these varied reasons, "it has not been possible for missionaries to come to village India and plant churches similar to those from which they came." The consequence was regrettable: "The result was that instead of there being churches where many shared in preaching responsibilities and in the worship services (as is Brethren tradition), there were churches where the missionary (and sometimes one or two Indians) were the sole participators in church meetings. The end was that as soon as the missionaries left… the Christians in these places ceased to gather as a church."[5]

This brief analysis raises the question of why the Brethren missionaries in Mysore failed to stimulate a spontaneous expansion of indigenous fellowships, whereas Rhenius and Arulappan had been able to do so. The reason probably lies in the strategy adopted. Brethren missionaries in Mysore State chose to establish a

---

[1] *Mysore*, 35
[2] *Mysore*, 35
[3] Kollegal Church Roll, 1898, 58 (cited by Newton, *Mysore*, 39)
[4] *Mysore*, 39
[5] *Mysore*, 41-2

foreign denomination in India, using methods learned from the missionary societies that preceded them. There is no sign that they drew upon the thinking or example of Anthony Norris Groves. Only when political changes in the 1970s demanded the withdrawal of foreign leadership did Indian Christians begin to play a significant part in the leadership of the assemblies they had created.

Elsewhere in India it seems that Brethren missionaries adopted a less authoritarian role and were more successful in seeing Indian Christians taking responsibility. A recent article describes how "the movement of Brethren churches in Kerala" was launched in early 1872 by an evangelist called Mathai from Tamil Nadu. The writer notes that "Mathai was a disciple of John Arulappan, who himself was attached to Anthony Norris Groves."[1] This would appear to be a more thoroughly Grovesian initiative, and in Kerala there are now six hundred groups identified as Brethren assemblies.

Recent reports indicate that five hundred Brethren assemblies are found in Andhra Pradesh, the state in which Groves spent twenty years of his life, four hundred in Tamil Nadu, where Arulappan had his base, and three hundred in the Godavari Delta, pioneered by Bowden and Beer.[2] The Brethren in India currently support at least 1300 missionaries and evangelists sent out to other parts of the country and further afield.[3] In describing their origins, these fellowships generally see themselves as the fruit of indigenous initiatives rather than the offspring of foreign missions. As such, we might think they effectively fulfil Groves's vision for the spontaneous growth of biblical Indian churches.

Conclusion: Brethren Missions

Groves's influence on Brethren missions has been both direct and indirect, through the dissemination of his own writings, and through the missiological application of an ecclesiology that owed much to him.

It was the direct influence of Groves in 1829 that encouraged his brother-in-law George Müller to resign from a missionary society and "live by faith", looking directly to God for guidance and provision. We can see Groves's views reflected in the principles adopted by Müller for his Scriptural Knowledge Institution, and in his choice of like-minded missionaries to support, and then in the advice and encouragement he sent them during a period of fifty-two years.

Brethren missions, since Groves's day, have been largely identified with the magazines, *The Missionary Reporter* and *The Missionary Echo* (renamed *Echoes of Service*). The former originated with an exhortation of Groves himself shortly before his death, and the latter was founded and edited by his eldest son Henry. To Groves can also be attributed the working principle that, in publishing information and forwarding gifts, these magazines and their editors should support, but not direct, missionary activity.

In other respects, however, the influence of Groves on Brethren missions can be considered less clear-cut. Following his own initial call to Baghdad and the enthusiasm it aroused, some forty years passed before significant numbers of Brethren missionaries were being sent overseas. Then his own writings, his

---

[1] Kerala Brethren History, <http://www.brethrentoday.com/keralahistory.htm> (accessed 6th July 2003).
[2] Rowdon, *International Partnership Perspectives*, No.3, 40
[3] Daniel, *Prayer Handbook*, 375

widow's *Memoir*, and Lang's biography, all failed to become recommended reading for those associated with the magazines. Recruits, from the 1860s onwards, have been far more strongly influenced in practice by their personal experience of Brethren assemblies in the sending countries of the West than by Groves himself.

To the extent that Groves's influence was felt in the assemblies of the United Kingdom, his principles would be carried overseas. Dan Crawford, for one, appears to have used methods very similar to those of Groves, and the assemblies that he and others have established will reflect those principles. Groves's emphasis on liberty of ministry, active participation in the body, plural unpaid leadership, and his concepts of holiness, "light", faith and obedience, have all become characteristic of the Open Brethren around the world. In contrast, his non-denominationalism has been largely ignored, and the Brethren have become a denomination in many places, with a distinct style and tradition of their own, marked especially by a focus on the Atonement in both worship and evangelism (often to the exclusion of other subjects), and a requirement that women keep silence and wear a head covering during the weekly Breaking of Bread.

The tendency, during the final decades of the twentieth century, for distinctive Brethren tenets to be abandoned in the English-speaking nations has been slow to filter through to assemblies established by missionaries in other parts of the world. In consequence, we now find the majority of "Brethren churches" overseas far more recognisably "Brethren" than those in the West, and "Brethren missionaries", in general, far more conservative than the congregations that support them.

The fact that many of the earliest pioneers were not highly educated, and were at heart evangelists rather than teachers or pastors, undoubtedly contributed to the general weakness of Brethren missiology. Their tendency, moreover, to reject writings by both Brethren and non-Brethren suspected of unsoundness has deprived them of access to scholarship which would have helped them establish a more conscious strategy of mission.

In conclusion, we should recognise the role of Groves in the launching of the Brethren movement, the undoubted impact of *Christian Devotedness* and his own example on the earliest generation of Brethren, the ongoing influence of Müller in applying his ecclesiological principles to the Brethren and his "faith principles" to missionary support. But the exporting of Brethren tradition, the development of a quasi-denominational identity, the emphasis on missionary ministry, along with the imposition of administrative authority in certain places, has rendered these Brethren missions somewhat alien to Groves's primitivist ideals.

Faith Missions

Our study has identified a number of traits observable in the mission initiatives of Groves in Baghdad and India that differ markedly from the path traditionally followed by the classic denominational "voluntary societies", such as the CMS, LMS, BMS and the ABCFM. Turning our attention from the missionary societies that preceded Groves to those which commenced after his death, we must now enquire how far the new methods they adopted resembled his.

It is generally accepted that the launching of the China Inland Mission by Hudson Taylor in the year 1865 marked the beginning of a new age in Protestant missions.[1] The CIM was, in the words of Klaus Fiedler, "the first mission of a new

---

[1] See, for example, Taber, 58.

era, the era of interdenominational faith missions."[1] The founders of all subsequent "faith missions" drew inspiration and encouragement from the example of Hudson Taylor. But it has been suggested that Taylor himself was personally influenced by Groves.[2]

The title "father of faith missions" was first attributed to Groves in print by A Pulleng in 1958,[3] and it has reappeared occasionally since then. Chilcraft questions its aptness:

> Given Groves' deep antipathy to mission organisations, the claim that he is "the father of faith missions" is a little disingenuous; he might be better regarded as "the apostle of faith mission principles" or "the first modern faith missionary". Despite his deserved reputation for trusting God for material things, this is but one aspect of his achievements and must be seen as an integral part of the whole of his missiology.[4]

The question is thus raised as to how far the complete missiological package proposed by Groves was adopted by the CIM and other "faith mission" agencies.

Groves as a Model for "Faith Missions"

Groves and Hudson Taylor
Mission theorists have observed that, in the progress of the Christian Church from apostolic times onwards, each major historic movement of missionary expansion has received its inspiration from a spiritual revival in a so-called Christian homeland.[5] It is in the 1858-9 revival in Britain and America that Fiedler, for example, locates the origins of the remarkable series of Anglophone initiatives that followed the example of Hudson Taylor. The "faith missions", in his view, derived their vigour from the impetus generated in the revival, and they recruited the bulk of their workforce from its converts.[6]

Such a historical analysis can hardly be refuted, and yet the methods adopted by Taylor, and by the leaders of the revival, had their genesis in stirrings that we might locate somewhat earlier, stirrings indeed that could be traced back a full twenty years to fresh views of Christian ministry, unity and faith demonstrated by George Müller and, before him, by Groves.

It was prior to the revival, in 1857, that Hudson Taylor resigned from the Chinese Evangelisation Society "to become an independent missionary".[7] He

---

[1] Fiedler, 9. See also Bosch, 332-3; and Stanley, *The Bible and the Flag*, 76. For a comprehensive listing of agencies identifiable as "faith missions" see Fiedler, *passim*.

[2] See, for example, Lang, *Groves*, 19. One might suppose, in the light of subsequent theological trends, that both Groves and the "faith missions" were motivated, at least partly, by a desire to counteract liberal theology and to provide a sound alternative to older missions influenced by it. This would be an error. In Groves's case the reason is simply that his views were formed before liberal ideas had significantly infiltrated church circles known to him. In the case of the "faith missions", their early writings show no evidence, perhaps somewhat surprisingly, of any such ambition (Fiedler, 125).

[3] Pulleng (p.7) notes that others had attributed the title to Groves before his own use of it.

[4] Chilcraft, Ch.6

[5] Fiedler, 112-6

[6] Fiedler, 12-13. See also Walls, "Evangelical Revival", 310-1.

[7] Fiedler, 24. The early influence on Hudson Taylor of Müller, and of the Brethren in Hull led by Andrew Jukes, is documented and discussed in FOFM 510.

thereupon resolved to seek financial provision only "as an answer to prayer in faith".[1] At this point his position as a non-denominational missionary, without a contract or salary or even a recognised "home-church" to pledge continued support, was identical in every way to that of Groves. On his arrival in China, he adopted the habit of giving away everything surplus to immediate requirements, sharing a common purse with his closest colleagues, refusing to make his needs known, and refusing to enter into debt.[2] On this basis Taylor continued for the next eight years, and then, without changing his method at all, simply invited others to participate in it. Thus, in 1865, was founded the China Inland Mission. From this point onwards, the "faith missions" of the English-speaking world owe their fundamental principles to the model adopted and applied by Hudson Taylor. It was, we might suggest, a distinctively Grovesian model, for Taylor's early experiences in China resemble, to a remarkable degree, those of Groves in India.

Co-operation with All Denominations

Like Groves, the young Hudson Taylor sought and enjoyed fellowship with Christians of diverse agencies, various nationalities and all denominations. Indeed, newly arrived in China in 1853, he gave and received personal and practical assistance far beyond the call of duty, and formed warm and mutually appreciative friendships with other missionaries wherever he went. This did not save him from condemnation at the hands of the missionary community, and vehement opposition to his plans for marriage, on account of the fact that he was not ordained, that he was not attached to any church denomination, that he had no regular income, and (a point sometimes overlooked) that he did not observe conventional Sabbath restrictions.[3] These criticisms suffered by Taylor from missionaries in China were exactly the criticisms levelled at Groves by the missionary community in India. And just as Groves deliberately sought fellowship with those whose views differed from his,[4] so did Hudson Taylor.

Indeed, we might argue that Taylor had absorbed, from George Müller and from the assemblies in the London suburbs, a form of Brethrenism distinctly Grovesian in character and far removed from the narrower Darbyite influences prevailing elsewhere.[5] Throughout the months before the birth of the CIM, Taylor was in close touch with George Müller: "Many long talks J H T had with him. Felt

---

[1] Taylor, *Retrospect*, 95. Taylor's wavering resolve was strengthened at this time by his more mature CES colleagues John and Mary Jones, who deserve more notice than they have yet received as early advocates of "faith principles" (Broomhall, *Thousand Lives*, 64).

[2] *Thousand Lives*, 63-5, 110-1

[3] *Thousand Lives*, 91-2.

[4] See above, 81ff.

[5] In his application to join the CES in the summer of 1853, Hudson Taylor had asserted "the right of all Christians to preach, baptise and administer the Lord's Supper". He declared, "I do not believe in the division of the church into clergy and laity." Although such a view may owe something to the radical Methodism of his parents, in which they aligned themselves with the reformers against the clericism of Jabez Bunting, it more typically reflects Brethren influences. His acceptance on these terms by the CES committee was not something Taylor had taken for granted, "for the majority of the Committee are Clergymen, Ministers and others holding the opposite view" (Broomhall, *Treaty Wall*, 92).

him to be so wise, and a thorough man of business."[1] When Taylor took some of his earliest recruits to Bristol in August 1865, their first engagement on the day of their arrival was to take tea with "Mrs H Groves" and then accompany her to Müller's fellowship at Bethesda.[2] In 1872, Taylor and William Berger spent three days with Müller, "discussing the mission's problems", and later visited him again.[3] And likewise, in the London area, Taylor's particular friends, George Pearse, John and Robert Howard, the Bergers, and Miss Stacey (with whom both he and Groves stayed during their respective visits to Tottenham) represented a strand of Brethrenism largely or entirely uncontaminated by Darbyite negativism.[4] This circle also possessed an unusual gentleness and an element of mysticism probably attributable to the Quaker origins of its leading figures and reflected in the pacifistic responses of both Groves and Taylor to the "spoiling" of their goods.[5] It can be no coincidence that the financial support Taylor received during his first decade in China came almost entirely from Groves's friends: Müller, the Howards, Berger and Pearse.[6] We may thus see in Hudson Taylor an exponent, and a missionary exponent too, of Brethrenism in its most Grovesian form.

Mention of George Pearse brings to mind his response on first reading Groves's *Memoir*, and "how much the large-hearted catholic noble christian principles of Mr Groves's Brethrenism commend themselves to me, in contrast with that which is *called* Brethrenism in the present day."[7] We might feel justified in considering Hudson Taylor the truest heir and exemplar of "Mr Groves's Brethrenism" in its

---

[1] From verbatim notes of James Hudson Taylor's reminiscences taken by Dr & Mrs Howard Taylor in preparation for their biography (Broomhall, *Thousand Lives*, 428).

[2] Broomhall, *Survivors' Pact*, 64. This was almost certainly Harriet (widow of A N Groves), who was in Bristol at this time, rather than the wife of his eldest son Henry.

[3] Müller advised, in particular, that missionaries should move from place to place to avoid becoming permanent leaders of congregations (Broomhall, *Refiner's Fire*, 340, 344).

[4] The Tottenham assembly, indeed, was marked out by Darby for particular vilification, and was defended in print by Groves himself (see Groves, *The Tottenham Case*).

[5] Heb 10:34 AV

[6] Visiting the assemblies frequented by Pearse and Berger in Hackney, and the Howards in Tottenham, Taylor will have met James Van Sommer, who subsequently published his letters from China in *The Missionary Reporter*. At the assembly in Marylebone he will have known Groves's close friend (and former colleague in Baghdad and Madras) John Vesey Parnell, who had succeeded to the title Lord Congleton. Whilst staying as the guest of Pearse (who had recently moved to Brighton) Taylor made his momentous decision to launch the CIM, and it was in company with Pearse that he opened a bank account two days later in the name of the new mission (Broomhall, *Thousand Lives*, 436-7). Another independent missionary associated with this Tottenham circle was J G Bausum, beloved step-father of Hudson Taylor's first wife, Maria. Indeed, Bausum had been "a particular friend of A N Groves" (Broomhall, *Thousand Lives*, 338). This friendship may account for the fact that the widowed Mrs Bausum, almost alone among Ningbo missionaries, approved of Hudson Taylor as a worthy suitor to the hand of Maria despite the social stigma of his Brethren connections.

[7] Preface to *Memoir* 2nd and 3rd edns. Having some months' experience of a Darbyite assembly in Kennington, Surrey, Hudson Taylor himself recognised the difference between the two forms of Brethrenism. The Kennington assembly, would subsequently, in 1879, excommunicate Groves's former missionary colleague Edward Cronin, and Taylor remarked, "I saw enough of their spirit to keep me from ever joining them" (Broomhall, *Treaty Wall*, 62).

positive missionary vision and its application of primitivist principles to the world beyond the shores of the British Isles.

But "faith missions" were not limited, at this period, to the English-speaking world. Indeed, the first such agency in Germany was founded through the influence not of Taylor but of Müller. Visiting the Rhineland in the spring of 1877, Müller profoundly impressed the Reformed pastor Ludwig Doll, who then launched his "Waisen- und Missionsanstalt Neukirchen", often called the "Neukirchener Mission". Within five years of Müller's visit, Doll had also established, on the same faith principles, an orphanage, a mission magazine and a missionary training institute.[1] If a common origin be sought for German and English "faith missions" then that origin must be traced back to Müller and thence to Groves.

We shall now look in some detail at the ethos of the early "faith missions", as represented in particular by the CIM, and identify points where their approach resembles that of Groves.

Living by Faith

The term "faith missions" was one attributed to this new generation of missionary agencies by interested outsiders rather than one they deliberately propagated. Fiedler notes, "They did not claim that other missions worked without faith, nor did they claim to have more faith than other missions."[2] We might wonder why this particular title became so widely recognised, especially as other possible and appropriate titles might be suggested, such as "Bible missions", "premillennialist missions", "lay people's missions" or most aptly of all, "interdenominational missions". Yet it was the "faith principle" that evidently aroused the greatest interest and approval in the evangelical circles from which the friends and supporters of these agencies were drawn, and which then became attached to them collectively as a means of identification. Hudson Taylor's idea of "moving men through God by prayer alone"[3] was one that gave great encouragement to Christians. It offered a personal experience of providential intervention demonstrating the faithfulness of God in fulfilling the "promises" of Scripture.

Introducing the concept of "faith missions" to America, A T Pierson identified five principles which they all held dear. There was to be no solicitation of funds, no guaranteed salary, no debt; they were non-denominational, and they exercised faith in God alone to supply their needs.[4] Underlying these tenets was the basic idea of individually or collectively "living by faith" as an alternative to dependence on a committee for direction and financial support.

The economic history of overseas mission discerns four distinct methods adopted for the financing of Protestant initiatives, each largely replacing the other in chronological sequence during the past two hundred years. Mission was first attempted through the overseas appointment of salaried chaplains, then by subscriptions to voluntary societies, and then by the "faith principles" of Groves, Müller and Taylor. But a fourth method has largely superseded these in recent years. Originating in America, it may be traced back to the Student Volunteer

---

[1] Fiedler, 55-6, 199 n.84
[2] Fiedler, 11
[3] Taylor, *Retrospect*, 21
[4] Austin, 296. It is significant that four of the five relate to finance.

Movement (SVM) with its recruiting drives from 1886 onwards conducted by Robert Wilder and John Mott (assisted by Robert Speer and A T Pierson).[1]

These young men challenged their hearers to pledge either themselves for missionary service or their money (in the form of regular donations) for the support of missionaries.[2] And here is the origin of a system now widely accepted whereby the missionary engages in a periodic "home assignment" for purposes of raising support to an agreed level, and in which his or her supporters promise "pledged gifts" in the form of a fixed sum of money to be sent every month, quarter or year. Elizabeth Goldsmith comments, "This new challenge to give to the work of mission had an interesting result. Ever since this time, missionary giving in America has largely been directed towards the support of an individual, not towards the general expenses of a Society as was customary in Britain."[3]

This is no doubt true when one compares the American agencies, whose ranks were swelled through SVM recruitment, with the older voluntary societies and "faith missions" of British origin, such as OMF with which she herself is most familiar. But we should remember that many years previously Groves had likewise advocated the support of individuals rather than societies. The difference in his case was his belief that gifts would be forthcoming in response to constant prayer for constant guidance rather than as a single pledged commitment to be discharged like a business obligation, irrespective of unknown future circumstances. And Groves would pray for his needs to be met rather than ask his friends to meet them. In this respect, the traditional policy of the "faith missions" is seen to lie far closer to that of Groves than to the American system of "pledged support".

Recruitment of Unordained and Uneducated Men

In the early years of the nineteenth century the denominational missionary societies, especially in Britain, suffered from a serious shortage of suitably

---

[1] Pierson met George Müller in 1878 and was profoundly impressed by his premillennialism, and especially by his testimony of God's provision through faith and prayer alone. Resigning his lucrative Presbyterian pastorate in 1889, he supported himself "by faith", travelling widely to recruit missionaries in many countries. He wrote an early appreciation of Müller, and following Müller's death in 1898, was appointed his official biographer. Dana Robert's recent account of Pierson's life hints at an element of conflict between his own preference to "live by faith" and the more aggressive forms of fundraising introduced by his younger contemporaries (Robert, *Occupy*, 193-4). Pierson was identified by G H Lang as one of the two men of his acquaintance who most helped and influenced him (Lang, *An Ordered Life*, 59). For a discussion of Pierson's leading role in promoting mission and stimulating inter-mission co-operation, see Johnson, *Countdown to 1900*.

[2] Elizabeth Goldsmith describes how "Many of them used the highwayman's challenge, 'Your money or your life!', saying 'We have given our lives. Won't you give the money to support us?'" (*Roots and Wings*, 48). Such a blunt demand for money would be anathema to the "faith mission" founders, who much preferred "to move men through God by prayer alone". They would find no scriptural justification for such financial appeals, but rather the opposite when the apostle asserts, "not that I seek the gift" (Phil 4:17).

[3] Goldsmith, *Roots and Wings*, 48. Bonk points out that some agencies which originated as "faith missions" have followed this pattern by requiring candidates to "pray-in" a specified sum prior to their acceptance as members. But a recruit with limited means, from a small church, and who is rejected on these grounds, may thus be denied the opportunity genuinely to live, as a missionary, by faith (Bonk, "Between Past and Future", 131).

educated candidates for missionary service. This was the reason for the appointment by the SPCK and the CMS of German and Swiss Lutherans.[1] In 1799 (shortly before the foundation of the CMS), Henry Venn's father, John, had proposed the creation of a class of unordained Anglican missionaries with the title of catechist. He hoped this would enable "a person of inferior station" to serve overseas despite his lack of such "talents, manners or learning as are necessary in an officiating minister in England". The majority of such men could be described as "skilled mechanics", a class newly fired with an individualistic desire for self-improvement and usefulness. Many were self-taught and strongly self-motivated.[2] In the Nonconformist sphere, the LMS were led as early as 1796 to send out a shipload of artisans as evangelists to the South Seas.[3]

We thus find most of the early Scots and English missionaries unordained and from a relatively modest social background. They were commissioned simply to preach to the unconverted, under the authority of local Anglican superintendents and committees, not being entitled to officiate in church services or to administer the sacraments.[4] The artisan-missionaries of the LMS likewise operated under the strict supervision of ordained and educated "ministers".[5] The Pietist craftsmen of the Basel Mission were even more carefully supervised, and formally required to follow the instructions and disciplines imposed by "duly constituted authority" – an "inspector", a home committee, and field leaders drawn from higher social ranks.[6] In each of these agencies there was a clear distinction between the ordained and the unordained missionary, and in most cases this represented the deep social divide between the upper-middle class and the working class.

For a while the CMS, following John Venn's proposal, was willing to appoint men with little education, and without clerical ordination, to posts of inferior responsibility, but this was a reluctant policy and was abandoned as soon as practicable. In 1854 Henry Venn noted, "It may be asked whether there be not inferior positions in a Mission which humble but pious Catechists or Scripture

---

[1] Max Warren points to "the terrible devastation of the wars, the disorganisation of life [through agricultural and industrial innovations], and widespread poverty" as reasons why English recruits were not forthcoming (Warren, *Social History*, 52). See also Jenkins, *The CMS and the Basel Mission*, 43-50.

[2] *Social History*, 39, 44-6

[3] The twenty-five artisans included bricklayers, carpenters, tailors, weavers, a blacksmith, and a gunner of the Royal Artillery. They were accompanied and supervised by four ordained ministers, two of whom were also craftsmen (Lovett, I, 127; Horne, *LMS*, 23; Warren, *Social History*, 41-2). This diversity was probably intentional, for a century later (in 1899), the chronicler of the LMS suggested, "The reason why there was so undue a proportion of handicraftsmen and tradesmen was, undoubtedly, the belief that the natives would speedily see the value of European civilization and be glad to learn trades" (Lovett, I, 127).

Analysing the social origins of several hundred early nineteenth-century British missionaries in India, Piggin finds the large majority to have come from lower professional or artisanal classes. In the hierarchical society of contemporary Britain, these were the most socially ambitious classes, in which individuals would often anticipate a path of upward social mobility through religious ministry or school teaching (Piggin, *Making Evangelical Missionaries*, 40-41).

[4] Walls, *Missionary Movement*, 164-5

[5] Walls, Ibid, 166

[6] Miller, 32, 84, 95

Readers may fill. The reply is that, though the Society did at one time send out such, the advanced state of the Missions has compelled the Committee to raise their standard." From then on, unordained candidates might apply to the London committee for work as schoolteachers, "but as Missionaries they send forth only clergymen."[1]

Groves himself, whilst still under the aegis of the CMS, had been willing to delay his entry into missionary service until his ordination and the completion of a theological degree. After the severance of his CMS connection, however, there is no hint in Groves's writings that he valued academic study as a preparation for missionary work. Although he welcomed the accession of Gundert to his missionary party, newly honoured with a doctorate in theology, he gave an equal welcome to the stonemason Bowden and the shoemaker Beer and their wives. He fully expected the Bowdens and Beers, along with his own wife and other recruits, to pick up necessary knowledge on the voyage out, commencing their language studies with Gundert and their Bible studies with himself. In India he recruited converted British soldiers and Indian Christians for evangelistic itineration, without any preparatory training, and saw them preaching the gospel over substantial areas with significant success.

Faith missions in general followed this pattern, hastening recruits directly to their field of service and placing no great emphasis on prior training. Although Hudson Taylor advised the Guinnesses to launch their East London Training Institute, the focus there was on "spiritual development" and "practical Christian service" rather than academic achievement.[2] Like Groves's recruits, the first generation of "faith missionaries" consisted mainly of working men and women without much formal education – people in fact who could, by then, no longer gain ready acceptance in the denominational missions. The first CIM party with Hudson Taylor on the *Lammermuir* included a blacksmith, a mechanic, an agricultural engineer, two carpenters and a mason.

In recruiting men such as George Beer and William Bowden, and then encouraging their location beyond the reach of his personal supervision, Groves was departing from the traditional class-based system of authority. He considered these Devonshire artisans to be independent missionaries and church leaders in no lesser sense than the aristocratic Parnell and the theologically trained Gundert. They were accountable not to him, or to any human organisation, but directly to God. He expected them to seek their guidance and their daily bread from their "heavenly Father". The CIM likewise found some of its best regional leaders in working-class men and women, strongly and independently motivated, and able to take initiatives without officious regulation from higher mission authorities.

Recruitment of Single Women

It was rare in the denominational missionary societies prior to 1830 to find a woman such as the gifted Baptist, Hannah Marshman, making opportunities for herself to be active in her own right as a missionary. With regard to the role of women as evangelists, Fiedler observes, "It was the faith mission movement which developed a completely new theological and practical approach. Here again, Hudson and Maria Taylor set the standard. Right from the beginning, married

---

[1] Venn, "A special appeal", 8th May 1854 (cited by Warren, *To Apply the Gospel*, 139)
[2] Fiedler, 136, 145

women [in the CIM] were counted as full missionaries, and single women were missionaries in their own right, not only being allowed to preach but expected to."[1]

Earlier than this, however, Groves had encouraged both single and married women to engage in missionary service. On his initial journey through Russia to Baghdad in 1829, he met only one unmarried woman missionary. She was a Quaker, Sarah Kilham, who was conducting a school for girls in St Petersburg. On that same trip his own missionary team included his unmarried sister Lydia and another young unmarried woman, Charlotte Taylor. The fact that Lydia's poor health forced a return to the UK, and that Charlotte left the party on receiving a proposal of marriage, does not detract from the significance of Groves's initiative in taking single women missionaries to a place of great potential danger, confident that they would make a significant contribution to the work of the team. Returning to Europe in 1835, Groves recruited three single women, Julie Dubois, Marie Monnard and Emma Groves, along with couples and single men, for the work in India. This again was unusual, and was made possible by Groves's preference for working as a team.[2]

There is no sign that the single or married women associated with Groves ever preached in public, either in the open air or in a church meeting.[3] Their ministry consisted essentially of personal work and Bible teaching among women, and, in some cases, teaching children in schools.[4] But Groves's dismissal of ordination and education as essential requirements for spiritual service must have freed his women recruits to do more than would be anticipated or approved by denominational agencies, who would naturally expect ministry to be conducted in a formal capacity by male clergymen. In this regard, he opened a door for the extensive evangelistic activity of women which became such a marked feature of the "faith missions".

Internationalisation

One particular problem faced by state churches in their overseas missionary efforts stems from their commitment to the concept of a "national establishment". The Rhenius Affair provides a striking illustration of the difficulties that can arise when missionaries ordained by the "religious establishment" of one nation are compelled to submit to those of another. As soon as it could, the CMS dispensed with the services of its potentially subversive German recruits, preferring the more predictable uniformity of ordained Englishmen. The Nonconformist denominations, too, were often tied together at a national level by synods or conventions, so that American Baptists were organisationally distinct, for example, from British Baptists. A church defined as a national church faces peculiar difficulties when it attempts to plant churches in other nations.

In contrast, we find internationalisation to be one of the distinctives of the "faith missions". Those that began in Britain or America quickly acquired

---

[1] Fiedler, 292
[2] See M247.
[3] A passing comment in his *Remarks* shows that Groves considered it contrary to nature to "make women teachers of men". Indeed, it would be "repugnant to God's word and all right moral feeling" (pp.6-7).
[4] Once delivered of her baby in Baghdad, Mary Groves had fully expected to take responsibility for the girls' school. During her husband's prolonged absence from Chittoor, Harriet Groves administered the school of boys and girls almost single-handed.

missionaries and supporters from other nations, and for many of these English was a second language. Within a few years similar missions had sprung up, through their influence, in every nation with a Protestant heritage, and "faith" missionaries arrived on the field speaking their own language but perfectly willing for full missionary co-operation. The fact that many recruits were the product of revivals that crossed national boundaries also contributed to the international flavour of the "faith missions".[1]

Groves was an internationalist from the start. When he wished to recruit like-minded workers, his thoughts turned not to his native England, but to German-speaking Pietists from Würtemburg and Geneva.[2] In this he was undoubtedly anticipating the "faith missions".

Premillennialist Stimulus

One of the most striking novelties shared by Groves and the "faith missions" was their almost universal adoption of premillennialism. Several practical consequences are evident. Noting that "this 'premillennial' eschatology was most widely disseminated by the Brethren movement," Brian Stanley comments, "There is some evidence that missionaries holding this theological position differed significantly in their political and cultural attitudes from missionaries in the postmillennial tradition."[3] They were more willing, in particular, to distinguish between Christian doctrine and Western civilisation, and to adapt their message and their lifestyle to the cultural context in which they lived. They were also less inclined, in the expectation of Christ's imminent return, to construct elaborate buildings.[4]

A premillennialist belief that the world was in hopeless decline would reduce any tendency to linger for the improvement of any small part of it. In general, the premillennialist desire was to offer "the simple Gospel" once to every human being, thereby "hastening the Day of the Lord"[5] in expectation of a better life in the age to come. Missionaries with this perspective would be reluctant to remain in one place establishing a static institution whilst other places were still waiting to hear.[6]

Although Groves did settle for a lengthy period in Chittoor, his emphasis there, and throughout the region, lay in "spiritual" rather than in medical or social work.[7]

---

[1] Fiedler, 134. The existence of an early nineteenth-century *International*, an informal network linking innovative Christians from diverse nations and denominations throughout Europe, is postulated by Jenkins, *The CMS and the Basel Mission*, 50.

[2] Müller, *Narrative*, I, 120

[3] Stanley, *The Bible and the Flag*, 76

[4] For the effect of eschatology on diverse views of mission, see Bosch, 313-27, and Weber, 65-81. Taber notes that the desire to "civilize" native peoples was a missionary motivation far more evident in the denominational societies than in the "faith missions". Furthermore, it was usually more characteristic of mission administrators and supporters at home than of missionaries on the field, and was more evident in missions sent from nations with an active colonial and imperial programme than from those without (Taber, 67).

[5] 2 Pet 3:12

[6] Recognising that this may have stifled some philanthropic inclinations, Fiedler nevertheless affirms with some warmth that "there was no missionary without a medicine box, and hardly ever a mission station in Africa without a school. Only in ignorance or prejudice can it be said that the evangelical missions did nothing but evangelistic work" (Fiedler, 226-7).

[7] See above, 128ff.

Even education he regarded as a means to an evangelistic end, rather than an end in itself. As an early and vigorous advocate of premillennialism, he might be considered a forerunner of the "faith missions" both in promulgating the doctrine and in demonstrating its practical effects.

Indigenous Evangelists

Hudson Taylor's early positive experience of itinerating with Chinese evangelists and colporteurs led him in future years to make full use of Chinese evangelists in the extensive work of the CIM. The practice of travelling and preaching two by two, in company with missionaries, was found to be effective for both on-the-job training and widespread outreach. It was the method marked out by Groves,[1] and earlier applied in a Chinese context by Gützlaff.[2]

Conclusion: Groves as a Model for "Faith Missions"

The fact that the new generation of mission agencies, established from 1865 onwards, were popularly called "faith missions" demonstrates that the principle of "living by faith" was what particularly caught the imagination of their friends and supporters. This "faith principle" can be traced back to Hudson Taylor, who derived it from George Müller, who in turn attributed it to the example and teaching of Groves.

From the time of his earliest association with the CES, Taylor's missionary support was provided by Groves's circle of friends in the London suburbs. Twenty years earlier, Groves had declared his earnest desire to "re-model the whole plan of missionary operations so as to bring them to the simple standard of God's word."[3] In so far as Hudson Taylor adopted Groves's form of "re-modelling", we can feel justified in considering Groves, in both intention and fulfilment, the "father of faith missions" and a radical influence on a movement defined in such terms.

In addition to this, he set an example of willing co-operation with missionaries from other denominations and agencies, proposed ideals of missionary self-support, recruited unordained and uneducated men and women (including single women), envisaged international co-operation, commended the practice of widespread evangelism and advocated on-the-job training of indigenous evangelists.

Groves in Contrast to "Faith Missions"

Anthony Norris Groves and Hudson Taylor had much in common. Neither was an ordained minister, neither claimed a denominational identity and neither could promise a penny to his co-workers. In other respects, however, their paths diverge, and the CIM along with other "faith missions" evolved in ways that eventually differed substantially from the principles advocated by Groves. In particular we might think of their focus on pioneering unevangelised fields, systematising financial support, establishing authority structures, securing interdenominational co-operation, ignoring ecclesiological issues and, perhaps unintentionally, perpetuating the church / mission organisational dichotomy.

---

[1] See above, 106ff.
[2] On Gützlaff, see below, 224f.
[3] M285-6

Pioneering Unevangelised Fields

The fact that Groves accepted for his initial sphere of activity "the Mediterranean" (as a base for reaching the Muslim Middle East), and then "Persia", might lead us to suppose that he deliberately directed his attention, like the "faith missions", to the "unreached". These locations, however, were chosen for him by the CMS after the London committee of the Society had identified them as desirable and strategic places for him to go.

It is true that when free to choose his own field of activity he still had his mind fixed on Persia, and then more specifically on Baghdad, "the headquarters of Islamism".[1] Once he was there, however, he suffered acutely from his sense of isolation. He was not by nature a loner preferring to plough a solitary furrow. When relocating to India four years later, his energies were directed not to pioneering unreached areas but to seeking out and supporting existing works wherever he could find them, and to persuading missionaries already present to adopt what he believed to be more biblical methods. In 1834 his intention was to settle in Calcutta, where he had found a number of active missionaries. He considered it an ideal base, not only for evangelism, but also, and more significantly, for the promotion of unity and co-operation in Christian service.[2] Shortly afterwards it was in Tinnevelly, an area already evangelised by Rhenius, that he hoped to locate his colleagues Parnell and Cronin. John Tucker of the CMS asked with some indignation why, when "the whole land of India, nay the whole world, is open to Mssrs. Groves & Parnell & Cronin," he felt it necessary "to fix upon a spot now under cultivation."[3] In the event, Groves chose to locate his newly assembled team in Madras, a city already enjoying a strong Christian presence, and finally in 1837 moved to Chittoor, not because this was unreached territory but almost certainly because he heard that John Bilderbeck of the LMS was pleading for reinforcements.

Unlike Groves, the early generation of "faith missions" showed little interest in India, no doubt because Protestant activity was relatively well established there. Fiedler notes that "None of the early faith missions wanted to work where other missions were already working. They even avoided working close to them, because they saw missionary work in the remaining unreached areas of the globe as the only reason for their existence."[4]

In 1813 there had been only thirty-six Protestant missionaries in India. By 1830 there were a hundred and thirty from eight societies.[5] But in 1850 more than a quarter of the worldwide Protestant missionary force was stationed there.[6] This fact alone means that in relative terms India was not an "unevangelised field", such as would interest a "faith mission". India was, however, the most strategic place in the world for anyone aspiring to influence missionaries and expatriate Christian

---

[1] Eadie, 191; Stern, 34, 40

[2] M321. In north-east India he sensed less willingness for missionary co-operation: "The tendency to sectarianism, however, is in these provinces much more marked than either in Bombay or Madras, and this is why I feel so thankful the Lord has given me such favour with so many, in endeavouring to show them the beauty and glory of being contented with Christ as a Head and his word as a guide" (M306-7).

[3] Tucker to Nelson, 23rd July 1835

[4] Fiedler, 73

[5] Ingleby, *Education and India*, 2

[6] Ingleby, Ibid, 33

communities. Indeed, the pioneering evangelistic concern of the "faith missions" contrasts rather strikingly with Groves's focus on leading professing Christians to a more wholehearted faith in Christ and encouraging denominational agents already on the field to rediscover apostolic methods and to co-operate more willingly together.

We should nevertheless avoid exaggerating this contrast. Whilst the so-called "forward movements" of the "faith missions" were certainly motivated by the perceived spiritual destitution of the unevangelised fields, and by the need to hasten the coming of Christ by offering the gospel at least once in every place, we should not overlook the fact that their founders generally felt it wise to establish an initial base before moving into unreached areas. Hudson Taylor's earliest missionary experiences were itinerations from his home in Shanghai. A decade later, he was seeking to establish a headquarters for himself in Ningbo, a city where a number of missions already had Chinese churches, and he resolved to create another there, from which well-prepared Chinese evangelists and foreign missionaries could in due course be sent out to unreached areas.[1] Groves, similarly, having established his base of operations in Chittoor, then encouraged itinerations into unreached areas. Although there is a difference of scale (for the CIM eventually established many secondary bases further afield), there is hardly one of method.

It is, moreover, sometimes forgotten that missionaries possess varied abilities. Whilst some are gifted evangelists, and thrive best when preaching to restless crowds in the open air, others exercise their calling through the pastoral care of converts or through Bible teaching in some formal or informal setting. Many of those associated with "faith missions", whilst entirely approving of evangelistic itineration, have in fact devoted their lives to the encouragement of converts and other missionaries in locations already well-exposed to the Gospel. In this they resemble Groves. Where the "faith missions" differ from him is in their strong motivation to reach the unreached. This became a stated justification for their existence, and an emotionally charged rationale for their support, to a far greater extent than is evident in Groves's personal references to his own missionary settlement in Chittoor.

Systematising Financial Support

Although he did not promote the concept of "living by faith" as deliberately as did George Müller, Groves undoubtedly chose to place himself in dependence on God and independence of man with regard to his financial support. Setting out for Baghdad, he had no expectation that the funds he carried with him would last for ever and no reason to suppose he would find generous benefactors along the way or in Baghdad itself. He and his party deliberately placed themselves in circumstances requiring them to put their trust entirely in God.

Once committed to the missionary life, Groves was not well-positioned to attract financial assistance. He himself spent only a few months in Britain, and when he did return, preoccupied with business matters, he addressed no conferences and spoke but rarely to the assemblies in Devon and London. Although his letters and journals found their way to his personal friends, they were not widely circulated: few in the homeland could say they had ever met him. The

---

[1] Broomhall, *Thousand Lives*, 66-7, 441

surviving documents show little or no evidence of funds sent to him from Britain, and even in India his widespread unpopularity in the expatriate communities meant that financial gifts could be no more than uncertain and erratic. It troubled him to see that, among his colleagues, Bowden and Beer found their income hardly adequate, and it was to facilitate more consistent interest in such workers that Groves urged the creation of a magazine to report on progress and to stimulate prayer. But the magazine itself made no promise of funds and made no appeals for the support of those whose work it mentioned.

Hudson Taylor, in contrast, embarked on his missionary career as a salaried agent of the Chinese Evangelisation Society. During the period 1853-7, he suffered on the one hand from the inconveniences of accountability to superiors in London ignorant of his circumstances in China, and on the other from their failure to give careful attention to his financial needs. In fact Taylor's first experience, as a missionary, of "living by faith" was an extremely reluctant one, under vigorous protest, when the CES reneged on its promise to provide a regular salary for its agents. Failing to attract adequate donations and heavily in debt, the committee was forced by circumstances to send instructions that Taylor and his colleagues in China should henceforth put their trust in God rather than the society. When informed of this, "none of the missionaries accepted the change".[1]

It was a situation in which Taylor seriously questioned the sense of trusting to God to provide when simple human means to secure that provision were neglected. His CES co-workers John and Mary Jones seemed perfectly content with this state of affairs, selling household items when necessary in order to buy bread, refusing (despite George Pearse's kind enquiry) to estimate their probable future expenses, and assuring the CES that whatever happened they would have enough.[2] Such sentiments no doubt reassured the well-intentioned but seriously overworked stockbroker that more careful attention to the transmission of remittances was not necessary. As honorary foreign secretary, Pearse was also hindered in his care for the CES missionaries by the woeful failure of its large multi-denominational committee and its paid secretary to administer the limited funds it did receive with sensible discretion.[3] It was not until the following year (1861), when Hudson Taylor visited the Brethren in London, and discussed the matter with William Berger, that "living by faith" would be seen by him in a more positive light.[4]

In some degree, the haphazard approach to missionary support manifested by the CES echoes the attitude of Groves himself. It reflects an overriding confidence that God will provide even if no human plans are made for such provision. But it was undoubtedly the slackness of the CES in this regard that determined Taylor to create a more efficient home office for the CIM, ensuring the regular transmission to China of whatever funds might be in hand, and arranging public meetings for potential supporters where reports might be given of current progress and opportunities in China. From its inception the CIM enjoyed the help of outstanding home directors: William Berger, and then Benjamin Broomhall and Richard Hill.

---

[1] *Thousand Lives*, 239
[2] *Thousand Lives*, 63
[3] *Thousand Lives*, 236-40, 438. The fact that the CES committee comprised sixty Members, with a Board of fifteen, representing a wide range of denominations, no doubt contributed to the confused and sluggish nature of its decision-making processes (Broomhall, *Treaty Wall*, 414-5).
[4] Broomhall, Ibid, 248

Contemporaries observed in the CIM a definite tendency towards "the use of means". Some criticised this as "leaning on the arm of man"; others commended it as an aspect of fellowship between "man" and God in fulfilling the Great Commission.

Self-support

In his early years, Hudson Taylor shared with Groves a readiness to support himself overseas through secular labour. Preparing himself for China, he reported, "I am studying medicine and surgery, that I may have more opportunity of usefulness and perhaps be able to support myself when there."[1] After his arrival in Shanghai, and his resignation from the CES, circumstances seemed likely to make self-support an urgent necessity:

> I did not know what means the Lord might use; but I was willing to give up all my time to the service of evangelisation among the heathen, if by any means He would provide the smallest amount on which I could live; and if He were not pleased to do this, I was prepared to undertake whatever work might be necessary to supply myself, giving all the time that could be spared from such a calling to more distinctly missionary efforts.[2]

Despite Taylor's early interest in "tent-making", he did not continue the practice and we do not find it favoured by "faith missions" in the nineteenth century.[3]

Establishing Authority Structures

Although "faith missions" in general owed much to Groves in breaking the old denominational mould with its entrenched hierarchy of command, they gradually reverted to the traditional model in developing an increasingly structured organisation of their own. Significant to this was the question of authority. Groves might be respected as the unofficial leader of the team in Baghdad, Madras and Chittoor, but Hudson Taylor went one stage further in compiling a list of principles to be accepted and obeyed, and requiring formal recognition of his overall control. Despite his strong advocacy for "faith missions", A T Pierson decried the tendency in some cases for a personality cult to develop around a gifted founder or leader. He warned, "It is the arbitrary and often tyrannical mode of carrying on independent missions that brings them into disfavour."[4] Groves's self-effacing modesty prevented him from ever assuming such a role.

We have noted that Groves's understanding of "living by faith" deliberately freed the missionary from the authority of those who provided financially for him. In contrast, the "faith missions", by channelling financial support to their missionaries from a central fund or common pool, retained a high degree of control. Failure to obey such regulations and directives as might be imposed by

---

[1] Broomhall, *Treaty Wall*, 29
[2] Broomhall, *Thousand Lives*, 69
[3] The twentieth century saw an increasing number of "faith mission" associates engaged in employment overseas for the sake of mission. One recent effect of this is to blur the distinction between ordained and unordained missionaries, a state of affairs that would be approved by Groves.
[4] *The Missionary Review*, cited by Robert, 187. This accounts for Pierson's "uneven relationship" with A B Simpson's Christian and Missionary Alliance among others.

field leaders and councils could lead to the dismissal of the missionary. In such circumstances, most appointees would feel it wise to defer to authority, even when such authority conflicted with a sense of personal guidance. In 1896 Edward Groves compared the Brethren missions he knew with those of the CIM: "Going out in dependence on the Lord alone was as true of members of the China Inland Mission as of those whose names were given in Echoes of Service. The real attraction among ourselves [i.e. the Brethren] was the independence of the worker of any control either from home or his elders in the same part of the mission field."[1] Issues of authority and accountability thus represent, in the "faith missions", a major divergence from Groves's original concept of missionary support and co-operation based on trust rather than obligation.[2]

The contrast is illustrated in the life of Henrietta Soltau. Born in 1843, she was brought up in a Brethren family in Plymouth, and her father was a well-known speaker among the Brethren throughout the United Kingdom. In 1889 she was asked by Hudson Taylor to open a residential home for women candidates preparing for service with the CIM, on the understanding that she would receive a regular allocation from CIM funds. Prior to this she had acted as house-mother to a number of missionary children in London, and later in Hastings, where, impressed by Taylor's example of "living by faith", she had been accustomed to meeting the needs of her household through prayer alone, without incurring debts or revealing their circumstances outside their own circle.[3] At Taylor's insistence, however, her new venture was tied into the CIM administration and received a regular allocation. She became increasingly unhappy, and later remarked, "The preparation of accounts for the Treasurer and Minutes for the Ladies' Council were my chief burdens."[4] Within a few weeks she had informed him that henceforth she would not require anything from CIM funds, for she and the candidates would look directly to God for provision of their daily needs. Although her expressed reason was to avoid depleting the monies sent to China, her biographer then adds a significant comment: "Seeing that Miss Soltau now accepted no financial support from the China Inland Mission, she was at complete liberty to arrange her own time and the details of her establishment as seemed best to herself."[5] There can be little doubt that for Henrietta Soltau, the personal option of "living by faith" was made the more attractive by the independence of decision it allowed her, along with freedom from tiresome administrative duties.

Here we have at least one individual, who, when faced with a choice between membership in a "faith mission" and living individually "by faith", chose the latter,

---

[1] Groves E K, *Successors*, 168
[2] See above, 154ff. This issue is one that affects all missionaries. Among those with personal cause to question the power vested in mission authorities is the author Elizabeth Goldsmith, whose husband was unexpectedly appointed to a ministry and then more unexpectedly dismissed from it. Earlier, her parents had "faced a sharp disagreement with their [CIM] mission leaders... Although they really wanted to remain in Chefoo where we six children were at school, they eventually acquiesced in the autocratic decision that they must go and lead the hospital in distant Lanchow." Her mother died in Lanchow and the children, interned by the Japanese, did not see their bereaved father for five years (*Roots and Wings*, 165-6).
[3] Cable & French (2nd edn.), 72-7.
[4] Ibid, 144-6
[5] Ibid, 164

and for reasons which no doubt appealed to many other men and women of independent character and strong personal convictions. Again we see a divergence in the paths marked out respectively by Groves and Taylor, revealing two significantly different ways of "living by faith", one far less tied into structures of human security, accountability and control than the other.

Respecting Denominational Traditions

Although Groves and Taylor shared the ideal that missionaries from diverse denominations could work happily side by side, there was a significant difference in the way they applied this principle. Groves had drawn together the Nonconformist Cronin, the Anglican Parnell and the radically independent Newman. But these three had each, before leaving Britain, abandoned their previous denominational loyalties in favour of a consciously non-denominational stance. Hudson Taylor had the harder task of uniting workers who still retained their original denominational identities and who saw no need to abandon them.

In Groves's mind, a missionary was called overseas to make disciples who would enjoy fellowship together, but no organisation beyond this was found in scripture or necessary in practice. It required the missionary merely to read the New Testament with his converts and ask them how they might follow apostolic precepts and example in their own cultural context. Hudson Taylor, on the other hand, faced the more complicated task of superintending missionaries with denominational loyalties who would want to see churches established according to the pattern of their denomination. He eventually decided to group his workers on the basis of their affiliation, allocating them to specific areas and allowing them to establish there the kind of churches to which they were accustomed in their homeland (in many cases under the authority of ordained clergymen). Following this pattern of intra-mission comity, Chinese converts were expected to conform to the denominational style that had been allocated to their area. Watchman Nee was one who questioned the validity of such a scheme. In fact, "The CIM Editorial Secretary, Norman Baker, had kindly shown Nee the current edition of the Mission's *Principles and Practice*, and Nee had had to point out that under the heading of 'church government' the document gave little or no room for Chinese opinion concerning the pattern of worship to be followed in any given case"[1]

This demonstrates a striking difference between the approach of Groves and that of the CIM in addressing their common desire to overcome denominational tensions. Groves envisaged unity through ignoring denominational identities; Hudson Taylor through respecting them. There can be little doubt that Groves's method would allow more freedom for the development of culturally sensitive fellowships with indigenous leadership.

Evading Ecclesiological Issues

Whereas the CIM chose eventually to group its missionaries according to denomination, other "faith missions" continued for the most part to ignore the varied denominational origins of their agents and, at least in their earliest years, to lay no great stress on the development of churches. In an African context, Fiedler remarks that "faith missions" were "quite weak in ecclesiology".[2] Indeed, with

---

[1] Kinnear, *Against the Tide*, 256 n.3
[2] Fiedler, 89

their focus on evangelism and the securing of conversions, rather than on the spiritual growth of Christian fellowships, "faith missions never produced an ecclesiology of their own."[1] The evidence shows that, "Issues of church order were minor matters for faith missions. They were not dealt with in their statements of faith or, at most, only in a negative way. The SAGM [South Africa General Mission] stated that neither workers nor converts would be tied to any special form of church order. The AIM [Africa Inland Mission] left it to the individual missionary to decide on church order. In the SIM, the field conference was to decide."[2]

Several reasons have been suggested for this alleged ecclesiological deficiency. Firstly, there is no doubt that premillennialist views encouraged widespread and rapid itineration. In some cases this may have led to a neglect of new converts and a failure to organize churches.[3] Groves, however, was also a premillennialist, and he cannot be accused of such pastoral neglect. Whilst appreciating the value of itineration, he devoted his own energies to teaching and establishing Christian fellowships where believers could grow together in love and in holiness. Whilst the premillennialist expectation of Christ's imminent return may inhibit major building projects there is no inherent necessity for it to stifle the care of converts and the planned development of functioning congregations.

Secondly, Fiedler notes that the majority of the early "faith missionaries" were converts of the revival.[4] Their early energies had been directed to the conversion of "the ungodly", and they were equipped neither by experience nor by education to provide systematic Bible teaching for believers. Many had acquired a tendency to criticise the rather formal meetings, sacraments and leadership of their home churches, without having any particular alternative to offer. Having led a sinner to faith in Christ, they might well be uncertain how to help him progress further towards spiritual maturity. Groves, in contrast, was a specialist in this form of ministry.

Thirdly, there is evidence that churches associated with "faith missions" were particularly slow to develop regional or central administrative bodies uniting and co-ordinating their activities. One reason for this, Fiedler suggests, is Brethren influence within the "faith missions", producing a general mistrust of administrative complexity.[5] Of greater importance may be the fact that in many places the "faith mission" itself fulfilled the role of a regional and in some cases supra-regional organisation. This lessened the need for a parallel church structure, especially when the leaders of the local churches were, for all practical purposes, the missionaries.

Fourthly, we should bear in mind that the founders and leaders of the "faith missions" were deliberately attempting to unite young missionary recruits from diverse denominational backgrounds in a common evangelistic task. This, of necessarily, obliged them to minimize potential friction by evading issues on which they might disagree, and to discourage discussion of matters that might be divisive. Questions relating to ordination, church leadership, forms of meeting, baptism, and

---

[1] Fiedler, 320
[2] Fiedler, 181
[3] Fiedler, 277-8
[4] Fiedler, 114
[5] Fiedler, 89, and 111n.

the Lord's Supper would undoubtedly prove controversial, and were for this reason rarely addressed. Pragmatic rather than scholarly considerations may thus underlie the commonly heard assertion that the apostolic writings allow of varied interpretations, and indeed that they offer little ecclesiological guidance.

The vague and inadequate ecclesiology of the "faith missions" has had long-term consequences in the kind of congregations they have created. In most cases, once a group of converts had been assembled, a church would develop almost by default, without any clear idea of what pattern its ministry should take. The tendency was simply for the senior missionary in each location to adopt a role similar to that of the pastor or minister familiar to him in his home church. His congregation would gradually develop along Baptist, Congregationalist or other lines in its form of meetings, discipline and ministry. Promising converts were generally encouraged to become evangelists rather than church leaders, and rarely was church responsibility placed from the start in the hands of national Christians. The "faith missions" were slow to ordain ministers, and in general granted this as a special honour to just a few. Fiedler comments, "Ordination is not the church's blessing at the beginning of the full-time pastoral ministry, but a reward for good service and a promotion to the higher ranks of the ministry."[1] In consequence the ordained "native pastor" was often somewhat elderly, exercising a benign and generally nominal superintendence over a number of junior mission employees.

Once a number of congregations had been established, a uniformity of style (reflecting a particular denominational tradition) would generally develop as they exchanged visits and preachers, and participated in regional conferences. A greater or lesser degree of administrative co-ordination, involving matters of discipline and finance, followed on from this. The centralising of financial administration then played a key role in the creation of inter-church structures. The appointment of individuals to oversee regions led inevitably to the development a power hierarchy.[2] Fiedler cites the example of a Presbyterian model imposed on a number of AIM related churches that had formerly each followed its own pattern, and similarly a network of congregations associated with the Christian and Missionary Alliance which were eventually required to follow the pattern formalised in the CMA congregations of the USA.[3] Elsewhere, the administrative structure operated by the mission organisation was simply taken over or replicated by the regional network of church congregations. Fiedler concludes, "The churches did not pattern themselves after the New Testament, nor after the *ideals* of the missionaries, first of all, but after their *organization*."[4]

The 1930s saw a growing desire among the missionaries to discuss the future of their congregations, and the writings of Roland Allen acquired a considerable vogue in "faith mission" circles. Times were changing, however, and the churches were soon to be overtaken by political pressures from the outside world, profoundly affecting church / mission relations. This was especially true in Africa. The "wave of independence" which, after 1950, swept the continent caught the "faith missions" unawares. The churches were rushed into a form of independence unplanned and largely unforeseen. The ecclesiological vacuum was rapidly filled

---

[1] Fiedler, 332-3
[2] Fiedler, 326
[3] Fiedler, 325-6
[4] Fiedler, 327

by the wholesale adoption of ready-made church structures observable in neighbouring congregations identifiable as "proper churches". Some of these had been created deliberately as denominational congregations by the older societies (CMS, BMS, American Presbyterian etc.). Others, with "faith mission" origins, had slipped by default into Western habits under the ministry of missionary pastors.

As far as we may conclude from Africa, the "faith missions" have produced a style of church recognisably Euro-American, and thus failed to introduce any positive and distinctive vision for indigenous fellowships with home-grown forms of leadership. In this respect they have profited little from the missiological thought of Groves.

Perpetuating the Church / Mission Organisational Dichotomy
The fact that the "faith missions" established themselves as para-church organisations meant that administratively and financially they stood apart from the churches they produced. In this they followed the example of the denominational societies that preceded them, regarding the mission organisation and the church organisation as two separate and independent entities, each with paid appointees accountable to superiors.

It has caused obvious and undeniable difficulties. With reference to Africa, Fiedler observes, "Faith missions, which had so severely criticised the churches in their home countries for their lack of missionary vision, produced churches that lacked exactly that... The missions introduced a clear dichotomy: mission is the foreigners' affair, the church is for the 'natives.'"[1] Henry Venn's scaffolding analogy was adopted by the "faith missions" to justify and perpetuate the dichotomy. The consequence is that the "natives" remain tied to the *church* whilst the foreigners move on with the *mission*. The social gulf between the foreign missionary and the indigenous Christian is rendered all the wider by the tendency for the missionary to feel a far greater personal attachment to the mission than to the local congregations.[2]

This problem is compounded by the principle of comity, which has rendered foreign missionaries reluctant to encourage local Christians to cross frontiers of language and culture lest they impinge upon territory belonging to a sister organisation or denomination. Furthermore, the principle that the churches must be self-supporting has fostered the idea that "'white money' should not be used for [the support of] black missionaries."[3] Then as the churches were generally too poor to provide for their own missionaries, such missionaries were almost never sent.

In regarding Church and Mission as two distinct organisational entities, the "faith missions" may have adopted the only course open to them as interdenominational societies. But in doing so, they diverged fundamentally from Groves's vision for indigenous churches engaged in mission on their own initiative. Groves expected local and foreign believers to co-operate on terms of equality, without any formal financial or institutional obligation to one another. He positively encouraged the sending of finance from the West for the support of Indian evangelists living "by faith", whilst expecting the evangelists to consider

---

[1] Fiedler, 364
[2] On this issue see Neill, *Creative Tension*, 84.
[3] Fiedler, 365

themselves dependent on and accountable to God rather than the donors. And he anticipated that the indigenous fellowships, coming into existence through their efforts, would be able to provide for their own modest requirements without foreign funds, for they would have no salaried ministers or elaborate buildings to drain their resources.[1]

The "faith missions", by creating organisational structures, undoubtedly added strong elements of pragmatic stability and efficiency to the "faith principles" they derived from Groves. But in the process, they proved hardly more successful than their denominational predecessors in creating genuinely indigenous churches. Groves's missiological principles would appear much better suited to this end.

Other Influences on "Faith Missions"

Our final assessment of Groves's influence on the "faith missions" must take into account the reality of other influences, and in particular of two spiritual movements that occurred after his death and added a certain flavour to the "faith missions" unknown to his own generation.

The first of these was the revival of 1858-9, which demonstrated not only the vast potential for working class missionary recruitment, but also the real possibility of interdenominational co-operation in evangelism. The second was the so-called "holiness movement" with its distinctive teaching of sanctification to be received as a "second blessing" subsequent to conversion. Though able to trace its theology back to Wesley, and its earliest phases to the end of Groves's own lifetime, this movement gained its major momentum through the Keswick Convention and its offshoots from about 1875 onwards. These new holiness and Keswick teachings were generally associated with an Arminian theology, in contrast to Groves's Calvinism, and they drew many "faith missionaries" overseas.[2]

In fact many such recruits identified themselves not primarily with a denomination or even a local church but with their happy memories of revival meetings or of Holiness Conventions. Such missionaries lived in what C P Williams has described as "a sort of spiritual no-man's-land".[3] The need to belong to some company of like-minded people led many to find their identity in the "faith mission" society to which they had devoted their lives. Amy Carmichael, for one, was sent out not by a church but by the Keswick Convention, and after many years in India undoubtedly felt more truly identified with her Dohnavur Fellowship than with the Presbyterianism of her Irish childhood. For such people, far from their roots in time and space, the missionary society became for all practical purposes a church and a denomination, and one towards which they felt a particularly strong loyalty and affection. These were elements distinctive to the "faith missions", owing little or nothing to Groves.

Conclusion: Groves in Contrast to "Faith Missions"

Despite their indebtedness to Müller, and thus to Groves, for their "faith principles", the missions that followed the example of Hudson Taylor diverged substantially from Groves's other missiological principles. In particular we have

---

[1] See above, 110ff.
[2] Fiedler, 116. On the role of the Keswick Convention in stimulating overseas mission, see Price and Randall.
[3] quoted by Fiedler, 200 n. 87

noted their disinterest in missionary self-support through secular labour, their systematising of financial supply, establishing authority structures, maintaining denominational traditions, evading ecclesiological issues and, most crucially, in perpetuating the longstanding and hazardous dichotomy between Church and Mission. In securing greater administrative efficiency the "faith missions" gained stability, public confidence and support, but may, at the same time, have lost some of the ecclesiological focus that a more rigorous primitivist missiology might have offered. The reality is that they often struggled to create viable indigenous churches.

Conclusion: Faith Missions

It is to Groves that the "faith missions" primarily owe the principle of individually and collectively "living by faith", passed on to them through George Müller and Hudson Taylor. The example of Groves in co-operating with individuals of all denominations and varied nations should also not be forgotten. In addition the "faith missions" learned from him to place confidence in recruits unordained and largely uneducated (and in some cases single women), and they shared his premillennialist emphasis on the salvation of individuals rather than the civilising of nations.

But just as Groves's early and idealistic influence on Brethren missions became overlain by later and more pragmatic considerations, so his influence on the interdenominational "faith missions" became somewhat dissipated through their desire to maintain unity and to secure a degree of administrative stability and efficiency. What remained with them, however, was his concept of "living by faith", and this became the distinctive mark of a generation of missions, both in the thinking of their own members and supporters, and in the more scholarly analyses of subsequent historians and theologians. It is to Groves that we owe this distinctive phrase, and to him that we may look for its earliest and simplest application.

Indigenous Missions

In mission conducted under Western auspices, the really effective work has probably always been done by indigenous Christians, whose names have gone largely unreported in our official histories.[1] It is only recently that the subject of indigenous mission (either in association with or independent of Western agencies) has become recognised as a matter worthy of extensive research. One reason for this is that mission administrators have tended to see indigenous initiatives as a threat rather than a fulfilment to their own work.[2] The fact that indigenous evangelistic activities often operate without any significant accountability to secretaries and treasurers also means that little of their activity has been documented. Western missiologists simply lack adequate information about non-Western missionary initiatives, and in consequence only a minute proportion of missiological writing is devoted to the subject of independent indigenous church movements.

Concerted efforts to produce a major *Dictionary of African Christian Biography* are currently directed to redressing this imbalance, at least in so far as

---

[1] Bonk, "Between Past and Future", 122
[2] See, for example, Cliff, "Church Planter", 291; Rajamani, 76.

that continent is concerned. In support of this project Jonathan Bonk has recently observed,

> Despite the very modest results accruing from the prodigious efforts of nineteenth-century missionaries like David Livingstone, Robert Moffat, Mary Slessor and C T Studd, these names are household words today; in contrast, while Christian numerical growth in Africa has burgeoned from an estimated 8.8 million in 1900 to 382.8 million in 2004, scarcely anything is known about the persons chiefly responsible for this astonishing growth – African catechists and evangelists.[1]

Throughout his time in India, the news which most excited Groves was always the news he received of indigenous evangelistic initiatives.[2] In this regard, it has taken a century and a half for missiographers to catch up with him.

John Arulappan (1810-67)

In the course of our study, mention has often been made of Groves's young disciple John Christian Arulappan and the movement in southern India associated with him, whereby he and his Indian friends, without denominational affiliation or guaranteed financial support, engaged in widespread evangelistic itineration resulting in the creation of a network of informal fellowships comprising at least 30,000 Indian Christians, entirely free of foreign control, and at least thirty-three, largely self-supporting, Christian villages.[3]

From 1840 onwards, Groves's vision for the spontaneous growth of indigenous churches was amply fulfilled in these remarkable initiatives. The death of the gifted Arulappan in 1867, however, marked a turning point and the beginning of a rapid degeneration in the movement associated with him. Several reasons may be suggested for this. Firstly, it is evident that Arulappan had not adequately shared leadership tasks and responsibilities with other men or prepared his associates for the time when he would no longer be with them. In particular we find that gifts, arriving regularly from Britain for the support of Indian evangelists, were sent to him personally and distributed by him. This system no doubt developed from the trust reposed in Arulappan himself by the donors, who had confidence in his judgement, his integrity and his ability to arrange means for money to be carried safely to appropriate people during the years when the Indian postal service was still rudimentary. But it also meant that, on his death, the system of support entirely broke down. Then secondly, and perhaps more importantly, we find that Arulappan's final years were burdened by the secular "tent-making" aspects of his movement, involving him in conflicts over lands, properties and debts that in some cases involved costly legal action. Then thirdly, in his concern to co-operate cheerfully with Christians of all denominations, and especially with the neighbouring Anglicans of the CMS, he perhaps failed to emphasize strongly enough the vision for independent indigenous Indian churches that he had inherited from Groves.

The consequences were almost inevitable. Having enjoyed a good education in a Church of England school, a son of Arulappan arranged in 1875 for the Indian

---

[1] Bonk, "Ecclesiastical Cartography", 153-4
[2] See for example his reaction to news from Serkies (M360), Mokayel and a friend of Serkies (M360), and Arulappan and Andrew (M393).
[3] M467; Lang, *Aroolappen*, 90-1. See above, 110ff.

churches and villages to be placed under the authority of the English bishop. Although Arulappan himself had "declined any form of salary, because the people... would not cease to tell him that he preached because he was hired,"[1] a new generation of church leaders evidently saw greater benefit in a salaried post with a foreign mission, and perhaps some comfort in relinquishing responsibility to a foreign committee.

Three local churches chose to remain independent, in association with another of Arulappan's sons, and among these was his original base at Christianpettah.[2] A visitor in 1925 found this fellowship still active on the same financial basis as when it commenced eighty-five years earlier.[3] But the widespread network of Indian congregations engaged in spontaneous indigenous mission, launched by Arulappan and inspired by Groves, had become a thing of the past. Here we may observe a familiar pattern: pragmatic interests overriding missiological ideals and translating a spiritual movement into a religious institution.

Watchman Nee (1903-1972)

Ni To-sheng[4] is known in the West primarily through a series of books published in the mid-twentieth century by means of which his verbal Bible teaching, transcribed and translated, has found wide acceptance in the English-speaking world.[5]

As a young man in China we find Nee "greatly influenced by accounts of the faith of George Müller of Bristol and Hudson Taylor of the China Inland Mission."[6] These biographies persuaded him that, in contemplating a life devoted to Christian ministry, he should never ask for money from anyone or accept gifts from the unconverted: he should live, like these men, "by faith".

In a subsequent commentary on the book of Revelation, Nee quoted the words of Groves in Dublin, in the drawing room meeting of 1827 and the following year in Lower Pembroke Street.[7] He went on to describe the Brethren movement as "the church which returns to the orthodoxy of the apostles,"[8] and claimed, "This movement was greater than the movement of the Reformation."[9]

Visiting London in 1938, Nee met a number of Open Brethren, including George H Lang, who was then working on his biographies of Groves and Arulappan.[10] Immediately afterwards Nee wrote his influential book *Concerning*

---

[1] M392

[2] *Aroolappen*, 216-8

[3] *Aroolappen*, 218

[4] At his birth in Swatow, 4th Nov. 1903, he was called Ni Shu-tsu or Henry Ni, and later renamed Ni Ching-Fu. Once engaged in active Christian work, he adopted the style of Ni To-sheng, that is, Watchman Nee.

[5] The most recent major study of Nee's thought is Cliff, *Life and Theology of Watchman Nee*. See also Cliff's "Watchman Nee: Church Planter and Preacher of Holiness".

[6] Kinnear, *Against the Tide*, 69

[7] Nee, *The Orthodoxy of the Church*, 1994 edn., 66

[8] Nee, Ibid, 61

[9] Ibid, 70. Though impressed with the doctrinal teaching of J N Darby, Nee was disenchanted with the divisive tendencies of his followers.

[10] Lyell, 75. During this visit Nee attended the Keswick Convention. He also had close contact with Theodore Austin-Sparks at his Honor Oak fellowship, and, of course, with those who had originally invited him, the "London Meeting" of Exclusive Brethren, who

our Missions, in which he advocated mission strategies very much akin to those envisaged by Groves.

Nee observed missionaries in his native China promoting Henry Venn's "three-self" values in their frustrated attempts to hand over leadership of their congregations to the Chinese, and he commented, "Such problems would never have come up for consideration if the principles shown us in God's word had been adhered to from the very beginning...Wherein lies the failure of missions today? They keep the results of their work in their own hand. In other words they have reckoned *their* converts as members of *their* mission, or of *their* mission church."[1]

Though Nee was careful to honour the sacrificial work of many missionaries in China, he regretted the Western accretions they had brought with them: "According to the present-day conception, three things are regarded as essential to the existence of a church... These three are a 'minister', a church building and 'church services'... But what is considered essential to a church these days was considered totally unnecessary in the early days of the church's history."[2] Rather than adopting Western forms of Christianity, he advised, "Let us see what the word of God has to say on the matter."[3] He then observed,

> The apostolic procedure was quite simple. The apostles visited a place, founded a church, left that church for a while, then returned to establish it. In the interval, certain developments would naturally take place. When the apostles left, some of the professing believers would leave too. Others... would make no appreciable progress. Others again would eagerly press on... Those who had more spiritual life than others would spontaneously come to the front and take responsibility for their weaker brethren. It was because they had proved themselves to be elders that the apostles appointed them to hold office as elders, and it was *their* business to shepherd and instruct the other believers.[4]

Nee's study of the New Testament convinced him that churches should be led by a group of unpaid elders, that these should be "local brothers" rather than men trained elsewhere, that full-time workers should be evangelists rather than pastors, and that these evangelists should look directly to God for guidance and support without salary or obligation to man. He observed that all who are born of the Spirit are automatically members of the church, that every member has a vital function in the body, that meetings will be informal with much spontaneous participation, and that they will generally take place in the homes of the believers. Although a hall or public place may be rented or borrowed for occasional conferences, "we must remember," he said, "that the ideal meeting places of the saints are their own private homes."[5]

For Watchman Nee this was not just abstract missiological theory; it was the practical basis of an indigenous movement that grew rapidly from small beginnings in the early 1920s. It evidently satisfied a widely felt need, for within a short time

---

condemned his evident willingness to enjoy fellowship with other Christians (Kinnear, *Against the Tide*, 85-160).

[1] Nee, *The Normal Christian Church Life*, 1980 edn., 109-10
[2] Nee, Ibid, 163-4
[3] Ibid, 164
[4] Ibid, 40
[5] Ibid, 171

the loose network of house fellowships associated with Nee had more adherents than any other Christian group in China. The title "Little Flock" was given to the movement by those outside it, although Nee himself believed that no distinguishing title should be used for any group of Christians, other than the name of their locality.

Although some undoubtedly transferred to his fellowships from other churches, most were conversions. He described how he and his co-workers would take the gospel to an unreached town and start a church. "Suppose we go to Kweiyang to work, what should be our procedure? On arrival in Kweiyang, we either live in an inn or rent a room, and we begin to preach the gospel. When men are saved, what shall we do? We must encourage them to read the word, to pray, to give, to witness and to assemble for fellowship and ministry… We should teach them to have *their own* meetings in *their own* meeting place."[1] This approach differed fundamentally from that of the missionary societies known to Nee. He commented, "One of the tragic mistakes of the past hundred years of foreign missions in China (God be merciful to me if I say anything amiss!) is that after a worker led men to Christ, he prepared a place and invited them to come there for meetings, instead of encouraging them to assemble by themselves."[2]

Nee expected his converts to take responsibility from the very moment of their conversion: "The worker [i.e. evangelist] must leave the believers to initiate and conduct their own meetings in their own meeting place, and then he must go to *them* and take part in *their* meetings, not ask them to come to *him* and take part in *his* meetings."[3] A positive consequence of this is that new converts will identify immediately with the body of Christians in their locality, rather than with any national or international organisation, for, in Nee's words, "there is no such thing in scripture as the building up of denominations; we only find local churches there."[4]

By 1949 the "Little Flock" had over 70,000 members in five hundred fellowships,[5] and by 1956 it was believed to outnumber any other Christian group in China.[6] Following what they believed to be New Testament principles, these groups closely resemble the earliest Brethren assemblies in Britain and elsewhere, and they continue to flourish in most difficult circumstances, without a paid ministry, recognised buildings or set times of worship.[7]

Their inspiration is obviously the New Testament rather than any identifiable writing of Groves, Müller or Hudson Taylor. Yet the idea of turning to the New Testament as a manual of missionary methods may certainly be traced back, in Nee's earliest thought, to these ecclesiological and missiological pioneers, the first and most radical of whom was Groves.[8]

---

[1] Ibid, 107
[2] Ibid
[3] Ibid, 108
[4] Ibid, 135
[5] Cliff, "Church Planter", 291. The source of the figures is not stated.
[6] Ecumenical Press Service, Geneva, 22nd Nov. 1957, cited by Kinnear, *Against the Tide*, 254. See also Adeney, 146-8.
[7] See Cliff, "Church Planter", 296.
[8] On the mission strategy of Watchman Nee, see below, 247ff.

Bakht Singh (1903-2000)

The indigenous missionary movement associated with John Christian Arulappan was largely appropriated, as we have seen, by the CMS. Yet Arulappan himself had a granddaughter, whose husband was "an evangelist associated with the Christian Brethren".[1] They had two sons, named Rajamani and Dorairaj. In 1935 Rajamani returned to the village of Christianpettah to help bury a beloved younger sister, and here he and Dorairaj prayed at the grave of their distinguished ancestor. Rajamani recalled, "It seemed that something of the influence of his remarkable life of faith clung to the place... On our return from the south Dorairaj and I felt a new awakening of our love for the Lord and we began to pray much together."[2]

The pair began preaching publicly, distributing tracts, marching with banners and musical instruments through the streets of Madras, and before long had been joined by "an increasing number of young men from various denominations". This "Gospel League" possessed "no constitution, nor membership, nor subscription list, but found its unity and strength in our love for the Lord Jesus Christ and our free wholehearted committal to him."[3]

It was in 1938 that Bakht Singh, a converted Sikh from the Punjab, first came to Madras, and Rajamani and Dorairaj became two of his closest friends.[4] As he preached publicly, many bystanders came to faith in Christ and a number were miraculously healed. Through his open-air campaigns in the 1930s, Bakht Singh became "the spiritual father of tens of thousands",[5] and the leader of another remarkable indigenous movement.

In 1941, Bakht Singh was refused permission to preach on a church compound in Madras. The reason given was simple: "We in the Indian Ministers' Conference have met and passed a resolution never again to make any place available to this Punjabi preacher. Our objection is that he is not an ordained minister and therefore has no right to baptise anyone."[6]

Many of those who responded to the preaching of Bakht Singh and his friends had no church background; others were disillusioned with existing churches and missions increasingly influenced by liberal theology. Bakht Singh's biographer describes the course of events: "By his side were godly and experienced men like Dorairaj and Rajamani. They felt the need of a new solution to India's pressing problem. With prophetic insight they could see the inevitable crumbling of the missionary system. If the Lord's interests were to be secured in the land there was need for a far stronger foundation."[7] After much prayer they were led to rent a

---

[1] Rajamani, 13
[2] Rajamani, 45
[3] Rajamani, 47
[4] Prior to 1936, Bakht Singh had served as an agent of the CMS in Karachi and elsewhere. In the early period of his independent ministry (Madras, 1940-1), he received much encouragement from the Brethren missionaries Wilfred and Christina Durham, and later from C Raymond Golsworthy and Alfred J (Fred) Flack of Honor Oak fellowship, London, along with Leslie Carter of WEC and Dennis E Clark of the Brethren in what is now Pakistan (Koshy, *Brother Bakht Singh of India*, 136-7).
[5] Koshy, "A Saint of God"
[6] Rajamani, 76
[7] Smith D, 45-6

large dilapidated house in Madras, and here they launched a new fellowship with the name Jehovah Shammah.

By this time, Lang's biography of John Arulappan had found its way to India, and the example of Arulappan was introduced to a fresh generation.[1] Searching the scriptures for the apostolic principles of church life, they agreed that the first priority was to insist on the need for new birth. A true church, they observed, will consist of committed believers, not people "baptised" as infants or made "members" by signing a piece of paper. Secondly, their fellowship must be "free from foreign control and direction, and also from the slavish rule of foreign finance."[2] And thirdly, the meetings should be like those described in the New Testament, where all who believed might freely participate, devoting themselves to the apostles' teaching, fellowship, breaking of bread and prayer.

A contemporary describes how, from this point on, Bakht Singh "founded churches based on New Testament principles."[3] In addition to being "scriptural" churches, they were thoroughly "Indian" churches.

> He built simple bamboo sheds (as against the pretentious stone buildings of Western design); he sat his people on floor mats, native style (and not on Western-style benches); he had gifted fellow-workers compose their own hymns and psalms, and set them to native lyrics [sic]; he brought in Indian instruments of music to lead congregational singing; he kept meetings going for long hours, which Indians love (to debunk the infamous Western one-hour service); he taught believers to give and not to beg; he showed them how to seek guidance about every matter direct from the Lord instead of slavishly following the orders of the missionary. Bakht Singh ruthlessly brought the externals back to simplicity and placed the emphasis on "life", the resurrection life of the Lord Jesus, lifting believers into a realm far above the cold dead things of religious formality.[4]

Over the next eighteen years, more than two hundred such churches sprang up in places he visited, and these rapidly became the fastest growing churches in India.[5] At the present day they number at least two thousand.[6] Most were the result of a gospel campaign conducted by a team of several dozen volunteers. Arriving in a town they would first of all rent a house. Then, with literature distribution and open-air processions during the day, and a major evangelistic meeting every evening, the whole population was soon introduced to the gospel. When the team left, after a week or a month, a few workers would remain to answer questions and advise those who had responded until local leaders had emerged from among them.[7] Once established with recognised elders, the new assembly, meeting in a home or a rented house, would only rarely receive a visit from Bakht Singh himself or from a leader associated with him.

Two or three thousand believers from these assemblies in many parts of India would gather periodically in Madras for a "Holy Convocation" of worship,

---

[1] Rajamani himself refers directly to Lang, quoting Lang's extracts from Arulappan's diaries (Rajamani, 107-8).
[2] Ibid, 48
[3] Koshy, "A Saint of God"
[4] Smith D, 52
[5] Ibid, 53
[6] Koshy, "A Saint of God"
[7] Smith D, 56-7

teaching and fellowship, but Bakht Singh never created an organisation to oversee or direct them. Financial needs were never mentioned, and the cost of the campaigns and conferences, and the support of the evangelists, were covered by unsolicited freewill offerings. Visiting Hyderabad in the 1950s, Norman Grubb of the Worldwide Evangelisation Crusade remarked, "In all my ministry experience I think these churches on their New Testament foundations are the nearest I have seen to a replica of the early church, and a pattern for the birth and growth of the young churches in all the countries which we used to talk about as the mission fields."[1]

Some observers might judge that with the passage of time the assemblies associated with Bakht Singh have lost some of their earliest ideals. This too may provide a salutary example of a movement slowly turning into an institution, distracted, as is often the case, by administrative issues relating to properties and finance. But as a historic example of a doctrinally orthodox and thoroughly successful indigenous missionary initiative it deserves the fullest attention of ecclesiologists and missiologists. And in so far as it derived its fundamental principles from John Arulappan and his descendants (using the New Testament as its pattern and guide), we can trace its origins to the primitivist influence of Groves.[2]

Conclusion: Indigenous Missions

We may feel entitled to see in the movements associated with John Arulappan, Watchman Nee and Bakht Singh a clear fulfilment of Groves's missiological vision. To the extent that these men were influenced by him we can indeed consider him a radical influence on Protestant mission in the nineteenth and in the twentieth century. Arulappan knew him personally, and both Nee and Singh knew of him through others who thought highly of him.

It is significant that Groves's principles have found their warmest acceptance not among his own fellow-countrymen, with their strong ecclesiastical traditions, but among indigenous Christian leaders who observe, with a measure of scepticism or scorn, the efforts of Western missions and decide, like him, that the New Testament offers a better model for their emulation than any so far introduced from Europe or America.

Conclusion: Groves's Missiology Applied

The missiological influence of Anthony Norris Groves has been both direct and indirect. His ideas were advanced directly through personal relationships and the dissemination of his writings, and indirectly through the work of missionaries who, whilst knowing little of him, made similar missiological applications of an ecclesiology they held in common, and derived in part from him. These include Brethren initiatives in many countries, a wide range of "faith missions" and some highly significant indigenous movements, notably those associated with John Arulappan, Bakht Singh and Watchman Nee.

Groves's influence is most evident in the commitment of all these to "faith principles", communicated to them especially through the writings and example of George Müller and Hudson Taylor. Although Brethren missionaries have been

---

[1] Grubb, *Once Caught*, 152
[2] On the mission strategy of Bakht Singh see below, 250ff.

more strongly influenced by their experience of Brethrenism in a Western context than by Groves himself, their spiritual heritage owes much to his encouragement of the early leaders of the Open Brethren (through letters, publications and occasional visits) in their opposition to J N Darby and their adoption of an ecclesiology closely akin to his own. Although failing, in some cases, to follow his non-denominational principles, the generality of missionaries recruited from the Open Brethren have been more inclined to a primitivist ethos than those from other church backgrounds.

Outside Brethren circles, we can identify traces of Groves's influence in the principles and practices of the so-called "faith missions". The willing co-operation of missionaries from diverse church denominations (including many Brethren), the recruitment of unordained and uneducated men, and of single women, the internationalisation of missionary teams, the frugal lifestyle that allowed for closer identity with the local populace, the premillennialist impetus, and the prospect of self-support through secular employment – these were ideas proposed by Groves and then developed by the "faith missions". In other respects, however, these new societies followed a path divergent from his. In particular we should note their authority structures, their financial accountability, their respect for denominational loyalties and traditions, their focus especially on evangelism in unreached fields, their avoidance of ecclesiological issues, and their perpetuation of the organisational dichotomy between foreign society and national church.

Missionaries of both Brethren and the "faith missions" have, to some extent, encouraged "liberty of ministry" in their congregations, although their meetings have often been led by a single individual, of either foreign or indigenous race, acting more or less like an ordained minister and allowing little opportunity for "every member ministry". Evangelistic outreach has often been initiated and financed by the foreign missionary, although many, like Groves, have trained and encouraged local evangelists in the course of their itinerations together.

Comity agreements adopted by both Brethren and "faith missions" have allowed for interdenominational co-operation, which would have pleased Groves, whilst perpetuating denominational distinctions, which would not have pleased him at all. His non-denominational influence in this regard could be considered minimal.

Brethren and "faith missions" have, in general, consciously adopted the "three-self" and "scaffolding" models for transferring ecclesiastical responsibility. In this respect, both have ignored Groves's missiological alternative. Interest has frequently been expressed by both in the ideas of Roland Allen, but the evident novelty of Allen's thought demonstrates the extent to which Groves's earlier advocacy of the same principles has been generally unknown in Brethren and "faith mission" circles.

In fact, the rigorous primitivism of Groves is seen at its strongest not in these Western agencies but in the indigenous works initiated by John Arulappan, Watchman Nee and Bakht Singh. We can trace the primitivist missiological emphasis of these movements back to the personal influence of Groves himself, or to those who knew him, or to others influenced by him.

Our conclusion must be that, with the passage of time, Groves's early and largely indirect influence on Anglo-American missions became substantially overlain and dissipated under pressure from later and more pragmatic considerations. Evidence suggests, nevertheless, that indigenous movements, independent of foreign control and finance, proved better able to apply and preserve the primitivist missiological ethos they derived directly or indirectly from Groves.

2. Mission Thinkers, Grovesian and Other

The corpus of missiological writing produced during the past century manifests a profound and almost universal ignorance of Anthony Norris Groves. He can hardly be considered a known or recognised influence in circles professing either an academic or a practical interest in Christian mission. For this reason we might be inclined to deem him little more than a bygone voice crying in the wilderness, significant only to those who go deliberately seeking him.

In order to establish Groves as a missiologist of significance, we will need to assess not only the extent of his personal influence on others, but also the significance of his missiological principles in their own right, irrespective of his own success, or lack of it, in advocating them. We have considered how far Groves's ideas were influential in Brethren missions, in the so-called "faith missions" and in some indigenous missions. But history shows us that the same ideas have appeared elsewhere, and have been proposed, attacked, dismissed and defended by missionaries and missiologists whose personal awareness of Groves may or may not be evident.

In fact Groves has much to contribute to current debate on a wide range of missiological issues. Almost every matter of current controversy will find some point of contact with his thought – the perpetual gulf between rich and poor, the continued difficulty in dismantling foreign "scaffolding", the ongoing struggle to secure "three-self" autonomy, the perplexing frustrations in training and supporting "national pastors", the distressing tensions between mission executives and indigenous leaders, the perceived risk of financial dependence, the recent fashion for "direct sending" and the marginalisation of missionary societies, the growth of mission tourism, the dangers of indigenous syncretism on the one hand and hedonistic consumerism on the other, the increasing dominance of Anglo-American management methods, the ongoing demand for accountability, and the continuation of manipulative foreign control in guises both subtle and crass. These are issues that a Grovesian missiologist might approach quite differently from one following different principles.

Primitivism

Lesslie Newbigin has identified three basic elements, three corners to a triangle, which in varying proportions combine to determine the essential strategy adopted by any missionary or missiologist. They are firstly, foreign church custom; secondly, local culture; and thirdly, New Testament principle and practice.[1] Taken individually, we may define these as institutionalism, culturalism and primitivism, and we will consider each in turn, as represented by missions of the past and present that have leaned heavily in one direction or another.

Groves clearly stands in the primitivist "corner", and, indeed, we could consider him the first major primitivist, or biblicist, among mission strategists. For him, New Testament principles and practice should be the supreme determinant of strategy for church and mission in any age and any culture. Throughout history, a primitivist approach has been an uncommon one, and as we discuss the ebb and

---

[1] Newbigin, *The Open Secret*, 147. These three categories might be equated with those identified by Ingleby in an Indian context as Anglicist, Orientalist and Vernacularist. The Vernacularists were essentially concerned with teaching the Bible (Ingleby, 25).

flow of missiological thought from his day to ours, we will observe the points where primitivist, and thus Grovesian, principles come to bear. We will also note instances of direct and indirect contact with Groves himself, affecting policies and choices in spheres at a considerable distance from his own. In particular, we will compare Groves's primitivism with that of Charles Gützlaff, Thomas Walker and Roland Allen.[1]

Eight years younger than Groves, Charles Gützlaff (1803-51) was a German Lutheran serving in China as a translator for the British governor of Hong Kong. In 1844 he drew together a number of Chinese evangelists in what he called the Chinese Christian Union, and intimated its daring ambition to reach the whole of inland China by means of itinerant preaching. By 1849 reports spoke of a hundred and thirty evangelists proclaiming the gospel, selling books over a wide area, and leading hundreds of Chinese to faith in Christ. Although many of Gützlaff's "evangelists" proved to be confidence tricksters, some were genuine, and through their efforts groups of Chinese Christians came together in various places. One of these groups gained as many as eighty-seven members within the space of five years.[2]

Gützlaff's evangelists were supported largely by Brethren from the circles in England closest to Groves, especially Richard Ball of Taunton and George Pearse. It is likely that Gützlaff had read Groves's *Christian Devotedness*, for we know that among his close friends in China another influential government translator, Robert Morrison, had studied the booklet carefully and had been moved to commend its message.[3] In April 1834 Groves had been greatly encouraged by a letter from Gützlaff, sent either to himself or to a mutual friend in Calcutta, which spoke of "extensive openings for publishing the gospel" in China.[4] Gützlaff also corresponded regularly with Karl Rhenius, another supporter of indigenous evangelists, and was probably aware of Groves's involvement in Rhenius's conflict with episcopal authority.[5]

Gützlaff, like Groves, was a person of outstanding spirituality, energy and vision. Like Groves, a single error of judgment undermined the influence he might

---

[1] On the concept of "primitivism", see above, 77ff, and PEANG, 38ff. Forty years ago, a primitivist missiology was proposed by Grassi. More recently, the New Testament has again been offered as a model for mission, and Paul as a model missionary, by Nissen. For an alternative view, arguing that Paul, in particular, should not be considered a valid model for modern missions, see Strijdom, 612-22.

[2] An account of Gützlaff's life appears in Broomhall, *Barbarians*, 180-7, 315-61, and an assessment of his Chinese Union in Lutz & Lutz, 269-91.

[3] In his private journal for 20th November 1827, Morrison remarked, "A tract entitled 'Christian Devotedness' has appeared a little in my way with views as some deem them fanatical, of devoting all to God and not laying up treasures in the earth." Although a current periodical, the *Eclectic*, "opposed it fiercely," Morrison defended Groves's position: "Christ's precepts, high spun impracticable dogmas? Oh no; let it not be said! I think them the words of truth and soberness" (M16).

[4] M294

[5] Gützlaff's acceptance for missionary training at the Moravian Missionary Institute in Berlin was the result of a personal letter from Rhenius to the King of Prussia (Rhenius, *Memoir*, 258-9, 440).

otherwise have exerted on his and subsequent generations.[1] In a number of respects the missiological visions of the two men coincide. Gützlaff, too, had little interest in management. Like Groves, he encouraged national believers to meet together without waiting for a foreigner to lead them. He argued that the task of reaching a people would be most effectively accomplished by their own compatriots, and he believed that the role of the foreigner was simply to encourage and facilitate their efforts. According to Broomhall, "Gützlaff recognised the missionary's task as tuition short of tutelage, the helping but not the controlling hand – *autonomy from the very start of the relationship*, yet with close spiritual and pastoral oversight of the emerging church."[2]

Another point that Groves and Gützlaff had in common was their view that the missionary should adapt to the economic and social condition of those amongst whom he lives. Gützlaff proposed that the young missionary don Chinese clothes and devote himself to the task of discipling twenty or thirty Chinese believers. In his own words, "It is necessary that he should entirely live with the natives, identify himself with them... penetrate further and further in the country and give up all foreign society and connections... Local opposition will always be experienced wherever the gospel of salvation is announced... His pay therefore will be small, his troubles many and unless he be a heavenly minded man, he will soon sink under them."[3] Gützlaff was confident that God would provide: "No real workman will ever be left to starve, no great enterprise for the glory of God be allowed to stand still for want of means, for God who is rich above all that call upon him never abandons his own... How little is required when one can live with contentment among the natives; what happy hours can be passed in sharing a meal with them."[4]

A frugal lifestyle, identifying with the indigenous people, training evangelists by taking them out on evangelistic treks, and living by faith: these ideas are all strongly reminiscent of Groves. Although Gützlaff's efforts proved a disappointment to him in his own lifetime, the historian of the CIM considers that no less than eleven missions were founded through his influence.[5] Hudson Taylor later called him the grandfather of the CIM, and his vision for reaching inland China through Chinese evangelists was amply fulfilled through the hundreds subsequently associated with the CIM and the thousands who have been active since the Communist takeover.

Gützlaff, although he wrote less than Groves about mission strategy, might be considered a primitivist from the same school, and of great significance in the history of Protestant mission.

We turn our attention now from China to India. In 1885, eighteen years after the death of John Christian Arulappan, an English clergyman, Thomas Walker, was appointed by the CMS to be "Superintendent of the Tamil Church". He faced a situation in which a period of famine had given the Christians an opportunity to

---

[1] Groves considered he had erred in borrowing a substantial sum of money for the extension of his silk manufactory at Chittoor. The failure of this enterprise left him with crippling debts. See FOFM 247-8.
[2] Broomhall, *Barbarians*, 330 (italics added)
[3] Gützlaff, quoted by Broomhall, *Barbarians*, 333
[4] Ibid
[5] *Barbarians*, App.6. It was through an appeal by Gützlaff that David Livingstone received his initial missionary call in 1834 (Fiedler, 66).

feed and clothe the poor, and 30,000 grateful beneficiaries had flooded into the churches. Though warmly disposed towards Christianity, these had only the scantiest knowledge of its precepts and obligations. Caste prejudice, marriage with Hindus, and problems of drunkenness and litigation, soon compromised the newcomers. Many names had to be removed from the church rolls, and church officers relieved of their responsibilities. Walker admitted, "It is no light task to superintend fifty-five thousand Christians, specially when along with it you have to introduce and write a new set of rules."[1]

Much of the Superintendent's time was taken up with requests by Indian Christians for money, and this led him to observe, "The power of the rupee in our Indian missions has sometimes been more strongly felt than the power of the Holy Ghost. From personal experience I do not hesitate to say that our most living congregations are those which have received the least financial aid; and the converse is also true."[2] Elsewhere he confided, "I had close work today at the new regulations for Council. What a pity that such elaborate organisation is needed. One wonders how the Pastoral Department was managed in apostolic times."[3] On another occasion, "Conference of missionaries; much talk about Councils and Bodies, but oh, for a good apostolic prayer meeting!"[4] And again, "You often have to pay unspiritual people to do spiritual work – would the apostles have done that?"[5] Finally he asked, "Have we not, all of us, deviated sadly from the lines laid down in the Acts of the Apostles?"[6]

Walker's frustration led him to consider afresh the missionary methods described in the New Testament, and he wrote a small book on the subject, entitled *Missionary Ideals*.[7] He attempted to sift out the "unsuitable pastors, schoolmasters, catechists", and he challenged the pervasive influence of caste. Soon he faced a "torrent of remonstrances... much bitterness, finally furious anger." "His strong convictions concerning the growth of the Indian church were not shared by the home committee."[8] Appeals were made against him, authority was brought to bear, and eventually he was compelled to resign.[9] He admitted, "I feel that I have reached a point when my obedience to the Committee is in danger of clashing with my obedience to God."[10] Directing his energies to itinerant evangelism, Walker had returned to the path marked out by Rhenius, Groves and Arulappan. For his insistence on a frugal and spiritual lifestyle, he became "a very unpopular person in certain quarters".[11]

He was grieved in particular by the denominational jealousies that surrounded him: "In India all the unhappy divisions of the home Church are being rapidly introduced, and thus the spread of the gospel is hindered... Satan's choicest

---

[1] Carmichael, *This One Thing*, 55
[2] Ibid, 143
[3] Ibid, 55
[4] Ibid, 123
[5] Ibid, 73
[6] Ibid, 133-8
[7] first published in 1911
[8] Houghton, 96
[9] *This One Thing*, 73-4
[10] Ibid
[11] Ibid, 126

weapon is the blade which cuts asunder the union of the Christian Church itself."[1] Bishops still forbad Anglicans to take the Lord's Supper with fellow Christians unless the bread and wine could be administered by an ordained Church of England minister, and Walker would not accept this. Amy Carmichael recalls, "It was quite impossible for him to join his fellow servants in service and then to draw back from going to the Lord's Table with them. It is not the Table of any Church was his feeling. 'It's the *Lord's* Table.'"[2]

There is no evidence that Thomas Walker knew of Groves or of his writings, although he probably knew about the Rhenius affair and may have mixed with Brethren at university in England. Walker's form of Anglicanism, with its strong "Keswick" leanings and its interest in apostolic methods, was one that Groves would have found particularly congenial. Indeed we might think Walker far more akin to Groves than to Venn or the bishops of Calcutta.

Among recognised missiologists, the closest to Groves in letter and in spirit is undoubtedly Roland Allen (1868-1947). This may seem surprising, given the fact that Allen identified himself as a High Church Anglican. It reflects his substantial disillusionment with his own denomination.[3]

It was evident to Allen that, after the death of Henry Venn in 1873, the Church of England overseas had increasingly promoted its denominational traditions and asserted the authority of its bishops. In 1910, Anglican participants in the celebrated International Missionary Conference in Edinburgh had placed renewed emphasis on the call for western religion and civilisation to transform the world for the better. As Allen's grandson and biographer observed, "The conference epitomized all Roland's worst misgivings about the current attitudes of western missionaries – their conscious and unconscious paternalism, their clericalism, their colonialism."[4] Two years later, and largely as a reaction to the conference, Allen's classic work was published with the title *Missionary Methods, St Paul's or Ours?* The author was acclaimed as "prophetic", "one of the most seminal missiological and ecclesiological minds of this century". He was reckoned to be fifty years ahead of his time.[5]

Roland Allen's views were undeniably radical. He advised a return to what he identified as the methods of Christ and the apostles. He warned that national church leaders would not long tolerate the dominion of foreign church leaders, that technological progress and social justice should not be confused with faith in Christ, that truly indigenous churches cannot be established by foreign mission boards, that Christian institutions cannot turn people into Christians. He argued that evangelism must be the task of ordinary people rather than paid professionals, that the best way to train disciples is by living with them, that unordained

---

[1] Ibid

[2] Ibid, 123. Amy Carmichael joined Thomas Walker and his wife in Tinnevelly in 1896.

[3] It is remarkable to observe how many Anglicans in successive generations express themselves profoundly unhappy with the Church of England, whilst refusing to forsake it. No other Protestant denomination seems able to retain the loyal allegiance of such a high proportion of malcontents.

[4] Allen H J B, 85-6.

[5] Kenneth G Grubb in foreword to Allen, *Spontaneous Expansion* (World Dominion Press, 4th edn. 1960); review by William J Danker, quoted on back cover of Allen, *Missionary Methods* (American edn. 1962, Eerdmans reprint 1987).

indigenous Christians must be trusted to preach and teach and celebrate the Lord's Supper, that Christian unity is unity of life rather than organisational control.

Above all, he argued that the frustration experienced by missionary societies in their efforts to plant churches must be attributed to the fact that they have started with a society rather than a church. He declared,

> The natives always speak of "the Mission" as something which is not their own. The Mission represents a foreign power, and natives who work under it are servants of a foreign government. It is an evangelistic society, and the natives tend to leave it to do the evangelistic work, which properly belongs to them. It is a model, and the natives learn simply to imitate it. It is a wealthy body, and the natives tend to live upon it, and expect it to supply all their needs. Finally it becomes a rival, and the native Christians feel its presence as an annoyance... It always keeps the native Christians in check, and its relations with them are difficult and full of perils. A large part of modern books on Missions is concerned with the attempt to justify these relations and to find some way of escape from these difficulties. For St Paul they did not exist, because he did not create them. He set up no organisation intermediate between his preaching and the establishment of a fully organised indigenous church.[1]

The difficulties identified by Allen had all been foreseen eighty years earlier by Groves, as indeed were the solutions he advocated. Groves too had earnestly wished to bypass all the complications that followed from the administrative separation of "church" and "mission".

Their similarity of view is evident in many points of detail. Chilcraft has noted one example among many: "Both Groves and Allen thought it a scandal that many mission churches went months without celebrating communion because there was no ordained clergyman available. This drove Allen to the dramatic conclusion that in the absence of an ordained minister, any suitable man should be allowed to conduct it. This was the very issue that occasioned Groves' split with CMS and was at the heart of his response to the Rhenius affair."[2]

Chilcraft's comparative assessment of Groves and Allen suggests that the reason their ideas so closely coincide is because they both challenged church tradition in the light of New Testament practice. Few Anglicans of Allen's generation would be willing to do this so ruthlessly and so publicly, and it may be of significance that among Allen's childhood influences were an aunt and other relatives who were active participants in Brethren assemblies.[3] If Allen's distinctive views can be traced back to Brethren rather than Anglican roots, they will owe much to Groves. It is by no means unlikely that he had actually read Groves's *Memoir*, for as Chilcraft points out, "Allen is notoriously reluctant in his early works to attribute his sources or to betray the influences on his thought."[4]

But whereas Allen, from the comfort of his private study, offered his theories in print to the most contemplative and literate members of the missionary community, Groves conveyed them directly and verbally to indigenous believers. Indeed, while Allen's version was being perused, debated and disputed in conventions and common rooms, Groves's had already been accepted and applied by highly

---

[1] Allen, *Missionary Methods*, 83
[2] Chilcraft, Ch.8
[3] Allen H J B, 12
[4] Chilcraft, Ch.8

motivated and gifted indigenous leaders such as John Arulappan, Watchman Nee and Bakht Singh. Viewed in this light, we might go so far as to consider Groves's practical influence greater than Allen's. Although Groves wrote less on the subject, he deserves at least a share of the missiological esteem granted to Allen. Indeed, as a primitivist he takes precedence by eighty years.

We shall now turn our attention to the "institutionalist" corner of Newbigin's triangle.

Institutionalism

An institutionalist missiology will assume the need for administrative structures and a hierarchy of command to oversee the initiation and management of cross-cultural spiritual ministry in both missionary society and indigenous church. Desiring to promote their own Western denominations overseas, Henry Venn, Rufus Anderson and John Nevius are the best known representatives of this school. We have discussed their principles and seen some of the difficulties they faced in transferring administrative and financial responsibilities from foreign societies to national churches.[1]

Among institutionalists however, Venn's "three-self" indigenisation scheme was not the only methodology on offer, and Roland Allen was not alone in thinking it ill-adapted to the circumstances facing the Church of England overseas. Stephen Neill (1900-84) preferred to envisage an ongoing foreign / national partnership rather than a formal handover of properties and responsibilities from one to the other. Indeed, he considered Venn's distinction between "church" and "mission" ill-advised, and favoured the strategy of Bishop A R Tucker in Uganda who, from 1897 onwards, encouraged both national Christians and foreign missionaries to identify with the "Native Anglican Church" rather than with the CMS.[2] In Cairo, Temple Gairdner (1873-1928) also emphasized the partnership of foreign missionaries and local Anglican clergy, working together as equals in the ongoing life of the church.[3] Likewise in Lahore, Thomas French (1825-91) endeavoured to draw together the divergent Indian and English wings of the Anglican Church, and pressed for the creation of Indian synods to oversee all spiritual activities.[4]

As an Anglican missiologist, Lesslie Newbigin regrets the continued tendency of the younger churches around the world to defer to the older churches of Europe and America. He remarks, "The modern missionary movement has depended, in a manner unparalleled in the New Testament, upon the continuing guidance, support, and direction of the 'daughter' church by the 'mother' church. There is no parallel to that in the Acts of the Apostles."[5] In 1995 he optimistically observed that both Protestant and Roman Catholic leaders evidenced a "new readiness to acknowledge the missionary character of the church",[6] and he commented, "The struggles

---

[1] See above, 87ff.
[2] Tucker met with vehement opposition among his missionary colleagues and was not able to carry his point (Neill, *Christian Missions*, 260, 387; Shenk, *Venn*, 113-5).
[3] William Henry Temple Gairdner was an ordained clergyman serving as a CMS missionary in Cairo between 1899 and 1928. He was a gifted Arabist, an outstanding church leader and a key figure in the Edinburgh Conference of 1910.
[4] Vander Werff, 51
[5] Newbigin, *A Word in Season*, 12
[6] Newbigin, *The Open Secret*, 1

through which the younger churches born of Western missions have had to pass in order to graduate from 'mission' to 'church' have forced the older churches to recognise that this separation of church from mission is theologically indefensible."[1]

But, as Anglicans, these men all took for granted the idea that their foreign denomination (considered catholic or universal) should be exported to other continents and then directed by foreigners until such time as local leadership could maintain its distinctive ecclesiastical traditions, with its liturgy, its forms of dress, its Prayer Book and its articles of faith. In 1939 Stephen Neill became bishop of Tinnevelly (Tirunelveli), an event which led Amy Carmichael to sever her connection with the diocese.[2] Gairdner too, though strongly committed to inter-mission and interdenominational co-operation, deliberately directed his energies to the establishment of an "Egyptian Anglican Church".[3] Thomas French, as Bishop of Lahore, though wary of High Church rituals likely to stifle the growth of Indian forms of worship, strongly upheld the idea of apostolic succession through the Anglican episcopacy.[4] Mission strategy for these men was defined by the nature of the Church to which they belonged, and they could not easily escape it. Only Roland Allen among recognised Anglican missiologists has been bold enough to question, like Groves, the very existence and validity of the denomination itself.

The "three-self" formula for indigenisation has become so widely respected that subsequent generations of missiologists and missionaries have almost taken it for granted. Like John Nevius, they have simply tinkered with it in various ways to make it work a little better. A recent example is Tom Steffan, who suggests that foreign missionaries should plan their phase-out even before commencing their work in a new field. Deriving his model from experience in Latin America, Steffan advises that the missionary's role will progress in the course of time from apostle, to administrator, to partner, to servant, to consultant.[5] His concept of "phaseout" requires the missionary to plant a fully functioning church and then gradually withdraw, so that its maintenance falls by default on others. He advocates "the planned absences of church-planters over time, so that believers can develop their own spiritual roots and grow strong, as responsibility for the church *shifts* to them from the church planters."[6] The word "shifts" is significant, for it places Steffan in the school of Venn and Anderson rather than that of Groves. He assumes that leadership must pass from missionaries to converts after a certain period of time,

---

[1] Newbigin, Ibid, 2

[2] Some fifteen years earlier Neill had spent twelve months assisting in her work at Dohnavur, during which time there were marked tensions between the two strong personalities (Daughrity).

[3] In 1921 Gairdner wrote, "We decided to have one real shot at getting *on*: to take stock of our members, quasi-members, adherents, see who was who, have a campaign of explaining what the Anglican Church is, what it stands for in Egypt, what is its order, liturgy, aim, spirit: regularize, take hold, take stock, rekindle, and finally ordain the first Egyptian pastor, as a first step towards building up a really indigenous non-foreign church" (Padwick, *Temple Gairdner*, 263, 282). See also Vander Werff, 204.

[4] Vander Werff, 51

[5] Steffan, *Passing the Baton*. Peter Wagner and Harold Fuller have proposed similar sequences, assuming that new churches need continued paternal oversight from the foreign missionaries who started them.

[6] Steffan, "Phasing out" (italics added)

and that indigenous converts will be unable to meet and minister responsibly from the beginning.

The institutionalist approach has been well-tested over time, and especially in southern India. One well qualified to comment on its progress is Michael Hollis (1899-1986), formerly Bishop of Madras and then Moderator of the Church of South India. In 1962, Hollis wrote to warn his successors of weaknesses in both church and mission, which "seriously hinder their work and witness."[1] Among these was a tendency for Indian Christians to attach more importance to personal spirituality than church ordinances. Some had claimed that "the corporate life of the Church is so unspiritual that no true Christian can have anything to do with it."[2] Hollis admitted that something had gone seriously wrong: "Somehow there has been much building up of organization, structure, forms of worship, patterns of ministry and machinery of administration, but, often, a strange absence of the living God." He suggested that "the causes of these weaknesses lie in the past,"[3] and represented, in effect, a conflict between institutionalism and pietism:

> Our eighteenth century beginnings in South India were rooted in Continental Pietism... it turned men's attention away from the corporate life of the Church to the cultivation of their own inner spirituality. The general business of the Church, its activity through constitutional machinery, committees and elections, appeared to them as something external and in a considerable degree irrelevant to true Christianity... The effect of this still remains. Too many Christians in South India have never been taught to see their Christianity as essentially concerned with their corporate life... They do not attend Church meetings, they will not take part in the choice of the Church's committees nor are they prepared to hold office.[4]

Hollis did not examine the possibility that the Indians' preference for pietism over institutionalism might be a strength rather than a weakness.

He turned instead to another long-standing frustration: the deeply rooted church / mission dichotomy: "We have to ask just how far there ought to be any such thing as a mission organisation, in distinction from the Church, at all. What truth, or falsehood, about the real meaning and vocation of the Church is communicated by the existence side by side of two organizations, Church and mission?... We may conclude that, under a particular set of conditions and for a period while they lasted, it was the least unsatisfactory pattern."[5] But the problems faced by Thomas Walker, in handling church and mission employees, had grown in the course of time even worse. Now, in 1962, Hollis reported,

> At every level, from elections for the local church committee up to the choice of members of the highest councils of the Church, we are accustomed to find canvassing

---

[1] Hollis, 91. Newbigin notes, "Michael Hollis played a decisive part in bringing into one body the Anglican, Methodists and Reformed Christians in south India to form a single church, the Church of South India... It was Bishop Hollis who had the courage to cast the decisive casting vote which settled the matter. He earned thereby the deep and lasting displeasure of many and he had to live with this for the rest of his life" (foreword to Millington, *Led by the Spirit*).
[2] Hollis, 89
[3] Hollis, 91
[4] Hollis, 89
[5] Hollis, 3

and intrigue... Where appointments have to be made, we speak of candidates, even for bishoprics, and too often men set about the gaining of them as they would seek election to Parliament... All this is more intelligible if we realise that from the beginning the mission pattern accepted without question the principle of a gradation of importance among its Christian workers and assumed without serious examination that these varying degrees of importance must be marked by differences in salary and other privileges.[1]

The village teacher hoped for promotion to the status of catechist, the catechist hoped for ordination as a pastor, the pastor hoped for selection to an administrative post with the mission or with an institution such as the YMCA, the National Christian Council or the Bible Society. Promotion almost inevitably took a man progressively away from spiritual ministry into administration.[2] Finally Hollis concluded, "The pattern of organization, whatever its local variations, remains fundamentally a Western pattern. The complaint that Indians capable of working the particular system in vogue are hard to find seldom seems to make people ask themselves whether, if Indian Christians find it hard to work a particular system, it is necessarily the fault of the Indian Christians rather than of the system."[3]

The wheel thus turns full circle. A century after Groves had suffered bitter condemnation from Anglicans in Madras for daring to question the system and offer an alternative, we find the Bishop of Madras himself questioning the same system and wistfully wondering whether an alternative might have been the wiser course to take.

Above all, Hollis deplored the visible pomp and wealth of Anglican institutions and dignitaries. He recalled with regret how "Claudius Buchanan, in pleading for an Anglican episcopate in India, was insistent that it should be maintained with sufficient magnificence to impress upon the Indians the value which the English set upon their religion and its ministers."[4] But even at a local level, the foreign missionary still occupied a position to which the poor Indian could never aspire: "The Indian villager might respect and admire the missionary. He might envy him. He might try to exploit him. He might in a real sense love him. But he did not easily see him as an example of self-sacrifice and of humility. He did not see him as a servant."[5]

At the time when Hollis wrote, the severest handicap suffered by the churches was still a shortage of suitable Indian candidates for ordination. The few Indian ministers that were available found themselves responsible for congregations in twenty, forty or even eighty different villages. Most such clergy were from low castes, and their upbringing had not accustomed them to read, to think for themselves, to question traditions or to take initiatives. The majority were middle aged or elderly: "Ordination was regarded as a reward for faithful service, and those were selected who had been content to do what they were told rather than

---

[1] Hollis, 30. Hollis noted that a man qualified as a Bachelor of Divinity from an English-language institution would be paid more than one with an equivalent qualification in an Indian language (Hollis, 31-2).
[2] Hollis, 92
[3] Hollis, 66
[4] Hollis, 43
[5] Hollis, 46

those who thought for themselves."[1] It all tended towards a deeply-rooted conservatism in the local churches: "The Indian minister was trained to carry on the worship of the Church according to the particular pattern introduced by the missionary. He was trained to work the administrative machine which the missionary had established."[2] Hollis, in his retirement, could do no more than regret the entrenched evils of a system requiring salaried clergy to provide spiritual services to a passive and apathetic laity whose individual circumstances were largely unknown to them. Consecrating sacraments from village to village, conducting marriages and funerals, overseeing financial arrangements, the Indian clergy lacked any real spiritual or pastoral involvement in the lives of the local believers.

There could surely be no better vindication of Groves's early protest against Anglican church policy in this very part of India. But equally clear is the evidence of how impotent he was to change it or to prevent the imposition of an institutionalist system he abhorred.

We turn now to the "culturalist" corner of Newbigin's triangle.

Culturalism

From the early 1950s onwards a significant new trend of thought relating to Protestant overseas mission became evident in evangelical circles. Originating in America, and still largely represented there, it has been strongly influenced by anthropological scholarship. Its interest is directed particularly towards previously unreached ethnic groups, and its mission strategy is derived not from institutional considerations, nor from scriptural precept and precedent, but from the culture of the people with whom the missionary is attempting to engage.

The earliest impetus towards a more anthropological view of mission came in the1940s from circles involved in Bible translation (the Summer Institute of Linguistics / Wycliffe Bible Translators, and later the United Bible Societies). Although the focus of people such as Kenneth Pike and Eugene Nida was essentially linguistic, their translation initiatives required a clear perception of anthropological issues. Owing much to Nida's stimulus, a new missionary journal was launched in 1952, with the title *Practical Anthropology*. Two years later, Nida's book *Customs and Cultures* was published and rapidly became essential reading for American missionary candidates, especially those associated from 1961 onwards with the School of World Mission at Fuller Theological Seminary.[3]

In 1953 Melvin Hodges (1909-88) of the Assemblies of God published a short manual for missionaries associated with his denomination. Entitled *On the Mission Field: The Indigenous Church*, it reaffirmed the long-accepted three-self ideals, but recommended a greater respect for local cultures. Although Hodges was not a lucid or original thinker, he successfully popularised views that were becoming increasingly heard in more erudite circles.[4]

---

[1] Hollis, 87
[2] Hollis, 68
[3] Taber, 131
[4] At times, Hodges appears quite paradoxical. He asserts, for example, that "We must seek the New Testament approach and follow the New Testament pattern." But he then proposes organisational complexities at a local and a national level which have no New Testament basis whatsoever. He advocates church procedures for accepting members, holding business meetings, voting, and compiling records, and he takes for granted the

In 1958-9, two influential articles appeared in *Practical Anthropology* from the pen of William Smalley (b.1923). He noted that that the appointment of national pastors and the payment of their salaries by national believers will be no guarantee that an indigenous church has come into being, for the cultural style of the minister and congregation could still be entirely foreign. He remarked, "It may be very easy to have a self-governing church which is not indigenous... All that is necessary to do is to indoctrinate a few leaders in western patterns of church government, and let them take over. The result will be a church governed in a slavishly foreign manner."[1] Drawing on his experience of the Hmong people in Laos, Smalley went on to suggest that a church should be moulded by the culture in which it grows, rather than expecting the opposite. He admitted that, entering the culture from outside, Christianity is inevitably intrusive, and in consequence there is "no such thing as an absolutely indigenous church in any culture."[2] But he argued that the intrusion should be as sensitive and as discreet as possible, and that the church should retain as much as it can of the culture in which it is located.

The year 1972 marked a further development in this anthropological approach to mission, with the introduction of the term "contextualisation" to a consultation of the World Council of Churches. The January 1978 issue of *Evangelical Missions Quarterly* was devoted to the issue of contextualisation. After this, throughout the 1980s, Charles Kraft popularised and developed the concept, proposing that a church should resemble as closely as possible the existing social assemblages of the host community. In preference to both the classic denominational model of mission and the "three-self" indigenisation model, Kraft applied his concept of "dynamic equivalence", whereby the structure and activity of the church will be determined supremely by the local culture. He argued that "A truly indigenous church should look in its culture like a good Bible translation looks in its language."[3] Indeed,

> A contemporary church, like a contemporary translation, should impress the uninitiated observer as an original production in the contemporary culture, not as a badly fitted import from somewhere else... A church that is merely a "literal" rendering of the forms of one church – be it an American church or a first-century Greco-Roman church – is not according to the dynamic-equivalence model, for it is not structured in such a way that it can appropriately perform the functions and convey the meanings that should characterise a Christian church.[4]

With this statement, Kraft carries the "anthropological" approach to mission to its logical conclusion. For him, the current local culture in any place will determine the nature of mission strategy and of church activity in that place. This means that Kraft can reject, in a single breath, the culture of both the missionary and of the New Testament. Again he states his case: "A church in Africa or Asia that is

---

promotion of his own denomination as an body independent of other denominations. He surely rebukes himself when he says, "We might be shocked if we could bring ourselves face to face with the discrepancies between our methods and the New Testament pattern" (Hodges, *The Indigenous Church*, 2002 edn., 58).

[1] Smalley, "Cultural Implications"; also in Winter, *Perspectives* (1992 edn.)
[2] Smalley, *Practical Anthropology*, Vol.6 (1959), 137
[3] Kraft, "The Church in Culture", 219
[4] Kraft, *Christianity in Culture*, cited by Thomas, 215

merely a 'literal' rendering of an American church in the twentieth century (or even a Greco-Roman church in the first century) should be rejected. Such a church slavishly copies the foreign church that founded it."[1]

The effect of this approach is to elevate culture to a position of authority and to render both procedural and ethical issues relative, negotiable and temporary. "Good" and "bad" will change through both time and space. In practice it means replacing a wide spectrum of New Testament moral teachings, practices and associated beliefs with more "culturally appropriate" morals, practices and beliefs. Serious difficulties will always arise, however, within the social community itself, when opinions differ with regard to setting constraints and limits on behaviour of any sort. With culture as their only guide it will be hard for a community to reach a consensus and harder still to enforce conformity to a particular view.[2]

Commenting on these tendencies, Charles Taber suggests that, through anthropological influence, "Malinowskian functionalism pressed missions in the direction of excessive relativism, in over-reaction against the ethnocentrism and iconoclasm of earlier periods."[3] He comments,

> Functionalism was strongly biased in favour of what is, because "it works". This led in missions to an over-reaction against the older ethnocentric judgmentalism and to an excessive readiness to approve almost anything and everything. It also led missionaries as it did anthropologists to be gullible in taking at face value the explanations and interpretations of those persons in each society who were privileged and to discount the perspectives of those persons who were not favoured or rewarded by the culture, persons who might even be grievously oppressed.[4]

This, in Taber's view, has tended to encourage syncretism and to obscure the traditional Protestant view of culture. In his words, "The fall has fatally infected every aspect of culture, no matter how much good it expresses, so that nothing fully escapes the perversion of sin... All cultures, our own included – or perhaps

---

[1] Kraft, "The Church in Culture", 223

[2] The obvious difficulty lies in determining where to draw the line. For example, the condemnation of fornication in the first-century churches of Asia Minor and southern Europe (1 Cor 5:9-11; 1 Thess 4:3) might be regarded as the religious application of a pre-existing cultural taboo, appropriate for the people of that time and place but not necessarily for other times and places. A dynamically equivalent form of Christianity in a different society might conceivably allow or even encourage fornication as a normal and acceptable activity in church youth groups. To take a less extreme example, we may find the qualifications required for male elders and deacons in Ephesus (1 Tim 3:1-13) liable to reinterpretation, so that a church leader in a different time and place may be a woman with a considerable love of money, an aggressive temperament, a reluctance to welcome strangers in her home, and a complete inability to control her children. If Kraft's line of reasoning is logically applied, this will not matter in the least so long as she is a typical representative of her culture (see "The Church in Culture", 226-30). Missiologists of this school will rarely carry their ideology to such an extreme, yet the possibility of doing so is a real one, and on occasion the tension is felt when missionaries influenced by this approach interact with churches beyond the shores of Britain or America.

[3] Taber, xxi

[4] Taber, 142. Expressing his frustration with modern British Christianity, Lesslie Newbigin comments, "Ours is an advanced case of syncretism. In other words, instead of confronting our culture with the gospel, we are perpetually trying to fit the gospel into our culture" (Newbigin, *A Word in Season*, 67).

our own especially, since it is the one we are prone to absolutize – must be seen to be under the judgment of God. One important dimension of not being 'conformed to this age' (Romans 12:2) is that our minds are transformed, with the result that it is the will of God rather than the (cultural) patterns of this world that are seen to be good, and acceptable and perfect."[1] It is interesting here to see a leading figure in the anthropological school of missiology pulling back from a position where culture determines strategy to one where Scripture recovers a large element of authority.

A conscious policy of deference towards culture is a distinctly modern one, and yet we have seen precedents in the early southern Indian missions (both Roman Catholic and Lutheran / Anglican), who opted to maintain in their churches the caste distinctions approved by the prevailing culture.[2] It was Rhenius, supported by Groves, who found scriptural reasons to reject the local culture in his desire to inculcate standards of justice and equality that he considered more truly Christian, because derived directly from the Bible as he understood it.

It is hardly necessary to emphasize that Groves, whilst possessing an unusual sensitivity to the feelings and preferences of people from other cultures, held the practical doctrines of the New Testament to be the necessary "rule of life" for all Christians in all ages.[3] He expected human traditions and customs to give way before what he considered the written revelation of "the mind of the Lord".[4] In addition to this, Groves believed apostolic practice, as described in the New Testament, to be a God-given model for church and mission, worthy of emulation in every age and every culture.[5] He is unlikely to be greatly appreciated by the "anthropological" school of modern American missiology.

Church Growth

A leading "anthropological" mission thinker was Donald McGavran (1898-1990) founder of the School of World Mission at Fuller Theological Seminary. His ideas were derived from his personal experiences as a third-generation missionary in India during the 1930s and 40s. Expressed especially in terms of "church growth", they will require further analysis in their own right.

McGavran became famous for his motto, "Men like to become Christians without crossing racial, linguistic or class barriers."[6] His particular concern was to concentrate evangelistic effort on key tasks among receptive peoples, and thus to see more rapid and more numerous conversions. He was particularly interested in "people movements", involving the spread of the gospel within existing homogeneous social groupings.

In an Indian context this meant respecting and indeed, making use of, the caste system. In his own words, "If we can conceive of these castes as arranged like the strata of sandstone in a vertical series, then it is easy to see that Christianity easily spreads horizontally within the caste from relative to relative throughout the homogeneous mass, and with great difficulty to the different strata vertically."[7]

---

[1] Taber, 170-1.
[2] See above, 48ff.
[3] Groves, *Remarks*, 80-1 etc.; see PEANG, 136ff.
[4] M43, 316; see also PEANG, 175ff.
[5] M285
[6] McGavran, *Understanding Church Growth*, 98
[7] McGavran, *Founders*, 36-7,

McGavran advocated proclamation of the Christian message to families and communities rather than to individuals, and he urged the importance of converts remaining in their existing social setting rather than relocating to Christian villages or institutions. In this way, "Men become Christians without social dislocation, so that the resulting churches have leaders and loyalties intact. Churches are therefore likely to be more stable and self-supporting, and to bear up better under persecution."[1] They will also tend to grow more rapidly and spread more widely through numerical conversions from within their own social strata.

For McGavran (as for Kraft), local culture assumes a place of authority in determining the form of Christianity which will develop in each locality. He speaks of humanity as a vast mosaic of different cultures, each of which is "psychologically closed to the rest of the world." For this reason, "adaptation of Christianity to the culture of each piece of the mosaic is crucially important." And in consequence, "the true goal is to multiply, in every piece of the magnificent mosaic, truly Christian churches which fit that piece, are closely adapted to its culture and recognised by its non-Christian neighbours as 'our kind of show'."[2]

An important aspect of McGavran's scheme was his concept of "discipling", introduced in 1955. Missionaries had long sought to fulfil the Great Commission by "making disciples" (Gk. *mathēteusate*) of their individual converts, baptising them and teaching them to observe all that Jesus had taught them. For McGavran, however, the verb "to disciple" meant the teaching of unconverted collectivities in the hope that they might accept what they heard and start to believe in Christ. For him, "discipling" was a form of evangelism rather than a means of strengthening committed Christians.[3]

McGavran's ideas have influenced his generation to think in terms of "people groups", and have stimulated many mission initiatives. Yet the optimism they initially aroused has not been entirely justified by results. Since the period in which he first developed his ideas, the world has experienced a massive transformation in forms of communication. In the age of television and the internet, it is questionable whether individual cultures have remained as "psychologically closed to the rest of the world" as McGavran expected. In most countries there are highly educated leaders of society who are in close touch with other cultures, and in particular with the form of urban materialism that has been exported so successfully from the West. In fact social boundaries are generally far less sharp than McGavran was inclined to assume. There is often a considerable amount of upward and (less commonly) downward mobility, and this flow is dramatically increased wherever urbanisation has taken place. In the towns there is much social interaction across social boundaries, especially in the context of commerce and of administrative and religious activity. In positively discouraging such interaction, and by insisting on ancient traditions and customs, McGavran and his school have been considered reactionary and obscurantist by the very people they are attempting to please,

---

[1] McGavran, in Neill, *Concise Dictionary*, 479

[2] McGavran, "The Dimensions of World Evangelisation". Peter Wagner suggests that the idea of "people groups" has been particularly helpful for missionaries from America, where generations of immigrants have been encouraged to abandon their original culture and language in order to become "American". Respect for other cultures is therefore not a normal American attribute (Wagner, *Acts of the Holy Spirit*, 133).

[3] One consequence of this has been considerable confusion among missionaries whenever the term "discipling" is used. See *Understanding Church Growth*, 3rd. edn., x, xi, 123.

accused of deliberately resisting the natural development of social communities, and even of fostering racial prejudice and social discrimination.[1]

In fact, McGavran's hopes for "people movements" transforming successive strata of society in India have not materialised to anything like the extent he envisaged. In India itself mass movements along caste lines have only taken place in the lowest strata of society, among people whose wish is not to preserve caste identity but rather to escape it.[2] The major mass movements, moreover, have been associated with Protestant missions that deliberately repudiated caste. Bishop Azariah, the first Indian bishop of the Anglican communion, strongly opposed distinctions of caste and condemned the denominational rivalry that so often followed caste lines. He observed the dire consequences when "separate castes merge into separate denominations and once more continue their unholy warfare of generations."[3] In a village where the Baptists have one caste and the Anglicans another, the Christians can even now appear as deeply divided as the Hindus.[4]

The toleration of caste is a significant application of the principle that cultural expectations should carry more weight than scriptural principles. Groves, in contrast, would teach his Indian pupils, friends and converts that the way of Christ infinitely surpasses all other ways and should be accepted in its entirety for the well-being of the individual and the society. As he himself expressed it, "When I think of this subject of caste, in conjunction with the humiliation of the Son of God, I see in it something most unseemly, most peculiarly unlike Christ... It is truly hateful that one worm should refuse to eat with, or touch another worm, lest he become polluted."[5] In the New Testament, although we find the apostles preaching to the Jews and Gentiles in different places and with different forms of address, we do not find separate churches for Jews and for Gentiles, or separate churches for masters and for slaves, nor for the speakers of diverse languages and dialects. The apostolic example would be a sufficient model for Groves. Indeed, it can be argued that in apostolic times "the breaking down of social and racial barriers in the New Testament was considered an essential part of the gospel, and not merely the result of it."[6]

Like Donald McGavran, his contemporary, Lesslie Newbigin (1909-98), speaks with the benefit of long experience in India. Indeed, he served as a bishop in the combined Church of South India during the period 1947-57, and then as Bishop of Madras between 1965 and 1974.

Newbigin takes issue with some particular aspects of McGavran's thought, especially his overriding desire for numbers of converts, pointing out that "church growth" is not an emphasis evident in the New Testament. Indeed, beyond Luke's obvious delight in the response to the early apostolic preaching, there is no reference in the other apostolic writings to numerical growth. On the contrary, "the emphasis falls on the faithfulness of the disciples rather than their numbers."[7]

Perhaps Newbigin, as an Englishman, finds McGavran, in his confident strategy for assured success, a little too triumphalistically "American". Indeed,

---

[1] Newbigin, *The Open Secret* (2nd edn. 1995), 145.
[2] See Laing, 8.
[3] cited by Harper, *In the Shadow of the Mahatma*, 239
[4] Koshy, *Brother Bakht Singh of India*, 273, 481
[5] M271
[6] Laing, 12
[7] Newbigin, *The Open Secret*, 125

"When numerical growth is taken as the criterion of judgment on the church we are transported with alarming ease into the world of the military campaign or the commercial sales drive."[1]

Newbigin questions McGavran's insistence that Christianity must always defer to the local culture and conform to traditional expectations and constraints. He advises,

> In every community there are conservatives and there are reformers, and there are different issues upon which the members of the society will take different sides. The danger inherent in all programs for the "indigenisation" or "acculturation" of the gospel is that they involve the church with the conservative and backward-looking elements in the society. A study of the missionary history of the nineteenth century will show, on the other hand, that some of the foreign elements that were accepted by the converts from the missionaries were welcomed precisely *because* they made a break with the traditional culture and therefore came as reinforcement for younger elements in society who were impatient of old tradition. And where foreign missionaries, bearers of a culture considered (rightly or wrongly) to be "advanced", have tried to confine the "indigenous" church to the traditional language and culture of the past, they have been deeply and rightly resented.[2]

There is no doubt that many Indians from lower castes have been drawn to Christianity precisely because the new religion offered an alternative to the traditional system. But in questioning McGavran's supreme respect for local cultures, Newbigin seeks a balance avoiding all evils. He hopes to find "the proper path between a kind of accommodation that robs the gospel of its power to challenge traditional ways of life and a kind of intransigence that either fails to communicate altogether or else alienates the converts from their culture."[3]

For Newbigin, the answer lies, as we have seen, in the triangular relationship between the traditional culture, the Christianity of the missionary, and the convert's own response to the Bible. The third of these "corners" is most crucial. He comments, "The Bible has operated as an independent source of criticism directed both against the Christianity of the missionaries and against the traditional culture of the tribe."[4] In places where converts have personal access to the written scriptures, "the missionary may find that the point at which the conscience of the convert has been awakened is far away from the point that seemed to the

---

[1] Newbigin, Ibid, 127

[2] Ibid, 145. In theological terms, the missiological school represented by Kraft and McGavran would side with Richard Niebuhr in adapting the Church (and some might say, the Gospel) to the culture, with the ultimate aim of transforming the culture, rather than with Jürgen Moltmann, who argues that the Church is essentially alien. Newbigin consciously aligned himself with Moltmann (Newbigin, *Unfinished Agenda*; see also Yates, *Christian Mission*, for a useful summary of Newbigin's thought).

[3] Ibid, 145-6. John H Yoder notes that even the most ardent Christian culturalists will reject certain aspects of culture, such as cannibalism, slavery, pornography, and the death penalty for petty offences, whilst those most critical of culture will entirely approve of the use of such cultural features as literacy, money and languages. Other aspects of culture will be adapted, or even created, by Christians for purposes they consider beneficial. In practice, we are all selective in our attitude to culture (Yoder, 69; see also Newbigin, *Pluralist Society*, 184-6).

[4] *The Open Secret*, 147

missionary to be crucial."[1] It was, of course, exactly this use of the Bible by the Indians themselves that Groves encouraged.[2]

Reviewing the history of Christian mission, Newbigin observes a progression of thought evident in successive conferences of delegates from many countries:

> The World Missionary Conference of 1910 was already thinking in truly global terms and was aware of the deeply evil elements in the impact of Western power on the peoples of Asia, Africa and the Pacific. But the younger churches were only marginally acknowledged, and there was a still unshaken confidence in the future of Western civilisation as the bearer of the gospel to the "backward peoples". At Jerusalem in 1928 there was a fuller acknowledgement of the younger churches and a much more acute awareness of the ambiguities of Western power and of the worldwide impact of Western secularism. At Tambaram ten years later there was a new awareness of the worldwide church as the people entrusted with the gospel and called to do battle with a paganism that was showing its power in the heart of old Christendom. In the years following World War II, the church-centred concept of mission was further consolidated. At Willingen (1952) there was a strong affirmation of mission as central and essential to the life of the whole church seen as a world fellowship, but in the course of that meeting a new insistence began to be felt upon the need for a missiology that was not domesticated in the church.[3]

Following from this, at the 1960 conference in Strasbourg, "the assembled students were challenged 'to move out of the traditional Church structure in open, flexible and mobile groups' and 'to begin radically to de-sacralise the Church'."[4]

Described in these terms, we might think that mission leaders in these conferences had gradually shifted towards a stance resembling that of Groves. This was not the case, for parallel with these developments went an increasingly liberal theology which meant that "Mission was primarily concerned with doing God's justice in the world and not primarily with increasing the membership of the church."[5] Indeed, a number of missionary societies had redefined their aims since the days of their founders: "The literature of many of those missionary agencies that were the bearers of the great expansion of the nineteenth century now give the impression that they are mainly concerned with cultural exchange within the Christian fellowship."[6] There was little thought of converting people to a different faith or adding numbers to the churches. The gospel had become political, social, medical – essentially secular rather than religious. The consequence, as Newbigin saw it, was to "marginalize the role of the church".[7]

If Groves were an observer of all this, he would no doubt view it as a manifestation of worldliness in a degenerate religious establishment, whilst finding some participants with whom he could enjoy warm personal fellowship, "those fair

---

[1] Ibid, 138

[2] We should not assume that Newbigin himself considered the Bible infallible or ultimately authoritative. As a "modern Western theologian", he expected it merely to offer some stimulus in one's personal quest for "the Christ of faith", who will be perceived very largely in terms of one's own culture (Ibid, 153-9).

[3] Ibid, 8

[4] Ibid

[5] Ibid

[6] Ibid, 10

[7] Ibid, 18. Newbigin's missiological influence is discussed by Goheen and by several contributors in Foust (ed.).

pearls which lie within what seems to me so naughty a shell."[1] But Groves, we should remember, moved in circles as yet untouched by modern or liberal theology. His ability to conceive of church and mission as a single entity with a single aim stemmed from his interest in simply doing what the apostles did, rather than from a respect for nationalistic aspirations or a pragmatic fear of administrative conflict between "older" and "younger" churches.

An early and articulate disciple of Donald McGavran was his fellow American C Peter Wagner (b.1930), who did much to promote and popularise the "church growth movement", focusing particularly on the use of modern methods in order to ensure success.

In one of his earliest published writings, dated 1971, Wagner asserted "Effective missionary strategy must be kept relevant... many of the methods which missions are using today are obsolete already... today's missionary strategy must be updated."[2] In his unashamed use of terms such as "modern" and "updated" and "scientific", Wagner introduced, at this point, a subtle shift in focus. Granted that his interest lay primarily in the application of McGavran's ideas to America itself, his Americanisation of the "church growth movement" as a whole severely reduced its sensitivity to multiple cultures and, at the same time, shifted its emphasis away from McGavran's own essentially evangelistic concern for disciple-making in other parts of the world.[3]

To be sure, we might expect liberal theologians such as John Hick, in defining a Christian worldview, to advocate the adoption of a "modern" and "scientific" outlook rather than a biblical outlook,[4] but it is more surprising to observe so-called Evangelicals following the same path, and especially at a time when the spiritual emptiness of Western culture is increasingly manifested in the breakdown of European and American society. Newbigin remarks, "For those who have never lived in any other cultural world than that of the contemporary West it is very hard to see that theirs is only one of the tribal cultures of humankind. They are inclined to see it simply as the 'modern scientific world view'."[5] This is exactly the trap into which Wagner appears to have fallen.

Wagner's position naturally led him to deny the normative value of the New Testament as a model for mission strategy, and indeed he condemned those who held this view: "Some missionary leaders continually stress the need to return to the first century. They have created a nostalgia so strong that in some circles all that is done today must be evaluated as to how nearly it approaches what was done nineteen hundred years ago. Two of the most distinguished missiologists of the twentieth century, Alexander Hay and Roland Allen, both show tendencies in their writings toward over-sanctifying the first century."[6] Wagner considered this unwarranted:

---

[1] M297
[2] Wagner, *Frontiers*, 48
[3] McGavran, *Effective Evangelism*, 57
[4] Hick, *God and the Universe of Faiths*, 97-8. Hick describes a "sifting process" whereby science has progressively modified religious belief during the past hundred and fifty years: "As a result we have learned to distinguish between the central message of the gospel and its expression in the now obsolete thought forms of earlier ages" (p.104).
[5] Newbigin, *The Open Secret*, 152
[6] Wagner, *Frontiers*, 48-9

> Hay's tendency is to take the apostles' methods as principles. This is one reason he insists on one particular type of church government (the brethren assemblies pattern) rather than admitting that the church government used by Paul and his colleagues was simply a wise and strategic use of certain first-century cultural patterns. These patterns were relevant to first-century Christians, but they may have little relevance to Christians who come from other cultures at other stages in history.[1]

Wagner is by no means alone in commending the apostles for adapting to their culture, but his confidence in the superior perspective provided by his own culture led him to judge Paul's method, on at least one occasion, in Athens, not "a wise and strategic use of first-century cultural patterns", but on the contrary, a foolish and regrettable mistake. He asserted, "Paul was as human as any of us. He too was subject to error. While supernatural inspiration by the Holy Spirit protected him from error when he wrote his epistles, it does not follow that his missionary strategy was equally inspired or inerrant."[2] No scholarly reason is offered by Wagner for this opinion, and few serious commentators would feel justified in judging so confidently, from the New Testament narrative, whether or not Paul was guilty of strategic error in Athens.

For Wagner, it was his own culture that provided him with a standard by which the New Testament should be judged and to which it must adapt. He stated this quite baldly: "When thinking through missionary strategy, it is much more helpful to attempt to fit New Testament principles into twentieth-century patterns than to attempt the reverse... It is much more profitable to accept ourselves as we are now, and see how best to adapt New Testament principles to our present situation."[3] And Wagner did not hesitate to carry this into effect. He proposed rewriting the Acts of the Apostles:

> To help out in this process, someone ought to do a new paraphrase of the book of Acts, writing it in contemporary language. One could refer to Paul's terms rather than journeys. His time in Jerusalem and Antioch was furlough. The Jerusalem Council could have been a meeting of the mission board. Timothy could be called a junior missionary, and Mark a missionary intern. The Corinthians were a group of nationals. Paul's epistle to the Philippians was a prayer letter. If this were done, Acts would become a much more helpful book for contemporary strategy.[4]

With the book of Acts rewritten, its missions and churches will appear much more like twentieth-century American missions and churches. So what did Wagner look for in them? "Vital sign number one of a healthy church is a pastor who is a possibility thinker and whose dynamic leadership has been used to catalyse the entire church into action for growth."[5] At a stroke Wagner consigned the majority of evangelical fellowships throughout the world to a condition of inevitable mediocrity, for they simply cannot afford to support a dynamic "pastor" of the type familiar to him in America.

In recent years, Wagner's pragmatic approach to "church growth" has continued to downplay the role of the New Testament in forming church and

---

[1] Ibid, 49
[2] Ibid, 50
[3] Ibid, 50-1
[4] Ibid, 51
[5] Wagner, *Your Church Can Grow*, 57

mission strategy, and to emphasize the value of secular academic research: "Church growth... looks to social sciences as a cognate discipline... The classical approach judges the validity of any experience on the basis of previously established theological principles. In contrast, Church Growth leans toward a phenomenological approach which holds theological conclusions somewhat more tentatively and is open to revising them when necessary in the light of what is learned through experience."[1] On these terms, just as current science regulates one's understanding of creation, so current sociology conditions one's view of church and mission.

In his earliest presentation of these views, Wagner hardly disguises the cultural imperialism at the heart of his remodelled "church growth" programme. It is all but impossible to be "modern" without technology, and it is absolutely impossible to have technology without being rich. Never was there a more rigid caste system than this separation between the wealthy mission executive and the poor Indian or African Christian.[2] It is this that moves Taber to admit that anthropological missiologists like himself are disappointed to see how little their exhortations to cultural sensitivity have been heeded by Protestant missionaries throughout the world. He identifies a reason: "The factor which worked most strongly against the beneficial effect of anthropology was the captivity of missions to high technology"[3] Missionaries have felt justified in making use of every new invention – cars, planes, two-way radios, air conditioning, electric light, computers: "Each of these steps could be, and was justified quite satisfactorily, given that efficiency, defined in very Western terms, was the supreme desideratum." The problem for the anthropologist is that local cultures often eagerly desire such technology, and when given the opportunity will embrace it with enthusiasm. But the source of the technology is perceived, at least initially, as foreign, and the use to which it is put follows foreign methodologies as a matter of course: "Looking exclusively at tasks and programs and goals, missions too often lost sight of the human dimension... And, most clearly, programs involving mission funding and high technology required mission control for 'accountability' and 'efficiency'".[4]

---

[1] Wagner, *Church Growth*, 33. See also Wagner, *On The Crest of the Wave*.

[2] Wagner's pragmatism has, in recent years, been somewhat constrained by the requirements of scholarship. In his *Acts of the Holy Spirit* (1994), a commentary on the Acts of the Apostles, revised and reissued in 2000, he describes Luke's text as "God's training manual for modern Christians" (p.9). Here the discipline of drawing missionary principles directly from the New Testament restrains some of his revisionist tendencies. Only occasionally does he now define first-century activities in modern American terms, and when doing so, manifests a measure of embarrassment. Referring to Acts 20:18, "Although it is hard to read the details of our twentieth century back into the first century, it is not far-fetched to say that those whom Paul was teaching in his seminar would be the functional equivalent of what we regard today as ordained ministers" (p.501). But commenting on the prophets and teachers in the church at Antioch (Acts 13:1), he asserts with some confidence that "The five, perhaps along with others, functioned as what we call today a 'para-church organisation' – the Cyprus and Cyrene Mission" (p.287). Following Ralph Winter, Wagner identifies Barnabas as a modality (church) leader and Paul as a sodality (mission) leader, which in his view explains the conflict between them (pp.374-5). The temptation to read modern problems into ancient texts is one he still cannot entirely resist.

[3] Taber, 133

[4] Taber, 133-4. See also Walls, "American Dimension".

The "church growth" emphasis on numerical success has often been questioned,[1] and David Smith has recently expressed disquiet with the triumphalism evident in much modern church and mission propaganda. Indeed, "This heightened sense of expectation can create what might be charitably called wishful thinking, bordering on self deception."[2] A sincere and passionate longing for success, for recruits, for funds, fired in some cases by a renascent postmillennialism, seems sometimes to produce a willingness to proclaim impossible visions, and to exaggerate petty achievements, ignoring inconvenient realities and playing down the real difficulties and frustrations of missionary labour in a hostile environment. Smith suggests that gullible excitement, whipped up by slick communicators with advanced technology, may ultimately lead to disillusionment and cynicism.

The other strikingly modern phenomenon in Protestant missions is the proliferation of international conferences, many of which offer an invitation, all-expenses-paid, to Christians from some of the poorest countries in the world, with a five-star-hotel experience in an exotic setting that neither they nor other members of their church could possibly afford in the normal course of life. Borthwick, among others, has questioned how far this really helps them.[3]

When "church growth" at all costs becomes the goal, then the influence of local culture is as irrelevant as that of Scripture. The culture of the missionary once more determines his strategy. We recall Groves's words as he contemplated "the gentlemanly and imposing aspect which our present missionary institutions bear", and his conclusion that "much will not be done till we go back again to primitive principles and let the nameless poor and their unrecorded and unsung labours be those on which our hopes, under God, are fixed."[4]

Primitivism Revisited

A recent challenge to some of these missiological trends has come from the current editor of the *International Bulletin of Missionary Research*. Observing that "the gap now between rich nations and poor nations is far wider than it was in the nineteenth century," Jonathan Bonk sees little cause to suppose that Christianity will be able to spread technology and prosperity from the West to the whole world as was once optimistically believed:

> We now know with terrifying certainty that for 999 out of 1000 of our fellow human beings, there is no possible road to our way of life in the foreseeable future. The stark and brutal truth is that the natural resources of our planet are sufficient to support "civilised" life for only a tiny fraction of its human population. Accordingly, Western

---

[1] For a recent and multi-faceted critique of the Church Growth Movement see McIntosh. A critical view of the movement's syncretistic tendencies is offered by Van Rheenen, "Contrasting Missional and Church Growth Perspectives". He suggests that the essential question is not "What makes the church grow?" but "What is the Gospel?", and he argues that mission should be driven by theology and by the Spirit (God's "surprises") rather than by anthropology and strategic planning.
[2] Smith D, "Fundamentalism", 272
[3] Borthwick, "Reflections", 184-6
[4] R22

missionaries must be prepared as never before to test the truthfulness of their assertion that "Christ is the answer" in the context of personal material want.[1]

Wealthy Western missionaries are already finding it difficult to offer a relevant gospel to the multitudinous peoples of the world trapped in a cycle of poverty. Bonk suggests that for most Christians in the West,

> Our affluence and our security make God necessary in only an academic or theological sense. Prayer, as a biblical study of the subject quickly reveals, is not the activity of people who are in reasonable control of their lives. It is the resort of weak, overwrought, desperate people whose life circumstances call for resources beyond those they possess. A "good" missionary society will take every possible step – by means of elaborate medical, financial, educational and logistical support systems – to ensure that most of life is well under control most of the time. This is a natural, commendable and – humanly speaking – desirable course to follow. But it does leave God with, apparently, very little to do in our lives.[2]

A faith taught by missionaries who appear secure and comfortable is unlikely to be a source of great comfort to people living in circumstances of poverty, persecution and misery. Bonk warns, "The reassuring words of a salesman who, for whatever reason, has never tested his own product under adverse conditions, and who is, furthermore, unwilling to do so personally, can and should be treated with scepticism."[3] Indeed, to preach in such circumstances can come perilously close to institutional hypocrisy, and one might ask, "Is it possible to maintain both credibility and an affluent lifestyle when teaching the poor what God says about the stewardship of possessions?"[4] Bonk's answer is clear: "The missionary cannot challenge converts to a way of life that he himself is unwilling to live."[5] Indeed, "The money and power-based strategies and statuses generated by the institutional and personal affluence of Western missionaries contradict principles which are at the very heart of Christian mission as prescribed in the New Testament."[6]

In fact, the most recent observable trend in mission is for so-called "independent" movements to take over the task of evangelising the world: "Affluent missions are becoming increasingly marginalized in the great spiritual mission of the church."[7] So, "While missionaries from the affluent West get on with the expensive and complicated process of living comfortable and secure lives in a Third World context, their national counterparts take the Word and make it flesh, dwelling among peoples who see in their frail flesh the glory of a living Saviour full of grace and truth."[8] And finally comes Bonk's most damning critique: "Preaching the Gospel of spiritual salvation with their lips, and the gospel of abundance with their lives, Western missionaries have frequently expressed annoyance with the fact that their presence, while creating little hunger and thirst

---

[1] Bonk, *Missions and Money*, 113. See also Bonk, "Missions and Mammon".
[2] Bonk, *Missions and Money*, 81-2
[3] Ibid, 61
[4] Ibid, 79
[5] Ibid, 83
[6] Ibid, 82
[7] Ibid, 107
[8] Ibid, 14-15

for righteousness, has stimulated within indigenes hearty appetites for the wood, hay and stubble of Western material culture."[1]

Bonk's analysis leaves us with the suspicion that Western mission agencies have become an expensive anachronism, noisy and very visible but of minimal spiritual significance, and unable to understand why: "Becoming accustomed to doing missions with technology, Western missionaries find it difficult to conceive of engaging in mission without it."[2] Hence the desperate appeals for funds to buy equipment. Without the equipment, it would seem, the mission of the Church must cease. Recruiting potential missionaries has become equally difficult. Societies offer comprehensive support packages in order to make the sacrifice required of their recruits as painless as possible, and their publicity materials sometimes give the impression that the prospective missionary is making a sensible career choice rather than forsaking all for the service of Christ. One wonders how such recruits will fare when faced with the need to learn a complex language and co-operate in uncongenial circumstances with difficult people.[3]

This brief summary of Bonk's work on missions and money suggests he is considerably more in harmony with the principles introduced by Groves than are most contemporary missiologists. It will be interesting to see whether his future missiological writings reflect additional themes introduced by Groves.

. One such issue could be the continued frustration of Western agencies trying to plant indigenous churches. Keith Eitel of the South-eastern Baptist Theological Seminary reminds us that this issue remains as controversial as ever: "How to accomplish the task of establishing healthy indigenous churches that reflect the ongoing, biblically balanced contextualisation process is still the point of much debate and requires serious analysis in any modern mission context."[4] According to Eitel, tensions between foreign missions and "national conventions" (committees of indigenous church leaders) remain the major missiological problem of the modern age. It is a situation inherited by our generation through policies in the past which we may regret but cannot change. And he confides, "Assuming they eventually sit together and lay all their concerns on the table, the mission leaders might realise that there is a sense of long-term abuse in the way the mission has acted towards the nationals."[5] The issue is plainly stated, and the existence of two separate institutions, foreign and national, with two separate leaderships and two distinct agendas, evidently lies at the heart of the problem. But one wonders whether the introduction of a table on which concerns are laid reflects an American rather than a biblical solution to it. Other, less confrontational, methods might be suggested.

In the course of his analysis, Eitel identifies five possible models for church / mission relations, and it is significant that these vary according to "the degree of mutual trust between a mission and a national church"[6] The fifth of his models represents a church "separated from a founding mission work". It has "grown independently of both the mission and historic Christianity." For Eitel, the

---

[1] Ibid, 67
[2] Ibid, 70
[3] Ibid, 119
[4] Eitel, "To Be or Not to Be", 313
[5] Eitel, Ibid, 313-4
[6] Ibid, 314-5

separation is regrettable and will be less beneficial than first supposed. He anticipates that, in separating from "the mission", the indigenous church will have drifted from "historic Christianity".[1] Indeed, he fears that, "In this model, there is a real danger of syncretistic tendencies that may cause a set of distorted religious forms and functions to develop which appear more cultic than biblical."

No grounds are offered to justify such a fear, and Wilbert Shenk's observation may be aptly quoted: "The conventional wisdom was that indigenous forms of Christianity in Africa, labelled variously as Zionism, prophetism, separatism, or Independent Churches, were aberrant forms and must be rejected." Only rarely did an outside observer "judge such movements on their own terms, thereby opening the way for the introduction of non-Western categories and standards."[2] The fact is that indigenous leaders such as John Arulappan, Bakht Singh and Watchman Nee derived much initial benefit from foreign missionaries, and then, separating from Western agencies, remained firmly attached to "historic Christianity", more firmly perhaps than some missionaries whom they thought to have abandoned it.[3]

Eitel's preferred alternative assumes an official partnership between an institutionalised "national convention" and an institutionalised mission agency. This is perhaps something taken for granted in the denomination he represents, and indeed he is currently engaged in controversy with his Southern Baptist colleagues, advocating a stronger role for national leaders in decision-making processes.[4] On reflection he might consider such leaders competent to decide the nature of "historic Christianity" and to avoid "distorted religious forms and functions". Groves was willing to place such trust in them.

In fact, Eitel offers a suggestion that would have pleased Groves. He counsels, "National believers ought to participate in the decision to implement indigenous concepts *from the beginning*. This procedure helps ensure a sense of ownership over the decision to be autonomous."[5] Indeed, the attitude of the missionary to his very first convert will substantially determine the form of leadership emerging in the church: "A partnering spirit can and ought to develop *very near the beginning*. The attitude is the essential factor. Missionaries who utilise a partnering spirit from the beginning of the process find that churches are more willing to engage in the task of local and global evangelism early in the process."[6]

As this was exactly the practice advocated by Groves (and then by Gützlaff), twenty years before Venn and Anderson had systematised an alternative, it might behove modern missiologists to give some attention to the history of the idea and to study its earliest application.

Indigenous Primitivism

It is when we turn away from Euro-American missions to the indigenous movements of the past and the present that we discover the greatest interest in primitivist methods such as those advocated by Groves.[7] Many such movements,

---

[1] Ibid, 316
[2] Shenk, "Toward a Global Church History"
[3] For Bakht Singh's perspective on the "social gospel" discussed at Tambaram, see Koshy, *Brother Bakht Singh*, 177-8.
[4] See Eitel, *Paradigm Wars*.
[5] Eitel, "To Be or Not to Be", 309 (italics added)
[6] Eitel, Ibid, 316 (italics added)
[7] Newbigin, *A Word in Season*, 68

taking the precepts and practice of the apostles as their guide and model, have proved to be vigorous and effective. Far from displaying a naïve literalism in their use of the New Testament, they demonstrate an intelligent and well-developed strategy undergirded by soundly reasoned exegesis. One such indigenous leader is Watchman Nee (1903-1972), who avoided creating a church / mission dichotomy by refusing to countenance the existence of two separate organisational entities. The New Testament, in his view, offered a much simpler alternative:

> In Scripture we find no trace of man-made organizations sending out men to preach the Gospel. We only find representatives of the ministry of the Church, under the guidance of the Spirit and on the ground of the Body, sending out those whom the Spirit has already separated for the work. If those responsible for the sending out of workers sent them out, not as their own representatives or the representatives of any organisation, but only as representatives of the Body of Christ, and if those sent out stood on the ground of no particular "church" or mission, but on the ground of *the* Church alone, then no matter from what places the workers came or to what places they went, co-operation and unity would always be possible, and much confusion in the work would be avoided.[1]

On the same principle Nee forestalled the problems of control, inhibition and manipulation that have so often followed from administrative accountability to superiors: "In divinely constituted companies of workers there is no organization. Authority *is* exercised among them, but such authority is spiritual, not official... an authority which is the outcome of a deep knowledge of the Lord and intimate fellowship with him"[2] Whilst experienced and gifted leaders might teach, advise and exhort, they would not command:

> After the apostles were called by the Spirit and were separated for the work by the representative members of the Body, what did they do? We need to recall that those who separated them only expressed identification and sympathy by the laying on of hands; they had no authority to control the apostles. Those prophets and teachers at the base assumed no official responsibility in regard to their movements, their methods of work or the supply of their financial needs. In Scripture we nowhere find that apostles are under the control of any individual or any organised company. They had no regulations to adhere to and no superiors to obey. The Holy Spirit called them, and they followed his leading and guidance; he alone was their director.[3]

It was obviously to the New Testament that Nee looked for his model of leadership: "The word of God makes it clear that the oversight of a church is not the work of apostles, but of elders... the characteristic of an apostle is *going*; the characteristic of an elder is *staying*."[4] Although he encouraged the recognition of travelling evangelists and local elders, Nee rejected the foreign custom of appointing a salaried pastor to minister to the congregation: "The present day pastoral system is quite unscriptural; it is an invention of men."[5] In contrast to most

---

[1] Nee, *The Normal Christian Church Life*, 31
[2] Nee, Ibid, 124
[3] Ibid, 31
[4] Ibid, 41
[5] Ibid, 49

of his contemporaries, "Nee concentrated on training all the believers to do the work of God."[1]

The financial tensions, abuses and jealousies that so commonly marred the work of Western missions were circumvented by Nee through following Jesus's advice to look to God rather than man as a source of supply. He observed that "He who holds the purse holds authority. If we are supported by men, our work will be controlled by men... If we are supported by men, then we must seek to please men, and it is often impossible at the same time both to please men and God."[2] And he affirmed, "We dare to be utterly independent of men in financial matters, because we dare to believe utterly in God."[3]

For a primitivist such as Nee, apostolic precedent is sufficient to justify any course of action, and a lack of apostolic precedent will be a sufficient reason to question or reject it. Following the apostolic model, an evangelist, for example, will devote his time to preaching, only engaging in secular labour when circumstances demand it: "To work with our hands may be very good, but we need to note that Paul does not regard that as the usual thing. It is something exceptional, a course to be resorted to in special circumstances."[4]

The New Testament even provided guidance for Nee concerning the buildings to be used: "In our assemblies we must return to the principle of the upper room. The ground floor is a place for business, a place for men to come and go; but there is more of a home atmosphere about the upper room, and the gatherings of God's children are family affairs. The Last Supper was in an upper room; so was Pentecost, and so again was the meeting [at Troas]. God wants the intimacy of the upper room to mark the gatherings of his children."[5]

As for Christian unity, Nee sees no difference in principle between the unity of Christians in the first century and those in the modern age: "If you have the Spirit of Christ and I have the Spirit of Christ then we both belong to the same Church... God has never told us to become one with other believers; we already *are* one... We cannot *make* this oneness, since by the Spirit we *are* one in Christ, and we cannot *break* it, because it is an eternal fact in Christ."[6]

The ecclesiological and missiological thought of Watchman Nee is profound and extensive. Sufficient has been said to show that indigenous Christian leaders like him have a major intellectual contribution to make in these areas, a

---

[1] Cheung, *The Ecclesiology of the "Little Flock"*, 6.

[2] Nee, Ibid, 141-2. By way of contrast we find the Anglo-Catholic missionary in China, David M Paton, pointing out as late as 1952 that even in dioceses where self-support was greatest, twenty per cent of the budget was still consistently required to be paid by the foreigners, with no sign of change: "This uneasy equilibrium had disastrous spiritual results: Chinese were aware of their dependence, and resented it (and us), but could not face doing without our help, nor take the risk of wholly ignoring our opinions" (Paton, 44). He then observed, "The question of standards and manners of living was worse still. The writer was paid about three times as much as a Chinese of comparable age and responsibility in the Church; and there were comparable missionaries of other missions paid three times as much as he." The result for many missionaries was, according to Paton, "a guilty conscience, and a guilty conscience is inhibiting and frustrating" (Paton, 44-5).

[3] Nee, Ibid, 143

[4] Ibid, 145

[5] Ibid, 168

[6] Ibid, 76-7, referring to Eph 4:3.

contribution which has been substantially neglected – a contribution which, as we have seen, owes much to the direct and indirect stimulus of Anthony Norris Groves.[1]

Like Watchman Nee, Bakht Singh (1903-2000) was what we might call a practical missiologist. He did not propose a method so much as follow one. His missiology is proved to have worked in the real world.

We have seen that it was after discussions with Rajamani and Dorairaj, great-grandsons of Groves's disciple Arulappan, that Bakht Singh entered a new phase of ministry in deliberately starting churches modelled on those described in the New Testament.[2] He went on to create hundreds of local fellowships. Each was an autonomous "house-church", meeting for the most part in rented accommodation, and always "on the basis of Acts 2:42".[3] Like Nee, he refused to create separate organisations for church and mission, and the local fellowships bore full responsibility for the periodic gospel marches that took the church through the streets, and for public evangelistic preaching campaigns.[4]

Bakht Singh himself appointed individuals as "God's servants" to assist new initiatives and to advise local fellowships that had particular needs, following the example of the apostle Paul who sent Timothy and Titus on similar errands. Such men were not encouraged to become settled "pastors",[5] for he recognised no spiritual distinction between clergy and laity.[6] Many of the so-called Bakht Singh assemblies were not started by him at all, but rather by individuals and groups who attended one of his "Holy Convocations" and, on returning to their hometown, decided to meet for fellowship on the same principles.[7]

Bakht Singh's stance on almost every issue echoes that of Groves. Regarding the true church as a single worldwide spiritual body (the "one new man" of Ephesians 2:14-15),[8] he refused to be identified with any denomination or society.[9] "He insisted that there is no Indian Church or Chinese Church or American Church but one single universal Church,"[10] and he would not accept any form of "membership" beyond that which every believer has in the universal body of Christ.[11] He disliked the term "indigenous" which, to his mind, "savours of nationalism".[12] He suggested, moreover, that the appointment of Indians to

---

[1] See above, 213ff.
[2] See above, 213ff, and also Koshy, *Brother Bakht Singh of India*, 354, 94, 208-26.
[3] Koshy, Ibid, 323, 325, 459, 463 etc.
[4] Ibid, 493, 495
[5] Ibid, 299, 443-4
[6] Ibid, 433
[7] Ibid, 298
[8] Ibid, 231-2, 463, 541
[9] Koshy comments, "Following the Lord's Table, one of the Brethren would lead in intercessory prayer, reminding all that the broken pieces of bread which remain speak of the members of the Body worldwide" (Ibid, 438).
[10] Ibid, 447
[11] Ibid, 260, 432, 434
[12] Ibid, 455. Nationalism (patriotism) is not a quality advocated in the New Testament. Indeed Lesslie Newbigin has questioned whether the ethnocentrism of "national churches" (the legacy of Establishment missionary agencies) is any more justified than the colonial ethnocentrism seen in past generations of missionaries. He regrets that sometimes "we applaud in the younger churches a synthesis of nationalism and Christianity which we deplore in our missionary grandparents" (Newbigin, *Pluralistic Society*, 143).

positions previously held by foreigners was no proof of "indigenisation", for a church led by Indians could still be thoroughly alien to the Indian mentality if established on a foreign plan and led by men trained in foreign ways. He insisted that the need in India was not for "indigenous churches" but "scriptural churches".[1]

Like Groves, he had a strong confidence in the sovereignty of God, overruling all circumstances for good.[2] He sought financial support and direction in his personal ministry from God alone.[3] He "did not believe in any formal Bible school or seminary training as a prerequisite to the work or the ministry of the Lord."[4] He preferred the method used by Jesus and by Paul, providing on-the-job training for Christian ministry (for both men and women) through participation in evangelistic campaigns and outreach teams.[5]

Bakht Singh allowed no racial distinctions in ministry or in finance, maintaining that there is no such thing as Eastern or Western money for it is all the Lord's money.[6] Whatever their nationality, his co-workers lived together and shared whatever they had; foreign participants lived at the same social and economic level as the Indians.[7] He taught the local believers "to contribute generously and joyfully to the work of the Lord,"[8] but he made no appeals for funds, took no subscriptions and accepted nothing from the unconverted.[9] His assemblies were self-supporting from the start, launched as local initiatives and maintained by local funds.[10] He remained free from any form of Western control or accountability, and was in no way dependent on the gifts he sometimes received from Britain or America.[11]

Bakht Singh's assemblies met to "break bread" every Sunday, welcoming "all true children of God" to partake, irrespective of caste or denomination, encouraging them to share "the common cup".[12] Communal meals or "love-feasts" also served as a visible demonstration that caste has no validity in the family of God.[13] They encouraged every believer to develop his or her gifts for the corporate functioning of the Body.

Like Groves, Bakht Singh had little interest in administration. His biographer comments, "Because most denominations go to the extreme of doing everything based on their constitutions and man-made laws, Bakht Singh seemed to have gone to the other extreme... He paid very little attention to legal requirements and infrastructure."[14] One reason for this was his conviction, shared with Groves, that

---

[1] Smith D, 48-50
[2] Koshy, Ibid, 411
[3] Ibid, 148-9, 421-2, 424
[4] Ibid, 446
[5] Ibid, 252-3. Bakht Singh periodically arranged three-week communal retreats for more formal Bible study, fellowship and prayer (Ibid, 446).
[6] Ibid, 455
[7] Ibid, 252-3
[8] Ibid, 445, 457
[9] Ibid, 254, 414-5, 457
[10] Ibid, 457, 463
[11] Ibid, 457-8
[12] Ibid, 257, 438, 455, 538-9
[13] Ibid, 482
[14] Ibid, 520

Christ's return was imminent.[1] Some have considered this a weakness, and it has undoubtedly caused difficulties within the movement, especially after his death, with regard to properties.

In other respects Bakht Singh diverges from Groves. Although both were temperamentally prone to shyness, Bakht Singh overcame this so far as to become an essentially confident character. His success added to his confidence and in time he became a dominant public figure. Although he required unanimity before reaching a decision with his inner circle (often after many hours of prayer), his associates became increasingly reluctant to oppose his personal convictions. Bakht Singh himself exercised absolute authority in the appointment of workers to particular places, even when contrary to the wishes of the individual.[2] There can be little doubt that he became something of a "guru", dispensing divine guidance on matters ranging from marriage decisions to job applications, expecting deference and submission to his personal control.[3] This contrasts strongly with Groves's far more subtle and diffident form of leadership.

Nevertheless, as a decided primitivist, Bakht Singh stands firmly in the camp of Groves rather than the institutionalist school of denominational missions or the culturalist school of American anthropologists. Like Groves himself, primitivists such as Arulappan, Nee and Singh have taken to its logical conclusion the evangelical belief that the New Testament is inspired, authoritative and endued by right with a status above foreign church custom and local culture. For these indigenous leaders, the New Testament will represent genuine Christianity, untainted by either Western or Eastern accretions. Bakht Singh's stance, as described by his biographer, is typical of them all:

> He did not compromise the Word of God with Indian culture, customs or the traditions of men. He vehemently taught against any culture or custom that was contrary to, or in conflict with, the Word of God. 'What we needed in the Body of Christ was not Western or Eastern culture but Biblical culture,' he emphasized.[4]

And he was certainly no armchair missiologist. Like Groves, he devoted his life to active participation in church and mission. He learned from his experience and applied what he learned.

In conclusion, we should note that a primitivist ecclesiology, based on New Testament principle and practice, will tend to produce forms of church meeting and leadership of a similar nature in any cultural context. Groves himself did not expect Indian churches to be very different from English churches, for both would be modelled upon the churches of the apostolic age described in the New Testament. Among the perceived advantages of this scheme might be a stronger sense of international unity and an ease of adaptation to ministry in any part of the world.

Support and Dependence

The missiological theme arousing most passion at the present time is probably that relating to the financing of worldwide mission. Gary Corwin has observed the bitter resentment suffered by foreign agencies who attempt to force

---

[1] Ibid, 534
[2] Ibid, 444, 529
[3] Ibid, 531
[4] Ibid, 456. See also 537.

"indigenisation" upon associated national churches and ministries by simply terminating their financial support. Such a policy has appeared "contrary to the biblical teaching on interdependence in the Body, and simply seemed an excuse for rich Western Christians to withhold essential and appropriate assistance to their less fortunate brothers and sisters." He judges that "The 'indigenous principles' are largely out of favour today as a result."[1]

Western money still seems essential to the task, and speaking for a current generation of Indians, K P Yohannan has argued that, whilst the evangelisation of Asia can be readily accomplished by her own people, ongoing financial support from the West remains crucial. Indeed, "The primary role for Westerners now should be to support efforts of indigenous mission works through financial aid and intercessory prayer."[2] And again, "I believe it is wiser to support native missionaries in their own lands than to send Western missionaries."[3] He cites several reasons:

1. Western missionaries are very expensive to support, even when they attempt to live frugally (air fares, medical insurance, taxes, language classes, school fees etc.).

2. The presence of Western missionaries perpetuates the idea that Christianity is a Western religion, and it preserves inappropriate Western organisational frameworks.

3. Western agencies and denominations tend to promote their own programme, hiring gifted indigenous Christians to fulfil a foreign agenda.

4. Many nations, especially those where unreached people live, will not allow the entry of Western missionaries.

5. Westerners are generally far less effective in evangelism than local believers (and one reason for this is anti-Western prejudice).

Yohannan's solution is to use Western wealth for indigenous evangelism. Through the agency he has founded, Gospel for Asia, Yohannan channels funds to some ten thousand Indian evangelists.[4] The American face of this agency is culturally American, and the Indian face culturally Indian. To satisfy his American constituency he affirms that the evangelists are tested, trained and accountable (doctrinally, morally and financially);[5] to reassure his Indian constituency he emphasizes that they are free from foreign control.

An early advocate of this approach was Lawrence Keyes, who noted that in 1978 an astonishing 96% of Western missionaries were engaged in "perfecting ministries", that is, in ministry to Christians rather than direct evangelism.[6] He advocated greatly increased Western support for a new generation of mission agencies, initiated by the churches of the "third world", whose evangelists were often highly effective and pitifully underpaid. Like Groves, he argued that the worldwide Church has ample resources to complete the Great Commission but that

---

[1] Corwin, "Church Planting", 101
[2] Yohannan, 147
[3] Yohannan, 148
[4] Yohannan, 208
[5] Yohannan, 199-200
[6] Keyes, *The Last Age of Missions*, 111

the resources are unevenly distributed and thus largely unproductive. The solution is simply to release and redistribute them.[1]

Critics claim that this will undermine the long-held principle of indigenous self-support. Indeed, it would seem likely to exacerbate the problem of dependence on the West.[2] Yohannan replies, "It is not outside money that weakens a growing church, but outside control. Money from the West actually liberates the evangelists right now and makes it possible for them to follow the call of God."[3] Yohannan accepts that local *churches* should be self-supporting in their own ministry, but argues that the support of the numerous *evangelists* willing to travel to distant unreached areas simply lies beyond the limits of their resources. He points out, "These are people from among the one-fourth of the world's population who live on just a few dollars each week... The rapid growth almost always outstrips the original congregation's ability to support additional workers."[4]

Yohannan suggests that dangers can be avoided, firstly, by selecting only such evangelists as give evidence of a genuine desire to serve God sacrificially, and secondly, by distancing them from their supporters. Funds received by Gospel for Asia offices in the West are forwarded to a committee of "indigenous leaders" in India, who then allocate the funds. Yohannan notes that "This procedure is being followed by several other organisations... and it seems to work very well."[5]

We have seen that Groves, in a similar fashion, encouraged churches and individuals in Britain to send financial support to Arulappan and other Indian evangelists, and Arulappan himself became the channel for gifts to his co-workers. Where Groves and Yohannan differ is in the willingness of Yohannan to move far beyond the simple conveyance of funds to evangelists. He is now developing his own denominational network of "Believers' Churches" to care for the converts of his evangelists. The consequence of this is the growth of two increasingly formal organisations (a missionary society and a church denomination) and the transformation of a spiritual *movement* into two organised *institutions* (one largely American and one Indian). This is a pattern we see repeated many times in church and mission history. Groves, as we have noted, disapproved of denominational identities and of the institutional separation of "church" and "mission".

The year 1990 saw the publication of an influential book, *Partnering in Ministry* by Luis Bush and Lorry Lutz. It advocated links of fellowship and sponsorship between Western congregations and unconnected congregations and ministries overseas.[6] A perceived advantage of this approach was a more efficient use of funds, as no properties and administrative offices were required. The intention was no doubt excellent, but the scheme suffered from the fact that such "partnerships" are never between equals. In most circumstances, a flow of money from the West will be welcomed on almost any terms by Christians in poorer parts of the world, and elements of acquiescence and manipulation are almost always

---

[1] Keyes, 115; Groves, *Influence*, 60, and M244, citing 2 Cor 8:14: "Then there will be equality." See PEANG, 174f, and above, 77ff.
[2] See, for example, Schwartz, below.
[3] Yohannan, 208
[4] Yohannan, 207
[5] Yohannan, 209
[6] On the influence of Lutz & Bush, see especially Rickett, and also Rickett and Welliver. For a balanced and more cautious assessment of this type of "partnership", see Van Rheenen, *Missions*, 189-202.

evident. To start with, the relationship is generally defined according to Western values – clearly defined goals, regular communication and detailed accountability. Then along with the money goes an expectation of doctrinal conformity, often including the use of programmes and resources developed by the Western church.[1] The recipients, when communicating with their benefactors, can hardly avoid the temptation of suggesting that without the provision of funds nothing can be done. Congregations fortunate enough to be selected for largesse become the envy of those around them, and the regular arrival of wealthy white tourists on "short term missions" simply adds to the confusion. Such visitors enjoy a "cultural experience" whilst attempting, in some cases, to assist in work that might be better done by the local believers or by skilled craftsmen of their own social community. This is undoubtedly part of a modern trend which Ralph Winter calls the "amateurisation" of mission.[2]

Whether this form of "partnership" helps or hinders the task of world evangelisation and the growth of indigenous churches is the subject of vigorous debate. It may function well when the receiving church is located in an urban context with modern, westernised expectations. But it may do much harm if the recipients have a more traditional culture and an attitude of deference to their alien benefactors.[3]

Modern trends of this sort owe much to the relatively recent availability of comfortable air travel and the wealth that provides access to it. In his own generation, as we have seen, Groves was profoundly concerned to diminish the social and economic gap between rich foreigner and poor indigene. He would adapt to local circumstances so far as to share the poverty of his Indian friends and colleagues. He lived with them, and lived like them, and one might think this a more healthy form of partnership. Groves was also aware that the Church throughout the world comprises both rich and poor, and he desired all to be involved in the Great Commission. In general, he expected that the rich would provide the finance, and the poor the labour.[4] He encouraged expatriates with a substantial income to use it for the support of both indigenous and expatriate evangelists, and he would surely encourage Yohannan in his initiatives.

But the issue remains a controversial one. Glenn Schwartz takes the opposite line from Yohannan and Bush, arguing that indigenous evangelism should be self-supporting, and that the sending of Western funds merely creates a relationship of dependence ("dependency" in American English). He is also highly critical of Western attempts to "partnership" with existing indigenous churches in poorer parts of the world, for reasons we have seen above. The term "dependency" has become something of an anathema to Schwartz, and he describes a conference in Kenya where a group of about ninety church leaders "confessed the sin of dependency on foreign funding." He comments, "They referred to it as an addiction – 'the more you get, the more you want'."[5]

But Schwartz draws no evident distinction between support for churches and support for evangelists: he opposes all foreign support for indigenous Christians.

---

[1] McQuilkin, "Avoiding Dependency"
[2] Winter, "The Re-Amateurisation of Mission"
[3] Van Rheenen, *Missions*, 202
[4] See above, 131ff.
[5] Schwartz, "How the Current Emphasis…"

When he argues that indigenous churches should support themselves, few would disagree, although this may require the dismantling of Western-style buildings and organisations. But in opposing all Western funding, he surely risks stifling evangelistic initiative such as that envisaged by K P Yohannan. And in equating foreign funding with foreign control, he misses the point made by Yohannan that the two do not have to go together. Despite this, Groves would certainly agree that "independent churches" should remain independent, with no attempt made to adopt them into Western denominations.

The historical origin of Schwartz's view that non-Western churches must stand on their own feet lies, of course, in the traditional three-self model for independence. Bonk, among others, considers the basic concept of "independence" to be flawed. He suggests, "Only a biblically rigorous ecclesiology of *interdependence* can ensure the credibility of the church globally." He adds, "We need to remind ourselves constantly that our Scriptures do not ever speak of the 'bodies' of Christ, only of the body... The interdependence described and advocated in our Scriptures has not only mystical but also practical dimensions, including economic ones."[1] With this in mind, the challenge remains for the richer Christians of the West to find ways of supporting indigenous work around the world without controlling, manipulating and distracting the workers.

Another recent trend has been for large "charismatic" churches in the West to send their own missionaries overseas for the purpose of creating similar churches elsewhere. Terry Virgo is a modern advocate of this form of "direct sending", and a critic of the tendency for "so-called para-church organisations" to do the work that churches should be doing.[2] His view that missionary societies are unnecessary would no doubt meet with Groves's approval.[3] But Virgo's "worldwide family of churches", bearing the New Frontiers International label, is a foreign denomination, seeking to establish possessive relationships with existing churches overseas that were previously independent or linked with other organisations.[4] The desire for control, for imposing a denominational identity and for inculcating particular doctrines and practices, all run counter to Groves's basic ecclesiological and missiological principles.

Most recently of all, the increasing globalisation of the "world Christian movement", along with vastly improved international communications (internet) and transport links (air travel), has opened the way for any Christian with access to the necessary technology to establish personal contact with a fellow-believer in another country, and to initiate ministry to that individual and his or her circle. A multiplication of competing influences will be the almost inevitable result. If Groves could comment, he would probably consider this a mixed blessing – a good opportunity for making disciples but a regrettable means of inculcating Western ways.[5]

Recent commentators such as Ted Ward and Darrell Whiteman have highlighted some of the current challenges facing modern Western mission

---

[1] Bonk, "Between Past and Future", 135-6
[2] Virgo, 304.
[3] See Chilcraft, Ch.5.
[4] Their ethos is very evident from their website <http://www.newfrontiers.xtn.org> (accessed 17th March 2005).
[5] On the significance of this trend, see Stackhouse *et al.*, 204-5. Other recent analyses are Jenkins, *The Next Christendom*, and Escobar, *The New Global Mission*.

agencies. Ward notes the persistence of denominational rivalry in Europe and America, a phenomenon largely irrelevant to churches elsewhere, yet still motivating much missionary recruitment and financial support. He observes that denominational co-operation seems to work better overseas than at home, a fact that the home constituency may find hard to understand and approve.[1] Groves long ago recognised that co-operation was easier overseas, and made this a fundamental aspect of his missiology.[2]

Whiteman has recently reminded us of the extent to which money still drives policy in American missions. The president of a large Protestant denominational mission board in the United States admitted his frustration: "The problem I face in trying to move our mission toward a more contextualized approach is that I am held accountable to a board of trustees, and they don't understand anything about contextualization. They are interested only in extending our denomination across the face of the globe, sincerely believing that this is the best way to win the world for Christ." As Whiteman observes, "Contextualization and denominational extension are two very different agendas, but if most of us are committed intellectually to the former, we frequently draw our paycheck from the latter, and this creates the problem.[3] The issue is an old one. Groves had attempted to free the missionary from the control of those who financed him, and he absolutely denied the validity of denominational extension.[4] The fact that our generation still struggles with these issues shows how little we have heeded what he said.[5]

A number of younger writers are seeking methods for more guaranteed success. David Garrison offers a useful analysis of some successful church planting movements, where "missionaries consciously progress along a four-stage process of Modelling, Assisting, Watching and Leaving (MAWL)."[6] Although he may underestimate the crucial importance of social instabilities in predisposing people groups to religious conversion, the method he approves follows the track marked out by Groves a century and a half ago, encouraging missionaries to mentor rather than manage indigenous converts.[7] Roland Muller finds that many young missionary recruits, drawn from post-modern Western societies, respond poorly to the traditional leadership methods of the established mission agencies. He

---

[1] Ward T, "Repositioning Mission Agencies"
[2] See above, 81ff.
[3] Whiteman, "Contextualization"
[4] See above, 81ff, 139ff.
[5] The limited scope of this thesis has not allowed us to pursue lines of thought that might be opened up by other writers such as Peter Beyerhaus and Roger Hedlund. We have also been unable to give attention to several missiological writers who could be considered summarizers and popularisers rather than original thinkers. Amongst the latter we might mention Alan Tippet, who noted the importance of the local church's self-image as representing the body of Christ in its locality, and who especially criticised missionaries' reluctance to let go the reins of authority. Another would be Charles Brock, who emphasized that foreign missionaries should do only what the local people can reproduce or imitate. In recent years David J Bosch, John Mark Terry, J Verkuyl, Gailyn Van Rheenen and Arthur F Glasser have written and edited major works of general missiological interest.
[6] Garrison, 194
[7] See above, 110ff.

advocates a much looser form of leadership, with a style essentially relational and motivational, and much more akin to that exercised in his own day by Groves.[1]

Gene Daniels has recently advocated a greater sensitivity to culture in his *Searching for the Indigenous Church*. On the other hand, an excessive reverence for culture is critiqued by Dave O'Brien, who finds the New Testament writers positively resisting culture in their exhortations to love not the world, and in the contrast they draw between the wickedness of this present evil age and the anticipated blessings of the age to come. O'Brien argues that "The gospel is and must remain essentially countercultural."[2] He suggests that the Gospel offers what may be considered a culture of its own, foreign to all worldly cultures. In the past this inherent strangeness has been sadly misunderstood, with dire consequences: "This essential foreignness of the gospel can heighten the misperception that Christianity is a Western religion."[3] Groves, of course, expressed no interest in culture, and we might think him deliberately and biblically "counter-cultural".[4]

In the same issue of the *Evangelical Missions Quarterly*, Larry W Sharp suggests that in Western missions, "the focus on church planting has detracted from our real business." He points out that the New Testament does not instruct us to plant churches. The commands of Jesus are to "make disciples," "preach the word," "follow me," "feed my sheep," "be my witnesses." And Sharp suggests, "Missionaries who define themselves as a traditional 'church planter' have difficulty avoiding transplanting their culture's idea of church. But if they simply teach the word, make disciples and encourage those disciples to 'do church' in their own contextually appropriate way under the guidance of the Holy Spirit, they will avoid the many pitfalls of church planting." Then he adds, "If church planting becomes the work of national believers, missionaries don't have to pass a baton; the baton is in national hands from the beginning." His conclusion is a striking one: "How about instead of being good at planting churches, we strive to be good being disciples, making disciples and encouraging nationals to do the same?"[5] It would be hard to find, in recent years, a better expression of Grovesian missiology than this.

Conclusion: Mission Thinkers, Grovesian and Other

Introducing a number of missiological themes in harmony or in conflict with the thought of Anthony Norris Groves, we have considered Lesslie Newbigin's threefold paradigm, in which he identifies three basic elements that in varying proportions combine to determine the essential strategy adopted by any missionary

---

[1] Muller, *Missionary Leadership*. In a second book (*Missions*), Muller offers to provide formal administrative support for independent missionary teams. Groves envisaged something similar, and in Brethren missions the magazines have long fulfilled this function whilst minimizing the laborious paperwork that Muller assumes necessary (see above, 177ff).

[2] O'Brien, 359

[3] Ibid

[4] See above, 115ff. On Groves as a man who ignored culture, see also above, 119, and PEANG, 156ff.

[5] Sharp, 280-1. In a recent study of successful church planting movements, David Garrison repudiates the idea of passing the torch of church leadership to indigenous Christians, advising that "you begin with the torch in their hand" (Garrison, 188). The same point is made more briefly by Shenk, *Transfiguration*, 9-10.

or missiologist. They are firstly, foreign church custom; secondly, local culture; and thirdly, New Testament principle and practice. Mission strategists who emphasize one element above the others may be identified as follows:

1. *Institutionalist*. The supreme importance of foreign church custom is held by Henry Venn, Rufus Anderson, John Nevius, Stephen Neill, Michael Hollis, Tom Steffan and perhaps by Keith Eitel and Luis Bush.

2. *Culturalist*. The determinative role of local culture is advocated by Charles Kraft, Donald McGavran, Peter Wagner, Melvin Hodges, William Smalley, and perhaps by Glenn Schwartz.

3. *Primitivist*. The overriding authority of New Testament principle and practice is maintained by A N Groves, Charles Gützlaff, Roland Allen, Watchman Nee, Bakht Singh, and perhaps by Jonathan Bonk and K P Yohannan.

Defined in these terms, we can consider Groves the earliest major exponent of the third, or primitivist approach. For him, New Testament principles and practice were the supreme determinant of strategy for church and mission in any age and every culture.

The history of Christian mission shows, in general, that a primitivist approach is valued more highly by indigenous Christians than by the agents of foreign societies.[1] To indigenous Christians, the denominational peculiarities and organisational structures preoccupying Western mission leaders (institutionalists) can appear quite irrelevant to their own circumstances. And again, to indigenous Christians, the intense interest shown in local cultures by some foreign missionaries (culturalists) can seem entirely misdirected, for the culture is something they take for granted and, in some cases, despise. Of far greater interest to them is the quest for "genuine Christianity", as originally practised in its best and earliest days. We should not be surprised, therefore, to find Groves's ideas reappearing more frequently in the verbal exhortations of indigenous leaders than in the written expositions of Western mission leaders and missiologists.

Indeed, Alan Kreider observes an increasing primitivist tendency in churches originally attached to Western missions, largely as a reaction against a perceived failure of foreign structures and methods to meet the real spiritual needs of the local congregations: "Churches in many countries were founded by Western missionaries who imported Christendom assumptions and institutions as an integral part of the Gospel... People in these churches often find that pre-Christendom is fascinating. For them pre-Christendom patterns can provide a means of critiquing the Christendom practices and assumptions that are weighing their churches down and can point forward towards a hopeful future."[2] Groves advocated exactly this rediscovery of "pre-Christendom patterns".[3]

Introducing a number of current missiological issues, we have seen that the principles identified by Groves bear strongly upon a range of contemporary controversies. His emphasis on a frugal lifestyle, Christian stewardship, and "living by faith" will have many applications in a world where the gulf between rich and poor is evident both within the universal Church and outside it. His indigenous principles, if adopted by pioneer missions today, might enable them to avoid the difficulties faced by successive generations in dismantling foreign "scaffoldings".

---

[1] Newbigin, *A Word in Season*, 68
[2] Kreider, "Beyond Bosch"
[3] M285

His on-the-job training of indigenous evangelists could still prove an ideal method for the development of local leadership. His encouragement for converts to initiate their own activity and take full responsibility from the beginning might serve to mobilize many a frustrated indigene and obviate many an institutional power struggle. His congregations with no salaried "pastor", meeting simply in homes and schools, would have no need for elaborate finance and no thought of dependence on foreign budgets. His evangelists, living "by faith and prayer" and supported by generous Christian friends, would carry the Gospel far beyond the regular congregations. His "direct sending" of missionaries, with the concomitant marginalisation of foreign societies, would encourage spiritual rather than institutional links between local fellowships. His advocacy of New Testament principle and practice as a model applicable to every age, overriding both foreign tradition and indigenous culture, could effectively protect local congregations from the excesses of indigenous syncretism and of Western consumerism.

There are advocates among modern missiologists for all the views Groves expressed a century and a half ago. Many such writers are likely to think highly of him when given the opportunity to assess his strategic approach to church and mission.

3. Groves's Primitivist Missiology: a Hermeneutical Critique

In every age, pietists, romanticists and primitivists are vulnerable to the accusation of naïvety, and we must consider whether or not this would be fair in the case of Groves. In particular, we should consider his use of scripture and assess how far his practice may be justified.

Groves's writings demonstrate that he considered the Bible to be a comprehensible book, and relevant to his own circumstances. When troubled by worldly expectations, he advised, "Against all this overwhelming influence, there is but one remedy, to read the word of God with a single view to know His will, by whom it was inspired."[1] Theories, traditions and prejudices must give way, in his view, to the divine wisdom revealed in scripture: "I know that ten thousand arguments, plausible and powerful in various degrees, may be brought against this view of the subject; but my simple answer is: the Lord hath spoken, what can I say? – the Lord hath acted, what can I do? Shall a man be wiser than his Maker?"[2] Groves took for granted the perspicuity and the normativity of scripture.

A contemporary British or American student of hermeneutics will be inclined to consider this naïve. As Callahan observes,

> There is a sincere distrust of perspicuity, and a praise of obscurity, afoot in modern hermeneutics. Either perspicuity is regarded as the epitome of precritical naïveté and sacrificed on the altar of modernity, or it is regarded as a gnostic theme and a code available only to the privileged... Perspicuity is quickly and easily dismissed as nothing more than an illusion, a fideistic commitment to a religious fallacy that ancient texts are coherently understood with a realism uncommon even in our own day.[3]

A contemporary critic might feel equally justified in accusing Groves of overconfidence in assuming that scripture could be lifted from the context in which it was written. As Bosch observes, "There never was a 'pure' message, supracultural and suprahistorical."[4] We might wonder whether Groves, as a nineteenth-century reader, would understand the first-century context of the New Testament sufficiently to make universal applications of the teachings and practices recorded in its pages. And was he also, perhaps, ignorant of the extent to which his own cultural background influenced his interpretation of scripture and the manner in which he sought to apply it to the circumstances he faced? We might expect his exposition of biblical texts to unconsciously legitimize presuppositions drawn from his own cultural and religious heritage and from his personal experiences.[5]

It is, of course, natural that Groves's hermeneutical assumptions would follow the Protestant custom of his day. As a general principle, the perspicuity of scripture was assumed, largely in reaction against Roman Catholic assertions that the Bible was incomprehensible to the layman and required interpretation by the church.[6] Luther had taught that in the papal kingdom "nothing is more commonly stated or more generally accepted than the idea that the Scriptures are obscure and

---

[1] M11
[2] Groves, *Influence*, 27
[3] Callahan, "Claritas", 362
[4] Bosch, 422
[5] Thiselton, "Biblical Studies", 108; Bosch, 423
[6] Callahan, "Claritas", 354

ambiguous, so that the spirit to interpret them must be sought from the Apostolic See of Rome."[1] Following Luther's lead, Protestants had long argued that any reader possessing the Spirit of God should be able to understand what he or she read. Indeed, "Perspicuity was a necessary article to sustain distinctively Protestant hermeneutics."[2] As such, it formed part of the "broader philosophical assumption of the perspicuity of truth generally."[3]

Significant to this was the related belief that the divinely inspired Bible should be accepted as a unity. Obscurities could thus be cleared up by comparing one verse or passage with another, and drawing a conclusion that would be consistent with both. Pietists, such as Spener, Bengel and Francke, applied this principle as they encouraged "the means of proper Bible reading" for "simple pious readers".[4] It was the "literal" and "historical" sense of scripture that readers were encouraged to accept, without any concern for the "interpretation" of mysteries, allegories or cultural peculiarities. Thiselton has noted that "in certain strands of Christian pietism", the certainty of perspicuity was taken "as a signal that hermeneutical theory and endeavour is scarcely necessary."[5] Indeed, the ability to understand scripture was considered the mark of a true Christian, freed from childish dependence on spiritual authorities. A basic Reformation principle was "the right to ask whether the Bible really means what the Church says it means."[6]

In an age when John Henry Newman observed that Bible reading was the religion of the English people,[7] "the assumption was that the text was clear and accessible... The Bible should be read, simply read, rather than interpreted."[8] Moreover, "biblicist primitivists claimed that the simpler one is in approaching the Bible, the more likely one is to acquire its true message."[9] In 1871 Charles Hodge declared, "the Bible is a plain book," "intelligible by the people". Indeed, "to them are directed these profound discussions of Christian doctrine.... They are everywhere assumed to be competent to understand what is written."[10]

On this basis, the Bible reader could be largely independent of others. A sense of freedom to engage in independent investigation was a relative novelty at this period, and identified by historians as a trait characteristically "modern".[11] In Groves's habit of seeking fresh interpretations of scripture, we may discern in him what is termed "a hermeneutic of suspicion", a willingness to question generally accepted beliefs and practices.[12] This stands in contrast to the "hermeneutic of

---

[1] Luther, *On the Bondage of the Will*, cited by Callahan, "Claritas", 354. See also Thiselton, *New Horizons*, 179-81.

[2] Callahan, "Claritas", 357. The democratic concept of the "priesthood of all believers" inclined Protestants to resist suggestions that a scholarly magisterium must interpret the meaning of scripture for the mass of believers (Noll, *Between Faith and Criticism*, 151-3).

[3] Marsden, 80

[4] Spener, "The Spiritual Priesthood", in Erb, 55, 71-2

[5] Thiselton, *New Horizons*, 179

[6] Barton, 16

[7] Newman, J H, 96.

[8] Callahan, "The Bible Says", 455

[9] Ibid

[10] Hodge, 183-4

[11] Thiselton, *New Horizons*, 143. Attempts to classify Groves's thought in this way are inevitably anachronistic. He could also be credited with "post-modernist" affinities in his resistance to "systems" of thought and practice (PEANG, 102ff).

[12] Thiselton, *New Horizons*, 143; Goldingay, 106-7

trust", characteristic of an earlier age assuming the correctness of traditional interpretations.[1] Groves's independence of thought, separating himself (partially, at least) from the religious consensus of his day, marks him, in this regard, as a "modern" man, as well as a biblicist and a primitivist.[2] Then again, Groves might equally well be considered an "Enlightenment" man, that is, one seeking cumulative information enabling him to understand the exact meaning of the ancient texts and the intentions of their original writers.[3]

With this kind of background and disposition, Groves made it his aim throughout life to discover "the mind of the Lord" through painstaking study of the Bible. He remarked, "I feel that there is no time more usefully employed than in searching God's word, unless it be by living it… I cannot tell you the interest I feel in my analysis of the New Testament. This is something that steadily occupies my mind many hours a day."[4] And again, "I have very little confidence in man. My great desire has been to cast myself on the word of God, that every judgment of my soul concerning all things may be right, by being, in all, the mind of God."[5] In Groves's various writings, the scarcity of reference to published commentaries would lead us to assume he was not in the habit of referring to such. He expected to receive "light" on a verse or passage by means of studying it himself, intelligently and prayerfully.

In New Testament passages, it seems clear that he sought the literal sense, that is, the "original" and "historical" meaning. In the Old Testament (after 1831), he especially sought types that might confirm New Testament teachings.[6] It was in 1831 that the traumas he suffered in Baghdad led him to the realisation that he had been mistaken in his belief that the whole Bible contained principles applicable to Christians in the present age. He admitted, "This error arose from considering the temporal promises of the 91st Psalm, and other similar ones in multitudes of places, as the legitimate objects of faith, whereas I have been now led to see that they… are but 'typical' representations of that kingdom in which the saints of the Lord shall rejoice and be safe when his enemies are swept away as the chaff of the summer threshing floor."[7] Developing a dispensational view of scripture, he now carefully distinguished between the Old and New Covenants: "I found I must not follow Moses if I would live according to Christ."[8] He came to the view that the principles of Jesus had replaced those of Moses as "a rule of life" for God's people. He saw these principles lived out by the first generation of Christians in an exemplary manner, which should thus be considered normative for every age and culture.[9]

In the confidence that they could comprehend the Bible on their own, numerous individuals and groups had, before Groves, attempted to replicate in their own day

---

[1] Thiselton, Ibid; Goldingay, Ibid
[2] Thiselton, *New Horizons*, 143; Barton, 16
[3] Barton, 16; Bosch, 422
[4] M334
[5] M43
[6] This is discussed more fully in PEANG, 136ff.
[7] R220
[8] Groves, *The New Testament in the Blood of Jesus*, 13, quoted by A Minister, *The Perpetuity of the Moral Law*, 14
[9] These issues are discussed at length in PEANG,136ff.

what they found in scripture.[1] Like them, and like many since, Groves made a "conscious effort to sit down, figure out what the New Testament blueprint called for, then quite rationally reproduce it in the modern world."[2] By March 1827, he was seeking precedents in scripture to serve as a model for himself and his friends, as one of them testified: "Groves has just been telling me that it appeared to him from scripture that believers, meeting together as disciples of Christ, were free to break bread together as their Lord had admonished them; and that in as far as the practice of the apostles could be a guide, every Lord's Day should be set apart for thus remembering the Lord's death and obeying his parting command."[3] Eleven years later in India, he observed, "The constant reference to *God's Word* has brought, and is bringing, the questions connected with ministry and Church government into a perfectly new position in the minds of many."[4] It was his custom to draw both positive and negative conclusions from the New Testament, remarking on one occasion, "That it is not essential to have a bishop or elder to 'consecrate' the supper, I should unhesitatingly infer from the perfect silence of the Scriptures."[5]

Groves, of course, lived before hermeneutical studies had seriously questioned the common person's competence to understand biblical texts.[6] Underlying his desire to produce and distribute scripture portions in Mesopotamia lay his conviction that vernacular translations would be understandable to the local people. Both there and in India, he encouraged and indeed taught children to read by using the Bible as his text. His stated aim in his elementary schools was to "bring God's word before them in a form intelligible and clear."[7]

Callahan remarks that "the determination of which texts are attributed the status of 'clear' and which are labelled 'obscure' often indicates more about the prejudices of the interpreter than the actual clarity or obscurity of a given text."[8] Where present-day commentators might identify cultural presuppositions in the Sermon on the Mount, for example, and thus absolve the reader from literal compliance,[9] Groves considered its instructions perfectly lucid, and applicable literally as a "rule of life" to his own circumstances.[10] He remarked, "How beautifully all our blessed Lord's precepts hang together, and fit the one the other. If you consent to follow him in his poverty as he has commanded, you have little to fear in following his other commands of non-resistance."[11]

---

[1] Some are described in PEANG, 88ff.
[2] Wacker, "Searching for Eden", in Hughes, *Primitive Church*, 143
[3] M39
[4] M393
[5] *Liberty*, 73
[6] Noll, *Between Faith and Criticism*, 11-15
[7] J55
[8] Callahan, "Claritas", 369, citing J D G Dunn, *Baptism in the Holy Spirit* (London, SCM, 1970)
[9] See, for example, Rowdon, "The Concept of Living by Faith", 346. As early as 1838, a "Minister of the Establishment" similarly criticised Groves's "literal" view of the Sermon on the Mount, arguing that its basic ideas could be applied in various ways more suited to modern culture (A Minister, *Perpetuity*, 7-8, 17).
[10] M338, *Remarks*, 80, 81
[11] R226

As a child of his time, Groves can hardly be blamed for elements of hermeneutical naïvety shared with his contemporaries. But if we are to take him as a significant voice in ongoing missiological debate, we must assess how far his views may derive from an inadequate or misleading view of scripture and thus limit the degree to which we may feel able to support his conclusions. Did he fail, for example, to take sufficient account of the extent to which first century culture determined the views and methods described in the New Testament? Current hermeneutical scholarship would lead us to expect this.[1]

We should note that Groves gave very careful thought to matters of exegesis. He actively sought to understand what the writers of the biblical texts intended, and he studied significant portions in the original languages.[2] We have observed, for example, that this enabled him to achieve a sounder hermeneutic than Edward Irving in applying "apostolic" missionary methods in a cross-cultural as distinct from a purely Jewish context.[3] He also found fault with Irving's custom of identifying evangelists as messengers (angels) *to the churches*, that is, "evangelical clergy", "those who are to build up in knowledge and faith, comfort and charity, those who already do believe the Gospel."[4] Groves, on the contrary, found the evangelists in the New Testament to be preachers of the gospel to the unconverted. And whereas Irving considered Timothy to be a "pastor", Groves noted that Timothy was instructed to "do the work of an evangelist", and that both he and Titus were, in fact, missionaries sent for short periods to help establish new churches rather than clergymen sent to take permanent charge of old churches.[5]

Bosch, for one, defends the validity of a literalist approach like that of Groves, over against what he considers traditional "misinterpretations". He suggests, "Through the ages... Christians have usually found ways around the clear meaning of the Sermon on the Mount... Today, however, most scholars agree that these and similar interpretations are inadequate, that there is no getting round the fact that, in Matthew's view, Jesus actually expected all his followers to live according to these norms always and under all circumstances."[6] To a greater extent than many of his contemporaries, and many in our own day, Groves was concerned to discover exactly what was taught and practised in the first century, and he condemned those who sought to explain away what to him was clear, and to read back into scripture the familiar practices of their own generation.

But if this be granted, was Groves in fact blind to the assumptions and prejudices he himself brought to the Bible as he read it? Recent studies in hermeneutics would consider this likely.[7] An opponent in his own day thought him guilty in this regard, suggesting, for example, that he was predisposed to interpret scripture in a manner contrary to Anglican tradition: "He never condescends to

---

[1] Zuck, 79-90; Thiselton, *New Horizons*, 31

[2] The early Brethren, following Groves, gained a reputation for exegetical scholarship enhanced by published works such as *The Englishman's Greek Concordance of the New Testament*, edited by G V Wigram, and the *Hebrew and Chaldee Lexicon* of S P Tregelles. Tregelles and Henry Craik, among others, were outstanding writers on academic issues relating to the biblical texts.

[3] See above, 23f.

[4] Irving, *For Missionaries*, xxiii

[5] Groves, *Liberty*, 78; 2 Tim 4:5

[6] Bosch, 69

[7] Goldingay, 36-55; Thiselton, *New Horizons*, 35, 44-6

refer to any authority. He is above such a mode of settling a question. His interpretations of scripture are generally his own... Where an opinion or a practice is more anciently or more generally followed... it is the more liable to exception [i.e. rejection]."[1] The charge is a natural one. Groves's conviction that Anglican tradition was at variance with apostolic practice is one he would not deny, but his attempt to demonstrate this in a scholarly fashion cannot be condemned *a priori* as a matter of presupposition or prejudice. His argument must be judged on its merits. It is difficult to find any evidence in his writings that unconscious assumptions influenced his interpretation of the New Testament, apart from his evident belief in the perspicuity, unity and normativity of scripture.

Let us return briefly to Newbigin's threefold classification of missiological parameters, and consider its hermeneutical implications. A missiologist with "institutionalist" or "culturalist" leanings will almost inevitably express more interest in hermeneutics than would a "primitivist" colleague. Institutionalist, culturalist and primitivist are all likely to place high value on exegesis, and of the three, the primitivist will be especially concerned to understand the biblical texts, for he is seeking to replicate what he has understood. On the other hand, there are considerations important to the institutionalist drawn not from scripture but from his denomination or sending agency. The culturalist likewise brings to his reading of scripture attitudes and beliefs to which he is committed, derived not from scripture but from the expectations of the world around him. Granted that every Bible reader brings to his reading pre-suppositions and prejudices, this will be especially so, and perhaps deliberately so, for the institutionalist and culturalist. They will seek to interpret passages that the primitivist will be inclined to accept at face value and implement directly. Whilst seeking principles in scripture, the institutionalist and culturalist will seek applications conformed to the institution or the culture, whilst the primitivist will draw both principles and applications from scripture itself. In reality, the primitivist is likely to find his opponents approving his diligence in exegesis and regretting his disinterest in hermeneutics. We would expect Groves to be admired and condemned on this basis.

Groves, of course, was a pioneer missionary, not an academic theologian. An itinerant evangelist, preaching to unruly crowds and gathering first-generation converts into local churches, faces circumstances similar to those of the apostles to a far greater degree than would be the case for a hermeneutician located in a land with a long Christian history. We might judge such a missionary better qualified, in this respect, to understand the context in which the New Testament was written, and also better qualified to relate its content relevantly to present-day circumstances. The possibility is thus raised that the gap between the "two horizons" (ancient text and modern reader) could be somewhat smaller for a person like Groves than for a scholar in a modern British or American university.[2]

---

[1] A Minister, *Perpetuity*, ii. For details of Groves's debate with this Minister, especially on the issue of pacifism, see PEANG, 189ff.

[2] The standard university texts take little or no account of hermeneutics as practised by pioneer missionaries and indigenous Christians in circumstances similar to those of the first-century apostles and their converts in the Mediterranean Basin. This we might regret. Such works also take little account of past and present primitivist theory that deliberately presumes the perspicuity, unity and normativity of scripture with significant consequences for the primitivist reader of biblical texts.

By way of summary we should note that Groves's presuppositions, in his approach to scripture, were those common to Protestants of his day. He assumed the perspicuity and unity of the Bible as a divinely inspired book. To this he added a further presupposition: that New Testament doctrine and practice should be taken as normative for Christians in every age and cultural context. On this basis, Groves probably read the Bible with a more open mind than most of his generation. Indeed, he constantly sought for fresh "light" through his own exegetical efforts, and he made it his aim to replicate primitive practice as closely as possible in his missionary initiatives, without concession to institutional custom or local culture. His interest in exegesis was marked, his awareness of hermeneutical issues limited, but his experience as an active cross-cultural missionary would undoubtedly aid his understanding of issues addressed by the New Testament writers.

4. Groves's Primitivist Missiology: a Historical Critique

We have frequently referred to Groves as a primitivist and a restorationist. He is therefore vulnerable to allegations that his methodology was merely a "naïve attempt to avoid the power of history and culture", an "effort to deny history", "a rejection of any sense of history".[1] He might appear guilty of exactly this tendency to "historylessness" when he declared to a friend, "Oh! my brother, let us not put the experience of 1500 years against the word of God. If we believe, we shall have what we ask for."[2]

Groves, however, was by no means inclined to ignore history. In his most scholarly work, *Remarks on a Pamphlet*, he cites several Church Fathers, along with Anabaptists, Mennonites and Waldenses. He once noted, "I have been occupied with the history of the periods connected with the Reformation and the time of Constantine, or rather with the events which transpired within one century of both; and in this study I hope I may learn some lessons in Church matters: The formation of new ideas, and the modification of old ones, distinguished both these remarkable periods."[3] He was, throughout his life, an avid reader of religious biography, and he became an admirer, in particular, of Tyndale, Cranmer and Wesley. His studies in church history led him to commend certain individuals and movements, and to censure others. His interest in the subject was a discerning and practical one, and in seeking to draw a line under the past and make a fresh start, he hoped to see better results in his own day than were evident in former ages. This approach cannot be fairly described as "ahistorical". On the contrary, "It takes history seriously, but treats history's outcomes as needing critique, rather than as traditions to invest with authority."[4]

Historians in our own day are inclined to consider any quest for the recovery of primordial blessings as entirely illusory, arguing that the past simply cannot be restored.[5] Yet Groves was probably less naïve in this regard than we might suppose. He shows no sign of imagining that the past could be literally recreated, or that churches and missions in his own day could exactly resemble those of the apostolic age. His primitivism was fostered by the failings he saw in contemporary institutions, which led him to seek alternative strategies in the New Testament, but he was not so foolish as to suppose that he or others would experience exactly what the apostles experienced. There is no sign of this in his writings.

At times, primitivists may "blatantly and uncritically project their own contemporary concerns on to the first age and unwittingly find their own reflections staring back at themselves from within the well of their own Christian history."[6] Was Groves guilty of this? As a young man, having seceded from the Anglican communion without joining or founding any other communion, he would seem to have no conscious system of beliefs or practices to justify or maintain. Indeed, having deliberately distanced himself from the "faith community" of his

---

[1] Hughes, *Primitive Church*, x
[2] M224
[3] M418
[4] Schlabach (citing J H Yoder), in Hughes, *Primitive Church*, 199
[5] Schleiermacher saw the Protestant Reformation, for example, as a step forward rather than a step back (Bosch, 422).
[6] Hughes, *Primitive Church*, xi

earlier years, he felt free to find fault with many of its beliefs and practices, dismissing them as "the rules of traditionary Christianity".[1] Within a basically Calvinistic framework, his genuine desire, as far as we can tell, was to ascertain exactly what Christ and the New Testament writers taught and did, and to conform himself to this.[2]

It is said that "primitivist / restorationist movements, by definition, enshrine the first age as a transcendent norm and, on that basis, stand in judgment on the contents of modern culture," and indeed, that "primitivists sometimes turn their energies in profoundly counter-cultural directions."[3] We might wonder whether this was true of Groves. In fact he was an essentially positive person. He declared, "The important question is not so much to know what is *wrong*, as to learn from the Lord what is *right*."[4] Culture, whether of West or East, simply did not engage his attention; at least, he took no trouble to write about it. His expectation was for the world-view of the early Christians to be adopted by his converts, and for the Bible rather than any culture of the world to determine their attitudes and behaviour. Beyond this, aspects of life untouched by scriptural principles were of no personal concern to him.

Here again he might be considered naïve. His lack of interest in Indian customs and beliefs could be thought to count against him as a missionary, as indeed would his inability to speak an Indian language. Despite this, critics in our own day may find his attitude preferable to the profound and patronising interest that some missionaries have taken in foreign cultures they considered either amusing or despicable. Groves's respect for individual Indians, and the trust he reposed in them, showed that he considered their culture no hindrance to the development of their Christian character.[5]

Studies of primitivism in general will question whether it is possible for a primitivist to be entirely consistent.[6] Groves himself could be accused at times of both deliberate inconsistency and inadvertent deviation from his principles. On occasion, he himself admitted as much. As an advocate of "apostolic" forms of church fellowship, he confessed, "In fact I do not see a single church existing that appears an exact transcript of what is evident in Scripture; and I should feel it to be my duty, and I hope my happiness, to submit to any discipline that did not violate the *spirit* and *essential nature of the gospel*, which my brethren in Christ thought it right to institute."[7] He was evidently wise enough to make the best of local circumstances that always, and inevitably, fell short of the primitivist ideal.

Particularly striking is his change in attitude over time towards educational missions. He had given no evident thought to the subject before leaving England in 1829, and indeed, on his way through eastern Europe, declared, "Education is one thing, which may or may not be a blessing; the knowledge of God's word is another. To forward the one, separated from the other, I would not put forth my

---

[1] *Liberty*, 39; see PEANG, 102ff.
[2] M11, 43
[3] Ibid, xiv
[4] Groves, "A Letter on Missions"
[5] See above, 115ff.
[6] We may observe tensions, for example, between primitivist (separatist) and modernist (fundamentalist) tendencies in modern American evangelicalism (Hughes, *Primitive Church, passim*).
[7] Groves, *Liberty*, 81

little finger; to the latter, all my strength."[1] Two years later, his experience in Baghdad led him to suggest that when it was impossible to preach openly (in an Islamic context for example), and when the populace seemed unresponsive to other methods, the pioneer missionary should not be "discouraged from attempting schools, for although they may not stand above a year or two, you may by the Lord's blessing be the instrument of stirring up their minds to think and examine for themselves, and without violence lead them to question the truth of some of their dogmas. And when you have once dislodged the principle of implicit faith you have at last opened the door for truth."[2] Then, following his visit to Alexander Duff's far more ambitious educational establishment in Calcutta, he confided, "My interest in boarding schools is very much increasing, not because I think it was the way in which the apostles propagated Christianity, but because I see the Lord now blessing it."[3]

His admiration for "apostolic methods" clearly did not prevent him from using other methods, as is demonstrated by the fact that he subsequently opened his own boarding school in Chittoor and taught there for many years. His views in this regard were strengthened by his conviction that "the days of the Spirit's energy" had ceased, and that, without accompanying miracles, preaching was now considerably less effective than in apostolic times. He remarked,

> I think direct preaching to the natives a much higher and more noble work; and one the aim after which my whole heart feels the overwhelming importance of; but if the aim, in truth, be Christ's honour, persons are often blessed of the Lord [through a long period of education], to effect what in the days of the Spirit's energy, was done by a single sentence brought home and sealed.[4]

In other matters, too, Groves felt a measure of uncertainty as to whether apostolic conditions could in practice be replicated. Hearing that a colleague was dangerously ill, he considered the possibility of miraculous healing through prayer, and commented,

> This I do feel – that the apostle Paul, in Corinthians 12 and 14, when speaking of supernatural gifts for the edifying of the Church and doing the work of God, points them out as things to be desired and prayed for then. And if they were desired to be prayed for then [*sic*], why not now?... Distinguishing between apostolic times and present times is to my mind so dangerous a principle, and puts into the hands of anyone so disposed a sword that seems to me to reach the very vitals of the gospel.[5]

On this occasion the sick person did gradually recover, but without causing Groves to develop any particular interest in the miraculous. Towards the end of his life, he expressed his agreement with a tract arguing that "the season of supernatural gifts was that of the *infancy* of the Church, and that their withdrawal took place when the Testament was complete and the Church left under the guardianship of the indwelling Spirit – in the period, in short, of her manhood." He commented, "That this is the doctrine of scripture, I have no doubt. And so far from the absence of

---

[1] J44-45; M59
[2] R192
[3] M326
[4] M326-7
[5] R302-3

those things... being a sign of decay, they mark the period of the Church's progress from infancy to manhood."[1] With regard to the miraculous, his primitivism had given way to a belief that the experience of the early church was not entirely reproducible in later times.

These are examples of Groves's flexibility and adaptability when primitivist ideals were impossible of exact fulfilment. But in his endeavour literally to obey the precepts of Jesus, there were occasions when his refusal to lay up treasures on earth, for example, actually made the missionary task more difficult. Once, travelling by sea, he admitted, "I miss very much the retirement of a closet [i.e. small room] which I enjoyed on shore. To avoid expense I allowed a Christian brother to have a third of my cabin, and I have up to this time slept on the floor of the cuddy. Sometimes I have felt the spiritual loss to be greater than the value of a few hundred rupees, yet I think again it is right."[2]

In this instance, his consistency can hardly be questioned, which leads us to enquire whether, throughout his missionary career, this was always the case. His greatest achievement was undoubtedly the training and mentoring of John Arulappan in Chittoor, in preparation for the Indian's indigenous initiatives in Madurai. But once Arulappan had left him in 1840, there is no indication that Chittoor continued to be a significant base for on-the-job training of Indian evangelists and church leaders for ministry in wider spheres. Although Indian Christians in Chittoor continued to engage in evangelistic itineration and to teach in the school, there was nothing unusual or distinctive about this compared with the work of missions elsewhere. Preoccupied by his industrial and commercial activities, Groves now seemed less effective in mentoring younger men than he had been in his earlier years. In ministering to English-speaking expatriates at major towns in the region, his role came to resemble that of a conventional nonconformist minister. In this he may be thought to have lost his earlier and more rigorous primitivist vision for the spontaneous expansion of indigenous congregations.

We have seen that early in his career, Groves hoped to encourage existing ecumenical initiatives and to stimulate "a missionary combination and service that, to some extent at least, will resemble what there was in the days of the apostles."[3] The frustration of these early hopes followed from the sudden death of the ecumenically inclined Rhenius, from the vehement rejection of Groves himself by the Anglican community in India, and by the refusal of the Congregationalist John Bilderbeck to work in harmony with him at Chittoor. The consequence was that, during the final decade of his life, Groves was ostracised by almost the entire church and mission community in India, a state of affairs particularly painful for a man who had anticipated, and endeavoured to achieve, the exact opposite.

We have noted the "tent-making" element in Groves's missiology, and there is no doubt that he always considered self-support to be the ideal for both foreign missionary and indigenous evangelist. We might suppose from the failure of his own industrial initiatives and his desire, shortly before his death, to be freed from them for "an uninterrupted ministry some where or in some form",[4] that he

---

[1] M443-4
[2] M328
[3] M270
[4] M421

ultimately rejected his "tent-making" model for mission. This is not the case, for with Groves's approval and encouragement, his sons continued to combine industry and mission, providing both employment for Indian Christians and support for evangelists. His widow commented, "Thus, in the providence of God, they illustrate the principle their father so desired to see carried out in India, of uniting spiritual and manual labour, and while availing themselves of the facilities the country affords for their support, they not only seek the blessing of the people among whom they dwell, but strengthen the hands of other missionaries."[1]

The great turning point in Groves's missionary career undoubtedly came when he contracted a substantial loan for extension of his farm colony at Chittoor in 1842. Shortly afterwards, disease wrecked his silk works, and then some further crushing losses attended his subsequent commercial investments. His widow recalled that he attributed his failure to "having been too much engrossed with the external affairs of the mission, which had hindered his enjoying his usual hours of retirement and communion with God."[2] But it might equally be considered a failure in consistency to maintain his primitivist resolve never to borrow money.[3] It brought him untold sorrow and regret, and distracted him throughout his final years from the missionary task he had originally set himself. His ideals remained unfulfilled and he died believing himself a failure.

Groves's unpopularity with the expatriate community in India undoubtedly stemmed from his primitivist view of unity and ministry. Voluntary societies and denominational agencies simply could not abandon the institutional identities and structures, and the doctrinal distinctives, that motivated and divided them. To imagine that they might do so must be considered naïve. As Kenneth J Newton observes, "In India, as in the missionary world of the day, it was the denominational polity of Venn and not the ecumenical dream of Groves which prevailed. Groves's vision was too idealistic, too impracticable in a protestant world still marking out its denominational missionary boundaries."[4]

Nevertheless, it would be facile in the extreme to attribute Groves's failure entirely to his primitivism. His encouragement of Arulappan to undertake independent indigenous initiatives might be thought equally naïve, and yet proved highly effective. His method of living "by faith", seeking guidance and provision directly from God, was adopted with success by thousands of foreign and indigenous missionaries in the generation that followed him. His concept of "tent-making" teams, following apostolic example, continues to find acceptance today. His vision for "liberty of ministry" and "the spontaneous expansion of the church" found an effective advocate in Roland Allen, and eventually received widespread acclaim. And in our day, we see a fulfilment of ecumenical hopes that, in his generation, seemed absurdly unrealistic.

It was, in fact, when he *abandoned* his primitivist principles, and followed the financial way of the world, that Groves faced his own greatest disappointment, clouding his final decade with commercial difficulties and debts: "the blank, as he

---

[1] M549
[2] M403
[3] On Groves's financial principles, see above, 139ff.
[4] Newton, *Anthony Norris Groves*, 13

calls it, of his ten years at Chittoor."[1] Preoccupied with problems in his farm colony, he must leave others to attempt the fulfilment of his vision.

The present-day reader's opinion of Groves will be determined very largely by his or her view concerning the perspicuity and normativity of the New Testament scriptures. If these two hermeneutical principles are denied, Groves himself will seem naïve and his methods out of touch with twenty-first-century reality. If they are accepted, he may offer some hope that the evangelistic success of apostolic times may be replicated by a generation applying his primitivist principles more consistently than he did himself. Such a hope has been forcefully expressed by a more recent and more widely regarded exegete and primitivist, J B Phillips: "There are thousands of people who are sick of narrowness and churchiness, and who long for the fresh air of the New Testament… I am firmly of the opinion that so great is the longing for New Testament Christianity that it will be along this line that true spiritual revival will come."[2]

---

[1] M437
[2] Phillips, *New Testament Christianity*, 20

Conclusion: The Missiological Influence of A N Groves

Anthony Norris Groves has been described as a "neglected missiologist", and this might lead us to suppose his influence rather negligible. He never created an organisation that would seek to honour his name or apply his methods. He was criticised and condemned during his own lifetime by Protestant mission leaders in India, which considerably restricted his influence there. His final years were clouded by the failure of his commercial projects. Since then, the inaccessibility of his missiological writings, and the failure of his biographer to attract a significant readership, have perpetuated his obscurity.

Despite this, the missiological influence of Groves is seen to extend far further than is commonly supposed. The principles that we associate with him were propagated both directly and indirectly. They were propagated directly through his personal relationships and the dissemination of his writings, and indirectly through the work of missionaries who, whilst knowing little of him, made similar missiological applications of an ecclesiology they held in common, and derived in part from him.

It was the personal influence of Groves in 1829 that led his brother-in-law George Müller to resign from a missionary society and "live by faith", looking directly to God for guidance and provision. From this point onwards, Groves's views are reflected in the principles adopted by Müller for his Scriptural Knowledge Institution, and in his choice of like-minded missionaries to support, and then in the advice and encouragement he sent them during a period of fifty-two years.

There were aspects of Groves's radical ecclesiology, conveyed largely through Müller, that found a significant place in the Brethren movement, and, through Brethren influence, far beyond it. His emphasis on liberty of ministry, active participation in the body, plural unpaid leadership, spiritual unity and co-operation, and his concepts of sacrificial stewardship, holiness, "light", faith and obedience, all became characteristic of the Open Brethren, and eventually found their way, especially through the university Christian Unions, into wider evangelical circles. From these circles were drawn many nineteenth and twentieth century missionaries, some identified as Brethren and others without such an identity. All owe something to Groves as an early advocate of principles they chose to follow.

In more than a hundred different nations, assemblies have now been planted by missionaries associated with Brethren missionary magazines. The first of these magazines was *The Missionary Reporter*, launched in response to exhortations from Groves himself shortly before his death. Its successor *The Missionary Echo* (*Echoes of Service*) was founded and edited by his eldest son Henry. To Groves may also be attributed the working principle that, in publishing information and forwarding gifts, these magazines and their editors should support, but not direct, missionary activity.

In other respects, the influence of Groves on Brethren missions is less clear-cut. Following his own initial call to Baghdad, and the enthusiasm it aroused, some forty years passed before significant numbers of Brethren workers were being sent overseas. The majority attempted to create assemblies similar to those at home, having no detailed knowledge of Groves's principles for cross-cultural ministry. His non-denominationalism was largely ignored, and the exporting of Brethren traditions, the adoption of methods used by other groups, the development of a quasi-denominational identity, the emphasis on missionary rather than indigenous ministry, and the imposition of administrative authority in certain places, has rendered Brethren missions somewhat alien to Groves's primitivist ideals.

Like Brethren missions, the interdenominational "faith missions" owe to Groves the principle of individually and collectively "living by faith", communicated through George Müller and Hudson Taylor. With some justification Groves has been called the "father of faith missions". These agencies shared his enthusiasm for co-operation with Protestants of all denominations and diverse nationalities, and his willingness to place confidence in recruits unordained and largely uneducated (and in some cases single women), and they followed his premillennialist emphasis on the salvation of individuals rather than the civilising of nations. But Groves's missiological primitivism could not be easily maintained in organisations requiring increasingly complex systems of administration and accountability, and whose agents wished to preserve foreign denominational identities and traditions.

In fact, Groves's idea of using the New Testament as a practical manual of missionary methods was taken up with greatest effect not by Anglo-American missionaries but by indigenous Christian leaders. Notable among these was John Christian Arulappan (who knew him personally), and Bakht Singh and Watchman Nee (who knew of him through others who thought highly of him). These men initiated significant primitivist movements through which many thousands were converted and gathered into flourishing self-propagating indigenous fellowships.

Our concluding assessment of Groves's missiology led us to consider a number of mission theorists, identifying their personal emphases as institutionalist, culturalist or primitivist. We have described Groves as the earliest major primitivist among mission strategists of modern times.

A primitivist approach has been most prominently advocated by Roland Allen, whose views may possibly derive from Brethren rather than Anglican influence and thus owe much to Groves. Nevertheless, primitivist principles have found their warmest acceptance, not among foreign missionaries or missiologists, but among indigenous Christian leaders. The interest of such leaders is focused neither on Western institutions nor their own culture, but on "genuine Christianity" as originally practised in its best and earliest days. This interest, which Groves shared and stimulated, was his single greatest contribution to the work of the Gospel overseas.

For two hundred years, Protestant mission has been largely shaped by the institutionalist principles that Groves abhorred. When he first challenged them, by intervening in the so-called Rhenius Affair, the consequence was to alienate him from the entrenched Anglican institutions of his contemporary India. And yet, in Michael Hollis, we have a former Bishop of Madras prepared to admit that the policies censured by Groves ultimately failed to produce a strong indigenous church, and for the very reasons which Groves identified.

In recent years, anthropological study has magnified the importance of local culture as a determinant of mission strategy, rendering both the institutionalist and primitivist approaches somewhat unfashionable. Only recently do we see a fresh awareness that "the gospel is and must remain essentially countercultural." If this view prevails, we may expect greater interest in Groves during the coming decade.

Indeed, current missiological writing suggests many points of contact with Groves. Bonk advocates a frugal lifestyle, and warns against "money- and power-based strategies and statuses". Eitel encourages "a partnering spirit" from the start of the missionary / convert relationship. Keyes observes that the Church worldwide has ample resources which simply need redistributing. Yohannan advocates the use of Western money for the support of indigenous evangelists. Schwartz warns against Western manipulation through financial dependence. Virgo recommends the "direct sending" of missionaries by congregations, without involving societies. Garrison approves mentoring rather than managing indigenous converts. Muller encourages a more informal style of leadership. Sharp proposes making disciples rather than planting churches.

We begin to see Grovesian missiological perspectives emerging wherever writers question accepted "institutionalist" and "culturalist" theory and practice. Indeed, an increasing awareness of Groves himself may serve to stimulate a more conscious revival of primitivist thought and method in mission circles not previously inclined to give them serious consideration.

Conclusion

The Primitivist Missiology of Anthony Norris Groves:
a radical influence on
nineteenth-century Protestant mission

On his initial tour of India in 1833-4, Anthony Norris Groves observed affluent missionaries amidst poverty, foreign denominations competing for Indian converts, and missionary societies preoccupied with issues of authority, property and finance. His conclusion was a disquieting one: "It must be obvious to all, if the native churches be not strengthened by learning to lean on the Lord instead of man, the political changes of an hour may sweep away the present form of things, so far as it depends on Europeans, and leave not a trace behind."

There followed a declaration of intent: "My earnest desire is to re-model the whole plan of missionary operations so as to bring them to the simple standard of God's word." Some might consider this statement presumptuous, subversive or simply naïve, but it was the first deliberate expression of a primitivist and biblicist strategy that would prove to be of enormous significance to the future history of Protestant cross-cultural mission. Groves asserted, "Much will not be done till we go back again to *primitive principles* and let the nameless poor and their unrecorded and unsung labours be those on which our hopes, under God, are fixed."

The missiology of Groves may be considered the practical application, in a cross-cultural context, of a primitivist ecclesiology reflecting pietistic and "Romantic" trends in contemporary Britain. With no connection to a church denomination or missionary society, he felt able to relate equally to every Christian he met simply on the basis of their common faith in Christ, and he could speak of Christ to a Muslim or Hindu without feeling any obligation to defend or justify the transgressions of churches ancient or modern. He taught from the Bible wherever he had the opportunity, and he stimulated others to do likewise, without attempting to recruit people to a society or a denomination or even a local fellowship. He advocated full co-operation between Protestant Christians for the development of indigenous congregations free from foreign affiliation or control. He denied the traditional distinction between clergy and laity, and he aspired to make disciples rather than organise churches. He encouraged Christians with secular jobs to engage in preaching, teaching and pastoral care, and he encouraged evangelists and Bible teachers to support themselves through secular work. He fostered a form of partnership between itinerant preachers, of any race, and Christians whose secular income could assist in their support. He envisaged the development of indigenous leadership through the participation of converts in church fellowship, ministry and outreach, rather than through enrolment in training institutions. He believed Christian influence to be best exerted, not through acquiring social prominence and political power, but by a frugal and sympathetic adaptation to the people around him. He established local schools, where English and the vernacular were used in teaching the Bible for the conversion of individuals rather than the promotion of Western civilisation. He shunned the forms of organisational accountability to be found in foreign missionary agencies, preferring to "live by faith", responsive to unforeseen circumstances, seeking guidance and provision directly from God.

These ideas and methods he discussed in his journals and especially in his "Letter on Missions to the Heathen" published in 1840, where he suggested that "the work societies endeavour to accomplish can be done better, because more scripturally, by the Church herself." He advised young Indian Christians to ignore Western customs and institutions and to follow, as closely as possible, the teaching and practice of Christ and his apostles, seeing this as a divinely inspired model applicable to every generation and every culture.

Fourteen years later, Henry Venn and Rufus Anderson would propose their "three-self" scheme for congregations to become self-governing, self-supporting and self-propagating, along with their concept of the foreign mission as a scaffolding which must remain until the national church has been firmly built. But Groves had foreseen the difficulties that would face mission executives wishing to transfer weighty administrative and financial responsibilities, and he did so eighty years before Roland Allen drew attention to the problem. Where Venn envisaged the creation by one institution (a foreign mission) of another institution (a national church), Groves drew no distinction between mission and church. And rather than projecting an eventual shift from foreign government, support and propagation to self-government, support and propagation, Groves would start with no organised government, support or propagation at all, expecting these to develop naturally as local believers helped one another develop their own abilities and ministries after the fashion described in the New Testament. With no organisation to oversee, no buildings to maintain, no salaries to pay, his emphasis from the start was on the freedom of local converts to meet together without foreign supervision, and to preach the gospel to their own people without being trained, authorised and paid to do so.

The influence of Groves on his own and subsequent generations has been seriously underrated. This may be attributable partly to the opposition he encountered during his own lifetime, partly to the commercial failures that clouded his final years, and partly to the inaccessibility of his own writings and works about him. Described twenty years ago as a "neglected missiologist", and largely unknown today, his significance might seem somewhat negligible, but to Groves we can trace back ideas that stimulated the birth of a new generation of missions following what have been called "faith principles".

There were aspects of his primitivist ecclesiology, applied especially by his brother-in-law George Müller, that found a significant place in the Brethren movement of the United Kingdom and then throughout the world. It was Groves himself who proposed moves for the support of missionaries living "by faith", through publication of their news in a periodical, *The Missionary Reporter*. A little later his son Henry became a founding editor of its successor, *Echoes of Service*. Brethren associated with these and similar magazines have planted assemblies in more than a hundred different nations, and there are now approximately 2.5 million Christians worldwide identifying themselves as Brethren.

The influence of Groves was equally significant to the founders of the great interdenominational "faith missions". All owe their inspiration to Hudson Taylor, whose "faith principles" can be traced back to Müller and through him to Groves. These three men moved in the same circles, and indeed, financial support for Taylor and his China Inland Mission in its early years came almost entirely from personal friends of Groves. The "faith missions" shared Groves's desire for co-operation with Protestants of all denominations and diverse nationalities, and his willingness to place confidence in recruits unordained and largely uneducated (and in some cases single women), and they followed his premillennialist emphasis on the salvation of individuals rather than the civilising of nations.

With some justification Groves has been called the "father of faith missions". Yet his idea of using the New Testament as a practical manual of missionary methods was taken up with greatest effect not by Anglo-American missionaries but by indigenous Christian leaders. Notable among these was his own disciple John Christian Arulappan, who, in 1840, initiated a rapidly growing network of entirely indigenous fellowships in Madurai province of Tamil Nadu. Arulappan encouraged self-supporting Indian evangelists to travel widely, preaching the gospel, gathering converts for informal meetings, and stimulating the emergence of local leadership. By 1859, he was overseeing work in thirty-three villages with eight hundred believers, and the following year the Anglican *Church Missionary Intelligencer* declared, "It is indeed a new era in Indian missions – that of lay converts going forth, without purse or scrip, to preach the gospel of Christ to their fellow-countrymen, and that with a zeal and life we had hardly thought them capable of." Here, the writer believed, was "the first entirely indigenous effort of the native church at self-extension." It was, in reality, the fulfilment of Groves's vision. At a later date, similar indigenous movements were associated with Bakht Singh in India (whose closest colleagues were great-grandsons of Arulappan), and Watchman Nee in China (who mentions Groves and the Brethren as an early influence).

Lesslie Newbigin has identified three basic elements, three corners to a triangle, which in varying proportions combine to determine the essential strategy adopted by any missionary or missiologist. They are firstly, foreign church custom; secondly, local culture; and thirdly, New Testament principle and practice. It is the third of these "corners" that interested Groves. Indeed, we might identify him as the first major primitivist, or biblicist, among mission strategists.

Newbigin suggests that, in general, the third "corner" will be valued more highly by indigenous Christians than by the agents of Western missionary societies. He comments, "The Bible has operated as an independent source of criticism directed both against the Christianity of the missionaries and against the traditional culture of the tribe." It was this use of the Bible by the Indians themselves that Groves encouraged, and which equipped them to take their own initiatives without waiting for foreign tuition, authorisation or finance.

Like Groves himself, primitivists such as Arulappan, Nee and Singh have taken to its logical conclusion the evangelical belief that the New Testament is inspired, authoritative and endued by right with a status above foreign church custom and local culture. For these indigenous leaders, the New Testament will represent genuine Christianity, untainted by either Western or Eastern accretions. Though generally neglected by missiologists, these primitivist movements have arguably achieved more, in a shorter space of time, than contemporaneous Protestant missions following different principles.

Our research concludes that Anthony Norris Groves should be considered a highly significant radical influence on Protestant mission in the nineteenth century, and indeed to the present day. His missiological thought has much to offer in the context of current controversies, and during the next decade we may anticipate a growing interest in him as an early missiological primitivist.

Stephen Neill, in his *History of Christianity in India*, judges Groves harshly and quite unjustly: "Wherever this man went he created division – frequently, it must be said, with intent." But even Neill will grudgingly admit, "Yet perhaps Groves was nearer to the ideal of independent Indian churches than the established bodies which he so much disliked."[1] This we may consider praise indeed and a fitting conclusion to our study.

---

[1] Neill, *Christianity in India*, 409

Bibliography

The location of rare and archive materials is noted as follows:

AWM	Arab World Ministries, Loughborough, UK
BL	British Library, London, UK
CBA	Christian Brethren Archive, John Rylands University of Manchester, UK
EL	The Evangelical Library, London, UK
EOS	Echoes of Service, Bath, UK
MF	George Müller Foundation, Bristol, UK
OLC	Orchard Learning Centre, University of Birmingham, UK
PP	In private possession of author or of persons known to author
SD	St Deiniol's Library, Hawarden, UK
SOAS	School of Oriental and African Studies, University of London, UK
UC	University of Cambridge Library, UK

Archive copies of *The Christian Witness*, *The Eleventh Hour*, *The Missionary Reporter* and other early Brethren publications are held at CBA.

[Anon], "Church Canons", *The Christian Witness*, Vol. 3 (April 1836), pp.105-146 [CBA]

Acland, Anne, *A Devon Family: The Story of the Aclands* (London, Phillimore, 1981)

Adeney, David H, *China: The Church's Long March* (Ventura, CA, Regal Books, 1985)

Allen, Hubert J B, *Roland Allen: Pioneer, Priest and Prophet* (Grand Rapids, Eerdmans, 1995)

Allen, Roland, *Missionary Methods: St Paul's or Ours?* (London, World Dominion Press, 1912; 2nd edn. 1927) (reissued, Grand Rapids, Eerdmans, 1962)

———, *The Spontaneous Expansion of the Church* (London, World Dominion Press, 1927; 2nd edn. 1960) (reissued, Grand Rapids, Eerdmans, 1962)

———, *Voluntary Clergy* (London, SPCK, 1923)

Allison, R C, *Leaves from the African Jungle* (Kilmarnock, John Ritchie, 1999)

Anderson, Allan, *An Introduction to Pentecostalism: Global Charismatic Christianity* (Cambridge, CUP, 2004).

———, "Signs and Blunders: Pentecostal Mission Issues at "Home and Abroad" in the Twentieth Century", Henry Martyn Centre, 2000; <http://www.martynmission.cam.ac.uk/CSigns.htm>, accessed 9th March 2005).

Appleby, R Scott, "Primitivism as an Aspect of Global Fundamentalism", in Hughes, Richard T (ed.), *The Primitive Church in the Modern World* (Illinois, University of Illinois Press, 1995)

Arnot, Frederick Stanley, *Bihe and Garenganze* (London, 1893)

Arnott, Anne, *The Brethren, an Autobiography of a Plymouth Brethren Childhood* (London and Oxford, Mowbray, 1969, 1982) [CBA]

Austin, Alvyn, "Only Connect: The China Inland Mission and Transatlantic Evangelicalism" in Shenk, Wilbert R (ed.), *North American Foreign Missions 1810-1914: Theology, Theory and Policy* (Grand Rapids, Eerdmans, 2004)

Baago, Kaj, "First Independence Movements", *Indian Church History Review*, 1 (1967)

Baker, Dwight P, "William Carey and the Business Model for Mission", in Bonk, Jonathan (ed.), *Between Past and Future: Evangelical Mission Entering the 21st Century*, (Pasadena, William Carey Library, 2003), pp.167-202

Barabas, Steven, *So great salvation: The history and message of the Keswick Convention* (Marshall, Morgan & Scott, 1952)

Barclay, Oliver R, *Whatever Happened to the Jesus Lane Lot?* (Leicester, Inter-Varsity Press, 1977)

Barton, John (ed.), *The Cambridge Companion to Biblical Interpretation* (Cambridge, Cambridge University Press, 1998)

Bass, Clarence B, *Backgrounds to Dispensationalism: Its Historical Genesis and Ecclesiastical Implications* (Grand Rapids, Baker, 1960; paperback edn. 1977)

Bat Ye'or, *The Dhimmi: Jews & Christians under Islam* (London & Toronto, Associated University Presses, 1985)

Bateman, Josiah, *The Life of the Right Rev Daniel Wilson* (London, J. Murray / Boston, Mass., Gould & Lincoln, 1860)

Bawden, C R, *Shamans, Lamas and Evangelicals: the English missionaries in Siberia* (London, Routledge & Kegan Paul, 1985)

Beattie, David J, *Brethren, the Story of a Great Recovery* (Kilmarnock, John Ritchie Ltd, 1940) [CBA]

Beaver, R Pierce, *The Ecumenical Beginnings in Protestant World Mission: A History of Comity* (New York, Thomas Nelson & Sons, 1962)

──────, *To Advance the Gospel: Selections from the Writings of Rufus Anderson* (Grand Rapids, Eerdmans, 1967)

Bebbington, D W, *Evangelicalism in Modern Britain: A History from the 1730s to the 1980s* (London, Unwin Hyman, 1989; reprint, London, Routledge, 2002)

──────, *Holiness in 19th Century England* (Carlisle, Paternoster, 2000)

Beckett, J C, *The Anglo-Irish Tradition* (London, Faber, 1976)

Bellett, J G, *Early Days: A Series of Letters Showing How the Spirit of God Led in the Recovery of Various Great Truths Relating to the Church, Some Ninety Years Ago* (New York, Loizeaux Brothers, 1920) [CBA]

──────, *Interesting Reminiscences of the Early History of "Brethren", with Letter from J G Bellett to J N Darby* (Weston-Super-Mare, Walter Scott, c.1871) [CBA]

Bellett, L M, *Recollections of the Late J. G. Bellett by his Daughter* (London, Rouse, 1895) [CBA]

Bergin, G Fred, *Autobiography of George Müller*, 3rd edn. (London, 1914) [CBA]

Beyerhaus, Peter, *Die Selbständigkeit der jungen Kirchen als missionarisches Problem* (Wuppertal-Barman, Verlag der Rheinischen Missiongesellschaft, 1956); abridged English version, *The Responsible Church and the Foreign Mission* (Grand Rapids, Eerdmans, 1964)

Birks T R, *Memoir of the Rev Edward Bickersteth* (2 vols., London, 1852; reissued Vancouver, Regent College, 2001/2)

Blaikie, William G, *David Livingstone* (Dunbar, Labarum, 1985)

Bonk, Jonathan (ed.), *Between Past and Future: Evangelical Mission Entering the 21st Century*, (Pasadena, William Carey Library, 2003)

──────, "Ecclesiastical Cartography and the Invisible Continent", *International Bulletin of Missionary Research* 28:4 (Oct 2004), pp.153-4

──────, "Missions and Mammon: Six Theses", *International Bulletin of Missionary Research*, 13:4 (Oct 1989), pp.174-8, 180-1 (CD: *The Best of IBMR*, 2004)

──────, *Missions and Money: Affluence as a Western Missionary Problem* (Maryknoll, Orbis, 1991)

──────, *The Theory and Practice of Missionary Identification (1860-1920)*, (New York, The Edwin Mellen Press, 1990)

Borthwick, Paul, "Reflections on the Lausanne Forum: Seven Open Questions Concerning Global Christian Gatherings", *Evangelical Missions Quarterly*, Vol. 41, No. 2 (April 2005), pp.182-187

Bosch, David J, *Transforming Mission: Paradigm Shifts in Theology of Mission* (New York, Orbis, 1991)

Bowen, Desmond, *The Protestant Crusade in Ireland, 1800-70* (Dublin, Gill & Macmillan, 1978)

Bozeman, Theodore Dwight, *To Live Ancient Lives: The Primitivist Dimension in Puritanism* (Chapel Hill, Univ. of North Carolina Press,1988)

Bradley, Ian, *The Call to Seriousness: The Evangelical Impact on the Victorians* (London, Jonathan Cape, 1976)
Brady, David (ed.), "The Brethren: A Bibliography of Secondary Studies", <http://rylibweb.man.ac.uk/data2/spcoll/cba/sources.html> (accessed 18th July 2005)
Brady, Steve & Rowdon, Harold (eds.), *For Such a Time as This* (Milton Keynes, Scripture Union / London, Evangelical Alliance, 1996)
Brecht, Martin, "The Relationship Between Established Protestant Church and Free Church: Hermann Gundert and Britain", tr. David Meldrum, in Robbins K (1990)
Broadbent, E H, *The Pilgrim Church* (London, Marshall Pickering, 1931, 1989)
Brock, Charles, *The Principles and Practice of Indigenous Church Planting* (Nashville, Broadman Press, 1981)
Brock, P, "The Peace Testimony of the Early Plymouth Brethren", *Church History* 53 (March 1984)
Brockett, Allan, *Nonconformity in Exeter 1650-1875* (Manchester, Manchester University Press, 1962)
Brockington, John, *Hinduism and Christianity* (Houndmills, Macmillan, 1992)
Bromley, E B, *They were Men sent from God: A Centenary Record (1836-1936) of Gospel Work in India amongst Telugus in the Godavari Delta and Neighbouring Parts* (Bangalore, Scripture Literature Press, 1937) [CBA]
Broomhall, A J, *Hudson Taylor and China's Open Century*, Book 1, *Barbarians at the Gates* (London, Hodder, 1981)
——————, Book 2, *Over the Treaty Wall* (London, Hodder, 1982)
——————, Book 3, *If I had a Thousand Lives* (London, Hodder, 1982)
——————, Book 4, *Survivors' Pact* (London, Hodder, 1984)
——————, Book 5, *Refiner's Fire* (London, Hodder, 1985)
——————, Book 6, *Assault on the Nine* (London, Hodder, 1988)
Brown, Judith M and Frykenberg, Robert E (eds.), *Christians, Cultural Interactions and India's Religious Traditions* (Grand Rapids, Eerdmans, 2002)
Brown, Stewart J, *Thomas Chalmers and the Godly Commonwealth in Scotland* (Oxford, OUP, 1982)
Bruce, F F, *The Epistle to the Galatians, a commentary on the Greek text* (Exeter, Paternoster, 1982)
——————, *Paul, Apostle of the Free Spirit* (Exeter, Paternoster, 1977)
Buchanan, Claudius, LL.D., *Memoir of the Expediency of an Ecclesiastical Establishment for British India; both as a Means of Perpetuating the Christian Religion among our own Countrymen; and as a Foundation for the Ultimate Civilization of the Natives* (Cambridge, Mass.: Hilliard and Metcalf, 1805; 2nd edn. 1811); <http://www.wmcarey.edu/carey/buchanan2/est.htm#text> (accessed 12th March 2005)
Buchanan, James, *The religious belief of James Buchanan, British Consul to the United States of America, 1819-1843, formerly of Lisonally, Omagh, addressed to his children and grandchildren, May 1834* (Omagh, J. Quinn, 1955) [CBA]
Bull, Geoffrey T, *The Rock and the Sand: Glimpses of the Life of Faith* (London, Chapter Two, 1990)
Burgon, John William, *Lives of Twelve Good Men*, 3rd edn., Vol. 1 (London, John Murray, 1889)
Burnham, Jonathan David, *The Controversial Relationship between Benjamin Wills Newton and John Nelson Darby*, (Carlisle, Paternoster, 2004)
Burns, Arthur, *The Diocesan Revival in the Church of England c.1800-1870* (Oxford, Clarendon Press, 1999)
Bush, Luis & Lutz, Lorry, *Partnering in Ministry* (Downers Grove, Inter Varsity Press, 1990)
C. [Congleton], *The Open Meeting*, 2nd edn. (London, J E Hawkins, 1877) [CBA]
Cable, Mildred, & French, Francesca, *A Woman Who Laughed* (1st edn., London, CIM, 1934) (2nd edn., Basingstoke, Pickering & Inglis / OMF, 1984)

Caldwell, Robert, *Lectures on the Tinnevelly Missions* (London, Bell & Daldy, 1857)
Callahan, James Patrick, "Claritas Scripturae: The Role of Perspicuity in Protestant Hermeneutics", in *Journal of the Evangelical Theological Society*, 39:3 (Sept. 1996), pp.353-372
——————, *Primitivist Piety: The Ecclesiology of the Early Plymouth Brethren* (Lanham, The Scarecrow Press, 1996)
——————, "The Bible Says: Evangelical and Postliberal Biblicism", in *Theology Today*, Vol. 53, No. 4 (Jan. 1997)
Carey, S Pearce, *William Carey* (London, Hodder & Stoughton, 1926)
Carey, William, *An Enquiry into the Obligations of Christians to use Means for the Conversion of the Heathens* (reproduced in George, Timothy, *Faithful Witness*; Leicester, Inter-Varsity Press, 1991)
Carmichael, Amy, *This One Thing: The Story of Walker of Tinnevelly* (London, Oliphants, 1950)
Carpenter, Joel & Shenk, Wilbert (eds.), *Earthen Vessels: American Evangelicals and Foreign Missions, 1880-1980* (Grand Rapids, Eerdmans, 1990)
Carson, Penny, "The British Raj and the Awakening of the Evangelical Conscience: The Ambiguities of Religious Establishment and Toleration, 1698-1833", in Stanley (ed.), *Christian Missions and the Enlightenment* (Grand Rapids, Eerdmans, 2000), pp.45-70
Carter, Grayson, *Anglican Evangelicals: Protestant Secessions from the Via Media c.1800-1850* (Oxford, OUP, 2001)
Carus, William (ed.), *Memoirs of the Life of the Rev Charles Simeon* (London, Hatchard, 1847)
Cawston, Ray: "Accountability", in ed. Rowdon Harold H, *World Mission Today*, Christian Brethren Review Journal, 36 (Sep. 1985) pp.39-48 [CBA]
——————, "The Church and Mission" in ed. Rowdon Harold H, *Into All the World*, Christian Brethren Review, 40 (1989), pp.16-23 [CBA]
Chadwick, Owen, *The Victorian Church*, 2 vols. (London, A & C Black, 1966, 1970)
Chalmers, Thomas, *Lectures on the Establishment and Extension of National Churches* (London, William Collins, 1838)
Chatterton, Georgina, *Memorials, Personal and Historical of Admiral Lord Gambier* (2 vols., London, Hurst and Blackett, 1861)
Cheung, James Mo-Oi, *The Ecclesiology of the "Little Flock" of China Founded by Watchman Nee*, (Deerfield Ill, Trinity Evangelical Divinity School, unpublished thesis, 1970)
Chilcraft, Stephen J, *Anthony Norris Groves' Theory and Practice of Mission* (Birmingham Christian College, MA dissertation, 2003)
Clark, Henry Martyn, *Robert Clark of the Panjab: Pioneer and Missionary Statesman* (London, Andrew Melrose, 1907)
Cliff, Norman H, *Life and Theology of Watchman Nee: Including a Study of the Little Flock* (Kok Pharos, 1996)
——————, "Watchman Nee: Church Planter and Preacher of Holiness", *Evangelical Review of Theology*, Vol. 8, No.2 (Oct. 1984)
Coad, F Roy, *A History of the Brethren Movement* (Exeter, Paternoster, 1968); reprint (Vancouver, Regent College Publishing, 2001)
Collingwood, William, *The "Brethren": A Historical Sketch* (Glasgow, Pickering & Inglis, 1899) [CBA]
Corwin, Gary, "Church Planting 101", *Evangelical Missions Quarterly*, Vol. 41, No. 2 (April 2005), pp.142-3
Cracknell, Kenneth, *Justice, Courtesy and Love: Theologians and Missionaries Encountering World Religions, 1846-1914* (London, Epworth, 1995)
Cragg, Kenneth, *The Arab Christian: A History in the Middle East* (London, Mowbray, 1991)

Craik, Henry, *New Testament church order: five lectures* (Bristol, W Mack / London, Snow, 1863) [CBA]
Crutchfield, Larry V, *The Origins of Dispensationalism: the Darby Factor* (Lanham, Univ. Pr. of Amer., 1992)
Crawford, Daniel, *Thinking Black*, 2nd edn. (London, 1912)
Dale, R W, *History of English Congregationalism* (London, Hodder & Stoughton, 1907)
Dallimore, Arnold, *The Life of Edward Irving* (Edinburgh, Banner of Truth, 1983)
Daniel, Robin, *This Holy Seed: Faith, Hope and Love in the Early Churches of North Africa* (Harpenden, Tamarisk Publications, 1992)
Daniel, Roy T (ed.), *Prayer Handbook: Indian Commended Workers Working in India and Abroad* (Bangalore, Operation Barnabas, 2002)
Daniels, Gene, *Searching for the Indigenous Church: a missionary pilgrimage* (Pasadena, William Carey Library, 2005)
Danker, William, *Profit for the Lord: Economic activities in Moravian Missions and the Basel Mission Trading Company* (Eugene, Wipf & Stock Publishers, 2002)
Dann, Robert Bernard, *Father of Faith Missions: The Life and Times of Anthony Norris Groves* (Authentic, Waynesboro, 2004)
———, "The Legacy of Anthony Norris Groves", *International Bulletin of Missionary Research*, Vol. 29, No. 4 (Oct. 2005), pp. 198-202
———, *The Primitivist Ecclesiology of Anthony Norris Groves: a radical influence on the nineteenth-century Protestant church in Britain* (Chester, Tamarisk Books, 2006)
Darby, John Nelson, *Collected Writings of J N Darby, ed. W Kelly* (Kingston-on-Thames, Stow Hill Bible and Tract Depot, c.1960) 34 vols [CBA]; CD-Rom, *The Darby Disk*, Stem Publishing
———, The Apostasy of the Successive Dispensations (*Collected Writings*, Vol. 1)
———, The Bethesda Circular (*Collected Writings*, Vol. 15)
———, Considerations on the Nature and Unity of the Church of Christ (*Collected Writings*, Vol. 1)
———, Evidence from Scripture of the Passing Away of the Present Dispensation (*Collected Writings*, Vol. 2)
———, The Hopes of the Church of God, in Connection with the Destiny of the Jews and the Nations, as Revealed in Prophecy: Eleven Lectures delivered in Geneva, 1840 (*Collected Writings*, Vol. 2)
———, The Irrationalism of Infidelity: Being a Reply to "Phases of Faith" (*Collected Writings*, Vol. 6)
———, The Notion of a Clergyman Dispensationally the Sin against the Holy Ghost (*Collected Writings*, Vol. 1)
———, The Rapture of the Saints and the Character of the Jewish Remnant (*Collected Writings*, Vol. 11)
———, Remarks on the State of the Church, in Answer to the Pamphlet of Mr. Rochat (*Collected Writings*, Vol. 1)
———, Separation from Evil God's Principle of Unity (*Collected Writings*, Vol. 1)
———, What the Christian has Amid the Ruin of the Church, being a Reply to Certain Articles in the "Jamaica Magazine" (*Collected Writings*, Vol. 14)
Daughrity, Dyron, *Researching Bishop Stephen Neill*, Henry Martyn Centre, Cambridge, 2003; http://www.martynmission.cam.ac.uk/CDaurighty.htm (accessed 16th July 2005)
Davenport, Rowland A, *Albury Apostles, the Story of the Body Known as the Catholic Apostolic Church* ([Birdup]: United Writers, 1970/3)
Davis G C B, *The Early Cornish Evangelicals 1735-60* (London, SPCK, 1951)
Dickson, Neil, *Brethren in Scotland 1838-2000* (Carlisle: Paternoster, 2003)
———, *Modern Prophetesses* (Records of the Scottish Church History Society, Vol. 25, 1, 1993); reissued (London, Partnership Publications, n.d.) [CBA]
Drummond, Andrew Landale, *Edward Irving and his Circle* (London, James Clarke, 1935)

Drury, Elizabeth & Lewis, Philippa, *The Victorian Household Album* (London, Collins & Brown, 1995)
Duff, A, *India and Indian Missions* (Edinburgh, J Johnstone, 1839)
Dyer, Helen S, *Pandita Ramabai* (Glasgow, Pickering & Inglis, n.d.) [CBA]
Eadie, John, *Life of John Kitto, DD, FSA* (Edinburgh, Oliphant, Anderson & Ferrier, 1886)
Edwardes, Michael, *A History of India* (London, New English Library, 1967)
Edwards, David L, *Christian England*, Vol. 3, From the 18th Century to the First World War (Glasgow, Collins, 1984)
Edwards, Victor, *Concepts of Inculturation in Roland Allen's Missiology: A Critique*, MTh dissertation, University of Liverpool, 1997
Eitel, Keith E, *Paradigm Wars: The Southern Baptist International Mission Board Faces the Third Millennium* (Oxford, Regnum, 2000)
————, "To Be or Not to Be: The Indigenous Church Question", in Terry et al. (eds.), *Missiology: An Introduction to the Foundations, History and Strategies of World Mission* (Nashville, Broadman & Holman, 1998)
Elliot, Elizabeth., *The Journals of Jim Elliot* (Grand Rapids, Fleming H Revel, 1978)
Elliot-Binns, L E, *Religion in the Victorian Era* (London, Lutterworth, 1936)
Embley, Peter L, "The Early Development of the Plymouth Brethren", in Wilson, Bryan R (ed.), *Patterns of Sectarianism* (London, Heinemann, 1967)
Erb, Peter C (ed.), *Pietists: Selected Writings* (London, SPCK, 1983)
Escobar, Samuel, *The New Global Mission: The Gospel from Everywhere to Everyone* (Downers Grove, IVP, 2003)
Ex-Member of the Society of Friends, An, *Open Communion with Liberty of Ministry, the Only Practicable Ground for Real Union amongst Christians*, 4th edn. (London, Central Tract Depot, 1840) [CBA]
Fiedler, Klaus, *The Story of Faith Missions* (Oxford, Regnum, 1994)
Fielder, Geraint, *Lord of the Years* (Leicester, Inter-Varsity Press, 1988)
Fife, Eric S & Arthur F Glasser, *Missions in Crisis* (London, IVF, 1962)
Firth, Cyril Bruce, *An Introduction to Indian Church History*, revised edn. (New Delhi, Indian Society for Promoting Christian Knowledge, 1976)
Fleming, Kenneth C, *Essentials of Missionary Service* (Carlisle, Paternoster, 2000)
Flikkema, B, *Edward Irving, A Bibliography* (Appingedam, Netherlands, privately printed, 1997)
Flood, Gavin, *An Introduction to Hinduism* (Cambridge, CUP, 1996)
Forrest J W, "The Missionary Reporter", *Journal of the Christian Brethren Research Fellowship*, No. 21 (1971), pp.24-42 [CBA]
Foust, Thomas F (ed.), *A Scandalous Prophet: The way of mission after Newbigin* (Grand Rapids, Eerdmans, 2002)
Frykenberg, Robert Eric (ed.), *Christians and Missionaries in India: Cross-Cultural Communication Since 1500* (London, Routledge, 2003)
————, "Christians in India: An Historical Overview of Their Complex Origins", in Frykenberg (ed.), *Christians and Missionaries in India: Cross-Cultural Communication Since 1500*
————, "The Impact of Conversion and Social Reform upon Society in South India during the Late Company Period: Questions Concerning Hindu-Christian Encounters, with Special Reference to Tinnevelly", in Philips, C H & Wainwright, M D (eds.), *Indian Society and the Beginnings of Modernisation c.1830-1850* (London, School of Oriental and African Studies, 1976)
Gairdner, W H T, *"Edinburgh 1910", an account and interpretation of the world missionary conference* (Oliphant, Anderson & Ferrier, 1910)
————, *The Reproach of Islam* (London, Student Volunteer Missionary Union, 1909)
Garrison, David, *Church Planting Movements* (Midlothian, VA, WIGTake Resources, 2004)
George, Timothy, *Faithful Witness: The Life and Mission of William Carey* (Leicester, Inter-Varsity Press, 1991)

Gibbs, M E, *The Anglican Church in India 1600-1970* (New Delhi, Indian Society for Promoting Christian Knowledge, 1972)

Gibson, Dan, *Avoiding the Tentmaker Trap* (Ontario, WEC International, 1997) (CD: *Roland Muller Books*)

Glasser, Arthur F, *Announcing the Kingdom* (Grand Rapids, Baker, 2003)

——— & McGavran, Donald, *Contemporary Theologies of Mission* (Grand Rapids, Baker, 1983)

———, "The Evolution of Evangelical Mission Theology Since World War II", *International Bulletin of Missionary Research*, 9:1 (Jan 1985), pp.9-13 (CD: *The Best of IBMR*, 2004)

Goheen, Michael W, *"As the Father has sent Me, I am sending you": J.E. Lesslie Newbigin's missionary ecclesiology* (Zoetermeer, Boekencentrum, 2000)

Goldingay, John, *Models for Interpretation of Scripture* (Grand Rapids, Eerdmans / Carlisle, Paternoster, 1995)

Goldsmith, Elizabeth, *Roots and Wings* (OM Publishing, 1998)

Grass, Tim, "Edward Irving: Eschatology, Ecclesiology and Spiritual Gifts", in Gribben & Stunt (eds.), *Prisoners of Hope? Aspects of Evangelical Millennialism in Britain and Ireland, 1800-1880* (Carlisle, Paternoster, 2004), pp.95-121

———, *Gathering to his Name: The Unfinished Story of Brethren in Britain and Ireland* (Carlisle: Paternoster, forthcoming)

———, introduction to *The Letters and Papers of Lady Powerscourt* (London, Chapter Two, 2004)

———, "Thomas Dowglass: Evangelist" (*Brethren Archivists and Historians Network Review*, forthcoming)

Grassi, Joseph, *A World to Win: The Missionary Methods of Paul the Apostle* (Maryknoll, Orbis, 1965)

Green, Michael, *Evangelism in the Early Church* (London, Hodder & Stoughton, 1970, 1978)

Gregory, Olinthus, *Works of the Rev Robert Hall* (3 vols., London, Holdsworth & Ball, 1831)

Gribben, Crawford & Stunt, Timothy C F (eds.), *Prisoners of Hope? Aspects of Evangelical Millennialism in Britain and Ireland, 1800-1880* (Carlisle, Paternoster, 2004)

Groves, Anthony Norris, *A Brief Account of the Present Circumstances of the Tinnevelly Mission* (Sidmouth, Harvey, 1835)

———, *Christian Devotedness* (Piccadilly, J Hatchard & Son, 1825); 2nd edn. (London, James Nisbet, 1829); reissued, Belfast, Raven Publishing Company, c.1970; reissued, Kansas City, Walterick, n.d.; Midwest Christian Publishers, n.d. [CBA]; <http://web.ukonline.co.uk/d.haslam/groves/Anthony%20Norris%20Groves.htm> (accessed 9th March 2005)

———, "Correspondence from the East", *The Christian Witness*, Vol. 1 (April 1834), pp.196-201 [CBA]

———, *Journal of a Residence at Bagdad during the years 1830 and 1831, by Mr Anthony N Groves, Missionary*, ed. A J Scott (London, James Nisbet, 1832) [EOS]

———, *Journal of Mr Anthony N Groves, Missionary, during a Journey from London to Bagdad through Russia, Georgia and Persia. Also a Journal of Some Months' Residence in Bagdad* [ed. A J Scott?] (London, James Nisbet, 1831) [MF]

———, "A Letter on Missions to the Heathen", *The Christian Witness*, Vol. 7 (April 1840), pp.127-141 [CBA]

———, *On the Liberty of Ministry in the Church of Christ* (Neyoor/Madras, Albion Press, 1834; Sidmouth, J Harvey, 1835) [CBA]

———, *On the Nature of Christian Influence* (Bombay, American Mission Press, 1833) [CBA]

———, *Remarks on a Pamphlet Entitled "The Perpetuity of the Moral Law"* (Madras, J B Pharoah, 1840) [CBA]

―――――, "Remarks on the Typical Import of the Kingly History of Israel", *The Christian Witness*, Vol. 4 (April 1837), pp.123-136 [CBA]

―――――, *The New Testament in the Blood of Jesus, the Sole Rule of Morals and Discipline to the Christian Church* (Madras, J B Pharoah, 1837)

―――――, *The Present State of the Tinnevelly Mission, Second Edition enlarged with an Historical Preface and Reply to Mr Strachan's Criticisms; and Mr Rhenius's (farewell) Letter to the Church Missionary Society (after receiving his dismissal)* (London, James Nisbet, 1836) [OLC]

―――――, *The Tottenham Case* (Brighton, printed for private circulation, 1849) [CBA]

Groves, Edward K, "An Apology for the Life of Professor F W Newman" (*The Faith*, Feb. 1905, Mar. 1905) [PP]

―――――, *Conversations on "Bethesda" Family Matters* (London, W B Horner, 1885) [CBA/MF]

―――――, *George Müller and his Successors* (Bristol, privately printed, 1906) [EL/MF]

[Groves, Harriet], *Memoir of the Late Anthony Norris Groves, containing extracts from his Letters and Journals, compiled by his Widow*, 1st edn. (London, James Nisbet, 1856; reprint, ed. Kulp, Sumneytown, PA, Sentinel Publications, 2002); 3rd edn. with supplement (London, James Nisbet, 1869) [EOS]

Groves, Henry, *The Battlefield of Faith: A Warning for the Times* (London, H A Raymond, n.d.) [CBA]

―――――, *Darbyism: Its Rise and Development* (London, Houlston & Wright, 1866); 3rd edn. (London, J E Hawkins, c.1880) [CBA]

―――――, *Echoes: A Memorial of the Late Henry Groves, consisting of Brief Expositions from "Echoes of Service"* (Bath, Echoes of Service, 1891) [CBA]

―――――, *Faithful Hanie, or Disinterested Service* (London, J Nisbet, 1866) [CBA]

―――――, *Living by Faith* (London, J F Shaw, n.d.) [CBA]

―――――, *Not of the World: Memoir of Lord Congleton* (London, J F Shaw, 1884) [CBA]

Grubb, Norman P, *C T Studd, Cricketer and Pioneer* (London, 1933); paperback edn. (Fort Washington, CLC, 1972)

―――――, *The Four Pillars of WEC* (London, Worldwide Evangelisation Crusade, 1963)

―――――, *Once Caught No Escape* (London, Lutterworth, 1969)

Gundert, Hermann, *Hermann Gundert: Quellen zu seinem Leben und Werk*, ed. Albrecht Frenz (Ulm, Süddeutsche Verlagsgesellschaft, 1991)

―――――, *Hermann Mögling, A Biography*, tr. C Steinweg and E Steinweg-Fleckner, ed. Albrecht Frenz (Kerala, Kottayam, 1997)

―――――, *The life of Samuel Hebich: by two of his fellow-labourers*, tr. J G Halliday (1876)

―――――, *Schriften und Berichte aus Malabar mit Meditationen und Studien, herausgegeben von Albrecht Frenz, Stuttgart* (Stuttgart, J F Steinkopf Verlag, 1983)

―――――, *Tagebuch aus Malabar 1837-1859, herausgegeben von Albrecht Frenz* (Stuttgart, J F Steinkopf Verlag, 1983) [PP]

Guthrie D, Motyer, J A, Stibbs, A M & Wiseman, D J, *The New Bible Commentary Revised* (London, Inter-Varsity Press, 3rd. edn., 1970)

Halévy, Elie, *History of the English People in the Nineteenth Century* (London, Benn, 1970)

Harper, Susan Billington, *In the Shadow of the Mahatma* (Grand Rapids, Eerdmans, 2000)

―――――, "Ironies of Indigenization: Some Cultural Repercussions of Mission in South India", *International Bulletin of Missionary Research*, 19:1 (Jan 1995), pp.13-16, 18-20 (CD: *The Best of IBMR*, 2004)

Harris, Harriet, *Fundamentalism and Evangelicals* (Oxford, Clarendon Press, 1998)

Harris, Paul William, "Denominationalism and Democracy: Ecclesiastical Issues Underlying Rufus Anderson's Three Self Program" in Shenk, Wilbert R (ed.), *North American Foreign Missions 1810-1914: Theology, Theory and Policy* (Grand Rapids, Eerdmans, 2004)

——————, *Nothing but Christ: Rufus Anderson and the Ideology of Protestant Foreign Missions* (New York, OUP, 1999)
Harrison, J F C, *Early Victorian Britain 1832-51* (Weidenfeld & Nicolson, 1971); (Glasgow, Fontana, 1979)
——————, *The Second Coming: Popular Millenarianism 1780-1850* (London, Routledge & Kegan Paul, 1979)
Haslam, W, *From Death into Life* (London, Morgan & Scott, c.1880); reissued (St Austell, Good News Crusade, 1976)
Hawker, Robert, *The Works of the Rev Robert Hawker D D, Late Vicar of Charles, Plymouth, with a Memoir of His Life and Writings by the Rev John Williams D D*, 10 vols. (London, Ebenezer Palmer, 1831) [SD]
Hawley, Monroe E, *The Focus of Our Faith: A New Look at the Restoration Principle* (Nashville, 20th Century Christian, 1985)
Hawthorn, J., *Dan Crawford* (Pickering & Inglis, London, nd)
Hay, Alex Rattray, *The New Testament Order for Church and Missionary* (Temperley, Argentina, New Testament Missionary Union, 1947)
Hedlund, Roger, *God and the Nations A Biblical Theology of Mission in the Asian Context* (New Delhi, Indian Society for Promoting Christian Knowledge, 2002)
——————, *Roots of the Great Debate in Mission* (McGavran Institute, 1993)
Hempton, "Evangelicalism in English and Irish Society", in Noll, Bebbington and Rawlyk (eds.), *Evangelicalism: Comparative Studies of Popular Protestantism in North America, the British Isles, and Beyond, 1700-1990* (Oxford, Oxford University Press, 1994), pp.156-78
Hendricksen, William, *New Testament Commentary, Romans* (Edinburgh, Banner of Truth, 1980)
Henry, Marie, *The Secret Life of Hannah Whitall Smith* (Grand Rapids, Zondervan, 1984)
Heschel, Abraham Joshua, *God In Search of Man: A Philosophy of Judaism* (New York, Farrar, Straus & Giroux, 1955, 1976)
Hick, John, *God and the Universe of Faiths* (Houndmills, Macmillan, 1988)
Hiebert, Paul, "Critical Contextualisation", *International Bulletin of Missionary Research*, 11:3 (July 1987), pp.104-6, 108-12 (CD: *The Best of IBMR*, 2004)
Hilborn D & Horrocks D, "Universalistic Trends in the Evangelical Tradition: A Historical Perspective" in Parry R and Partridge C (eds), *Universal Salvation*, (Carlisle, Paternoster, 2003)
Hodge, Charles, *Systematic Theology*, Vol. 1 (Grand Rapids, Eerdmans, 1952)
Hodges, Melvin L, *On the Mission Field: The Indigenous Church* (1st edn., Chicago, Moody, 1953); reissued as *The Indigenous Church* (Springfield, Missouri, Gospel Publishing House, 2002)
Hoefer, Herbert E, *Churchless Christianity* (1st edn., 1991; 2nd revised edn. Pasadena, William Carey Library, 2001)
Hollis, Michael, *Paternalism and the Church: A Study of South Indian Church History* (London, OUP, 1962)
Holmes, David L, "Restoration Ideology Among Early Episcopal Evangelicals", in Hughes (ed.), *The American Quest for the Primitive Church* (Illinois, 1995)
Hope, Lady Elizabeth Reid, *General Sir Arthur Cotton: His life and work, by his daughter Lady Hope* (London, Hodder & Stoughton, 1964)
Horne, C Silvester, *David Livingstone* (London, Macmillan, 1912)
——————, *The Story of the L.M.S. With an appendix bringing the story up to the year 1904* (London, London Missionary Society, 1908)
Horrocks, D, *Laws of Spiritual Order: Innovation and Reconstruction in the Soteriology of Thomas Erskine of Linlathen* (Carlisle, Paternoster, 2003)
Houghton, Frank, *Amy Carmichael of Dohnavur* (Fort Washington, Christian Literature Crusade, 1953, 1979)

Hudson, D Dennis, *Protestant Origins in India: Tamil Evangelical Christians 1706-1835* (Grand Rapids, Eerdmans / Richmond, Curzon Press, 2000)
Hughes, Richard T (ed.), *The American Quest for the Primitive Church* (Illinois, University of Illinois Press, 1988)
────── (ed.), *The Primitive Church in the Modern World* (Illinois, University of Illinois Press, 1995)
────── & Allen, C Leonard, *Illusions of Innocence: Protestant Primitivism in America 1630-1875* (Chicago, University of Chicago Press, 1988)
Hyland, K G, "Roland Allen: The Man who Understood New Testament Missionary Principles", *Journal of the Christian Brethren Research Fellowship*, No. 13, Christian Missions Today (Oct. 1966), pp.28-34 [CBA]
Hylson-Smith, Kenneth, *Evangelicals in the Church of England 1734-1984* (Edinburgh, T & T Clark, 1989)
Ingleby, J C, *Missionaries, Education and India: Issues in Protestant Missionary Education in the Long Nineteenth Century* (New Delhi, Indian Society for Promoting Christian Knowledge, 2000)
──────, review of Rowdon, "The Concept of Living by Faith", *Brethren Archivists and Historians Network Review*, Vol. 1, No.1, Autumn 1997, 61-2
Irving, Edward, *For Missionaries After the Apostolical School, A Series of Orations* (London, Hamilton, Adams and Co., 1825) [UC]
Isaacs, Albert A, *A Biographical Sketch Relative To The Missionary Labors of Emma Herdman in the Empire of Morocco* (London, S W Partridge & Co, 1900) [AWM]
Jenkins, Philip, "The Church Missionary Society and the Basel Mission: An Early Experiment in Inter-European Co-operation", in Ward, Kevin & Stanley, Brian (eds.), *The Church Mission Society and World Christianity 1799-1999* (Grand Rapids, Eerdmans, 2000)
──────, *The Next Christendom: the Coming of Global Christianity* (Oxford, OUP, 2002)
Johnson, Todd M, *Countdown to 1900: World Evangelism at the End of the 19th Century* (Birmingham, Alabama, New Hope, 1989);
<http://www.globalchristianity.org/books/c1900/toc.htm> (accessed 1st Aug. 2005)
Johnston, Anna, *Missionary Writing and Empire, 1800-1860* (Cambridge, CUP, 2003)
Johnstone P & Mandryk J, *Operation World* (7th edn., Carlisle, Paternoster, 2001)
Jones, M G, *Hannah More* (Cambridge, CUP, 1952)
Jorgensen, Jonas, "Among the Ruins: Dr. Kaj Baago's Theological Challenge Revisited", <http://www.religion-online.org/showarticle.asp?title=1634> (accessed 22nd April 2005)
Jowett, William, *Christian Researches in the Mediterranean from 1815 to 1820* (London, 1822)
──────, *Christian Researches in Syria and the Holy Land in 1823 and 1824* (London, 1825)
Jukes, Andrew John, "[Letter] to the gatherings of brethren, meeting in the name of the Lord, at Leeds and Otley in Yorkshire [concerning Bethesda Chapel, Bristol.]", Hull, [n. publ.,] 1848 [CBA]; http://mikevinson.home.mindspring.com/fellowshipletter.html> (accessed 9th March 2005)
Keener, Craig S, *A Commentary on the Gospel of Matthew* (Grand Rapids, Eerdmans, 1999)
Kelly, William, *The Brethren* (Jersey, Tract Depot, c.1852) [CBA]
Kerr-Jarrett, Andrew, *Life in the Victorian Age* (London, Reader's Digest, 1993, 1994)
Keyes, Lawrence, *The Last Age of Missions: A Study of Third World Missionary Societies* (Pasadena, William Carey Library, 1983)
Kinnear, Angus I, *Against the Tide: The Story of Watchman Nee* (Fort Washington, Christian Literature Crusade, 1973)
────── (ed), *A Table in the Wilderness: Daily meditations from the ministry of Watchman Nee* (Eastbourne, Kingsway, p/b edn. 1969)

Kirk, J Andrew, *The Mission of Theology and Theology as Mission* (Harrisburg, PA, Trinity Press International, 1997)

——————, *What is Mission? Theological Explorations* (London, Dartman, Longman & Todd, 1999)

Klausner, Joseph, *Jesus of Nazareth: His Life, Times and Teaching*, trans Danby, H (Boston, Beacon Press, 1964)

Klostermaier, K, *A Survey of Hinduism* (Albany, SUNY Press, 1994)

Knight, W, *The Missionary Secretariat of Henry Venn BD* (Longmans, London, 1880)

Knoepflmacher, U C, Introduction to Newman, F W: *Phases of Faith*, 6th edn. (Leicester University Press, 1970)

Koshy, T E, *Brother Bakht Singh of India: An Account of 20th Century Apostolic Revival* (Secunderabad, OM Books, 2003)

——————, "Brother Bakht Singh: A Saint of God", <http://www.BrotherBakhtSingh.org> (accessed 9th March 2005)

Kraft, Charles H, *Christianity in Culture* (Maryknoll, Orbis, 1979)

——————, "The Church in Culture: A Dynamic Equivalence Model", in Stott R W & Coote R (eds.), *Down to Earth: Studies in Christianity and Culture* (London, Hodder & Stoughton, 1980),

Kreider, Alan, "Beyond Bosch: The Early Church and the Christendom Shift", *International Bulletin of Missionary Research*, Vol. 29, No.2 (April 2005)

Laing, Mark, "Donald McGavran's Missiology: An Examination of the Origins and Validity of Key Aspects of the Church Growth Movement", *Indian Church History Review*, XXXVI/1 (2002)

Lang, George H, *Anthony Norris Groves, Saint and Pioneer: A Combined Study of a Man of God and of the Original Principles and Practices of the Brethren with Application to Present Conditions* (1939); 2nd edn. (London, Paternoster, 1949); reprint (Haysville, NC, Schoettle Publishing, 2001)

——————, *The History and Diaries of an Indian Christian, J C Aroolappen* (London, Thynne & Co. Ltd, 1939); reprint (Haysville, NC, Schoettle Publishing, 2001)

——————, *An Ordered Life: An Autobiography* (London, Paternoster Press, 1959; reprint, Miami Springs, Schoettle, 1988)

Larsen, Timothy, "'Living by Faith': A Short History of Brethren Practice", *Brethren Archivists and Historians Network Review*, Vol. 1, No. 2 (Winter 1998), pp.67-102 [CBA]

Latourette, Kenneth Scott, *Christianity in a Revolutionary Age*, Vol. 3, *The Nineteenth Century Outside Europe* (New York, Harper & Row, 1970)

——————, *A History of the Expansion of Christianity*, Vol. 6, *Northern Africa and Asia 1800-1914*, (New York, Harper & Brothers, 1944); reissued (New York, Harper & Row / Exeter, Paternoster, 1971)

Lee, Sydney (ed.), *Dictionary of National Biography* (London, Smith, Elder & Co, 1893)

Lehmann, Arno, *It Began at Tranquebar*, tr. M J Lutz (Madras, Christian Literature Society, 1956)

Lehmann, Hartmut, "'Community' and 'Work' as Concepts of Religious Thought in Eighteenth-Century Würtemburg Pietism", in Robbins K (1990)

Lewis A J, *Zinzendorf the Ecumenical Pioneer, A Study in the Moravian Contribution to Christian Mission and Unity* (London, SCM, 1962)

Lewis, Donald M (ed.), *The Blackwell Dictionary of Evangelical Biography 1730-1860*, 2 vols. (Oxford, Blackwell, 1995)

Livingstone, David, *Missionary Travels and Researches in South Africa* (London: John Murray, 1857)

Lovegrove, Deryck W, *Established Church, Sectarian People: Itinerancy and the Transformation of English Dissent, 1780-1830* (Cambridge, Cambridge University Press, 1988, 2004)

―――――――, "Unity and Separation: Contrasting Elements in the Thought and Practice of Robert and James Alexander Haldane", in Robbins K (1990)

Lovett, Richard, *The History of the London Missionary Society, 1795-1895*, 2 vols. (London, Henry Frowde, 1899)

Lutz, Jessie G & Lutz, R Ray, "Karl Gützlaff's Approach to Indigenization: The Chinese Union", in Bays, Daniel H (ed.), *Christianity in China, From the Eighteenth Century to the Present* (Stanford, CA, Stanford University Press, 1996), pp.269-291

Lutz, Lorry & Bush, Luis, "Partnership: The New Direction in World Evangelism", <www.qd2000.org/adoption/coop/fuldoc/fppart.htm> (accessed 4th Aug. 2004)

Lyell, Leslie, *Three of China's Mighty Men* (London, OMF, 1973); new edn. (Tain, Ross, Christian Focus, 2000)

[Mann, Horace], "Census of Great Britain, 1851: Religious Worship. England and Wales", 1853, *British Parliamentary Papers LXXXIX: Religious Worship (England and Wales): Report* (Vol. 10, British Parliamentary Papers, Irish University Press, 1970)

Marsden, George, "Everyone One's Own Interpreter? The Bible, Science, and Authority in Mid-Nineteenth-Century America," in Hatch N & Noll M (eds.), *The Bible in America* (New York, Oxford University Press, 1982)

Marsh, Charles, *Too Hard for God?*, 2nd edn.(Carlisle, Paternoster, 2000)

Marshman, John Clark, *The Life and Times of Carey, Marshman and Ward, Embracing the History of the Serampore Mission*, 2 vols. (London, Longman, Brown, Green, Longmans & Roberts, 1859)

Martin, Roger H, *Evangelicals United: Ecumenical Stirrings in Pre-Victorian Britain, 1795-1830* (London, Scarecrow Press, 1983)

Maxwell, Ian Douglas, "Civilization or Christianity? The Scottish Debate on Mission Methods, 1750-1835", in Stanley (ed.), *Christian Missions and the Enlightenment* (Grand Rapids, Eerdmans, 2000), pp.123-40

McCallum, Dennis H, "Watchman Nee and the House Church Movement in China", <http://www.xenos.org/essays/neeframe.htm> (accessed 9th March 2005)

McGavran, Donald A, *Effective Evangelism: A Theological Mandate* (Phillipsburg, Presbyterian & Reformed, 1988)

―――――――, *The Founders of the Indian Church* (Chennai, The Church Growth Association of India, 1998)

―――――――, "The Dimensions of World Evangelisation", Lausanne Congress strategy paper, 1974

―――――――, *Understanding Church Growth*, 3rd edn., ed. C Peter Wagner (Grand Rapids, Eerdmans, 1980)

McIntosh, Gary L (ed.), *Evaluating the Church Growth Movement* (Grand Rapids, Zondervan, 2004)

McLeod, Hugh, *Religion and Society in England, 1850-1914* (Basingstoke, Macmillan, 1996)

McQuilkin, Robertson, "Avoiding Dependency: Should We Stop Sending Missionaries?" at <http://www.missionsfestvancouver.ca/Common/articles.html> (accessed 6th Sep. 2005)

Millar, A A, *Alexander Duff of India* (Edinburgh, Cannongate Books, 1992)

Miller, Jon, *The Social Control of Religious Zeal: A Study of Organizational Contradictions* (New Brunswick, Rutgers University Press, 1994)

Millington, Constance M, *Led by the Spirit, A Biography of Bishop Arthur Michael Hollis* (Asian Trading Corporation, 1996)

Minister of the Established Church, A, *The Perpetuity of the Moral Law; being a Reply to Mr Groves's Book Entitled, The New Testament in the Blood of Jesus, the Sole Rule of Morals and Discipline to the Christian Church* (Madras, J B Pharoah, 1838) [CBA]

Mitchell, J M, *Memoir of the Rev Robert Nesbit* (London, Nisbet, 1858)

Moltmann, Jürgen, *Religion, Revolution and the Future* (New York, Charles Scribner's, 1969)

Morris, James, *Pax Britannica: The Climax of an Empire* (Harmondsworth, Penguin, 1979)
Morris, Jeremy, *F. D. Maurice and the Crisis of Christian Authority* (Oxford, OUP, 2005)
Müller, George, *A Narrative of Some of the Lord's Dealings with George Müller* (1837); 9th edn, 4 vols. (London, J Nisbet & Co, 1895) [CBA]; http://jcsm.org/StudyCenter/articles/1629.html (accessed 15th July, 2005)
──────, "The Second Coming of Christ" in [editor unknown], *The Second Coming of Christ* (Chicago, Moody Press, 1896), pp.58-72
Muller, Roland, *Missionary Leadership by Motivation and Communication* (Tinicum, Xlibris, 2000) (CD: *Roland Muller Books*)
──────, *Missions: The Next Generation* (Tinicum, Xlibris, 2003) (CD, *Roland Muller Books*)
Murray, Iain H, *The Puritan Hope, A Study in Revival and the Interpretation of Prophecy* (Edinburgh, Banner of Truth, 1971)
Murray, Stuart & Wilkinson-Hayes, Anne, *Hope from the Margins: New Ways of Being Church* (Cambridge, Grove Books, 2000)
Mutenda, Kovina L K, *A History of the Christian Brethren (Christian Missions in Many Lands) in Zambia* (Chingola, Christian Resource Centre, 2002)
Neatby, William Blair, *A History of the Plymouth Brethren*, 2nd edn. (London, Hodder & Stoughton, 1902); reprint (Stoke-on-Trent, Tentmaker Publications, 2001) [PP]; <http://www.schneid9.de/pdf/neatby.pdf> (accessed 9th March 2005)
Nee, Watchman, *Concerning Our Missions* (1939); reissued as *The Normal Christian Church Life* (Anaheim, CA, Living Stream Ministry, 1980)
──────, *The Orthodoxy of the Church* (1945); reissued (Anaheim, CA, Living Stream Ministry, 1994)
Needham, Nicholas R, *Thomas Erskine of Linlathen: His Life and Theology 1788-1837* (Edinburgh, Rutherford House Books, 1990)
Neill, Stephen, *Colonialism and Christian Mission* (London, 1966)
────────── et al. (eds.), *Concise Dictionary of the Christian World Mission* (London, Lutterworth, 1971)
──────, *Creative Tension, The Duff Lectures 1958* (London, Edinburgh House Press, 1959)
──────, *A History of Christian Missions* (Harmondsworth, Penguin, 1964)
──────, *A History of Christianity in India, 1707-1858* (Cambridge, CUP, 1985)
──────, *The Story of the Christian Church in India and Pakistan* (Grand Rapids, Eerdmans, 1970)
Neusner, Jacob, *Between Time and Eternity: The Essentials of Judaism* (Encino CA, Dickenson Publishing Company, 1975)
──────, *The Way of the Torah: An Introduction to Judaism*, 2nd edn. (Encino CA, Dickenson Publishing Company, 1974)
Nevius, John L, *The Planting and Development of Missionary Churches* (Monadnock Press, 2003)
Newbigin, Lesslie, "Cross-currents in Ecumenical and Evangelical Understandings of Mission", *International Bulletin of Missionary Research*, 6:4 (Oct 1982), pp.146-51 (CD: *The Best of IBMR*, 2004)
──────, *The Gospel in a Pluralistic Society* (London, SPCK, 1989)
──────, *The Household Church* (New York, Friendship Press, 1954)
──────, *The Open Secret: An Introduction to the Theology of Mission* (revised edn., London, SPCK, 1995)
────────── & Jackson, Eleanor (eds.), *A Word in Season: Perspectives on Christian World Missions* (Edinburgh, Saint Andrew Press, 1994)
──────, *Unfinished Agenda* (Edinburgh, St Andrews Press, 1993)
Newell, Jonathan, "'Not War but Defence of the Oppressed?': Bishop Mackenzie's Skirmishes with the Yao in 1861", *The Society of Malawi Journal*, Vol. 45/1 (1992) pp.15-46

Newell, J P, *A J Scott and his Circle* (Edinburgh University, PhD thesis, 1981)
Newman, Francis William, *Personal Narrative in Letters, principally from Turkey in the Years 1830-3* (London, 1856)
——, *Phases of Faith* (1850); 6th edn. reprint with introduction by U C Knoepflmacher (Leicester University Press, 1970)
Newman, John Henry, *Apologia Pro Vita Sua* (Glasgow, Collins, reprint 1977)
Newton, Ken J, "Anthony Norris Groves (1795-1853): A Neglected Missiologist", *Journal of the Christian Brethren Research Fellowship* (Australia), Vol. 60 (1985) [CBA]
——, *Brethren Missionary Work in Mysore State* (Scripture Literature Press, Malvalli, 1971; Christian Brethren Research Fellowship Occasional Paper No. 6, Pinner, 1975) [CBA]
——, "Christian Brethren, World Mission and an Australian Contribution", *Brethren Archivists and Historians Network Review*, Vol. 1, No. 1 (Autumn 1997), pp.3-9 [CBA]
Niebuhr, H R, *Christ and Culture* (New York, Harper, 1951)
Nissen, Johannes, *New Testament and Mission: Historical and Hermeneutical Perspectives* (2nd edn., Frankfurt, Peter Lang, 2002)
Noble, John, *A Memoir of the Rev Robert Turlington Noble, Missionary to the Telugu People in South India* (London, Seeley, Jackson & Halliday, 1867)
Nockles, Peter B, "Church Parties in the pre-Tractarian Church of England 1750-1833: the 'Orthodox' – some problems of definition and identity", in Walsh J, Haydon C & Taylor S, *The Church of England c.1689-c.1833: From Toleration to Tractarianism* (Cambridge, CUP, 1993) pp.334 -359
——, *The Oxford Movement in Context: Anglican High Churchmanship 1760-1857* (Cambridge, CUP, 1994)
Noll, Mark A, *Between Faith and Criticism: Evangelicals, Scholarship and the Bible* (Leicester, Apollos, 1991)
——, "Primitivism in Fundamentalism and American Biblical Scholarship: A Response", in Hughes, *The Primitive Church in the Modern World* (University of Illinois Press, 1995)
——, Bebbington, David W, Rawlyk, George A (eds.), *Evangelicalism: Comparative Studies of Popular Protestantism in North America, the British Isles, and Beyond, 1700-1990* (Oxford, Oxford University Press, 1994)
O'Brien, Dave, "Between the Dark and the Daylight", *Evangelical Missions Quarterly*, Vol. 41, No. 3 (July 2005), pp.354-60
Oddie, Geoffrey A, "India: Missionaries, Conversion, and Change", in Ward, Kevin & Stanley, Brian (eds.), *The Church Mission Society and World Christianity 1799-1999* (Grand Rapids, Eerdmans, 2000)
Oliphant, M O W, *The Life of Edward Irving*, 2nd edn., 2 vols. (London, Hurst & Blackett, 1862)
Orr, J Edwin, *The Second Evangelical Awakening in Britain* (London & Edinburgh, Marshall Morgan & Scott, 1949)
Oussoren, A H, *William Carey, Especially His Missionary Principles* (Leiden, A W Sijthoff's, 1945)
Padwick, Constance E, *Henry Martyn, Confessor of the Faith* (London, Inter-Varsity Press, 1922, 1953)
——, *Temple Gairdner of Cairo* (London, Society for Promoting Christian Knowledge, 1930)
Partridge, Christopher (ed.), *Fundamentalisms* (Carlisle, Paternoster, 2002)
Paton, David M, *Christian Missions and the Judgment of God* (London, SCM, 1952)
Perkin H, *The Origins of Modern English Society 1780-1880* (London, Routledge & Kegan Paul, 1969)
Peterson, Robert L, *Robert Chapman: A Biography* (Neptune, Lewis & Roth, 1995)
Pettitt, George, *Narrative of affairs in the Tinnevelly Mission, connected with the return of the Rev C. Rhenius* [BL]

——————, *Remarks on some parts of Mr Groves' Pamphlet on the Tinnevelly Mission* (1836)

——————, *The Tinnevelly Mission of the Church Missionary Society* (London, Seeleys, 1851) [BL]

Pfander, C G, Letter dated 20 Oct. 1829 in *Gazette des Missions Evangéliques*, 19, 1 Feb. 1830 (Basel, Basel Mission) [PP]

Philip, Johnson C, "The Brethren Movement in India", <http://www.biblebeliever.co.za/Brethren%20Assemblys/Brethren%20Information/Brethren%20Movement%20in%20Indiar.htm> (accessed 9th March 2005)

Philip, T V, *Edinburgh to Salvador: Twentieth Century Ecumenical Missiology* (Delhi, CSS/ISPCK, 1999); <http://www.religion-online.org/showbook.asp?title=1573> (accessed 11th March 2005)

Phillips, J B, *New Testament Christianity* (London, Hodder & Stoughton, 1956)

Pickering, Henry, *Chief Men among the Brethren* (London, 1918); reissued (Neptune, NJ, Loizeaux Bros, 1961) [CBA/MF]

Pierson, Arthur T, "Antagonism to the Bible", *Our Hope*, 15 (Jan 1909)

——————, *George Müller of Bristol* (London, Pickering & Inglis, 1899, 1972)

Piggin, F Stuart, *Making Evangelical Missionaries, 1789-1858: The Social Background, Motives and Training of British Missionaries in India* (Sutton Courtenay Press, 1984)

—————— & Roxborogh, John, *The St Andrews Seven* (Edinburgh, Banner of Truth, 1985)

Porter, Andrew, "'Commerce and Christianity': The Rise and Fall of a Nineteenth-Century Missionary Slogan", *Historical Journal* 28, 3 (1985), pp.597-621

—————— (ed.), *The Imperial Horizons of British Protestant Missions, 1880-1914* (Grand Rapids, Eerdmans, 2003)

——————, *Religion Versus Empire? British Protestant Missionaries and Overseas Expansion 1700-1914* (Manchester Univ. Press, 2004)

Potts, E D, *British Baptist Missionaries in India, 1793-1837*, Cambridge, CUP, 1967

Powell, Avril Ann, *Muslims and Missionaries in Pre-Mutiny India* (Richmond, Curzon Press, 1993)

Pratt J H (ed.), *The Thought of the Evangelical Leaders: Notes of the Discussions of the Eclectic Society, London, during the Years 1798-1844* (Edinburgh, Banner of Truth, 1978)

Price Charles & Randall, Ian M, *Transforming Keswick* (Carlisle, Paternoster, 2000)

Prickett, Stephen (ed.), *The Context of English Literature: The Romantics* (London, Methuen, 1981)

Pulleng, A, *Go Ye Therefore* (London, Paternoster, 1958)

Railton, Nicholas M, *Transnational Evangelicalism: The Case of Friedrich Bialloblotzky (1799-1869)* (Göttingen, Vandenhoek & Ruprecht, 2002)

Rajamani, R R (with Kinnear, Angus I), *Monsoon Daybreak* (London & Eastbourne, Open Books, Associated Christian Publishers, 1971) [PP]

Randall, Ian & Hilborn, David, *One Body in Christ: The History and Significance of the Evangelical Alliance* (Carlisle, Paternoster, 2001)

Read, William, Montserro, Victor & Johnson, Haron, *Latin American Church Growth* (Grand Rapids, Eerdmans, 1969)

Reardon, Bernard M G, *Religion in the Age of Romanticism: Studies in early Nineteenth-Century Thought* (Cambridge, CUP, 1985)

Rennie, Ian S, "Evangelicals and English Public Life 1823–50", unpublished thesis, Univ. of Oxford, Diss. Films 533 (microfilm),

——————, "Fundamentalism and the Varieties of North Atlantic Evangelicalism", in Noll, Bebbington and Rawlyk, (eds.), *Evangelicalism: Comparative Studies of Popular Protestantism in North America, the British Isles, and Beyond, 1700-1990* (Oxford, Oxford University Press, 1994), pp.333-350

——————, "Nineteenth Century Roots", in Carl Amerding (ed.), *Handbook of Biblical Prophecy* (Grand Rapids, Baker Book House, 1977)

Rhenius, Carl Gottlieb Ewald, *Reply to the statement of the Madras Corresponding Committee of the Church Missionary Society respecting the Tinnevelly Mission... To which is appended a narrative of occurrences which led to his return and renewed settlement in Tinnevelly, 1835* (Madras, Athenæum Press, 1836)

Rhenius, Josiah, *Memoir of the Rev C T E Rhenius, Comprising Extracts from His Journal and Correspondence, with details of Missionary Proceedings in South India* (London, Nisbet, 1841) [SD]

Richter, Julius, *A History of Protestant Missions in the Near East* (Edinburgh, Oliphant, Anderson & Ferrier, 1910)

Rickett David & Welliver Dotsey (eds.), *Supporting Indigenous Ministries, With Selected Readings* (Billy Graham Center, 1997)

————, *Building Strategic Relationships: A Practical Guide to Partnering With Non-Western Missions* (Wine Press Publishing, 2003)

Robbins, Keith (ed.), *Protestant Evangelicalism: Britain, Ireland, Germany and America, c.1750 - c.1950* (Oxford, Basil Blackwell, 1990)

Robbins, William, *The Newman Brothers* (London, Heinemann, 1966)

Robert, Dana L, "'The Crisis of Missions': Premillennial Mission Theory and the Origins of Independent Evangelical Missions" in Carpenter, Joel & Shenk, Wilbert (eds.), *Earthen Vessels: American Evangelicals and Foreign Missions, 1880-1980* (Grand Rapids, Eerdmans, 1990)

————, *Occupy Until I Come: A.T. Pierson and the Evangelization of the World* (Grand Rapids, Eerdmans, 2003)

Rogers, Richard Lee, "'A Bright and New Constellation': Millennial Narratives and the Origins of American Foreign Missions" in Shenk, Wilbert R (ed.), *North American Foreign Missions 1810-1914: Theology, Theory and Policy* (Grand Rapids, Eerdmans, 2004)

Rosman, Doreen, *Evangelicals and Culture* (London, Croom Helm, 1984)

Rowdon, Harold H, "The Brethren Contribution to World Mission", in Rowdon (ed.), *The Brethren Contribution to the Worldwide Mission of the Church* (Carlisle, Paternoster, 1994), pp.37-46

————, "The Concept of 'Living by Faith'", in Billington, Lane & Turner, *Mission and Meaning* (Carlisle, Paternoster, 1995)

————, (ed.) *International Partnership Perspectives* Nos. 3, 4 (Carlisle, Paternoster, 2001, 2002)

————, *The Origins of the Brethren 1825-1850* (London, Pickering & Inglis, 1967) [CBA]

Rowlandson, Maurice, *Life at the Keswick Convention* (Carlisle, Authentic, 1997)

Russell G W E, *Lady Victoria Buxton: A memoir with some account of her husband* (London, Longman, 1919)

Ryland, J E, *Memoirs of John Kitto DD, FSA* (Edinburgh, Oliphant, 1856) [SD]

Samuel, Vinay & Sugden, Chris, "Mission Agencies as Multinationals", *International Bulletin of Missionary Research*, 7:4 (Oct 1983), pp.152-5 (CD: *The Best of IBMR*, 2004)

Sandeen, Ernest R, *The Roots of Fundamentalism* (Grand Rapids, Baker Book House, 1970)

Sargent, John, *A Memoir of the Rev Henry Martyn* (12th edn., London, Seeley & Burnside, 1835); reissued as *The Life and Letters of Henry Martyn* (Edinburgh, Banner of Truth, 1985)

Schaff, Philip, *History of the Christian Church*, Vol. 3 (Grand Rapids, Eerdmans, 1910, 1989)

Schapera, I (ed.), *Livingstone's Missionary Correspondence 1841-1856* (London, Chatto & Windus, 1961)

Schlabach, Theron F, "Renewal and Modernization among American Mennonites, 1800-1980: Restorationist?", in Hughes, *The Primitive Church in the Modern World* (1995)

Schwartz, Glenn, "How the Current Emphasis on Dependency and Self-Reliance is being Perceived and Received" <http://www.wmausa.org/paper1-schwartz.htm> (accessed 19th July 2005)

Scotland, Nigel, *Sectarian Religion in Contemporary Britain* (Carlisle, Paternoster, 2000)

Serpel, R C F, "Some Plymouth Clergy of the Past", *Proceedings of the Plymouth Athenaeum*, v (1982)

Severn, Frank M, "Mission Societies: Are they biblical?", *Evangelical Missions Quarterly*, Vol. 36, No. 3 (July 2000), pp.320-6)

Sharp, Larry, "Are We Really about Church Planting?", *Evangelical Missions Quarterly*, Vol. 41, No. 3 (July 2005), pp.280-281

Shenk, Wilbert R, *Henry Venn: Missionary Statesman* (New York, Orbis, 1983)

——————— (ed.), *North American Foreign Missions 1810-1914: Theology, Theory and Policy* (Grand Rapids, Eerdmans, 2004)

———————, "Toward a Global Church History", *International Bulletin of Missionary Research*, 20:2 (April 1996), pp.50-4, 56-7 (CD: *The Best of IBMR*, 2004)

——————— (ed.), *The Transfiguration of Mission* (Scottdale, PA, Herald Press, 1993)

Short, Arthur Rendle, *A Modern Experiment In Apostolic Missions* (Bristol, W B Harris, n.d.)

Sibree, James, *London Missionary Society: a register of missionaries, deputations etc. from 1796 to 1923* (4th edn., London, London Missionary Society, 1923) [SOAS]

Sieveking, I Giberne, *Memoir and Letters of Francis W Newman* (London, Kegan Paul, Trench, Trübner & Co. Ltd, 1909)

Smalley, William A, "Cultural Implications of an Indigenous Church", *Practical Anthropology* Vol.5 No.2 (March-April 1958)

———————, "Some Questions about Missionary Medicine", *Practical Anthropology* Vol.6 (1959), pp.90-5

Smith, A Christopher, "A Tale of Many Models: The Missiological Significance of the Serampore Trio", *Missiology* 20, (1992), pp.479-500

Smith, Daniel, *Bakht Singh of India, a Prophet of God* (Washington, International Students Press, 1959) [PP]

Smith, David, "Fundamentalism and the Christian Mission" in Partridge, Christopher (ed.), *Fundamentalisms* (Carlisle, Paternoster, 2002), pp.264-78

Smith, George, *The Life of Alexander Duff*, 2 vols. (London, Hodder & Stoughton, 1879) [SD]

———————, *The Life of William Carey, Shoemaker and Missionary* (London, Murray, 1885) [SD]; <http://www.biblebelievers.com/carey> (accessed 9th March 2005)

Smyth, C, *Simeon & Church Order: A Study of the Origins of the Evangelical Revival in Cambridge in the Eighteenth Century* (Cambridge, CUP, 1940)

Spangenberg, A G, *The Life of Nicolas Lewis Count Zinzendorf* (London, Holdsworth, 1838)

Stackhouse, Max & Dearborn, Tim & Paeth, Scott (eds.), *The Local Church in a Global Era: Reflections for a New Century* (Grand Rapids, Eerdmans, 2000)

Stanes, Robin, *Stanes History 1771-1964, City of London and South India* (UK, privately printed, 2001) [CBA]

Stanley, Brian, *The Bible and the Flag: Protestant Missions and British Imperialism in the Nineteenth and Twentieth Centuries* (Leicester, Apollos IVP, 1990)

———————, "Christianity and Civilization in English Evangelical Mission Thought, 1792-1857", in Stanley (ed.), *Christian Missions and the Enlightenment* (Grand Rapids, Eerdmans, 2000)

———————, "'Christianity and Commerce': Providence Theory, the missionary movement and the Imperialism of Free Trade", *Historical Journal* 26, 1 (1983), pp.71-94

——————— (ed.), *Christian Missions and the Enlightenment* (Grand Rapids, Eerdmans, 2000)

———————, *The History of the Baptist Missionary Society, 1792-1992* (Edinburgh, Clark, 1992)

————, "Planting Self-governing Churches: British Baptist Ecclesiology in the Missionary Context", *Baptist Quarterly*, 34 (1992), pp.378-89.

Stassen, Glen H, Yeager, D M & Yoder, J H, *Authentic Transformation: a new vision of Christ and culture* (Nashville, Abingdon Press, 1996)

Steele, Francis R, *Not in Vain: The Story of North Africa Mission* (Pasadena, William Carey Library, 1981)

Steer, Roger, *George Müller, Delighted in God* (Wheaton, Harold Shaw / Sevenoaks, Hodder, 1981)

Steffan, Tom, *Passing the Baton* (Center for Organizational and Ministry Development, 2nd edn., 2000)

————, "Phasing out your work: Make it a plan not a crisis", *Evangelical Missions Quarterly* Vol. 27, No.3 (1991)

Stephen, James, *Essays in Ecclesiastical Biography* (London, Longmans, 1907)

Stern, Henry A, *Dawnings of Light in the East; with Biblical, Historical and Statistical Notices of Persons and Places Visited During a Mission to the Jews in Persia, Coordistan and Mesopotamia* (London, Charles H Purday, 1854)

Stewart, Kenneth J, "A Millennial Maelstrom: Controversy in the Continental Society in the 1820s" in Gribben & Stunt (eds.), *Prisoners of Hope? Aspects of Evangelical Millennialism in Britain and Ireland, 1800-1880* (Carlisle, Paternoster, 2004), pp.122-49

Stirling, A M W, *The Ways of Yesterday, Chronicles of the Way Family from 1307 to 1885* (London, Thornton Butterworth, 1930)

Stock, Eugene, *The History of the Church Missionary Society*, 3 vols. (London, Church Missionary Society, 1899)

Stoeffler, F Ernest, *The Rise of Evangelical Pietism* (Leiden, E J Brill, 1965)

Stott R W & Coote R (eds.), *Down to Earth: Studies in Christianity and Culture* (London, Hodder & Stoughton, 1980)

Strachan, C Gordon, *The Pentecostal Theology of Edward Irving* (London, Darton, Longman & Todd, 1973)

Strachan, J M, *Mr Groves' Brief Account of the Tinnevelly Mission Examined, in a Letter to a Provincial Member of the Church Missionary Society* (London, Hatchard & Son, 1835) [CBA]

Strijdom, Johan, "A Model not to Be Imitated? Recent Criticisms of Paul" (*Hervormde Teologiese Studies*, 57, No.1-2, 2001)

Stunt, Timothy C F, "Anthony Norris Groves (1795-1853) in a European Context: A Re-assessment of His Early Development", in Dickson, Neil T R (ed.), The growth of the Brethren movement: national and international experiences (papers presented at conference of Brethren Archivists and Historians Network, Gloucester, UK, July 2003) (Carlisle, Paternoster, forthcoming 2006?)

————, *Early Brethren and the Society of Friends* (Pinner, Christian Brethren Research Fellowship, Occasional Paper No. 3, 1970) [CBA]

————, *From Awakening to Secession: Radical Evangelicals in Switzerland and Britain 1815-35* (Edinburgh, T & T Clark, 2000)

————, "Influences in the Early Development of J N Darby", in Gribben & Stunt (eds.), *Prisoners of Hope? Aspects of Evangelical Millennialism in Britain and Ireland, 1800-1880* (Carlisle, Paternoster, 2004), pp.44-68

————, "Irvingite Pentecostalism and the Early Brethren", *Christian Brethren Research Fellowship Journal*, Vol. 10 (1965) pp.40-8

————, "James Van Sommer, an Undenominational Christian and Man of Prayer", *Journal of the Christian Brethren Research Fellowship*, No. 16 (Aug. 1967), pp.2-8 [CBA]

Stunt, W T, *Family Adventure* (Bath, Echoes of Service, c.1957) [EOS]

————, "James Van Sommer, Missionary Enthusiast", *Echoes Quarterly Review*, Vol. 9, No. 4 (Oct.-Dec. 1957), pp.18-23 [EOS]

―――, *Turning the World Upside Down: A Century of Missionary Endeavour* (1st edn., Upperton Press, Eastbourne, 1972), 2nd edn. (Bath, Echoes of Service, 1973) [CBA]

Summerton, Pauline, *Fishers of Men: the missionary influence of an extended family in Central Africa* (Kilmarnock, Brethren Archivists and Historians Network, 2003)

Sweetnam, Mark, "'Understand Before We Judge': Dan Crawford, Thinking Black, and the challenge of a missionary canon" (BA dissertation, Trinity College Dublin, 2004)

Symondson, Anthony (ed.), *The Victorian Crisis of Faith* (London, SPCK, 1970)

Taber, Charles R, *The World is Too Much with Us: "Culture" in modern Protestant missions* (Macon, Georgia, Mercer University Press, 1991)

Tatford, Frederick A, *A N Groves, the Father of Faith Missions* (Bath, Echoes of Service, 1979)

―――, *That the World May Know*, 10 vols. (Bath, Echoes of Service, 1982-6)

Taylor, Dr & Mrs Howard, *Hudson Taylor and the China Inland Mission, the Growth of a Work of God* (London, Morgan & Scott, 1918)

―――, *Hudson Taylor in Early Years, the Growth of a Soul* (London, Morgan & Scott, 1911)

Taylor, James Hudson, *A Retrospect* (London, Lutterworth, 1951 edn.)

Taylor, W Elfe, *Passages from the Diary and Letters of Henry Craik of Bristol* (Bristol, J F Shaw, 1866) [CBA]

Tennent, Timothy C, "William Carey as a Missiologist: An Assessment", *American Baptist Evangelicals Journal*, Vol. 7, No. 1 (Mar. 1999), pp.3-10

Terry, John Mark & Smith, Ebbie & Anderson, Justice (eds.), *Missiology: An Introduction to the Foundations, History and Strategies of World Mission* (Nashville, Broadman & Holman, 1998)

Tett, Mollie E, *The Road to Freedom: Sudan United Mission 1904-1968* (Sidcup, Sudan United Mission, 1968)

Thiselton, Anthony C, "Biblical Studies and Theoretical Hermeneutics", in Barton, *The Cambridge Companion to Biblical Interpretation* (Cambridge, 1998)

―――, *New Horizons in Hermeneutics* (London, Harper Collins, 1992)

Thompson, David M, *Denominationalism and Dissent 1795-1835: a question of identity* (London, Friends of Dr Williams's Library, 1985)

Thompson, Flora, *Lark Rise to Candleford* (Harmondsworth, Penguin, 1973)

Tilsley, George Edwin, *Dan Crawford, Missionary and Pioneer in Central Africa* (London, Oliphants, 1929)

Tippet, Alan, *Introduction to Missiology* (Pasadena, William Carey Library, 1987)

―――, *Verdict Theology in Missionary Theory* (Lincoln Christian College Press, 1969; Pasadena, William Carey Library, 1973)

Torjesen, Edvard P, *Fredrik Franson: A Model for Worldwide Evangelism* (Pasadena, William Carey Library, 1983)

Towlson, Clifford W, *Moravian and Methodist, Relationships and Influences in the Eighteenth Century* (London, The Epworth Press, 1957)

Tucker, Ruth A, *From Jerusalem to Irian Jaya: A Biographical History of Christian Missions* (Grand Rapids, Zondervan, 1983)

Turner, W G, *John Nelson Darby* (London, 1944)

Van den Berg, Johannes, *Constrained by Jesus' Love: An Enquiry into the Motives of the Missionary Awakening in Great Britain in the Period between 1698 and 1815* (Kampen, J H Kok, 1956)

Van Rheenen, Gailyn, "Contrasting Missional and Church Growth Perspectives" <http://www.missiology.org/mmr/mmr34.htm> (accessed 19th March 2005)

―――, *Missions: Biblical Foundations and Contemporary Strategies* (Grand Rapids, Zondervan, 1996)

Van Sommer, James (ed.), *The Missionary Reporter*, Vol. 1 (July 1853 to Dec. 1854); Vol. 2 (Jan. 1855 to Sep. 1856); Nos. 40-54 (Oct. 1856 to Jan. 1858) [CBA]

Vander Werff, Lyle L, *Christian Missions to Muslims, the Record: Anglican and Reformed Approaches in India and the Near East, 1800-1938* (Pasadena, William Carey Library, 1977)

Verkuyl, Johannes, *Contemporary Missiology: An Introduction* (Grand Rapids, Eerdmans, 1988)

Vidler, Alec H, *The Church in the Age of Revolution: 1789 to the Present Day* (Harmondsworth, Penguin, 1990)

Vine, W E, *The Divine Plan of Missions* (London, Pickering & Inglis, c.1940) [CBA]

Virgo, T, *No Well Worn Paths* (Eastbourne, Kingsway, 2001)

Vissert Hooft, W A, *The Meaning of the Ecumenical Movement* (London, SCM Press, 1953)

Wacker, Grant, "Searching for Eden with a Satellite Dish", in Hughes, *The Primitive Church in the Modern World* (1995)

Wagner, C Peter, *Acts of the Holy Spirit: A Modern Commentary on the Book of Acts*, Ventura, Regal, 2000

——————, *Church Growth: State of the Art* (Tyndale House, 1986)

——————, *Frontiers in Missionary Strategy* (Chicago, Moody Press, 1971)

——————, *On The Crest of the Wave: Becoming a World Christian*, (Ventura, Regal, 1983)

——————, *Your Church Can Grow* (Glendale, Regal, 1976)

Walker, Thomas, *Missionary Ideals* (London, CMS, 1911); 2nd edn. (London, IVP, 1969)

Wallace J A: *Lessons from the Life of the late James Nisbet, Publisher* (Edinburgh, Johnstone, Hunter & Co., 1867).

Walls, Andrew F, "The American Dimension in the History of the Missionary Movement", in Carpenter & Shenk (eds.), *Earthen Vessels: American Evangelicals and Foreign Missions, 1880-1980* (Grand Rapids, Eerdmans, 1990), pp.1-25

——————, *The Cross-Cultural Process in Christian History* (T & T Clark, 2001)

——————, "The Eighteenth-Century Protestant Missionary Awakening", in Stanley (ed.), *Christian Missions and the Enlightenment* (Grand Rapids, Eerdmans, 2000), pp.22-44

——————, "The Evangelical Revival, The Missionary Movement, and Africa", in Noll, Bebbington and Rawlyk, (eds.), *Evangelicalism: Comparative Studies of Popular Protestantism in North America, the British Isles, and Beyond, 1700-1990* (Oxford, Oxford University Press, 1994), pp.310-32

——————, *The Missionary Movement in Christian History: Studies in the Transmission of Faith* (New York, Orbis / Edinburgh, T & T Clark, 1996)

——————, "Missionary Societies and the Fortunate Subversion of the Church", *Evangelical Quarterly*, 88:2 (1988), pp.141-155

Walsh, John D, "'Methodism' and the Origins of English-Speaking Evangelicalism", in Noll, Bebbington and Rawlyk, (eds.), *Evangelicalism: Comparative Studies of Popular Protestantism in North America, the British Isles, and Beyond, 1700-1990* (Oxford, Oxford University Press, 1994), pp.19-37

——————, "Origins of the Evangelical Revival", in Bennett G V & Walsh J D (eds.), *Essays in Modern English Church History* (London, A & C Black, 1966)

——————, "The Yorkshire Evangelicals in the Eighteenth Century" (Cambridge Univ. PhD thesis, 1956)

—————— & Haydon, Colin M & Taylor, Stephen J C (eds.), *The Church of England c.1689-c.1833: From Toleration to Tractarianism* (Cambridge, CUP, 1993)

Ward, Kevin & Stanley, Brian (eds.), *The Church Mission Society and World Christianity 1799-1999* (Grand Rapids, Eerdmans, 2000)

Ward, Ted, "Repositioning Mission Agencies for the Twenty-first Century", *International Bulletin of Missionary Research* 23:4 (Oct 1999), pp.146-53 (CD: *The Best of IBMR*, 2004)

Ward, W Reginald, *The Protestant Evangelical Awakening*, (Cambridge, CUP, 1992)

Warren, Max A C, "The Church Militant Abroad: Victorian Missionaries", in Symondson, Anthony (ed.), *The Victorian Crisis of Faith* (London, SPCK, 1970)

———, *The Missionary Movement from Britain in Modern History* (London, 1965)
———, *Social History and Christian Mission* (London, SCM, 1967)
———, *To Apply the Gospel: Selections from the Writings of Henry Venn* (Grand Rapids, Eerdmans, 1971)
———, *"Why Missionary Societies and not Missionary Churches?" History's Lessons for Tomorrow's Mission*, (Geneva, WSCF, 1960)
Weber, T P, *Living in the Shadow of the Second Coming: American Premillennialism 1875-1982* (Chicago University Press, 1987)
Weinlick, John R, *Count Zinzendorf : The story of his life and leadership in the renewed Moravian Church* (New York/Nashville, Abingdon Press, 1956)
[Weitbrecht, M], *A Memoir of the Rev John James Weitbrecht* by his widow (London, Nisbet, 1854) [SD]
Whiteman, Darrell L, "Contextualization: The Theory, the Gap, the Challenge", *International Bulletin of Missionary Research*, 21:1 (Jan 1997), pp.2-7 (CD: *The Best of IBMR*, 2004)
Wilkens, Steve & Padgett, Alan G, *Christianity and Western Thought, Vol. 2: Faith and Reason in the Nineteenth Century* (Leicester, Inter Varsity Press, 2000)
Willey, Basil, *More Nineteenth Century Studies: A Group of Honest Doubters* (London, 1956)
Williams, C Peter, *The Ideal of the Self-Governing Church: a study in Victorian missionary strategy* (Leiden, E J Brill 1990)
———, "'Not Transplanting': Henry Venn's Strategic Vision" in Ward, Kevin & Stanley, Brian (eds.), *The Church Mission Society and World Christianity 1799-1999* (Grand Rapids, Eerdmans, 2000)
Wilson, Bryan R (ed.), *Patterns of Sectarianism: Organisation and Ideology in Social and Religious Movements* (London, Heinemann, 1967)
Wilson, J Christy, *Today's Tentmakers* (Seattle, Overseas Counselling Service, 1979)
Wilson, Elisabeth, "Your Citizenship is in Heaven: Brethren Attitudes to Authority and Government", *Brethren Archivists and Historians Network Review*, Vol. 12, No.2, Autumn 2003, pp.75-90
Winter, Ralph, *Perspectives on the World Christian Movement*, 3rd edn. (Pasadena, William Carey Library, 1999)
———, "The Re-Amateurisation of Mission", *Mission Frontiers*, March/April 1996
Wolff, Joseph, *Travels and Adventures of the Rev Joseph Wolff*, 2nd edn, 2 vols, (London, Saunders, Otley & Co, 1860, 1861)
Wolffe, John, "Anti-Catholicism and Evangelical Identity in Britain and the United States, 1830-1860", in Noll, Bebbington and Rawlyk (eds.), *Evangelicalism: Comparative Studies of Popular Protestantism in North America, the British Isles, and Beyond, 1700-1990* (Oxford, Oxford University Press, 1994), pp.179-97
——— (ed.), *Religion in Victorian Britain: Vol. V, Culture and Empire* (Manchester University Press, 1997)
Wood, Christopher, *Victorian Panorama: Paintings of Victorian Life* (London, Faber & Faber, 1976)
World Missionary Conference, 1910, the history and records of the conference, together with addresses delivered at the evening meetings, Reports of Commissions I-VIII (Edinburgh, Oliphant, 1910)
Yates, Timothy E, *Christian Mission in the Twentieth Century* (Cambridge, CUP, 1994)
———, *Venn and Victorian Bishops Abroad: the missionary policies of Henry Venn and their repercussions upon the Anglican Episcopate of the colonial period 1841-1872* (Uppsala, Swedish Institute of Missionary Research / London, SPCK, 1978)
Yoder, John Howard, "How H Richard Niebuhr Reasoned: A Critique of Christ and Culture," in Stassen, Yeager & Yoder, *Authentic Transformation: a new vision of Christ and culture* (Nashville, Abingdon Press, 1996)

Yohannan, K P, *Revolution in World Missions* (Carrollton, USA, Gospel For Asia, 1986, 1998)
Young, Florence S H, *Pearls from the Pacific* (London, Marshall Brothers Ltd, 1925)
Zuck, Roy B, *Basic Bible Interpretation* (Wheaton, Victor Books, 1991)
Zwemer, Samuel, "Karl Gottlieb Pfander", *The Moslem World*, Vol. 21, No. 3 (July 1941), pp.217-226 [BL]

Unpublished materials are held in the following archives:

Alnwick: Northumberland Archives, Alnwick Castle, Alnwick
Drummond Papers
    A N Groves to H Drummond, two undated letters [?April 1829]

Basel: Basel Mission Archives, Missionstrasse 21, 4003 Basel
    Extracts of German missionaries' conference minutes (Shushi), Oct 1829
    Letter from Dittrich (Shushee), 7 Oct. 1829
    A N Groves to R Pearson, 14 Oct. 1829
    Letter from C G Pfander, 14 Oct. 1829
    C G Pfander, C Taylor to C G Blumhardt, 1 Nov. 1829
    A N Groves to C G Blumhardt, 22 June 1834
    D Coates to C G Blumhardt, 17 Feb. 1835
    D Coates to C G Blumhardt, 20 Mar. 1835
    A N Groves to C F Spittler, 7 Apr. 1835
    Extract from Minutes of [CMS] Correspondence of May 11th 1835
    D Coates to C G Blumhardt, 6 Aug. 1835
    A N Groves to W Büchelen, 30 Nov. 1835
    D Coates to C G Blumhardt, 3 Dec. 1835
    A N Groves to C F Spittler, 24 Dec.[received] 1835
    D Coates to C G Blumhardt, 25 Jan. 1836
    A N Groves to W Büchelen, 22 Mar. 1836
    H Gundert to W Büchelen, 22 Mar. 1836
    D Coates to C G Blumhardt, 2 April 1836
    Extracts from Minutes of Correspondence Committee of November 1st, 1836
    [Coates's report of visit to Basel]

Basel Staatsarchiv
    A N Groves to C F Spittler, [received] 24 Dec. 1835

Birmingham: University Library, Edgbaston, Birmingham
Church Mission Society Archives (Formerly in CMS House, London)
    A N Groves to E H Bickersteth, 25 Mar. 1825, transcribed in CMS Minutes (20 May 1825)
    A N Groves to E H Bickersteth, 14 June 1825, transcribed in CMS Minutes (9 Aug. 1825)
    A N Groves to E H Bickersteth, 15 Sep. 1825
    A N Groves to E H Bickersteth, 14 Mar. [1826]
    A N Groves to E H Bickersteth, 10 Mar. 1827
    A N Groves to Rev W Jowett, 20 Feb. 1830
    A N Groves to Rev Thos. Woodroffe, 25 Oct. 1832
    A N Groves to J F Thomas, 2 Sep. 1836
    A N Groves to J Tucker, recd. 16 Oct. 1836
    J Tucker to Nelson, 23 July 1835
    L Schmid to J Tucker, 11 July 1835

Rev. J Tucker, "Notes on Mr Groves' letter, received 23rd July 1836"
The Minutes of the London committee of the Church Missionary Society contain several references to A N Groves between the dates of 20 May 1825 and 11 Nov. 1828.

Cambridge: University Library, Cambridge
British and Foreign Bible Society Archives (formerly in Bible House, London)
A N Groves to Rev Dr [Robert] Pinkerton, 23 May 1829
A N Groves to the Committee of the BFBS, 5 June 1829
A N Groves to Rev Dr [Robert] Pinkerton, 28 Aug. 1830
A N Groves to Rev A Brandram, 10 Sep. 1831, box 1832, 1
A N Groves to Rev A Brandram, 2 May 1832
A N Groves to Rev A Brandram, [?21 Oct.] 1832
A N Groves to Rev A Brandram, 21 July 1833

London: School of Oriental and African Studies
CWM/LMS archive, South India, Incoming Mail, boxes 3-8
W H Drew to Rev W Ellis (Foreign Sec. of LMS London), 10 July 1835
J Bilderbeck to Rev W Ellis, 20 Aug. 1835
J Bilderbeck to Rev W Ellis, 30 Dec. 1835
J Bilderbeck to Rev W Ellis, Chittoor, 1 Jan. 1837
J Bilderbeck to Rev W Ellis, 28 July 1837
J Bilderbeck to Rev W Ellis, 10 July 1838
A Leitch to Foreign Secretary of LMS, Chittoor, 19 Sep. 1840
J Bilderbeck to Directors of LMS, 8 Dec. 1840
J Bilderbeck to Directors of LMS, 22 Mar. 1841
J Bilderbeck to Directors of LMS, Arcot, 8 July 1841
A Leitch to Foreign Secretary of LMS, Chittoor, 21 Aug. 1841
J Bilderbeck to Rev Messrs A Tidman & J I Freeman (Foreign Secs. of LMS), 23 Sep. 1841
J Bilderbeck to Foreign Secs. of LMS, 19 Feb. 1842
Annual Report of LMS, 1837, 1838, 1839

Index

Acland, Thomas, 136, 177
Africa Inland Mission, 209-10
Allen, Roland, 168, 186, 210, 221, 227-9, 230, 241, 259, 273, 276
American Board of Commissioners for Foreign Missions, 41, 77-8, 85-96, 151, 159-60
Anabaptists, 44, 269
Anderson, Rufus, 15, 40, 77-8, 85, 87, 91-107, 115, 125-6, 151, 159-60, 229
Arnot, F S, 183, 185-6
Arulappan, John Christian, 16, 69, 73-4, 108, 110-4, 120, 127, 133, 137, 139, 150, 154, 157, 165-7, 178-9, 190-1, 214-5, 218-21, 225, 247, 252, 272, 281
Austin-Sparks, Theodore, 215
Azariah, V S, 68, 107, 110, 238
Baago, Kaj, 87
Bakht Singh, 16, 128, 154, 218-21, 229, 247, 250-2, 276, 281
Ball, Richard, 224
Baptist Missionary Society, 35-6, 38, 76-8, 81, 84, 106, 127, 156, 164
Basel Mission, 10, 32-4, 41, 48, 82, 121, 157, 159, 166, 198
Beaver, R Pierce, 40, 85, 91
Bebbington, David, 7, 43
Beer, George, 65, 83, 85, 131, 133, 137, 139, 145, 167, 177-9, 183, 191, 199, 205
Bellett, John, 177
Berger, William, 195, 205
Bickersteth, Edward, 11, 20-1, 73, 91, 155
Bilderbeck, John, 60, 65-72, 203, 272
Billy Graham Organisation, 86
Blumhardt, Christian Gottlieb, 34, 82
Bonk, Jonathan, 15, 117, 197, 214, 244-6, 256
Bosch, David J, 22, 39-40, 77, 79, 261, 265
Bowden, William, 65, 83, 85, 131, 133, 137, 139, 145, 167-8, 177-9, 185, 191, 199, 205
British and Foreign Bible Society, 19-20, 73, 150
Broadbent, Edmund H, 181
Broomhall, Benjamin, 205
Buchanan, Claudius, 88, 232
Bush, Luis, 254-5
Caldecott, William, 154
Calman, Erasmus, 29

Carey, William, 15, 21, 34-8, 49, 56, 77-8, 80-1, 83-5, 98, 107, 122, 142, 159, 164-6, 177
Carmichael, Amy, 212, 227, 230
Cawston, Ray, 160-2
Chase, Philander, 21
Chilcraft, Stephen, 24, 31, 41, 53, 60-2, 88, 90, 115, 183, 186, 193, 228
China Inland Mission, 106, 144, 148, 180, 192-5, 196, 199-208, 215, 225, 280
Chinese Evangelisation Society, 79, 180, 193-4, 203, 205-6
Christian and Missionary Alliance, 206, 210
Christian Missions in Many Lands, 182, 187
Church Missionary Society, 9-10, 15, 19-21, 31, 34, 37, 40, 48-50, 52-3, 57-65, 69, 72-3, 76-7, 79-82, 85-9, 92-4, 96, 99-102, 106-7, 110, 120, 123, 126, 128, 155-6, 164, 198-200, 203, 214, 218, 225, 228-9
Clark, Denis E, 168
Clark, Robert, 100, 166
Coates, Dandeson, 40, 62, 64
Congleton, Lord, see Parnell,
Corrie, Daniel, 59
Cotton, Arthur, 49, 168
Corwin, Gary, 252
Craik, Henry, 174-5, 265
Crawford, Dan, 183-6
Cronin, Edward, 10, 48, 62, 65, 68-9, 177, 195, 203, 208
Crowther, Samuel, 100, 110
Daniels, Gene, 258
Darby, John Nelson, 13, 42, 69, 159, 174, 178, 195, 215, 221
Darbyites, 42, 194-5, 215
Doll, Ludwig, 196
Dorairaj R P, 218, 250
Drummond, Henry, 11, 23-4, 46, 136
Dubois, J A, 50
Duff, Alexander, 41, 56, 65, 122-5, 127, 271
Echoes of Service, 180-2, 186, 190, 207, 280
Edinburgh conference (1910), 83, 87, 110, 227, 229
Eitel, Keith, 246-7
Elliot, Jim, 186-7
Evangelical Alliance, 179

Fiedler, Keith, 86, 143, 193, 196, 199, 201, 203, 208-10
Fisher, Walter, 186
French, Thomas, 229-30
Gairdner, W H Temple, 229-30
Garrison, David, 257
Goldsmith, Elizabeth, 79, 197, 207
Groves, Henry, 180, 186
Grubb, Norman, 220
Guicciardini, Piero, 178
Guinness, Henry Grattan, 180
Gundert, Hermann, 61, 64, 73, 82-3, 137, 157, 165, 199
Gützlaff, Karl, 224-5, 247
Hay, Alexander R, 181, 241-2
Heber, Reginald, 53, 56, 58, 88
Hebich, Samuel, 73
Hill, Richard, 205
Hodge, Charles, 262
Hodges, Melvin, 233
Hollis, Michael, 231-3, 276
Hough, James, 52
Howard, John and Robert, 195
Ingleby, Jonathan, 123, 126-7, 147-8, 223
Interdev, 86
Irving, Edward, 11, 23-30, 43, 46, 115, 265
Irvingites, 68
Jones, John and Mary, 194, 205
Jowett, William, 31-2, 34
Judson, Adoniram, 85, 117
Kennaway, John, 38, 88, 136
Kilham, Sarah, 121, 206
Kitto, John, 10, 32, 47, 79
Klausner, Joseph, 115
Kraft, Charles, 234-5
Kreider, Alan, 259
Lang, George H, 149, 181, 183, 192, 197, 215, 219
Larsen, Timothy, 143-6, 150-3
Leitch, Alexander, 66, 71-2
Livingstone, David, 41, 119, 182, 185, 225
London Missionary Society, 23-4, 37, 40, 53, 60, 65-8, 70-2, 76, 92, 123, 164, 187, 198
London Society for Promoting Christianity amongst the Jews, 31, 150
Lutz, Lorry, 254
Mackenzie, Charles F, 184
MacLean, John Lindsay, 186
Marshman, Hannah, 199
Marshman, Joshua, 34-8, 74, 156

Martyn, Henry, 19, 48
McGavran, Donald, 236-9, 241
Mennonites, 269
Middleton, Thomas Fanshaw, 53, 88
Moffat, Robert and Mary, 67, 185
Morrison, Robert, 166, 224
Mott, John, 196
Müller, George, 10, 13, 52, 61, 65, 112, 128, 135, 137, 139, 142, 144-5, 150-4, 159, 173-7, 179, 186, 193-7, 204, 215, 275-6
Muller, Roland, 162, 257
Nee, Watchman, 16, 126, 154, 206, 215-8, 220-1, 229, 247-9, 276, 281
Neill, Stephen, 229-30, 282
Nesbit, Robert, 155
Nevius, John, 15-6, 99-100, 105, 229
New Tribes Mission, 181
Newbigin, Lesslie, 56, 116, 223, 229, 235, 238-41, 250, 258, 266, 281
Newman, Francis W (Frank), 10, 208
Newman, John Henry, 262
Newton, Kenneth J, 186-90, 273
Nida, Eugene, 233
Niebuhr, Richard, 115, 239
Nissen, Johannes, 162
Noble, Robert, 85
O'Brien, Dave, 186, 258
Overseas Missionary Fellowship, 197
Owen, John, 20, 73
Parnell, John Vesey, 10, 29, 37-8, 62, 65, 177, 195, 199, 203, 208
Paton, David M, 249
Pearse, George, 195, 205, 224
Pfander, Karl Gottlieb, 10, 32-4, 47-8, 74, 82, 121, 165
Phillips, J B, 274
Pierson, Arthur T, 177, 196-7, 206
Pike, Kenneth, 233
Plütschau, Heinrich, 51-2
Pulleng, A, 193
Ragland, Thomas, 101
Rajamani, R R, 218, 250
Redwood, W A, 189
Rhenius, Karl Gottlieb Ewald, 10, 49-50, 52, 67, 69, 72, 83-4, 94, 104, 106, 122, 137-9, 190, 200, 224, 236
Rowdon, Harold, 78, 139, 143-9
Sastri, 57
Sathianathan (Satyanathan), 52
Schmid, L B E, 52, 54, 139
Schwartz, Christian, 52, 57
Schwartz, Glenn, 255-6
Scott, Alexander J (Sandy), 23-4, 29

Scott, Thomas, 52
Severn, Frank, 78, 161
Sharp, Larry W, 258
Shenk, Wilbert, 247, 258
Short, Arthur Rendle, 181
Simeon, Charles, 19, 88
Simpson, A B, 206
Smalley, William, 234
Smith, David, 244
Smith, John, 67
Society for Promoting Christian Knowledge, 52, 85, 89, 94, 120, 196
Society for the Propagation of the Gospel, 85, 89, 123
Soltau, Henrietta, 207
South Africa General Mission, 209
Speer, Robert, 196
Stacey, Miss, 195
Stanley, Brian, 41, 118, 127, 164, 201
Steffan, Tom, 230
Stock, Eugene, 15, 48, 102
Strachan, James Morgan, 59-60
Student Volunteer Movement, 196-7
Stunt, Timothy C F, 81-2, 155
Sweetnam, Mark S, 183, 185
Taber, Charles, 201, 235, 243
Taylor, James Hudson, 39, 61, 79, 106, 118-9, 139, 144-5, 148, 153, 158, 167, 169, 177, 179-80, 186, 192-6, 199, 202, 204-8, 212-3, 215, 225, 276, 280
Trad, Mokayel, 49, 108, 120
Tregelles, Samuel P, 265
Tucker, Alfred R, 229
Tucker, John T, 59, 61-2, 203
Turner, John Matthias, 53, 58
Van Sommer, James, 179, 195
Vedanayagam Pillai, 57
Venn, Henry, 15-6, 40, 62, 64, 77, 84-5, 87, 102, 107, 110, 114, 119, 125-6, 164, 172, 198, 211, 216, 227, 229, 286
Venn, John, 198
Virgo, Terry, 256
Wagner, C Peter, 230, 237, 241-3
Waldenses, 269
Walls, Andrew, 15, 78
Ward, Ted, 256-7
Warren, Max, 89-90
Wesley, John, 19, 45, 212, 269
Whiteman, Darrell, 257
Wigram, George V, 265
Wilberforce, Samuel, 89-90
Wilberforce, William, 37, 40-1
Wilder, Robert, 196
Wilson, Christy, 168

Wilson, Daniel, 53, 56, 58-9, 62, 88
Winter, Ralph, 255
Wolff, Joseph, 11, 21, 31-2, 46, 49, 54, 57, 74
Yoder, John H, 239
Yohannan, K P, 253-6
Ziegenbalg, Bartholomaeus, 51-2
Zinzendorf, Nikolaus Ludwig von, 21-2, 40

A companion volume by the same author:

The Primitivist Ecclesiology of Anthony Norris Groves:
a radical influence on
the nineteenth-century Protestant church in Britain

The decade in which Anthony Norris Groves developed distinctive views about church and mission coincided, between 1825-35, with a turning-point in the religious history of the British Isles. The eighteenth-century belief in order, design and gradual development was yielding to the free, dynamic, iconoclastic spirit of the nineteenth century. This book suggests that Groves was a significant participant in the rise and spread of these new spiritual forces.

Seceding from the Anglican communion in 1828, Anthony Norris Groves adopted a consciously non-denominational identity. With little interest in buildings, services, finances, organisation, training or ceremony, he developed a radically primitivist ecclesiology, taking the principles and practice of the early churches in the New Testament as a model to be followed by every generation in every cultural context.

These ideas came at a time when the "romantic" and the "primitive" were newly fashionable. The publication of Groves's tract *Christian Devotedness* in 1825, followed by his suggestion that Christians of diverse denominations might partake of the Lord's Supper without the presence of an ordained minister, and then his own resolve in 1829 to launch a mission to the Muslim world "by faith" without the support of a recognised church or missionary society, challenged and enthused his circle of personal friends. Some of these were soon to become leading figures in the Brethren movement, sometimes known as Plymouth Brethren.

Moving to India, Groves continued to write controversial tracts and to correspond with friends and former colleagues such as John Parnell, Henry Craik, Robert Chapman, John and Robert Howard, and especially his brother-in-law George Müller.

The eventual schism within the Brethren movement reflects an early divergence of view between Groves and J N Darby. Whereas Darby condemned the church on earth as apostate, Groves constantly sought to recover its primitive ideals. Where Darby looked to a pre-tribulation secret rapture of the saints, Groves anticipated the return of Christ in visible glory, after the great tribulation, to redeem his own. Whilst Darby considered the present "church age" to be a mere interlude in God's ongoing purposes for the Jews, Groves saw it as a fulfilment of God's eternal purpose for all nations.

Groves's primitivist ecclesiology became characteristic of the open Brethren, and through Brethren influence in university Christian unions and "faith missions" entered the mainstream of British evangelical life. For a century and a half, "the early church" was offered as a model for the emulation of evangelical congregations. The history of this period cannot ignore the key role played by Anthony Norris Groves in formulating and popularising these elements of evangelical primitivism.

ISBN 142511001-0